HB
21
M37   The Market and the state...

JUL   2000
Date Due   JUN   2004

JUL X X 2015			
		JUN 09	
	WITHDRAWN		

THE MARKET AND THE STATE

THE MARKET AND THE STATE

Essays in Honour of Adam Smith

EDITED BY

THOMAS WILSON

AND

ANDREW S. SKINNER

OXFORD
AT THE CLARENDON PRESS
1976

Oxford University Press, Walton Street, Oxford OX2 6DP

OXFORD LONDON GLASGOW NEW YORK
TORONTO MELBOURNE WELLINGTON CAPE TOWN
IBADAN NAIROBI DAR ES SALAAM LUSAKA ADDIS ABABA
KUALA LUMPUR SINGAPORE JAKARTA HONG KONG TOKYO
DELHI BOMBAY CALCUTTA MADRAS KARACHI

ISBN 0 19 828406 3

© *Oxford University Press 1976*

*Printed in Great Britain
at the University Press, Oxford
by Vivian Ridler
Printer to the University*

Preface

The Market and the State may be regarded as an appropriate title for a volume of papers in honour of Adam Smith. Although there is no need to stress Smith's historical role as an exponent and advocate of the price system, it may be in place to observe that much of what he had to say retains sufficient relevance two hundred years later to warrant attention from a practical as well as from a historical point of view. Admittedly specialised knowledge of the market economy has been greatly advanced in many directions since Smith's day, and specialised techniques for its analysis have been greatly improved; but the increased depth of understanding does not appear to have been matched by a corresponding extension of its scope. It may indeed be the case that no other great social institution of anything like comparable importance is so imperfectly understood and so inadequately appreciated as is the market. Smith's own contribution to economics is, of course, to be found mainly in this field, but his interests also extended to the economic role of the state. Thus not only was he interested in the principles of taxation, but, like his friend David Hume, he presented the concept of public goods at an early stage in the development of thought on these matters. It is almost unnecessary to add to these remarks that Smith was also much concerned with delineating the respective roles of state and market.

The papers contained in this volume were presented—with some minor modifications—at a conference convened at the University of Glasgow in April 1976 in order to mark the bicentenary of the publication of the *Wealth of Nations*. Their primary object was not, however, to elucidate and assess Smith's contribution nor to celebrate his importance as a historical figure. Another volume of papers devoted to his contribution in different fields of thought, philosophical as well as economic, had already been prepared by the editors of the present volume and published by Oxford University Press in association with the Glasgow edition of Smith's complete works. The authors of the conference papers were rather invited to direct their attention to some of the central themes discussed in the *Wealth of Nations* or in Smith's other works and to discuss these themes from the viewpoint of economists writing in 1976. It is true that these papers are very properly devoted in some measure to the presentation of Smith's own ideas and will be seen to reflect in varying degree sympathy with his point of view or detachment from it. The main concern of the authors, however, is not with the history of thought but with the contemporary discussion of certain issues that continue to be of central importance to economists. The procedure followed for each lecture, with one exception, was to invite two other distinguished scholars to add their comments. The exception was the oration delivered by Sir Alexander Cairncross, Chancellor of the University of Glasgow, which also bears the title 'The Market and the State'.

The conference was organised by the University of Glasgow in association with the Royal Economic Society and the Scottish Economic Society. The guests invited to the conference included distinguished figures from politics, industry, the trade unions, and some international economic organisations, as well as economists from several countries. A list of those who actually attended is to be found at the end of the book. The oration by Sir Alexander Cairncross was followed by an official reception given by H.M. Government where the guests were received by the Rt. Hon. William Ross, then Secretary of State for Scotland.

ACKNOWLEDGEMENTS

The Conference during which these papers were given would not have been possible without generous financial assistance from the Scottish Banks, Imperial Chemical Industries, the Shell Transport and Trading Company Ltd. and a number of other firms which include the British Oxygen Co. Ltd.; Goldberg & Sons Ltd.; James Finlay & Co. Ltd.; Grampian Holdings Ltd.; Melville Dundas & Whitson; Unilever Ltd.; The British Aluminium Co. Ltd.; Christian Salvesen (Managers) Ltd.; The Weir Group Ltd., and Scottish Television.

The editors would also like to acknowledge their indebtedness to Mr. Walter Ballantyne, acting on behalf of the Scottish Economic Society, for his continuing support, and to thank Miss McGill, Miss Lovell and Mrs. Boutineau for their part in coping with the arrangements for the Conference. We should also like to thank Miss MacSwan and Mrs. Campbell, our respective secretaries, whose unremitting efforts made possible the final preparation of the papers for publication.

T. WILSON

Glasgow, May 1976 A. S. SKINNER

Contents

Abbreviations

Corr.   *Correspondence*

LJ(B)   *Lectures on Jurisprudence*: Report dated 1766. This edition
was originally published by Edwin Cannan (Oxford, 1896)

TMS   *The Theory of Moral Sentiments*

WN   *The Wealth of Nations*

Stewart Dugald Stewart, 'An Account of the Life and Writings of
Adam Smith, LL.D.' in *Collected Works*, ed. Sir William
Hamilton (Edinburgh, 1858)

Essays   *Essays on Adam Smith*, ed. A. Skinner and T. Wilson
(Oxford, 1975)

There are a number of editions of Smith's major works, and for
the purposes of this volume the original references to the different
editions used by the contributors have been retained. We have,
however, added to these a set of references which supply part,
section, and paragraph number to Smith's works. For example,
the reference 'TMS I.iii.2.2.' indicates a reference to Part I,
section iii, chapter 2, paragraph 2. The statement 'WN I.x.b.1
indicates a reference to WN Book 1, chapter x, section b, paragraph 1. 'Stewart, IV. 3' supplies a reference to section IV paragraph 3 of the 'Account of the Life and Writings'. By following
this procedure, it should be possible to trace references to editions
other than those used by individual contributors and to the
Glasgow Edition of the Works and Correspondence of Adam Smith.

In the *Lectures on Jurisprudence* we have cited the volume and
page reference from the original manuscript while retaining page
references to the Cannan edition as supplied by the original
contributors. References to the *Correspondence* include date of
letter and letter number from the new edition.

I

The Historical Background Adam Smith and the Industrial Revolution

BY C. P. KINDLEBERGER*

I

An early version of this paper focused on the dispute, if one may call it that, between historians of economic thought who sometimes seek to demonstrate that Adam Smith was fully aware of the industrial revolution taking place around him as he wrote the *Wealth of Nations*, and economic historians who think he was not. It is true, as Samuel Johnson put it, that 'in lapidary inscriptions, a man is not upon oath' and piety demands that the guest of honour be given the benefit of the doubt. Nonetheless, I propose to dismiss this question quickly, with an open-and-shut verdict for the economic historians.

It is first necessary to establish that Adam Smith could have known, or should have known about the industrial revolution. The timing of the industrial revolution is not fully agreed. Rostow, for example, puts 'take-off' in 1783 which is too late for a book published in 1776, and even, allowing for publication lag, for the new Chapter VIII of Book IV and the new material of Chapter I of Book V which appeared in the third edition of 1783. But neither the *Wealth of Nations* nor the Industrial Revolution had production functions with point-input/point-output. The former as we shall see was twenty-five years in the writing, and the timing of the industrial revolution varies among observers as Charles and Richard Tilly indicate in the following table:

* Massachusetts Institute of Technology. The author is indebted for ideas, references, corrections, and comments to Mark Blaug, Kenneth Carpenter, Ronald Coase, Larry Neal, and Charles Staley.

Various Starting Dates for the Industrial Revolution[1]

Author	Date(s)	Indicator(s)
T. S. Ashton	1760s	Major Inventions
T. S. Ashton	1782	Cotton Exports; Cloth Production
Deane and Cole	1740s	Industrial Production
Deane and Cole	1780s	Output Per Head
Walther Hoffmann	1780	Industrial Production
W. W. Rostow	1783	Exports and Imports
J. A. Schumpeter	1787	Price Level

Ashton notes that for those that like to be precise in such matters the lighting of the first furnace at the Carron iron works in 1760 may serve to mark the beginning of the industrial revolution in Scotland.[2] Technology change turned sharply upward in the 1760s. The number of patents which had seldom been a dozen a year prior to 1760 rose to 31 in 1766 and 36 in 1769, the year in which James Watt took out his patent on the steam engine and Arkwright his on the waterframe.[3] Halévy notes that all the important inventions were crowded into the decade from 1766 to 1775.[4]

Assume for the sake of argument that the industrial revolution was in the making from 1760 to 1782. These are roughly the dates of the *Wealth of Nations*. Dugald Stewart held that its fundamental principles go back to Adam Smith's lectures delivered in Glasgow in 1752–3, in his first year as professor of moral philosophy. W. R. Scott claims that his Edinburgh period from 1748 to 1751 was of the greatest importance for the central principle of his system, and that by 1749 at the latest he had begun to apply the idea of natural liberty—which emerged directly from the Naturalism of the 18th century—to commerce and industry. The lecture of 1755 at the Club dominated by Andrew Cochrane, provost and merchant, contained an important early statement of his ideas. The manuscript of about 1763 discovered by Scott contains a well

---

[1] Charles and Richard Tilly, 'Emerging Problems in the Modern Economic History of Western Europe', unpublished paper (January 1971), 7.

[2] T. S. Ashton, *The Industrial Revolution, 1760–1830* (London, Oxford University Press, 1948), 65.

[3] Ibid. 90, 68.

[4] Elie Halévy, *A History of the English People in 1815*, Book II, Economic Life (Harmondsworth, Middlesex, Penguin, 1937; first published in English, 1924), 102.

worked-out version of the opening chapters of Book I on the division of labour, most of it preserved in the final version published 13 years later, but with one alteration in illustration significant for our purpose.[5] In the thirteen years between this draft and 1776, Smith spent two years in France, six years at Kirkcaldy in Scotland, and four years in London, the last 10 writing, finishing, and publishing the book, as well, at Kirkcaldy, in studying botany and some other sciences. Writing to Andreas Holt in October 1780, Smith said:

My own life has been extremely uniform. Upon my return to Great Britain, I retired to a small town in Scotland in the place of my nativity, where I continued to live for six years in great tranquility and almost complete retirement.[6]

Scott makes clear that Smith's technique of writing with a closely reasoned argument made revision difficult, as the text would have to be altered for a considerable distance.[7] It may well be true, as Viner says, that 'Smith was a keen observer of his surroundings and used skilfully what he saw to illustrate his general argument'— though Viner, puzzled by his unawareness of the bondage of Scottish colliers and salters and by the absence of references to the general economic state of the Highlands, excuses his failure to respond to his immediate Scottish background by saying his loyalties were largely to a wider Britain.[8] But it is surely going too far to say with Max Lerner in his introduction to the Modern Library edition:

Smith kept his eyes and ears open . . . Here was something that gave order and meaning to the newly emerged world of commerce and the newly emerging world of industry . . . Smith took ten more years.

[5] William Robert Scott, *Adam Smith as Student and Professor* (New York, August M. Kelley, 1965; originally issued 1937 to mark the bicentennial anniversary of Adam Smith's matriculation as a student at Glasgow University), 57, 61, 81, 82, 312–29.
[6] Ibid. 283. Letter 208 dated 26 October 1780.
[7] Ibid. 423.
[8] Jacob Viner, *Guide to John Rae's Life of Adam Smith* (New York, Augustus M. Kelley, 1965), 15, 101. For a debate on another instance in which Smith may or may not have been an astute observer of the contemporary scene see John Rae, *Life of Adam Smith* (London, Macmillan & Co., 1895), 229ff, in which Rae takes exception to McCulloch's judgement that Smith did not perceive any foreshadowing of the French Revolution in his long stay in France from 1764 to 1766.

He could not be hurried in his task. He had to read and observe further. He poked his nose into old books and new factories.[9]

The last sentence is half right.

The text of the *Wealth of Nations* supports Smith on 'great tranquility and almost complete retirement' against Viner and Lerner on contemporaneous illustrations. There is virtually no mention of cotton textiles, only one reference to Manchester in a list of cities, nothing on pottery, nothing on new methods of producing beer. Canals are dealt with under public works, but illustrated by the canal of Languedoc, finished in 1681, rather than with the Bridgewater canal of 1761, which initiated the spate of canal building and improvement in Britain culminating in the canal mania of the 1790s. Turnpikes are referred to without notice of the fact that travel times were falling rapidly: the first stage-coach from Birmingham to London in 1731 took $2\frac{1}{2}$ days; by 1776 the time had been reduced to 19 hours.

An historian of economic thought argues ingeniously that Smith was 'fully aware' of the technical change about him, citing for example, his text of the use of coal and wood as fuel, and the use of coal in iron and all other metals.[10] But Smith does not discuss the spread of coal in industrial use. Coal is mentioned to illustrate

[9] Max Lerner, 'Introduction' to Adam Smith, *An Inquiry into the Nature and Causes of the Wealth of Nations*, Edited with an Introduction, Notes and Marginal Summary, with an Enlarged Index, by Edwin Cannan (New York, The Modern Library), viii. All text references to the *Wealth of Nations* are to this edition. The London years from 1772 to 1776, however, were devoted to considerable revision. See Rae, op. cit., 256–58. Rae controverts Thorold Rogers' view that the book lay 'unrevised and unaltered during four years in the author's desk'. Ginzburg assumes that revisions were required by political events: 'He (Smith) must have realised that his prolonged isolation in the small Scottish town was a mistake, in that he had failed to keep informed on many contemporary problems. The sixties and seventies were important decades in English political history.' (Eli Ginzburg, *The House of Adam Smith* (New York, Columbia University Press, 1934), 135.) The revisions detailed by Rae, however, dealt with a variety of economic matters—the price of hides, the decline in sugar-refining in colonies taken from the French, American wages, extensive additions in the chapter on revenue—but not with methods of industrial production.

The literature on the Duke of Bridgewater canal, on Boulton and Watt's plant at Soho, and on the Wedgwood factory Etruria is replete with accounts of visitors from all walks of life, including such distinguished personages as the King of Denmark, Baron von Stein of Prussia, Samuel Johnson, Benjamin Franklin, the Duke of Buccleugh, etc. but no Dr. Smith.

[10] Samuel Hollander, *The Economics of Adam Smith* (Toronto, University of Toronto Press, 1973), 105.

points about rent[11] or consumer taxes,[12] primarily about space heating. From a discussion of producing iron with charcoal in the United States where wood is abundant[13] and a mention of iron in a list: 'In some manufactures, besides, coal is a necessary instrument of trade; as in those of glass, iron and all other metals' (825-26; V. ii. k. 12) I find it difficult to infer that Smith had a full appreciation of Darby's contribution in substituting coke for charcoal. Nor is it credible on the basis of the fact that Smith and Watt were acquainted, even friends, and had close friends in common, Dr. Joseph Black, the chemist and Dr. John Roebuck, an owner of the Carron Iron Works, to hypothesize a conversation in which Watt explained to Smith the machine-operated devices of the Soho plant of Boulton and Watt.[14] There is no evidence that Watt and Smith met after Smith left Glasgow in 1763, and the evidence for their friendship in Smith's Glasgow period is slight, resting largely on Smiles' *Lives of Boulton and Watt*, unsupported by anything in the surviving papers of Watt or Smith.[15] The minutes of Glasgow University do record that Smith was the chairman of a committee in 1762 to get back from Watt, and from the University printer Foulis, some of their considerable number of rooms.[16] To go from these contacts to a suppositious post-1768 conversation is an heroic leap.

Moreover, Smith's analysis is static. Manufactures using coal were 'confined principally to the coal countries; other parts of the country, on account of the high price of this necessary article, not being able to work so cheap' (825; V. ii. k. 12). He recognized the importance of transport costs in the delivered price of coal. What he failed to see was that the high price of coal away from the mines

[11] 165-6; I. xi. c. 15, 17-18. Part II of the chapter.

[12] 825-6; V. ii. k. 12. 'Taxes upon Consumeable Commodities.'

[13] 547; IV. vii. b. 37. Part II of the chapter.

[14] Ibid., note. A closer reading of this passage indicates that it does not explicitly state that Watt described Soho to Smith in 1767, although that inference was drawn and is possible. It is of interest that in discussing Smith's friends Viner (op. cit., Chapter 2) does not mention Watt, Boulton, Wedgwood, Arkwright, Darby, Wilkinson or any other leader of the industrial revolution, nor do the biographies of Boulton, Watt, and Wedgwood by H. W. Dickinson, Julia Wedgwood and Samuel Smiles (see footnotes 17, 19, 27, 28, 29 and Samuel Smiles, *Lives of Boulton and Watt*, Principally from the Original Soho Mss, Comprising Also a History of the Invention and Introduction of the Steam Engine (London, John Murray, 1865), 201 and Chapter xviii, mention Smith among the industrialists' friends who are explicitly discussed.

[15] Rae, op. cit. 98.   [16] Scott, op. cit. 149.

provided a strong incentive to reduce transport costs and to improve efficiency in coal consumption through invention, as in the Watt steam engine. In 1771 James Watt was working to install his new machines in Cornish copper mines where failures were being recorded because of the high price of coal and the inefficiency of the Newcomen engine.[17]

It is unnecessary to labour the point. The *Wealth of Nations* was the work of a literary economist, like some of us, who drew his examples from books, not from the world around him. The steam engine which replaced the plough and grain mills to illustrate the third source of improvement from the division of labour—invention—between the 1763 and the 1776 versions of WN I. i was a Newcomen engine, not a separate-condenser Watt, and the story of the invention is said by Cannan to be mythical and drawn from a book published in 1744 (9–10). Most of the books Smith relies on, moreover, are fairly old, published in the first quarter of the eighteenth century, and the bulk of his dated illustrations relate to this period as well, e.g. the detailed discussion on public debt in WN V. iii (865–7, 868–69 and 874–75 §§13–25, 27–30, 42–6). A detailed and up-to-the-minute discussion in the 3rd edition of 1783 concerns not industrial output but the impact of the herring bounty on the catch (485 ff; IV. v. a. 28–35 and Appendix I). Though it be heretical to say so, when he does go into the real world, he occasionally makes a slip. Smith believed, for example, that higher wages were paid in Birmingham than Sheffield because the former produced goods based on 'fashion and fancy', rather than the latter's 'use or necessity'.[18] Birmingham goods are 'continuously changing and seldom last long enough to be considered old established manufactures'. This implies that the higher wages are required because of the risks of unemployment, whereas Birmingham workers were paid more because new articles in the 'toy trade'—small metal articles, especially buckles and buttons—called for workmen with a capacity to adapt to new tasks, and to a continuous improvement in techniques.[19]

[17] James Patrick Muirhead, *The Origins and Progress of the Mechanical Inventions of James Watt*, Illustrated by Correspondence with his Friends and the Specification of His Patents (in three volumes, London, John Murray, 1854), vol. ii, 15.

[18] 114–15; I. x. b. 42. Part I of the chapter.

[19] H. W. Dickinson, *Matthew Boulton* (Cambridge, Cambridge University Press, 1937), 62–63.

I see no need to make the case that Adam Smith had a thorough understanding of the industrial revolution, and this for two reasons. In the first place, much of the substance of what he wrote was derivative; the division of labour goes back to Henry Martin's *Considerations on the East-India Trade* of 1701, and can be found worked out complete with references to pins in Carl's *Traité de la Richesse des Princes et de leurs états et des moyens simples et naturels* of 1722. Indeed, a powerful case has been made lately that much of the inspiration for Smith's emphasis on the division of labour came from Plato, rather than immediately earlier sources like the *Encyclopédie*, Harris, Locke, Mun or Mandeville (a list which omits Martin and Carl). Strong parallels are drawn between illustrations which Plato puts in the mouth of Socrates, and those used by Smith, along with the observation that the Smith library contained three sets of Plato's complete works.[20] Like Shakespeare who borrowed his plays, his originality was in how vividly and graphically he expressed ideas which were common currency.

Secondly, few are given to recognise the beginnings of great movements at their birth. Smith wrote throughout of 'improvements' in an age, as Samuel Johnson said, when the 'world was running mad after innovation'. A number of the inventors and entrepreneurs had large visions. In his well known letter to Watt in 1769, Boulton in reply to the Roebuck suggestion that he buy a licence to make the Watt steam engine for Warwick, Staffordshire and Derby, said that he wanted to make it for the whole world.[21] To James Boswell in 1776 he stated 'I sell here, Sir, what the world wants to have, Power'.[22] Similar exalted commercial ambition can be found in Josiah Wedgwood who wrote to his partner Thomas Bentley in November 1768, 'I have lately had a vision by night of some Vases, Tablets, &c with which Articles we shall certainly serve the *Whole World*'.[23] On a more technical level, note Watt's interest in 1769 in a patent for drawing a chaise by steam.[24] The idea had been advanced by his Glasgow colleague in 1759.[25] Boulton and Dr. William Small had many conversations on applying steam power to canal boats.[26]

[20] Vernard Foley, 'The Division of Labour in Plato and Smith', *History of Political Economy*, vi (1974), 220–42.

[21] Dickinson, op. cit. 76.   [22] Ibid. 73.

[23] *The Selected Letters of Josiah Wedgwood*, edited by Ann Finer and George Savage (London, Cory, Adams and Mackay, 1965), 68.

[24] Muirhead, op. cit. i. 53.   [25] Ibid. p. lxvii.   [26] Ibid. ii. 5.

The men associated with nascent industry were many of them caught up in the changes around them. Watt and Boulton visited the Bridgewater canal before undertaking the surveying of canal sites in Scotland in the former case, and the pushing for the Grand Trunk in the latter.[27] Thomas Bently 'participated in the new spirit. Canal-navigation, moss draining, new materials for manufacturers, improved processes for industry, new inventions of all kinds arrested and retained his attention.'[28] The 'spirit for enterprise and improvement in the arts' of (medical) Dr. John Roebuck, friend of Adam Smith and patron of James Watt, inventor of the lead chamber method of making sulphuric acid, entrepreneur of coal mines and the Carron iron works, 'was well known'.[29] Even Edmund Burke, as Koebner reminds us, in 1769 collected instances of the energies displayed in British manufactures, and praised the 'spirited, inventive, and enterprising traders of Manchester'.[30] From one viewpoint 'It was an age in which economic and industrial facts loomed large; they advanced new claims and offered new stimulus . . . a vast change had come over the general mind; the objects of knowledge, study and pursuit were seen in altered perspective and acquired altered values'.[31]

Adam Smith, as just noted, wrote continuously of improvements but without suggesting he was aware of their details on the one hand, or their collective import on the other. The reason is surely contained in a statement by a colleague of mine at M.I.T., a metallurgist, Cyril Stanley Smith, a statement which both sums up the nature of the industrial revolution and reveals how Adam Smith could have ignored it:

These and hundreds more materials and uses grew symbiotically through history, in a manner analogous to the S-curve of a phase transformation of the materials themselves. There was a stage, invisible except in retrospect, wherein fluctuations from the *status-quo*, involving only small localised distortion began to interact and consoli-

[27] H. W. Dickinson, *James Watt, Craftsman and Engineer* (Cambridge, Cambridge University Press, 1936) 46; Dickinson, *Matthew Boulton*, 50.

[28] Julia Wedgwood, *The Personal Life of Josiah Wedgwood* (London, Macmillan, 1915), 29.

[29] James Patrick Muirhead, *The Life of James Watt*, with Selections from his Correspondence (London, John Murray, 1858), 95.

[30] Cited by R. Keobner, 'Adam Smith and the Industrial Revolution', *Economic History Review*, Second Series, xi, No. 3 (August 1959), 386.

[31] Julia Wedgwood, op. cit. 28–29.

date into a new structure; this nucleus then grew in a more or less constant environment at an increasing rate because of the increasing interfacial opportunity, until finally its growth was slowed and stopped by depletion of material necessary for growth, or by the growing counter-pressure of other aspects of the environment. Any change in conditions (thermo-dynamic = social) may provide an opportunity for a new phase. We all know how the superposition of many small sequential S-curves themselves tend to add up to the giant S-curve of that new and larger structure we call civilisation . . . Because at any one time there are many overlapping competing sub-systems at different stages of maturity but each continually changing the environment of the others, it is often hard to see what is going on. Moreover, nucleation must in principle be invisible, for the germs of the future take their validity only from and in a larger system that has yet to exist. They are at first indistinguishable from mere foolish fluctuations destined to be erased. They begin in opposition to their environment, but on reaching maturity they form the new environment by the balance of their multiple interactions. This change of scale and interface with time, of radical misfit turning into conservative interlock, is the essence of history of anything whatever, material, intellectual or social.[32]

Adam Smith has a superb record for forecasting in his remarks on the subject of another revolution, that which started in the same year as the *Wealth of Nations* appeared, unless you take the parochial view of my fellow-citizens of Massachusetts that it started a year and a quarter earlier in the skirmishes at Lexington and Concord. Smith was, moreover, prescient in observing that after freeing the colonies 'Great Britain would not only be immediately free from the whole annual expence of the peace establishment of the colonies, but might settle with them such a treaty of commerce as would eventually secure to her a free trade, more advantageous to the great body of the people, though less so the merchants, than the monopoly which she at present enjoys'.[33] If one takes 1782 or 1783 as the date of ignition of the industrial revolution, the revolution Smith did foresee touched off the one he did not.[34]

[32] Cyril Stanley Smith, 'Metallurgy as Human Experience'. The 1974 Distinguished Lectureship in Materials and Society, *Metallurgical Transactions* A, vol. 6A, No. 4 (April 1975), 605.

[33] 582; IV. vii. c. 66. Part III of the chapter.

[34] C. R. Fay notes that Adam Smith was pre-industrial revolution and that his revolution with a capital R was 1688, adding that incidentally this was the telephone number of Trevelyan in old Cambridge days. *The World of Adam Smith* (Cambridge, W. Heffer, 1960), 81.

II

The industrial revolution is a well-squeezed orange, as Ashton has said, and my friend and former student, Charles Staley, on hearing that I was to write this essay, drew my attention to a quotation from an article on human evolution which he finds applicable to studies of Adam Smith:

> Human paleontology shares a peculiar trait with such disparate subjects as theology and extra-terrestial biology. It contains more practitioners than objects for study. This abundance of specialists has assumed the careful scrutiny of every bump on every bone.[35]

Despite the danger of strongly diminishing returns, however, it may be appropriate to touch on three aspects of the industrial revolution which currently interest me: the overtaking of Holland by Britain; the role of beauty in technical change; and Stephen Marglin's recent suggestion that the division of labour was practised under capitalism less for efficiency than for lowering the return to labour.

In a curious passage, Adam Smith claimed that England and France consisted in great measure of proprietors and cultivators, whereas Holland and Hamburg are composed chiefly of merchants, artificers, and manufacturers (632; IV. ix. 13). Hollander states that this remark is meant comparatively, but the basis for such a judgement is not evident.[36] Holland, Smith further thought, was a richer country than England in proportion to the extent of its territory and the number of its people (91; I. ix. 10). In a later passage he states that Holland is by far the richest country in Europe, and England perhaps the second richest (354; II. v. 35), which is not completely congruent with a still later passage in which he states that there is no country in Europe, Holland not excepted, of which the law is, upon the whole, more favourable to the interests of commerce and manufactures, which have been making more rapid progress than agriculture (393; III. iv. 20). Still later, Smith discusses the ruin of manufactures in Holland which is ascribed to high wages (826–27, 857; V. ii. k. 14, 79). This last view of Dutch industry is accepted by modern scholars.[37]

---

[35] David Pilbeoni and Stephen Jay Gould, 'Size and Scaling in Human Evolution', *Science*, vol. 186, No. 4167 (December 1974), 892.

[36] S. Hollander, op. cit. 97.

[37] Joel Mokyr, 'Industrial Growth and Stagnation in the Low Countries, 1800–1850' (doctoral dissertation, Yale University, 1974, to be published).

The picture could have been aided by a better historical sense. Holland was the richest country in Europe in 1675, after which its commerce and manufactures decayed and those of Britain advanced rapidly. By 1730 or at the latest 1750, according to modern interpretations, income per capita in Britain had outstripped that in Holland. A successful protectionist policy in Britain had stimulated linen production, especially in Ireland and in Scotland after union in 1707. Dutch potters moved to London to produce their Delftware there to exploit a patent taken out in 1671. Haarlem lost out in bleaching in 1730. Herring fishing and whaling declined. The staple trade of Amsterdam, moreover, had been replaced by direct exchanges of English woollens for German linen and Spanish and Portuguese wine and treasure, without the need for shipment through the intermediary of Amsterdam. Adam Smith was mistaken in relation to stapling. He thought that commerce or at least the carrying trade derived from opulence rather than led to it (354; II. v. 35) and stated elsewhere that merchants exchanging Koenigsberg corn for Portuguese wine brought both to Amsterdam and incurred the double charge for loading and unloading because they felt uneasy separated from their capital (421–22; IV. ii. 6), thus ignoring the stapling function of grading, packing, storing, and the economies of scale of broader markets.

It is odd that Smith should have thought Britain behind Holland in manufactures in the late 1760s. Josiah Tucker in 1757 wrote:

Few countries equal, perhaps none excell the English in the Numbers and Contrivance of their Machines to abridge Labour. Indeed the Dutch are superior to them in the Use and Application of Wind-Mills for sawing Timber, expressing Oil, making Paper, and the like. But in regard to Mines and Metals of all sorts, the English are uncommonly dextrous in their contrivance of the mechanic powers . . . Slitting Mills, Flatting Mills, Water Wheels, Steam Engines . . . Yet all these, curious as they may seem are little more than preparation or introduction for further operations . . . at Birmingham, Wolverhampton, Sheffield and other Manufacturing Places, almost every Master Manufacturer hath a new Invention of his own, and is daily improving on those of others.[38]

There is the view that it was not the decline of Holland so much that after 1648 she stood still and let other countries overtake her,[39]

[38] Quoted in Dickinson, *Matthew Boulton*, 12 and in R. Koebner, op. cit. 385–86.
[39] Charles Wilson, *The Dutch Republic and the Civilisation of the Seventeenth Century* (London, Weidenfeld and Nicholson, 1958), 230.

or that the Dutch economy did not decline absolutely until 1780.[40] This overlooks the deterioration of Leiden, Haarlem, Delft, Saandam in shipbuilding, and the loss of the Dutch monopoly in shipping and in the herring catch.

Most of all, however, Smith seems not to have appreciated how much of the advances in commerce and industry in Britain were the result of intervention in the economic process as opposed to the simple and obvious system of natural liberty. The Dutch monopoly in commerce was invaded by the Navigation laws of the seventeenth century, which Smith more or less approved of on the ground of national defence, though in this respect one view contends that he was being ironic.[41] Smith explicitly objects to the monopoly of the carrying trade with the colonies and insists that Britain was a great nation in trade before the Navigation laws (563; IV. vii. c. 23). This seems to overlook the basis for Glasgow's prosperity with the monopoly of tobacco trade with Maryland and Virginia; after its loss in 1776 Glasgow fell on hard times. And it especially ignores the position in textiles, where commercial policy was highly effective. It may well be that responsiveness of the economy is more important than the nature of the stimulus; under certain conditions, industry will be spurred either by an increase in a tariff or by a decrease. But the case of cotton textiles is instructive.

At the end of the seventeenth century Indian calicoes were beginning to eat into the market for woollens, and the latter interests persuaded Parliament in 1700 to prohibit the import of printed calicoes. In the interest of the printing industry, plain muslins were permitted entry under a heavy duty, but as these grew in volume, the woollen and linen interests agitated for an excise tax on calicoes printed, stained, painted or dyed, which affected local finishing. This was levied at the rate of 3d per yard in 1712 and raised to 6d in 1714. Demand kept rising, and such was the distress among woollen producers that in 1720 an act was passed prohibiting the use or wear of all printed or dyed calicoes except muslin, neck-

---

[40] H. R. C. Wright, *Free Trade and Protection in the Netherlands, 1816–1830* (Cambridge, Cambridge University Press, 1955), 9.

[41] Larry Neal, 'Adam Smith on Defence and Opulence', Faculty Working Paper no. 214, College of Commerce and Business Administration, University of Illinois at Urbana-Champaign (October 22, 1974). Smith's view that Britain was a great nation in trade prior to the Navigation Laws is controverted in Ralph Davis, *Rise of the British Shipping Industry* (New York, Rowman and Littlefield, 1962), Chapter 2.

cloths and fustians. None of these measures was effective. In 1736 the manufacture of calico was permitted with a linen warp. Walpole's tariff reforms of 1721–42 abolished duties on exports of manufactured goods, and on imports of raw materials, stimulating textile manufacturing of all kinds, though the import of raw cotton did not pick up until after 1748, well after Kay's 1738 invention of the flying shuttle, which could not help, given the yarn bottleneck. When this was broken by Arkwright's water-frame in 1769 and Hargreaves's spinning jenny in 1770, cotton was used first for stockings and then in 1773 for cloth. Arkwright petitioned Parliament to remove the duties, and by 1774 every kind of printed, stained and dyed stuffs made wholly from cotton became lawful.[42] As noted in the 1783 edition of the *Wealth of Nations*, this last year also saw the enactment of a prohibition on the export of utensils used in the cotton, linen, woollen and silk manufacture (624; IV. viii. 43).

Commercial policy equally played a role in the development of linen manufacture in Ireland and Scotland, and in iron.

Policy, as I have noted, was probably less important than the response to it. In the 1820s, Spitalfields would respond positively to a reduction in tariffs as Manchester responded positively to a reduction in imports. The difference between silk and cotton lay in the elasticity of the supply of raw material, low in silk, high (after 1790) in cotton. Entrepreneurs were ready to be stimulated by lower prices or higher, of outputs or inputs.

III

Smith's distinction between fashion and fancy and use or necessity, referred to earlier, had its echo in the division of Josiah Wedgwood's manufactures between Wedgwood and (Thomas) Wedgwood which produced useful wares at Burslem after the Etruria plant had been established for ornamental ware by Wedgwood and Bentley.[43] It survives today in Galbraith's distinction between

[42] Thomas Ellison, *The Cotton Trade of Great Britain* (first impression, 1886, new edition, New York, Augustus M. Kelley, 1968), 11–12; H. R. Fox Bourne, *English Merchants, Memories in Illustration of the Progress of British Commerce* (London, Richard Bentley, 1866), 152.

[43] Julia Wedgwood, op. cit. 123. In 1770, Josiah Wedgwood found the distinction between 'ornamental' and 'useful' ware overdrawn. It was not to be based on fineness, richness, price, colour, enamelling, or gilding, and it was important to avoid disputes such as those in France, where the King forbade

necessities and those goods forced on passive consumers by advertising, and in the lines drawn by developing countries between things they need and those like Coca-cola and breakfast foods which ignorant consumers waste their substance on. At every epoch it is of doubtful validity.

The usual view is that necessity is the mother of invention, or invention the mother of necessity, or both. Or that inventions leapfrog through disproportionalities, what Hirschman calls unbalanced growth, with expansion at one stage of production putting pressure on improved efficiency upstream in the production of inputs, and downstream in the consumption of its outputs. None of this can be denied. But Cyril Smith makes the point that a very large number of inventions, and particularly the improvement of materials, derives from the attempt to make goods more pleasing—softer, whiter, more brightly coloured, more beautiful,[44] better tasting. A great deal of the effort of merchants and manufacturers is in improving quality, and in standardizing it. Price is important, but so are quality and the assurance of quality which comes from standardization, a point largely missed initially in the Russian revolution and in economic development in the less developed countries, and one which was inherent in capitalist organization under both putting out and the factory system.

In another paper, I make the distinction between the 'gains-from-trade' merchant, who largely buys goods where they are cheap, and sells them where they are dear, and the 'value-added' merchant, who concerns himself especially with extending the market by insisting that the goods be made better so as to have greater appeal. These are ideal types, of course, since the purest of gains-from-trade merchants, buying spice, silk, or china in the East and selling it in London, will repackage and sort the goods to add some value; at the other extreme, the value-added merchant must still buy cheap and sell dear. The distinction is not quite identical with Adam Smith's separation of the speculative merchant, who exercises no one regular, established, or well known branch of business, who can sometimes accumulate a considerable fortune by

the use of gold to ordinary Potters, to reserve it for the Royal Pottery at Sèvres. 'Useful ware was that made use of at meals' (*Selected Letters of Josiah Wedgwood*, 95–96).

[44] Cyril Stanley Smith, 'Art, Technology and Science: Notes on their Historical Interaction', *Technology and Culture*, vol. ii, No. 4 (October 1970), 493–549.

two or three successful speculations, and the slow accumulator in
a single industry who seldom makes a great fortune but in consequence of a long life of industry, frugality and attention (113–14;
I. x. b. 38). The gains-from-trade merchant leaves goods much as
they are, save for sorting, perhaps curing, packing, refining, and
the like, relatively simple functions, while the value-added merchant puts pressure on his suppliers to make goods more efficient
for the task in hand, and in the cases of textiles, glass, china, 'toys'
more attractive, or cheaper for the same degree of attraction. The
chemical industry grew partly from pure science, the investigations
of Priestly and Lavoisier which fall within the period of the industrial revolution, and also from pressure of industry to find cheaper
methods of bleaching and dyeing, not for 'use or necessity' but for
'fashion and fancy'.

Adam Smith frequently failed to distinguish between commerce
and industry, treating them almost as one word, like 'damn Yankee',
and for the purpose of quality improvement and standardisation,
the differences are minimal. The merchant often retained the
finishing stages of textile manufacture in his own hands, or sub-
contracted it out under rigorous supervision. Such was the case
in Manchester,[45] Leeds,[46] Beauvais,[47] Le Mans,[48] Barman and
Elberfeld.[49] In toy-making there was a feverish search for novel-
ties, and designing advances was an important function of the
industry.[50] Wedgwood wrote to Bentley in 1770: 'I am fully
persuaded that the farther we proceed in it (ornament) the richer
crop we shall reap of *Fame and Profit.*'[51] The hunt for synthetic

[45] Alfred P. Wadsworth and Julia de Lucy Mann, *The Cotton Trade and Industrial Lancashire, 1600–1780* (Manchester, Manchester University Press, 1931), 250–52.
[46] R. G. Wilson, *Gentlemen Merchants, The Merchant Community of Leeds, 1700–1830* (Manchester, Manchester University Press, 1971), 65–70.
[47] Pierre Goubert, *Familles marchands sous l'Ancient Régime: les Danse et les Motte* (Paris. S.E.V.P.E.N., 1959), 69.
[48] François Dornic, *L'industrie textile dans le Maine et ses débouches inter-nationaux (1650–1815)* (Le Mans, Editions Pierre-Belon, 1955), 44.
[49] Wolfgang Köllmann, *Sozialgeschichte der Stadt Barmen im 19. Jahr-hundert* (Tübingen, J. C. B. Mohr (Paul Siebeck), 1960), 3.
[50] Dickinson, *Matthew Boulton*, 63.
[51] *Selected Letters of Josiah Wedgwood*, 97. In an early letter (October 1, 1769) he had put the matter in a more modern economic mode: 'Let us begin, proceed, and finish our future schemes, our days and years, in the pursuit of *Fortune, Fame,* and the *Public Good.*' (Ibid. 82.) In the pursuit of Fortune, Wedgwood and Bentley sought to keep their designs and materials secret; for the sake of the Public Good, they would welcome imitation.

dyes in the mid-19th century which ushered in the organic chemistry revolution had much the same spur.

It is of particular interest that import substitution and the search for economical beauty go hand in hand. The industrial revolution can be said to have resulted in large measure from the search for substitutes for cottons and china from the East. Calicoes in Britain have been discussed. 'Siamoises' were a cotton cloth in France devised to imitate the stuffs worn by the wife of the Ambassador of Siam when she was presented to the court of Louis XIV in 1684.[52] China ware was brought from the Orient by the early East India companies at the turn of the sixteenth to seventeenth centuries. Meissen ware in the first decade of the 18th century and Sevrès china in the 1750s were early responses. They were both supported by courts, and did not need to meet a market test. Delft provided a less elegant substitute for the earthenware of the ordinary household until Wedgwood took over,[53] in the same way that chemically bleached, dyed and printed cotton took over from unbleached or crudely bleached, and undyed or crudely dyed linens and woollens. Especially in the hot climates of the Mediterranean and Latin America lighter and brighter were better.

Standardization means value-added in various ways. To the modern consumer, homespun, handcrafted, tailor-made is superior to machine-produced goods, but that is because they are made to superior specifications. When all goods were homemade, the lack of standardization was a disability, whether in stacking plates which exerted unequal pressure on one another, and thus broke[54] or the cloth that did not meet specifications and was returned, thus increasing the need for investment in working capital.

One form of standardization is attention to delivery dates. In the eighteenth century this does not seem pressing, but infrequent sailings of ships, the fleet leaving Bristol for Newfoundland once a year, for example, made prompt delivery a capital-saving virtue, as did marketing through semi-annual or annual fairs.

The spectacular inventions in steam, waterframe, spinning jenny, coke, puddling and the like occupy front and centre of the stage of the industrial revolution. Firms like Boulton and Watt

[52] Pierre Dardel, *Commerce, industrie et navigation à Rouen et au Havre au XVIIIᵉ siècle* (Rouen, Société libre d'Emulation de la Seine-Maritime, 1966), 117.
[53] *Selected Letters of Josiah Wedgwood*, 3.
[54] Julia Wedgwood, *The Life of Josiah Wedgwood*, 22.

capable of contemplating steam-chaises and moving canal boats by steam engine in 1759 and 1770 capture the imagination. But the steady improvement of goods in quality and standardization was a vital part of the action. Search for quality frequently led to breakthroughs such as Wedgwood's creamware, and jaspar, which leads Cyril Smith to hold Wedgwood's science-based, market-oriented industry as a nucleus of English economic growth as much as the better known contributions of Darby and Cort to iron manufacture or of Watt to power production.[55]

IV

Adam Smith's contribution which is most clearly related to the industrial revolution is doubtless the opening discussion in Book I, chapters i to iii. This has recently been praised and damned, praised by Lord Kaldor who asserts that economics went wrong immediately in the middle of chapter iv when Smith abandoned his examination of the relationship between the division of labour and the extent of the market and moved off into money, the theory of value and the distribution of income, what most think his central contribution to our subject but Kaldor views as irrelevant;[56] damned by Stephen A. Marglin, a radical critic, who contends that the division of labour has nothing to do with efficiency and everything to do with the expropriation of income from the worker by the capitalist.[57] I leave the quarrel with Kaldor to others concerned with resource allocation and income distribution, and address Marglin's proposition. It is, I believe, of interest today because it makes a strong appeal to young people and to non-economist Marxists, such as Johann Galtung, who believe that all dependence, even interdependence, is exploitation.[58] Hierarchical organizations of all kinds are under attack, and the radical faith suggests that foremen and supervisors in a factory should be chosen arbitrarily, by lot, by election rather than by competitive means, and paid the same as those whom they supervise.

Marglin's argument proceeds along the same lines as Smith's, as he discusses the pin factory and the three sources of improve-

[55] Cyril S. Smith, 'Metallurgy as Human Experience', op. cit. 614.

[56] Nicholas Kaldor, 'The Irrelevance of Equilibrium Economics', *Economic Journal*, lxxxii (December 1972), 1240.

[57] Stephen A. Marglin, 'What Do Bosses Do, Part I', *The Review of Radical Political Economy*, vi, No. 2 (Summer, 1974), 60–112.

[58] Johann Galtung, 'The Future of Human Society', *Futures, The Journal of Forecasting and Planning*, vol. 2, No. ii (June 1970), 132–42.

ment: dexterity, the saving of waiting time between tasks, and the devising of inventions which abridge labour by workers concentrating on a single task. The last it is difficult to take seriously, and Marglin does not, pointing out that Smith himself observes that a workman engaged in repetitive tasks has no occasion to exercise his understanding or to exercise his invention in finding out expedients for difficulties which never occur (734; V. i. f. 50). Adam Smith indeed very quickly notes that 'All the improvements in machinery . . . have by no means been the inventions of those who had occasion to use the machines' but that 'in the progress of society, philosophy or speculation becomes, like every other employment, the principal or sole task of a particular class of citizens. Like every other employment, too, it is subdivided into a great number of different branches, each of which affords occupation to a peculiar tribe or class of philosophers; and this sub-division of employment in philosophy, as well as in every other business, improves dexterity and saves time. . .' (10; I i. 9).

Waiting time does not impress Marglin either. A farmer gains from staying with a task long enough to minimize set-up time. A pinmaker could undertake the first of ten operations for a day or days at a time, and then change, to reduce set-up time to an insignificant portion of total work time and then more to the second.[59] In this case, however, Marglin may have missed the point about the extent of the market. He claims that 'if each producer could integrate the component tasks of pin manufacture into a marketable product, he would soon discover that he had no need to deal with the market for pins through the intermediation of the putter-outer. He could sell directly and appropriate to himself the profit that the capitalist derived from mediating between the producer and the market.'[60] The pin producer now performs all the 10 manufacturing tasks and markets the product as well. Peasants perhaps can sell their produce above their own sustenance in a local market. It is not clear that the pin market is so organised. The pin is a 'very trifling manufacture'.[61] Any substantial number produced must be moved in what Smith calls 'distant sale'.[62]

[59] Marglin, op. cit. 66–67.   [60] Loc. cit.
[61] In the 1763 draft, the example is called 'a frivolous instance' (reprinted in W. R. Scott, 328). In Carl's *Traité de la Richesse des princes et de leurs états et des moyens simples et naturels*, the pin is called 'the least of our needs' (Paris, Chez Theodore Legas, three volumes, 1722), vol. i, 18.
[62] WN 359, 381, 382, 393 etc.; III. i. 5, III. iii. 17, 19, 20; III. iv. 20.

Distant sale requires knowledge of languages, commercial practice, credit standings, modes of transport, etc., forms of dexterity and skill which the home pinmaker may not readily achieve.

The matter is neatly put in a letter of August 23rd, 1772 to Thomas Bentley by Josiah Wedgwood who sought to lower piece-rates for workers:

I have had several *Talks* with our men at the Ornamental works lately about the price of our workmanships, and the necessity of lowering it, especially in Flowerpots, Bowpots (boughpots) and Teapots, and as I find their chief reason against lowering their prices is the small quantity made of each, which creates them as much trouble in *tuning their fiddle* as *playing the tune*, I have promised them that they shall make dozens and Groces of Flower, and Teapots, and of the Vases and Bowpots too, as often as we dare venture at such quantities.[63]

Wedgwood, of course, divided functions with the merchant Bentley, and Boulton with the merchant Fothergill. Scale sufficient to handle the waiting-time problem required distant sale which required merchants. On occasion distant marketing preceded efficient scale in production; often they grew side by side. Colonial trade provided important outlets: 'The process of industrialisation in England from the second quarter of the eighteenth century was to an important extent the response to colonial demands for nails, axes, firearms, buckles, coaches, clocks, saddles, handkerchiefs, buttons, cordage and a thousand other things goods, several sorts.'[64] To this list could be added pottery, both useful and ornamental, produced in the potteries of Staffordshire, the 'bulk' of which was exported to the Continent and the Islands of North America, as well as to every port in Europe.[65] Between Easter 1771 and Easter 1772, at the height, 72 per cent of Yorkshire's production of woollens was exported. While output was increasing four times between 1700 and 1780, the export proportion was rising from roughly 40 per cent (in 1695) to two-thirds (in 1800).[66] The notion of a producer selling his own output without the aid of specialists seems in these circumstances utopian.

[63] *Selected Letters of Josiah Wedgwood*, 130.
[64] Ralph Davis, 'English Foreign Trade, 1700–1774', *Economic History Review*, Second Series, vol. xv, No. 2 (May 1962), reprinted in W. E. Minchinton, ed., *The Growth of Overseas Trade in the 17th and 18th Centuries* (London, Methuen, 1969), 106.
[65] *Selected Letters of Josiah Wedgwood*, 24, 29.
[66] R. G. Wilson, *Gentlemen Merchants of Leeds*, op. cit. 19, 42.

Marglin has most difficulty in maintaining that the division of labour does not add to output per unit of input in improving dexterity. He makes several damaging concessions. Adam Smith would be difficult to counter if he had been dealing with musicians, dancers or surgeons;[67] to the extent that the skills at issue are difficult to acquire, specialization is essential to the division of labour into separate operations.[68] Later he suggests that factory employment can be attractive to men, whereas earlier he had said that whenever it is possible to avoid factory employment, workers had done so.[69] Most of his illustrations are drawn from the cotton-textile industry. In engineering, or in pottery, however, natural ability, training and practice are all needed:

My idea was to settle a manufactory for the steam engine near to my own by the side of the canal where I would erect all the conveniences necessary for the completion of the engines and from which manufactory we would serve all the world with engines of all sizes. By these means and your assistance we could engage and instruct some excellent workmen (with more excellent tools than would be worth any man's while to procure for one single engine) and could execute the engine 20 per cent cheaper than it would otherwise be executed and with as great a difference in accuracy as there is between the blacksmith and the mathematical instrument maker.[70]

I have trained up many and am training up more young plain Country Lads, all of which that betray any genius are taught to draw, from which I derive many advantages that are not to be found in any manufacture that is or can be established in a great and Debauched capital.[71]

We have not got thirty hands here, but I have much ado to keep the new ones quiet. Some will not work in Black. Others say they will never learn this new business, and want to be released to make Terrines and sauce boats again. I do not know what I shall do with them, we have too many *fresh* hands to take in at once, though we have business enough for them, if they knew, or would have the patience to learn to do it, but they do not seem to relish the thought of a second apprenticeship . . .[72]

---

[67] Marglin, op. cit. 68.   [68] Loc. cit.   [69] Ibid. 98 n.
[70] Letter of Matthew Boulton to James Watt, February 1769, in Dickinson, *Matthew Boulton*, 76.   [71] 1770 letter of Boulton, ibid. 60.
[72] Letter of Josiah Wedgwood to Thomas Bentley, November 1769, *Selected Letters of Josiah Wedgwood*, 84. See also 'It is this sort of *time loseing* with Uniques which keeps ingenious Artists who are connected with Great Men of taste poor, and would make us so too if we did too much in that way . . .' (ibid. 85).

You observe very justly that few hands can be got to paint flowers in the style we want them. I may add, nor any other work we do— *We must make them* . . . Where among our Potters could I get a complete Vase maker? Nay I could not get a hand through the whole Pottery to make a tableplate without training them up for that purpose, and you must be content to train up such Painters as offer to you and not turn them adrift because they cannot immediately form their hands to our new stile.[73]

You must have more Painters—You shall,—But remember that there are none *ready made* . . . So please give my respects to Mr. Rhodes, and tell him if any man who offers himself is *sober*, he must make him *everything else*.[74]

A strong case can be made that the division of labour has very little to do with capitalism. Plato's interest in the subject has been referred to earlier. Haley asserts that Dutch shipbuilding in the seventeenth century would have made a better illustration of division of labour than pin-making.[75] Standardized flyboats were built at Saandam using labour-saving machinery—wind-driven saw mills and great cranes which handled heavy timbers; inventories of timber for building four or five thousand ships were kept in hand. In the second war with England, Saandam turned out a ship a day.[76] A century earlier, moreover, in 1574, the Arsenal at Venice, a shipyard under public management, turned out a merchant galley for the edification of Henry the Third of France in less than an hour:

Mass production of ships of a standard design became the hallmark of the Venetian Arsenal. Workmen developed unusual skill and efficiency as a result of specialisation; standard replaceable parts made repairs easy; stockpiling such parts allowed the state to maintain a cadre of skilled men always available, who, in case of need, could direct the efforts of a suddenly enlarged workforce, such as might be required for building a new fleet in a hurry.[77]

[73] Letter of Josiah Wedgwood to Thomas Bentley, 19 May 1770, ibid. 92.
[74] Ibid., letter of 23rd May 1770.
[75] K. H. D. Haley, *The Dutch in the Seventeenth Century* (London, Thames and Hudson, 1972), 19.
[76] Violet Barbour, 'Dutch and English Merchant Shipping in the Seventeenth Century', *Economic History Review*, ii (1929–30), reprinted in E. M. Carus-Wilson, *Essays in Economic History* (London, Edward Arnold, 1954), 239, 242.
[77] William H. McNeill, *Venice, The Hinge of Europe, 1081–1797* (Chicago, University of Chicago Press, 1974), 6 and note 9, p. 244.

Marglin admits that evidence in support of his view that the division of labour represents not efficiency but an attempt to divide and conquer is 'naturally enough, not easy to come by', and 'not overwhelming'.[78] He cites in support a cotton textile manufacturer who kept his manager from knowing anything about mixing cotton, or costs, so that he can never take the business away from him.[79] Evidence that care was taken not to furnish industrial secrets to individuals considered as possible candidates for setting up rival establishments is abundant, however. Workmen who had been trained were not encouraged to take their skills elsewhere; on the contrary, manufacturers like Josiah Wedgwood petitioned Parliament to restrict their movement abroad, were wary of imitators, separated the different departments in Etruria and gave each one only outside entrances, so as to prevent workmen in one department from wandering about and picking up proprietary information.[80] At one point (1769) Wedgwood wrote:

If we get these new painters, and the figure makers, we shall do pretty well in those branches. But these hands should if possible be kept by themselves 'till we are better acquainted with them otherwise they may do us a great deal of mischief if we should be obliged to part with them soon.[81]

It is true enough that owners of proprietary information hung on to it under capitalism as long as they could. It is also true that competition tended to erode its scarcity value. The merchant started out with a monopoly of information, concerning where goods could be found, and where they were wanted. The monopoly over information was related to education, and when education became general, the merchant lost his pre-eminence, except to the extent that he innovated; direct buying and selling replaced him. His efforts to make goods of higher quality, more promptly and cheaper were part of the innovating process, and generally involved improvements which were unpatentable and insufficiently distinctive to be awarded prizes.

Marglin further insists that the move from the cottage to the factory was prompted by efforts to enforce the division of labour and thereby exploit workers, rather than by application of power,

---

[78] Marglin, op. cit. 72.   [79] Ibid. 74.
[80] *Selected Letters of Josiah Wedgwood*, 76.
[81] Letter of April 1769 to Thomas Bentley, ibid. 76.

prevention of pilferage and adulteration (the worker's only counter-vailing tactic, according to Marglin). The view is a familiar one. Charles Bray regarded the ordinary factory as a 'cunning device to cheat workmen out of their birthright' and justified the cottage factory which the Quakers set up in Coventry as Owenism.[82] One could equally refer to Karl Polanyi, a Christian Socialist, who excoriated the market but exonerated the factory,[83] or Lazlett who embraces the market but rejects the factory.[84] But to pursue these aspects of the industrial revolution would take us too far afield.

Smith was aware that the division of labour could lead to a dead end; in a passage far removed from Book I, he holds:

The man whose life is spent performing a few simple operations, of which the effects too are, perhaps, always the same or very nearly the same, has no occasion to exert his understanding, or to exercise his invention in finding out expedients for removing difficulties which never occur. He naturally loses, therefore, the habit of such exertion, and generally becomes as stupid and ignorant as it is possible for a human creature to become . . . His dexterity at his own particular trade seems, in this manner, to be acquired at the expense of his intellectual, social and martial virtues . . . In the barbarous societies . . . the varied occupations of every man oblige every man to exert his capacity, and to invent expedients for removing difficulties which are continually occurring. Invention is kept alive, and the mind is not suffered to fall into that drowsy stupidity, which, in a civilized society, seems to numb the understanding of almost all the inferior ranks of people.[85]

This emphasis on the social aspects of the division of labour antici-pates a line of argument found in Mary Wollstonecraft, who maintains that:

The time which, a celebrated writer says, is sauntered away, in going from one part of an employment to another, is the very time that preserves the man from degenerating into a brute . . . The very gait of the man who is his own master is so much more steady than the slouching step of the servant of a servant . . .[86]

[82] John Prest, *The Industrial Revolution of Coventry* (London, Oxford University Press, 1960), 104.

[83] See my essay on '*The Great Transformation*, by Karl Polanyi', in *Daedalus*, vol. ciii, No. 1 (Winter 1974), 45–52.

[84] Peter Lazlett, *The World We have Lost* (New York, Charles Scribner's Sons, 1965).

[85] WN, 734–35; V. i, Part III, Art. 2nd (V. i. f. 50, 51).

[86] Mary Wollstonecraft, *French Revolution*, 1795, the conclusion. This and the following reference were kindly communicated to me by Ellen Moers.

and in John Ruskin, who held that division of labour should be regarded as division of men:

Divided into mere fragments of men—broken into small fragments and crumbs of life, so that all the little piece of intelligence that is left in a man is not enough to make a pin, or a nail, but exhausts itself in making the point of a pin, or the head of a nail.[87]

These unhappy consequences may result from the division of labour, or what van der Wee refers to as 'excessive division of labour', though in the cottage textile industry, rather than the factory.[88] It is a fair point that the social consequences of the division of labour may be untoward, as Smith recognizes. It is quite a different matter to assert that the economic purpose of the division of labour was exploitation rather than efficiency.

Adam Smith's discussion of allocation, distribution, and the division of labour through the market was largely related to what is now called 'proto-industrialization', rather than the industrialization into large factories of the industrial revolution. Large-scale production had existed in isolation for centuries, and in Britain for decades. But proto-industrialization, the specialization by merchants, weavers, spinners, nailers, pinmakers, philosophers, and speculators was efficient rather than exploitative. Rudolf Braun has shown for the Zurich Oberland how proto-industrialization raised the level of living of peasants who were overcrowded on limited land, rather than lowering it. Cottage industry did not uproot men. On the contrary it gave them work and bread and enabled them not to migrate from their homeland.[89] The factory in the Zurich Oberland was a defensive measure to enable the area to meet the competition of British machine-spun.

In cotton textiles in Switzerland, the early factory pioneers were technical people, Wyss, Honneger, Wild, Oberholzer, who worked on making cloth cheaper, and not on impoverishing the workers who were impoverished by improved and cheaper British exports. The less efficient cottage workers moved into the factory and improved their standard. It was the more effective cottage workers,

---

[87] John Ruskin, *Stones of Venice*, vol. ii (London, 1853), Chap. vi.

[88] Herman van der Wee, 'Structural Changes and Specialization in the Industry of Southern Netherlands, 1100–1600', *Economic History Review*, 2nd Series, vol. xxviii, No. 2 (May 1975), 204.

[89] R. Braun, *Industrialisierung und Volksleben, Die Veränderungen der Lebensform in einem ländlichen Industriegebiet vor 1800* (Züricher Oberland), 241.

with greater dexterity, who held on in cottage industry too long when the higher efficiency of factories, as revealed by cheaper goods of a given quality, sealed their doom.[90]

Let us permit the division of labour between Adam Smith and, say, Josiah Wedgwood, though both in their way were protean. Wedgwood was a nucleus-maker and a man who understood nucleation:

> I have for some time been reviewing my experiments, and I find such *Roots*, such *Seeds* would open and branch wonderfully if I could nail myself down to cultivation of them for a year or two. And the Fox-Hunter does not enjoy more pleasure from the chace, than I do from the prosecution of my experiments when I am fairly enter'd in the field, and the farther I go, the wider the field extends before me.[91]

Smith was a man of wide interests in law, moral philosophy, criticism, rhetoric, and agriculture.[92] He approached the heart of the industrial revolution with his division of labour, specialization and exchange, and extent of the market, and planted the seed which has developed into the great social science of economics. That surely is glory enough.

COMMENT
by Asa Briggs*

As befits the first paper to be delivered at this Conference, Professor Kindleberger's interesting survey is concerned with large themes.

It is now a commonplace among historians that two long and continuing revolutions—an industrial revolution, which began with Wedgwood, Arkwright, Boulton and Watt, and a political revolution, which began in France in 1789—have transformed ways of working and thinking and feeling.

Yet it is an awkward commonplace, and it has not brought with it any general consensus among historians about motives, sequences and interconnections. Disagreement has started on the issue of the

[90] R. Braun, *Sozialer und Kultureller Wandel in einem ländlichen Industrie-gebiet im 19, und 20. Jahrhundert* (Erlenbach-Zurich and Stuttgart, Eugen Rentsch Verlag, 1965), chapter 2.

[91] *Selected Letters of Josiah Wedgwood*, 159.

[92] W. R. Scott, op. cit. 46.

* University of Sussex.

relationship between these two 'revolutions' and what went before. What was the relationship between the 'industrial revolution' and antecedent 'capitalism'? What was the relationship between the 'French revolution' and 'the Enlightenment'? These are fundamental questions which even when broken down into more detailed questions do not become much easier to answer. What was the relationship between the growth of 'trade and finance' in the eighteenth century—few would deny that this was Smith's main theme—and the growth of industry on which he said little that was explicit? What was the relationship between the French Revolution, which Smith lived to see only in its beginnings, and the American Revolution on which what he had to say, as Professor Kindleberger rightly points out in this bicentennial year of that Revolution, was direct and pertinent?

We are all caught in historiographical, if not in historical, thickets, when we turn to the questions raised in his paper, and we are not helped, in my view, by the division he draws between historians of economic thought and economic historians as guides. It was an economic historian, albeit a refreshingly unorthodox one, C. R. Fay, who provided evidence to qualify—if not completely to contradict—Professor Kindleberger's generalization that 'the *Wealth of Nations* was the work of a literary economist, like some of us, who drew his examples from books, not from the world around him': after beginning his *Adam Smith and the Scotland of His Day* with an account of Smith's library (as in the case of the other great book of 1776, Gibbon's *Decline and Fall*, we start with 'the womb of the classics'),[1] he goes on to show us that the books by themselves do not tell us enough. We have to turn to Smith's personal experience. On the other side of Professor Kindleberger's dividing line, not all historians of economic thought have gone so far as Professor Samuel Hollander has done in his lucid and persuasive advocacy of Smith's special claims to 'insight' into the processes of early industrialization: his footnotes abound with references to historians of economic thought who disagree with him.

Professor Hollander's use of the term 'insight'[2]—not foresight—provides us with clues to the significance of Smith's role. His conception of 'improvement'—a much-used eighteenth century term,

[1] C. R. Fay, *Adam Smith and the Scotland of His Day* (Cambridge, 1956), 1.
[2] S. Hollander, *The Economics of Adam Smith* (Toronto, 1973), 241.

which writers were to employ later when suggesting an alternative way ahead for mankind to the way of revolution—certainly involved a recognition that the progress in trade and finance would lead through market extension and market pressures to 'all such improvements in mechanics, as enable the same number of workmen to perform an equal quantity of work with cheaper and simpler machinery than had been usual before' (WN II. ii. 7). In other words, Smith saw a continuity in economic development which encompassed the growth of 'manufacturing' and of technical improvement to sustain it. 'Though the poor country, notwithstanding the inferiority of its cultivation, can, in some measure, rival the rich in the cheapness and goodness of its corn, it can pretend to no such competition in its manufactures: at least if those manufactures suit the soil, climate, and situation of the rich country' (WN I. i. 4).

Smith followed on from Hume who had written in 1752 that 'the same age, which produces great philosophers and politicians, renowned generals and poets, usually abounds with skilful weavers and ship's carpenters' and had noted how 'industry, knowledge and humanity' were 'linked together by an indissoluble chain' once men were roused from their lethargy and 'put into a fermentation'.[3] Hume caught the excitement of 'improvement', but Smith went further in his analysis of the relationship between commerce and 'manufacturing'—in his account, for example, of fixed capital and its maintenance and of the differential factor-saving consequences of technical change.

Nonetheless, if there was insight in his work there was no foresight. The sense of imminent economic revolution was just as absent from his thinking as the sense of imminent political revolution was absent from the thinking of most of the *philosophes* of the Enlightenment. They no more foresaw the rise of the Third Estate and the execution of the King than he foresaw the unprecedented upward movement of all the economic indicators during the 1780s, the use of new forms of power on a new scale— this was the great omission—or the far-reaching social consequences of technical invention. This does not mean to say, however, that we cannot find insights in the *philosophes* which in retrospect enable us to understand the French Revolution better than we otherwise would do or insights of a special order in Smith—many

[3] David Hume, *The Philosophical Works* (3 vols., London, 1882 edn.), iii. 301–21.

of them are singled out by Professor Hollander and other historians of economic thought—which enable us better to understand 'the industrial revolution'.

I emphasized how the two revolutions were interconnected from the 1780s onwards. It is necessary to add, of course, that Smith himself was in the middle of the pre-1780s interconnections. For John Millar 'the great Montesquieu pointed the road . . . He was the Lord Bacon . . . Dr. Smith is the Newton'.[4] Smith's memorandum of 1778 on 'the state of the contest with America' demonstrates (with more than a touch of irony, of course) what he would have thought of the French Revolution:

> The Americans, it has been said, when they compare the mildness of their old government with the violence of that which they have established in its stead, cannot fail to remember the one with regret, and to view the other with detestation. That these will be their sentiments when the war is over and when the new government, if ever that should happen, is firmly established among them, I have no doubt . . . [But] it was not until some time after the conclusion of the civil war that the people of England began to regret the loss of that regal govt which they had rashly overturned, and which was happily restored to them by such a concurrence of accidental circumstances as may not, upon any similar occasion, ever happen again. (op. cit. § 15.)

(The memorandum was first published in the *American Historical Review*, 1932–3.)

Surely the foresight was limited here, too. Smith may have been right in forecasting the effects on the British economy of the end of the American War and the Empire which went with it, but his *ad hominem* memorandum to Wedderburn, dwelt as much on 'the ulcerated minds of the Americans' as on the commercial advantages to Britain of the end of the struggle. To complete the interconnections it should be noted, perhaps, that the date of the first American edition of the *Wealth of Nations* was 1789.

In considering the contemporary relationship between 'manufacturing' and 'trade' Smith was less enthusiastic and less eloquent than many inferior thinkers, some of whom had technological interests and looked back to Francis Bacon as the pre-industrial

---

[4] J. Millar, *Historical View of the English Government from the Settlement of the Saxons in Britain to the Accession of the House of Stewart* (Glasgow, 1786), 528.

prophet of industrialism through 'the conquest of nature'. It was in 1776 itself that a jaunty versifier wrote:

> The time may come when nothing will succeed
> But what a previous Patent hath decreed
> And we must open on some future day
> The door of Nature with a patent key.[5]

There was, indeed, a whole popular or semi-popular literature on innovation and social change in the last thirty or forty years of the eighteenth century which must be set alongside the economic and philosophical literature of the period. Much of it was concerned with the relationship of the 'arts' to the 'sciences' (Hume's essay from which I have quoted was called 'Of Refinement of the Arts') and of both to 'useful technology' (a new term of the 1770s).[6] It has a direct bearing not only on Professor Kindleberger's first problem—the extent to which Smith was an economist of the industrial revolution—but on one of his subsidiary problems—the role of beauty in technological change.

Smith was not a prophetic writer, and there were many reasons, whether he was aware or not aware of the extent of contemporary technical change in 'manufacturing', why he did not move over the threshold into the future. First, he did not think in terms of 'revolutions'. Semantic history is necessary at this point. The word 'revolution', which has a very long history, only began to register in its modern sense as signifying an over-turning of an old order and the promise of a complete transformation of society *after* Smith had written the *Wealth of Nations*.[7] Paradoxically, its first meaning —a revolving movement in space and time—was retained by contemporaries for the movements of the steam engines which Marx was to see as the key inventions in the moves from capitalism to industrial capitalism. Second, the word 'industry' itself was only just beginning to be used in Smith's time to refer to a sector of economic life and not to a human attribute (of individuals or groups). Smith himself may have been a key figure in popularizing the change of usage: although he usually refers to 'industry' as an attribute and prefers to write of 'manufacturing' when we would

[5] Quoted in Witt Bowden, *Industrial Society in England Towards the End of the Eighteenth Century* (New York, 1925), 55.

[6] The word appears to have been coined by Johann Backmann (1739–1811); in 1777 he published his *Anleitung zur Technologie*, lectures delivered at his university, Göttingen.

[7] See R. Williams, *Keywords* (London, 1976), 226–30.

now say 'industry', nonetheless he does use the noun in something
like its modern sense in such sentences as: 'Every saving, therefore,
in the expence of maintaining the fixed capital, which does not
diminish the productive powers of labour, must increase the fund
which puts industry into motion' (WN II. ii. 25). There is no
movement in Smith's mind, however, towards the language of
'industrialism' or 'industrialization'. Both were soon to become
controversial value-loaded words within the specific context of
'carboniferous capitalism'.[8] Yet 'industry' with Smith was a human
value in itself, independent of its contexts, as it was for the Peel
family when they chose the Latin word 'industria' for their family
motto in 1792.[9] Third—and here conflicts of values cannot be left
out in Smith's own case—Smith did not much like the 'manufacturing interest' which within ten years was to seek to promote
the claims of industry in a collectivist sense. Many passages from
the *Wealth of Nations*, often quoted, condemn 'merchants and
master-manufacturers' for conspiring against the economic advantages due to society as a whole, and Smith was inclined to view
even the individual innovators among them as 'projectors' who
had little to offer to society as a whole. It could be argued that in
attitudes of this kind Smith was influenced by past experience
rather than by estimates of likely future contributions to human
improvement. There is no evidence that he sympathised with the
General Chamber of Manufacturers set up in 1785—I have argued
elsewhere that it marked an important landmark in changing
social consciousness—at the instigation of Wedgwood and Boulton.
Indeed, he wrote to the Duke of La Rochefoucauld in 1785 that
he anticipated 'all the bad consequences from the Chambers of
Commerce and Manufactures establishing in different parts of this
Country, which your Grace seems to foresee. In a Country where
Clamour always intimidates and faction often oppresses the
Government, the regulations of Commerce are commonly dictated
by those who are most interested to deceive and impose upon the
Public.'[10]

[8] This was a key phrase of Lewis Mumford in his *Technics and Civilization*
(London, 1934), 156–8. Adam Smith, he says, 'was too early to appraise the
transformation' (ibid. 152).
[9] See N. Gash, *Mr. Secretary Peel* (London, 1961), 23–4. A later Peel,
quoted by Gash, wrote 'the only ancestry we care about is the shuttle'.
[10] Letter 248, in Smith's *Correspondence*, dated 1 November 1785. Quoted
in Fay, op. cit. 147, from the *Athenaeum*, 28 December 1895.

Smith's attitudes on matters of this kind have been carefully considered by historians of his thought, and I am impressed by A. L. Macfie's argument that Smith did not think in terms of leaps of enterprise[11] and by J. J. Spengler's observation that in the Smithian system the 'undertaker' was 'a prudent, cautious, not overly imaginative fellow, who adjusts to circumstances rather than brings about their modification'.[12] And in collective action, when they worked together, as they were always tempted to do, Smith held that 'undertakers limited their enterprise still further: they were protective, not predatory'. It is not difficult to see why Schumpeter treated Smith with reserve.

There is a further interesting argument which Professor Hollander has used. Smith's belief that innate differences in ability were of little importance restrained him from advancing any theory of 'inventive genius'. He would have been shocked not impressed by a letter written by Wedgwood to Watt in 1785 just after he had visited Arkwright:

He [Arkwright] will be in Birmingham in a few days and I will ask him to call upon you. I told him you were considering the subject of patents, and you two great genius's may probably strike out some new lights together, which neither of you might think of separately.[13]

Smith would have been shocked, of course, not just because such a meeting of minds represented the opposite process to the division of labour. It is to such meetings of minds, however—modern sociologists would talk of 'networking'—that we must turn if we wish to understand the early 'industrial revolution', what was happening before the word itself was coined. Wedgwood was a key figure in the network, and it is fascinating to compare his language and style with that of Smith. When asked in 1792 by Lord Auckland how much the pottery industry had increased during the previous eighty years, he replied that even the idea of making an estimate made him feel giddy. 'I feel it just as impossible . . . as to number the sands on the seashore. The difficulties are nearly equal

---

[11] See A. L. Macfie, *The Individual in Society: Papers on Adam Smith* (London, 1967), a reprint of a paper 'The Scottish Tradition in Economic Thought' first published in the *Scottish Journal of Political Economy*.

[12] J. J. Spengler, 'Adam Smith's Theory of Economic Growth' in *Southern Economic Journal*, vols. xxv and xxvi (1951).

[13] Letter of 17 September 1785 printed in A. Finer and G. Savage (eds.), *The Selected Letters of Josiah Wedgwood* (London, 1965), 284.

with respect to the cotton trade; with this difference, indeed, that one must here shoot flying, for this darts forward with such an amazing rate as to leave all the others far behind.' Once again he came back to his great man—and the machinery. 'This business is supposed to have increased with ten times the celerity of any other; owing chiefly to the machinery invented by that truly great man, Sir Richard Arkwright.[14]

Professor Kindleberger was right to draw attention to Wedgwood and the pottery industry. Yet on the important, if neglected, question of the relationship between beauty and industrial change, I am surprised that he has not quoted Professor John Nef for whom it has been a central theme. It was in relation to an earlier 'industrial revolution', which Nef identified as occurring between 1540 and 1640, that he felt he discerned already a basic difference between Britain and France. In the former country there had been a shift, he thought, 'in the objectives for which considerable industrial capital and numerous workpeople were employed: the shift in the major resources of capital and labour away from production primarily for the sake of beauty, of delight in contemplation, toward production primarily for the sake of usefulness in the purely economic sense of substantial comforts in greater quantities.'[15] In his view what happened later only confirmed what had happened before. 'Since the American and French Revolutions [he took *the* industrial revolution for granted] the claims of utility and efficiency, of multiplication for its own sake, have obtained an increasing preponderance.'[16]

Nef's argument—one side only of a much bigger argument—has never been fully appreciated. Nor the apparent paradox that he would have praised Smith just because he was *not* a prophet of the nineteenth-century industrial society but a late representative of a cosmopolitan eighteenth-century 'civilization' which the industrial revolution and the long and wearing wars with revolutionary and Napoleonic France did much to destroy. I am reminded in conclusion of more words of Fay:

Britain after 1815 was very different from the Britain that had thrown up the Adamses [who came from Kirkcaldy]. Architecture

---

[14] Lady Farrer (ed.), *The Correspondence of Josiah Wedgwood* (privately printed, 1906), vol. iii, 188–94.

[15] J. U. Nef, *The Conquest of the Material World* (Chicago, 1964), 211.

[16] J. U. Nef, *The United States and Civilization* (Chicago, 1967 edn.), 40.

was decadent, ornament debased, things were in the saddle and rode mankind. The world now, in Wordsworth's phrase, knelt before 'the idol proudly termed the Wealth of Nations. The China vase of taste was cracked as badly as the China vase of empire.'[17]

For that huge shift, at least, Adam Smith could not be held responsible.

COMMENT

By R. M. Hartwell*

There are, I think, two meaningful ways in which Adam Smith can be associated with 'the industrial revolution': first, by determining his *awareness* of the industrial revolution, his explanation of it, and his reactions to it; second, by determining his *influence* in the making of the industrial revolution, especially the impact on public policy of his theory of the relationship between 'natural liberty' and 'the wealth of nations'. On 'awareness' Charles Kindleberger argues that Smith neither recognized nor anticipated the industrialization of Britain; thus, agreeing with Mark Blaug that Smith was not aware that 'he was living in times of unusual economic activity'.[1] On 'influence', which Kindleberger does not discuss, the modern conventional wisdom is to dismiss the once fashionable view that Smith was 'the great apostle of laissez-faire' (A. Gray) who enlightened and reformed the commercial policy of Europe, and to agree with J. Viner that 'Smith was not a doctrinal advocate of laissez-faire', and to argue that the *Wealth of Nations* was used more to rationalize than to create liberal economic policies.[2] I disagree both with Kindleberger and Viner. I believe that Adam Smith was aware of the economic changes

[17] Fay, op. cit. 8.

---

* Nuffield College, Oxford.
[1] M. Blaug, *Economic Theory in Retrospect* (Rev. Ed., Irwin, Homewood, Illinois, 1968), 39. For a similar view, see R. Koebner, 'Adam Smith and the Industrial Revolution', *Economic History Review* (2nd Ser., xi, 3, 1959), 382. For a contrary view, see S. Hollander, the *Economics of Adam Smith* (Heinemann, London, 1973), Chapter 7.
[2] A. Gray, *The Development of Economic Doctrine* (Longmans, Green, London, 1931), 142; J. Viner, 'Adam Smith and Laissez-faire', *Journal of Political Economy*, xxxv (1927), 231.

occurring during his lifetime, which coincided with the background and beginnings of the industrial revolution, and that his economic theory and his policy prescriptions were influential in the development of economic liberalism and the remarkable economic growth of the nineteenth century. I will deal at some length with Smith's awareness, but only briefly with his influence, not because I think that the one topic is more important than the other, but as a reaction to Charles Kindleberger, and because I think it is important, in a session on 'the historical background' to get quite clear what Smith *could have been aware of*, and that could only have been the widespread economic change and growth in Britain during his lifetime, and which culminated towards the end of the century in the faster economic growth generally known as 'the industrial revolution'.[3] It was impossible for Smith to have known much about 'the industrial revolution' thus defined and thus dated, but such definition and dating are misleading, as are assertions about Smith's ignorance of technological change. The industrial revolution is best defined as *sustained economic growth*, and Smith certainly recognized and analysed eighteenth century growth, not narrowly in terms of machine technology, but broadly, in terms not only of capital accumulation and the division of labour, but also of appropriate socio-political institutions and government.

II

The main evidence of Adam Smith's awareness of eighteenth century growth comes from his writings, especially from the *Wealth of Nations*, but this evidence can be supported by consideration of his life and career.[4] Indeed, Smith's awareness can be

[3] On eighteenth century growth and the industrial revolution, see R. M. Hartwell, *The Industrial Revolution and Economic Growth* (Methuen, London, 1971), especially Part 2.

[4] All accounts of Adam Smith's life and career stem from Dugald Stewart's memoir, written shortly after Smith's death. That, and J. Rae's *Life of Adam Smith* (Macmillan, London, 1895), which drew particularly on Smith's correspondence, are the principal sources for this paper. Also useful were: J. R. McCulloch, 'Life of the Author', *The Wealth of Nations*, ed. J. R. McCulloch (Edinburgh, 1849); J. E. Thorold Rogers, 'Adam Smith', in *Historical Gleanings* (Macmillan, London 1869); J. A. Farrer, *Adam Smith (1723–1790)* (Samson Low, London, 1881); R. B. Haldane, *Life of Adam Smith* (Walter Scott, London 1887); J. S. Nicholson, 'Introductory Essay', *The Wealth of Nations*, ed. J. S. Nicholson (Nelson, London, 1895); F. W. Hirst, *Adam Smith* (Macmillan, 1904); W. R. Scott, *Adam Smith as Student and Professor* (University of Glasgow, 1937); and articles by W. R. Scott.

documented conveniently by considering (a) his travel and observations of contemporary life, (b) his membership of clubs, and the discussions therein in which he participated, (c) his friendships, and his acquaintance with businessmen and politicians, (d) his library, and finally, (e) his writings. Each of these subjects deserves extended treatment, although here each will be discussed only briefly.

(a) *Travel and Observation.* Smith, for his times, travelled widely, and resided for relatively long periods in six important cities— Glasgow, Oxford, Edinburgh, London, Paris, and Toulouse; he also resided briefly in Geneva, Bordeaux, and Montpellier, and for much of his life, in Kirkcaldy. Residence in each of these cities, and travel within Britain and France, gave him insights into contemporary economy, and provided examples freely used in the *Wealth of Nations*. This continuous use of example gave his analysis a realistic and comparative flavour, with its interesting illustrations from contemporary life, and its telling comparisons between Scotland, England, and France. Residence in France undoubtedly gave Smith a vital broadening of education and experience, as whole sections of the *Wealth of Nations* demonstrate.[5] But all of Smith's travels and experiences are used to illustrate his great book, and examples from his personal observations enliven almost every page, whether discoursing on the difference between 'court' and 'mercantile' towns, on the relative nutritional merits of wheaten bread, oatmeal, and potatoes, on universities, on the grocery trade, or on infantile mortality.[6] It is quite impossible to read the *Wealth of Nations* without

[5] In Smith's own *Index* to the *Wealth of Nations*, France has one of the longest entries (along with agriculture, colonies, corn, labour, revenue, and trade), and in the Cannan edition (Ed. E. Cannan, The Modern Library, New York, 1937), where the Smith entries are expanded by more comprehensive indexing, France has the longest entry. All references from the *Wealth of Nations* in this Comment are from this edition.

[6] The *Wealth of Nations*, 79; I. viii. 38. WN 112; I. x. b. 36. WN 160–61; I. xi. b. 41. WN 320; II. iii. 12. WN 717–20; V. i. f. 6–15. On food, for example, Smith wrote: 'The common people in Scotland, who are fed with oatmeal, are in general neither so strong nor so handsome as the same rank of people in England, who are fed with wheaten bread. . . . But it seems to be otherwise with potatoes. The chairmen, porters and coal-heavers in London, and those unfortunate women who live by prostitution, the strongest men and the most beautiful women perhaps in the British dominions, are said to be, the greater part of them, from the lowest rank of people in Ireland, who are generally fed with this root' (WN 160–61; I. xi. b. 41).

recognizing that much of its description of politics, society, and economy arose directly from Smith's own experience, enriched by his reading and his intellect.

(b) *Clubs and Discussion.* Adam Smith sought, wherever he was, those clubs and salons which were a characteristic of eighteenth century social and intellectual life. In Glasgow he was a member of Andrew Cochrane's *Political Economy Club* and Simpson's Club; in Edinburgh, of the *Philosophical Society*, of *The Select Society* (formed in 1754, 'partly a debating society for the discussion of topics of the day, and partly a patriotic society for the promotion of the arts, sciences and manufactures of Scotland'), and of *The Poker Club*; and in London, of the famous *Literary Club* of Johnson, Burke, and Reynolds; and this list is not complete. Smith, also, was admitted to the *Royal Society* in 1773, and was a founding member of the *Edinburgh Royal Society* in 1783. During his visit to Paris in 1766 he was a regular guest at most of the famous salons, and this was a year of great literary activity among French economists. In the salons of Baron d'Holbach, Helvetius, Madame de Geoffrin, Comtesse de Boufflers, and Mademoiselle l'Espinasse, and probably Madame Necker, Smith met Turgot, Quesnay, Morellet, Diderot, D'Alembert, Necker, Dupont du Nemours, and Mercier de la Rivière. Many of Smith's leisure hours from 1750 to 1790 were spent participating in, or listening to discussion, much of which was concerned with economic affairs, and much of which was followed by correspondence.

(c) *Friends, Businessmen, and Politicians.* Adam Smith's life was full of friendship and company, but he did not choose his friends only from the professors he knew, but from businessmen, politicians, farmers, printers, doctors, lawyers, architects, teachers, clergymen, soldiers, sailors, artists, civil servants, and writers. Smith had the good fortune to have lived at a time when an able man like himself could comprehend a large part of human knowledge, and when the intellectuals of Europe were still a small enough group for many of them to know each other, to correspond regularly and even to visit each other. If Smith's writings prove the broad range of his interests, his friendships, correspondence and clubs expand those interests to cover every conceivable intellectual and topical problem of the eighteenth century. Thus, the comment of Sir John Pringle, reported by Boswell, that 'Dr

Smith, who had never been in trade, could not be expected to write well on that subject, any more than a lawyer on physic', deserved a different answer from the famous reply of Johnson.[7] Smith may not have been in trade, but he knew tradesmen, he knew a lot about trade and related matters, and he knew important politicians who were concerned with trade and economy. His closest association with businessmen was during his professorship in Glasgow. It was at this time, James Ritchie, a prominent Clyde merchant, told Dugald Stewart that Smith converted many of Glasgow's leading merchants to free trade.[8] After Glasgow, Smith's associations with businessmen lessened, while his association with other men of affairs, especially politicians, increased. Smith's list of political friends is long and distinguished: it included James Oswald, Lord Kames, Sir William Pulteney, William Eden (Lord Auckland), the Earl of Shelburne, Charles Townshend, Earl Stanhope, Sir John Sinclair, the Earl of Lauderdale, Henry Dundas (Lord Melville), William Wilberforce, Edmund Burke, H. Addington (Lord Sidmouth), and William Pitt, in Britain; and the Duke of Richelieu, the Abbé Colbert, Turgot, Necker, and Mercier de la Rivière, in France. On his visit to London in 1787, for example, Smith dined with Pitt, was consulted by Wilberforce, and had an ode written to him by Addington. On at least two occasions Smith was consulted directly about government policy, on the proposal for free trade with Ireland in 1779, when his views were sought by various members of the government, and on the American Intercourse Bill in 1783, when Eden approached him for advice. Smith was undoubtedly flattered by the attention of politicians (for example, of Pitt), but his comments on them, and on the art of politics, were as realistic as his comments on business.

(d) *Smith's Library.*[9] Charles Kindleberger is wrong when he says

[7] Johnson's reply was: 'He is mistaken, Sir; a man who has never been engaged in trade himself may undoubtedly write well upon trade, and there is nothing which requires more to be illustrated by philosophy than trade does.' *Everybody's Boswell* (Bell, London, 1930), 224.

[8] Dugald Stewart, op. cit. xli. See also, W. R. Scott, 'Adam Smith and the Glasgow Merchants', *Economic Journal*, xliv (1934), 506–8.

[9] J. Bonar, *A Catalogue of the Library of Adam Smith* (Macmillan, London, 2nd ed., 1932); H. Mizuta, *Adam Smith's Library. A Supplement to Bonar's Catalogue and Checklist of the whole Library* (Cambridge University Press, 1967). See, also, T. Yanaihara, *A full and detailed Catalogue of Books which belonged to Adam Smith, Now in the possession of the Faculty of Economics, University of Tokyo* (Kelley Reprints of Economic Classics, New York, 1966; first published 1951).

that 'most of the books [Smith] relies on ... are fairly old, published in the first quarter of the 18th century'. Smith's library was large (over 3,000 volumes) and its coverage, in language and contents, was impressive. Of the books from his library quoted by Smith in his published writings, the majority date from after 1750; excluding the classics, a fairly complete examination of the authors referred to, either in the *Theory of Moral Sentiments* or the *Wealth of Nations*, shows that only about a quarter of them were published before 1750, and that more than a half were published for the first time after 1750. The use of economists, both living and dead, is particularly extensive, and Smith's library contained most of the important authors on political economy; for example, Anderson, Cantillon, Chalmers, Child, Davenant, Gee, Hume, Law, Locke, de la Rivière, Morellet, Postlethwayte, Mun, Necker, Quesnay, and Tucker. Smith's library, indeed, indicates a widely-read man, and one who kept up to date with the latest publications (many volumes date from the seventies and eighties), and his writings prove the extensive use of the library for evidence and quotation. Smith would have had to ignore his books to be unaware of the changes of the eighteenth century, and this, we know, he did not do. He used his library, and he loved it. As he said to Smellie, 'I am a beau in nothing but my books'.[10]

(e) *Smith's Writings.* So much has been written about what Smith wrote, and what he meant, that further essays in interpretation might seem superfluous.[11] It is not difficult, however, to show that Smith was aware of eighteenth century growth, that he analysed it, and that he approved of it. Aggregate growth he saw in the advance of the whole economy, as for example, when he commented on English progress: 'The annual produce of the land and labour of England ... is certainly much greater than it was, a little more than a century ago, at the restoration of Charles II.'[12] Smith also recognized structural change and its importance for growth, noting the

[10] Rae, op. cit. 329.
[11] See, for example, B. Franklin and F. Cordasio, *Adam Smith. A Bibliographical Checklist. An International Record of Critical Writings and Scholarship Relating to Smith and Smithian Theory, 1876–1950* (Franklin, New York, 1950). This bibliography, selective, lists 446 items. For the most recent general analysis see the 'General Introduction' to The Glasgow Edition of *The Wealth of Nations*, ed. R. H. Campbell and A. S. Skinner (Oxford, 1976).
[12] WN 327, II. iii. 33.

differential progress of manufactures, trade, and agriculture.[13] As Smith was aware of growth, so he welcomed it, writing approvingly of 'the progressive state' in which 'the condition of the labouring poor, of the great body of the people, seems to be the happiest and the most comfortable. It is hard in the stationary and miserable in the declining state. The progressive state is in reality the cheerful and the hearty state to all the different orders of society. The stationary is dull; the declining melancholy.'[14] 'Servants, labourers, and workmen in different kinds', he also wrote, 'make up the far greater part of every great political society. But what improves the circumstances of the greater part can never be regarded as an inconveniency to the whole. No society can surely be flourishing and happy, of which the far greater part of the members are poor and miserable.'[15] In Great Britain, however, progress had been particularly marked in the eighteenth century. 'In Great Britain the real recompense of labour, . . . the real quantities of the necessaries and conveniencies of life which are given to the labourer, has increased considerably during the course of the present century.'[16]

Smith's explanation of growth stressed four factors: resources, the constitutional framework, the motivation for growth, and the growth mechanism. Given resources and an appropriate constitution, individual self-interest and the 'propensity to truck, barter, and exchange'[17] will set in motion the growth mechanism. The mechanism of growth is described in the first three books of the *Wealth of Nations*, with stress on capital accumulation and division of labour.[18] The constitution appropriate for growth is described

[13] Ibid. 19, 318, 863. WN I. iii. 4; II. iii. 10; V. iii. 9. Smith also recognized the relationship between industrial progress and growth: 'Our ancestors were idle for want of a sufficient encouragement for industry'; 'In a rude state of society, there are no great mercantile or manufacturing capitals.' (Ibid. 863 V. iii. 9.)

[14] Ibid. 81; I. viii. 43.   [15] Ibid. 78–9; I. viii. 36.

[16] Ibid. 200; I. xi. g. 20 ('Third Period').   [17] Ibid. 13; I. ii. 1.

[18] Smith also understood the importance of technological change and education in improving the quality of fixed capital and human capital. 'The productive powers of the number of labourers cannot be increased, but in consequence either of some addition and improvement to those machines and instruments which facilitate and abridge labour; or of a more proper division and distribution of employment. In either case an additional capital is almost always required.' (Ibid. 326; II. iii. 32.) On education, Smith linked the acquisition of necessary skills with an education partly subsidised by the state. (Ibid. 735–40; V. i. f. 51–61.)

in the fourth and fifth books, a constitution which guarantees
liberty, property, and contract, and which carefully defines and
limits the role of government. To Smith the limiting factor in
growth was the constitution; the motivation for growth was time-
less and universal. Differences in wealth between states, therefore,
can be explained by differences in constitutions and law. Thus,
China 'had . . . acquired that full complement of riches which the
nature of its laws and institutions permits it to acquire' and North
America prospered over the East Indies because of 'the genius of
the British constitution which protects and governs North America'
in contrast to 'the mercantile company which oppresses and
domineers in the east Indies'.[19] Throughout the *Wealth of Nations*
Smith argues on the basis of a comparative study of England,
Scotland, Ireland, France, Holland, Spain, China, India, and the
British colonies in North America, that a nation's constitution and
political institutions decisively affect its ability to increase its wealth.
It is, indeed, the firmest conclusion of Smith's 'inquiry into the
nature and causes of the wealth of nations'.

III

I think that I have shown that Adam Smith was aware of the
economic growth that was occurring in the eighteenth century,
and that he was concerned primarily in the *Wealth of Nations* with
explaining it in both economic and institutional terms. That his
knowledge and understanding were not complete is not surprising;
that his ability to foresee the future was not perfect makes him like
all other economists. But he did recognize that Britain's potential
for growth was greater than that of other European economies, and
he did define public policies that would ensure continued and even
greater progress. That Adam Smith prescribed a policy of economic liberalism cannot be seriously disputed; only a perverse mis-
reading of Book V can lead to any other conclusion. That the
various economies of Europe, those that successfully grew, adopted
more liberal constitutions and economic policies in the nineteenth
century is also undoubted. That, in justification of those policies,
Smith's name was frequently invoked is also true. In some cases,
the link seems direct and influential (for example, in Prussia);[20]

[19] WN 71, 73; I. viii. 24, 26.
[20] See C. W. Hasek, *The Introduction of Adam Smith's Doctrines into Germany*
(Columbia University, New York, 1925).

in other cases, the link seems obvious but less provable (for example, in the more liberal constitutional and civil codes of Europe which followed the French Code of 1804 and which generally enshrined 'property and liberty' as unassailable principles).[21] That liberalism was important in releasing remarkable economic initiative and energy, and hence economic growth, is also hardly to be doubted; even those who do not like the industrial revolution and the world it produced, rarely deny its economic success. At least in justification of economic liberalism, particularly in his insistence on the sufficiency of self-interest as the proper basis of economic and political policy, Adam Smith was influential.

[21] See A. Alverez, *et al.*, *The Progress of Continental Law in the Nineteenth Century* (Continental Legal History Series, Boston, 1919).

2

Smith's Contribution in Historical Perspective

BY R. D. COLLISON BLACK*

THE brief which has been given to me in the title of this paper might well be handled by giving my estimate of what exactly Smith's contribution was and then viewing it from the perspective of the present time. But in reflecting on my theme I have come to the conclusion that the very nature of historical perspective makes it difficult to be categorical about the nature of Smith's contribution. For we are all familiar with the illusions which perspective generates. As one writer on the phenomenon has said, 'Most people have observed that objects diminish in size as they recede farther from the eye, that parallel lines appear to converge, that in general the appearance of objects differs from the reality.'[1] Now just as the size and shape of objects appears to change in visual perspective as the position of the observer changes, so in historical perspective the significance of an event or an idea changes as it is seen from different points of time. So rather than add my own contemporary assessment of Adam Smith's work to the not inconsiderable number of such estimates which have already been offered in this bicentenary period, I have decided that it might be a more useful and valid interpretation of my brief to review the various ways in which it has been evaluated at various points in history, and to compare those earlier estimates with those presently being made.

In the hope of making my treatment of the theme both manageable and relevant I have limited it in a number of ways which it may be useful to make clear at the outset. First of all, I shall confine myself to Smith's contribution to the development of

* Professor of Economics in The Queen's University, Belfast.

[1] *Encyclopaedia Americana* (New York, Americana Corp., 1965), art. 'Perspective', vol. xxi, 632.

political economy—partly because it is only this aspect of his total contribution to knowledge that I am at all qualified to discuss, but also because it is the bicentenary of the *Wealth of Nations* which we are now celebrating.

In considering how perspectives on that great work have changed in the course of history, I shall limit myself to three points in time —1826, the golden jubilee of its publication, 1876, the centenary and 1926, the sesquicentenary. I shall not confine myself strictly to works written in those years with commemorative intent, but such writings will form the bulk of the material here surveyed and where I go beyond them it will be to look at works of these periods in which the authors did specifically indicate their view of Smith's system of political economy.

Not all writings commemorating the *Wealth of Nations* are included in this paper, for unfortunately I have not been able to discover copies of a number of the commemorative pieces published overseas; my survey is therefore largely devoted to Anglo-American writings and I do not claim that even when thus limited it is exhaustive. A further obvious and important omission is any reference to the treatment of Smith's political economy given by Karl Marx. Marx did not write anything directly commemorating the *Wealth of Nations*, but he did leave ample material for assessing his view of Smith's economic ideas. This, however, would provide the basis for a paper in itself and I have decided that it is better to omit the topic from this one than to treat it inadequately.

The contribution which Smith made in the *Wealth of Nations* can be said to have two major aspects—analysis and policy—and I shall examine how each of these was viewed at the three different periods considered. It should be pointed out, however, that while it is convenient and even perhaps essential to make that distinction now, it is one which commentators on Smith did not begin to make clearly until the centenary of the *Wealth of Nations* was approaching.

I

Half a century after the publication of the *Wealth of Nations* there appears to have been no thought of commemorating that anniversary of its publication; but that does not imply that its influence on the development of economic analysis at that time was small. Just as Keynes's *General Theory* remains today a work of continuing significance on which other authors are building by a process of action and reaction, so was the *Wealth of Nations* in or about 1826 a work of continuing significance.

The position has been very clearly stated by Lord Robbins:

> There is a vast extent of analysis and prescription which the genera-
> tion of Malthus and Ricardo more or less take for granted, the essential
> work having been done by Hume and Smith; and a great deal of what
> they do themselves is to be regarded, not as a series of propositions
> thought out in a void, but rather as an attempt to correct or improve
> propositions and explanations which are already to be found in the
> *Wealth of Nations*.[2]

In fact it is noticeable that the generation of Malthus and Ricardo, while always respecting the authority of Smith, were much more willing than later generations to point out what they considered to be mistakes in Smith and to offer corrections.[3] The *Wealth of Nations* was to them not so much a classical monument to be inspected as a structure to be extended and improved where necessary.

As to what was the most controversial feature of the structure in the view of this generation, an examination of the literature leaves no doubt that it was Smith's treatment of labour, especially in relation to the theories of value and distribution. Ricardo, re-reading Smith in the course of preparing his own *Principles* in 1816, found 'many opinions to question, all I believe founded on his original error respecting value'.[4] Ten years later the view of value and of labour in relation to it which Ricardo himself had put forward had served to split English economists into two camps. On the one side were those—a majority in influence if not in numbers—who accepted the Ricardian theory either in whole or in part. To them Smith's cost of production theory of value was

[2] Robbins, *Robert Torrens and the Evolution of Classical Economics* (London, MacMillan 1958), 233.

[3] Perhaps the best known example of this approach is contained in the Preface to Ricardo's *Principles*: 'The writer, in combating received opinions, has found it necessary to advert more particularly to those passages in the writings of Adam Smith from which he sees reason to differ; but he hopes it will not, on that account, be suspected that he does not, in common with all those who acknowledge the importance of the science of Political Economy, participate in the admiration which the profound work of this celebrated author so justly excites.'

[4] Ricardo to James Mill, 2 December 1816—*Works and Correspondence*, ed. Sraffa (Cambridge University Press), vii, 100.

essentially 'a more superficial approach' than Ricardo's attempt at a pure labour theory. Of this group the most influential perhaps was J. R. McCulloch, to whom it appeared in 1827 that:

I might advantageously employ myself in the publication of a new edition of the Wealth of Nations, subjoining such short notes to the text, as might serve to point out the changes that have taken place since the work was finally revised by the author . . . and . . . such more lengthened notes as might appear necessary to make the reader aware of the fallacy of the principles which Dr. Smith has sometimes advocated, and to furnish him with a brief, but distinct, account of the principal discoveries and improvements that have been made in the science. . . .[5]

Now Professor O'Brien has made clear that McCulloch's treatment of value proceeded on two levels and that while in his 'scientific' theory he departed considerably from Ricardo's example, particularly on the question of the invariable measure, in more popular expositions he remained always an uncomprising advocate of a straightforward labour quantity theory.[6] Although some of the significant modifications of his 'scientific' theory appeared in the 1838 as compared with the 1828 version of his edition of the *Wealth of Nations*, these were well concealed in the Notes[7] and to contemporary readers in general it must have appeared that McCulloch was replacing Smith's 'erroneous' cost of production theory with the 'superior insights' of Ricardo's labour theory. Certainly they were firmly informed by the editor that 'in consequence of the incorrectness of the opinions entertained by Dr. Smith, on two such important and fundamental points as the value of commodities and the nature and causes of rent, many of the principles which pervade other parts of his work are necessarily vitiated and unsound. This is particularly the case where he investigates the circumstances which determine the rate of wages and the rate of profit.'[8]

Influential as such statements may have been, the opposite view was not without its advocates. Thus the anonymous author of *The*

[5] J. R. McCulloch (ed.), *An Inquiry into the Nature and Causes of the Wealth of Nations, by Adam Smith LL.D. With a Life of the Author, an Introductory Discourse, Notes, and Supplemental Dissertations.* (Edinburgh, A. Black and W. Tait, 1828), Preface, I. ix.

[6] D. P. O'Brien, *J. R. McCulloch, a Study in Classical Economics* (London, Allen and Unwin, 1970), 126–46.

[7] Cf. 1838 ed., 436, and O'Brien, op. cit. 143.

[8] McCulloch, op. cit., (1828 ed.), I, lxxvi.

Opinions of the late Mr. Ricardo and of Adam Smith, on some of the leading doctrines of Political Economy, stated and compared,[9] while concluding that the systems of the two economists on the subject of value were not contradictory, went on to say:

> We must, however, own we prefer the view which A. Smith takes of the subject, as it is more comfortable to general experience, and serves to explain things under all the variations to which they are liable; whereas Mr. Ricardo's view seems designed to show how things should be under given circumstances rather than how they are in reality found to exist.[10]

This view must have commended itself to many readers of Smith and Ricardo at this period; but if the *Pamphleteer* articles came into the hands of Samuel Bailey he must have found the author's assertion that 'Value, as explained by Mr. Ricardo, is *relative* value, and as explained by A. Smith, *positive* or absolute value'[11] a curious one. For Bailey, whose critique of Ricardo rested on the proposition that 'value denotes merely a relation' set out from Smith's definition that the value of a good 'expresses the power of purchasing other goods, which the possession of that object conveys'[12] and claimed the authority of Smith for his relativist approach.

If we accept the view which has recently been put forward by Professor Bowley that Smith 'was not concerned primarily with physical inputs as the basis either of value or its measurement'[13] we may be inclined to think that Bailey and his followers were better interpreters of Smith than the Ricardians, but it was the Ricardian interpretation which became dominant. And perhaps the reason for this can be found in McCulloch's view that Smith's treatment of the relation of labour to value vitiated his account of the determinants of wages and profits. For as Professor Winch has said 'the questions which concerned Smith's successors were not merely more urgent, but more politically divisive as between the still dominant land-owning classes and the new commercial and industrial classes', and it was natural therefore that they should

---

9 *The Pamphleteer*, 23 (1824), 518–26, 24 (1824), 508.
10 *Pamphleteer*, 23, 525.   11 Ibid. 523.
12 Cf. R. M. Rauner, *Samuel Bailey and the Classical Theory of Value* (London, G. Bell & Sons Ltd., for L.S.E., 1961), 7.
13 M. Bowley, *Studies in the History of Economic Theory before 1870* (London, MacMillan, 1973), 116.

favour an approach which gave to distribution, and particularly the question of the relative shares of wage earners and profit receivers, a more central place than Smith had done.[14] For this, as Ricardo had realized, a theory of value such as Smith had used was not an appropriate foundation.

On the side of policy, the general impression left by the historical evidence is that by 1826 not only economists but a great many other influential public men were prepared to give assent and support to the system of natural liberty and the consequent doctrine of free trade set out by Adam Smith. Baring in 1820 had presented to an approving House of Commons the famous Merchants' Petition prepared by Thomas Tooke, one result of which was the establishment in 1821 of the Political Economy Club 'to support the principles of Free Trade'. By 1826 Parliament had begun the work of dismantling the Navigation Acts and other parts of the mercantile system, and of reducing protective tariffs. This was largely due to the influence of Huskisson, than whom 'Smith had no disciple more true to his doctrines in the sphere of statesmanship'.[15]

Nevertheless, free trade was still far from having triumphed, either in the sphere of doctrine or of legislation. In the eighteen-twenties probably even those economists who were firmest in their support of free trade principles would still have agreed with Smith's oft-quoted dictum that 'To expect, indeed that the freedom of trade should ever be entirely restored in Great Britain is as absurd as to expect that an Oceana or Utopia should ever be established in it.'[16] We may remind ourselves that when, in 1822, Ricardo wrote of a free trade in corn it was to say 'that is not, under our circumstances, the course which I should recommend.'[17] Instead he proposed a countervailing duty of 10 shillings per quarter to offset the 'peculiar burdens' on land. For similar reasons, McCulloch, who has been seen as an influential propagandist for free trade in the years 1825–30,[18] was not in favour of

[14] Cf. D. N. Winch, Introduction to the Everyman edition of Ricardo's *Principles of Political Economy* (London, Dent, 1973), ix.

[15] A. Brady, *William Huskisson and Liberal Reform* (2nd ed., London, Cass, 1967), 168. [16] *Wealth of Nations*, Book IV, Chap. II.

[17] D. Ricardo, On Protection to Agriculture (1822) Section VI, § 19; *Works and Correspondence*, ed. Sraffa, vol. iv, 243. And see also Ricardo to McCulloch, March 1821, op. cit., vol. viii, 355–60.

[18] Cf. L. Brown, *The Board of Trade and the Free Trade Movement, 1830–42* (Oxford, Clarendon Press, 1958), 18.

the complete removal of agricultural protection.[19] And even those, like Torrens in his early days, who were prepared to urge the abolition of the Corn Laws, did not extend their arguments to advocate a general free trade.[20]

Such caution may have been due in part to a recognition of the limits of what was politically feasible, although no one would now dispute the reality and importance of the *caveats* which many classical economists entered, on purely analytical grounds, against the free trade case. Thus when Huskisson and Ricardo served together on the Commons Committee on the Agriculture of the United Kingdom in 1821 they found themselves in complete agreement—yet the Committee's Report, which Huskisson wrote, endorsed the 'universally acknowledged' principles of free trade without recommending a free trade in corn, in order to 'spare vested interests' and 'deal tenderly with those obstacles to improvement which the long existence of a vicious and artificial system too often creates'.[21]

There was probably a great deal of truth in Greville's comment about Huskisson—'all the ablest men in the country coincide with him, and . . . the mass of the community are persuaded that his plans are mischievous to the last degree'.[22] Certainly both the tactical situation in Parliament and social conditions in the country as a whole did not favour pressing ahead too rapidly with far reaching reforms of trade policy in the later eighteen-twenties. Nevertheless the movement gained momentum in the next decade, with the appointment of Poulett Thomson as Vice-President of the Board of Trade in 1830; and as it did so, some of the reservations in the field of ideas were swept away also. So J. L. Mallet could write in his diary in 1834:

All the economists of my time and Ricardo at the head of them, held that the landlords were entitled to protection in respect of tithes, land tax and all direct charges on land. 'Mais nous avons changé tout cela.' As the times become more radical and the landlords and agricultural interests lose ground, the economists shift their quarters.[23]

[19] O'Brien, *J. R. McCulloch*, 225. [20] Cf. Robbins, *Robert Torrens*, 185.
[21] B. Semmel, *The Rise of Free Trade Imperialism* (Cambridge, Cambridge University Press, 1970), 137.
[22] *The Greville Memoirs*, 1814–60 (ed. Lytton Strachey and Roger Fulford) (London, MacMillan, 1938), vol. ii, 47. The entry is for 18 September 1830.
[23] From the diary of J. L. Mallet, 3 July 1834. *Proceedings of the Political Economy Club*, vol. vi (London, MacMillan, 1921), 262.

II

The centenary of the *Wealth of Nations* was duly celebrated with banquets, speeches, and articles in Britain, America, and on the Continent of Europe;[24] and half a century had produced no small difference in the way in which Smith's contribution was viewed. The distinction between its analytical and practical aspects was now consciously and deliberately made[25] and since, in Britain at least, it was the latter which tended to receive most attention in the discussions of 1876 it may be appropriate to reverse the order of the preceding section and take the policy side first.

The principal celebration of the centenary in Britain was the dinner given by the Political Economy Club on 31 May 1876, the proceedings of which were fully reported and made the subject of comment by a number of newspapers and reviews.[26] With Gladstone in the chair, Robert Lowe as the first speaker and the French Minister of Finance, Léon Say (grandson of J. B. Say) as second speaker it was, as Jevons said, 'true that the statesmen had it mostly their own way, and . . . the company appeared to care little what mere literary economists thought about Adam Smith'.[27]

The note which Lowe chose to strike was a confident one—so confident as now to appear complacent, but nevertheless fairly typical of the attitude of British public men of the day. After a somewhat facile and condescending survey of Smith's work in the course of which he declared that where Smith failed it was 'mainly because he had not sufficient confidence in the truth of the doctrines which he laid down', Lowe went on to deal with the question before the meeting—'What are the more important results which have followed from the publication of the *Wealth of Nations* . . . and in what principal directions do the doctrines of

[24] Cf. note 26 below, and *The Adam Smith Centennial to commemorate the hundredth anniversary of the publication of the Wealth of Nations* (New York, 1876); E. Nasse, 'Das hundertjährige Jubiläum der Schrift von Adam Smith über den Reichtum der Nationen' *Preussen Jahrbuch*, 38 (1876), 384–400 (Berlin, G. Reimer). K. T. von Inama-Sternegg, *Adam Smith und die Bedeutung seines Wealth of Nations für die Moderne Nationalökonomie* (Innsbruck, 1876).

[25] Notably by Walter Bagehot in his essay 'Adam Smith and our Modern Economy', *Economic Studies* (Longmans Green, London, 1879), 125–30.

[26] *Political Economy Club. Revised Report of the Proceedings at the Dinner of 31 May 1876, held in celebration of the Hundredth Year of the Publication of the 'Wealth of Nations'*. (London, Longmans Green, Reader and Dyer, 1876).

[27] W. S. Jevons, 'The Future of Political Economy', *Fortnightly Review*, vol. xx (1876), 617–31.

that book still remain to be applied?' His audience can scarcely have been surprised to hear him single out the achievement of free trade as the most important consequence of the work of 'this simple Glasgow Professor'. Quoting Smith's cynical comment about the prospects of free trade in Britain,[28] Lowe exclaimed 'He underestimated his own strength; Free Trade has found its way'.[29] But the corollary of this glowing account of the way in which the nineteenth century had learned and acted upon the lessons of Smith was a less encouraging view of the future of political economy—'I cannot help thinking that we must look rather to the negative than to the positive side, at least at present. . . . The controversies that we now have in Political Economy, although they offer a capital exercise for the logical faculties, are not the same thrilling importance as those of earlier days; the great work has been done.'[30]

This view that the mission of Political Economy, as Smith had presented it, had been accomplished, or soon would be, was echoed by several of the newspapers which commented on the occasion. 'It is perhaps true', *The Times* leader declared, 'that Free Trade has established itself more as a fact than a doctrine; but when the first position is firmly occupied the second must follow, and the time is not distant when the supremacy of Adam Smith's teaching shall surpass his largest hopes.'[31] What had seemed tentatively possible in 1826 was glorious reality in 1876, and ideas which had seemed sound but admitted of modifications and exceptions then had been raised to the status of incontrovertible truths half a century later.

George Warde Norman, the only survivor of the original members of 1821 to attend the Political Economy Club's centenary dinner, stated the position as he saw it unequivocally—'it seems to me that the real doctrines of Political Economy as they were first taught by Adam Smith . . . remain unimpeached; that they have never been successfully attacked; that they are in fact unattackable; that they are true now and will be true to all time'—and William Newmarch took Lowe's point about the future of political economy a stage further by predicting that 'there will be what may be called a large negative development of Political Economy tending to produce an important and beneficial effect; and that is, such a

---

[28] Cf. above, p. 47 and note 16.
[29] *Political Economy Club. Revised Report of the Proceedings . . .*, 11, 19, 21.
[30] Ibid. 20, 21.   [31] *The Times*, 1 June 1876.

development of Political Economy as will reduce the functions of government within a smaller and smaller compass'. Only W. E. Forster ventured to declare himself 'strongly of the contrary opinion, that we cannot undertake the *laissez-faire* principle in the present condition of our politics or of parties in Parliament, or in the general condition of the country'.[32]

This then was economic policy as the politicians of 1876 saw it; and had it not been for the hint dropped by Forster it would have been hard to realise, from the report of the Adam Smith centenary dinner that the 'mere literary economists' in the person of John Elliott Cairnes, had declared six years earlier that Political Economy 'has nothing to do with *laissez-faire* any more than with communism'.[33] Yet among the economists of the day there were many who shared Lowe's despondent view about the future of their subject in its second century, without sharing his optimistic idea of the reasons for it. For whatever men like Lowe and Norman might say there were, as Professor T. W. Hutchison has said,[34] unsettled questions in political economy in the eighteen-seventies on the three fronts of policy, theory, and method.

Political economy, said Bagehot at this time, 'lies rather dead in the public mind. Not only does it not excite the same interest as formerly, but there is not exactly the same confidence in it. Younger men either do not study it, or do not feel that it comes home to them, and that it matches with their most living ideas.'[35] Such lack of interest, bordering on hostility seems to have been a result of the tendency, which Lowe exemplified and which Cairnes opposed, to associate political economy with the doctrines of *laissez-faire* and free trade and to gloss over the social problems which urban industrialism had produced. If such policy issues were the basis for the disenchantment of the general public with political economy, the doubts and disillusionment expressed by the economists themselves arose also out of problems of theory and method.

It was the very fact that the principles of political economy—

[32] *Political Economy Club. Revised Report of the Proceedings . . .*, 26, 38, 50.

[33] J. E. Cairnes, 'Political Economy and Laissez Faire' in *Essays in Political Economy, Theoretical and Applied* (London, MacMillan, 1873), 255.

[34] T. W. Hutchison, *A Review of Economic Doctrines 1870–1929* (Oxford, Clarendon Press, 1953), 5–22.

[35] W. Bagehot, *Economic Studies* (1879, 2nd ed. Longman's Green, 1888), 3–4.

principles laid down by Smith, modified by Ricardo and restated
by J. S. Mill—seemed 'perfectly unattackable' to men like Norman
and Lowe which was so galling to economists of the younger
generation like Cliffe Leslie and Jevons. In their view if political
economy was to have a future as well as a past it must be freed
from what Jevons had called 'the noxious influence of authority'.[36]
Now I am disposed to think that this was a point which Jevons
exaggerated, and that his opposition to J. S. Mill particularly has
in turn been exaggerated by others;[37] but a study of the presentation of political economy to undergraduates at this period does
produce a strong impression of a stagnant subject.[38] Nor does
there seem any reason to question the view that this was the result
of the way in which John Stuart Mill had in 1848 given fresh life
and authority to Ricardian analysis set within a Smithian comparative framework.[39] Hence the very success of those revisions of
Smith's analytical system which the Ricardians had felt to be
necessary half a century after the publication of the *Wealth of
Nations* was in turn the source of that stagnation and dogmatism
which were tending to bring political economy into disrepute at
the time of the centenary.

The way in which economists of the historical stamp of Cliffe
Leslie on the one hand and of the mathematical stamp of Jevons
on the other, reacted to this state of affairs with proposals for the
reform and reconstruction of their discipline is a familiar story
which need not concern us here; what is relevant is the way in
which they viewed Smith's century-old contribution.

In fact, comparatively little of what was written at the time of
the centenary dealt with the *Wealth of Nations* directly, the
economists generally preferring to use the occasion to discuss their

[36] W. S. Jevons, *Theory of Political Economy* (London, MacMillan, 1871),
265–7.
[37] Cf. R. D. C. Black, 'W. S. Jevons and the Foundation of Modern Economics', in Black, Coats, and Goodwin (eds.), *The Marginal Revolution in Economics* (Durham, N.C., Duke University Press, 1973), 99–103; N. B. de Marchi,
'The Noxious Influence of Authority; a Correction of Jevons' Charge', *Journal
of Law and Economics*, vol. xvi (1973), 179–89.
[38] See, for example, W. P. Emerton, *Palaestra Oxoniensis; Questions and
Exercises in Political Economy, with references to Adam Smith, Ricardo . . . and
others. Adapted to the Oxford Pass and Honour and the Cambridge Ordinary
B.A. Examinations.* (Oxford, Thornton, 1879).
[39] Cf. S. Hollander, 'Ricardianism, J. S. Mill and the Neo-Classical Challenge'
(Toronto, 1973). In this working paper, Hollander sets out to challenge Schumpeter's contention that J. S. Mill was not really a Ricardian economist.

current pre-occupations; but serious consideration was given to Smith's theoretical work by both Cliffe Leslie and Walter Bagehot, while Jevons dealt with it more incidentally.

Cliffe Leslie's treatment of 'The Political Economy of Adam Smith'[40] was perhaps the most subtle of the three, and the one which is most interesting today because of its parallels with modern studies. Attacking the crude stereotype put forward by Robert Lowe of Adam Smith as the founder of a political economy which is 'a body of necessary and universal truth, founded on invariable laws of nature, and deduced from the constitution of the human mind', Cliffe Leslie stressed that the *Wealth of Nations* must be interpreted as a part of Smith's whole system of moral philosophy. Leslie indeed was exceptional amongst economists of his time in showing both familiarity with, and respect for, the *Theory of Moral Sentiments*. After a scholarly account of the origins of the doctrine of natural law and its place in Smith's philosophical system Leslie went on to argue that 'there ran thus through the political economy of both Adam Smith and the Physiocrats, though much more extensively and systematically in the former, a combination of the experience philosophy, of inductive investigation, with *a priori* speculation derived from the Nature hypothesis'. Hence, he contended, 'Adam Smith has been preserved by the inductive method which he combined with *a priori* deduction from enormous fallacies into which the school of Ricardo has since been betrayed by their method of pure deduction'.[41]

Coming from a leading exponent of the historical method, such conclusions are hardly surprising, and it was entirely consistent with the historical approach that Leslie should argue that Smith's theories were influenced by the early phase of industrial development in which he lived and hence could not be accepted and applied without modification a century later. All this is very much what we would expect but it leads on to a little-noticed conclusion which seems to have fresh relevance in the world of 1976:

Although 'the obvious and simple system of natural liberty' is the foundation of Smith's whole system, though he regarded it as the law of the beneficent Author of Nature, it turns out that he applied it

---

[40] *Fortnightly Review*, N.S. vol. viii (November, 1870), 549–63. Reprinted in *Essays in Political and Moral Philosophy* (Dublin, Hodges, Foster, and Figgis, 1879), 148–66.   [41] Leslie, *Essays*, 160–61 and 163.

only to one-half of mankind . . . He seems to have been perfectly content—though it involves an inconsistency which is fatal to his whole theory—with the existing restraints on the energies of women; and the only effort on the part of a woman to better her own condition which he has in view is 'to become the mistress of a family'.[42]

So far as I am aware, none of the redoubtable women economists of the nineteenth century made this point[43] and there is a certain piquancy in Adam Smith, the eighteenth century bachelor, being berated by Cliffe Leslie, the nineteenth century bachelor, for his neglect of women's rights.

Jevons was the foremost of the economists who used the centenary not for a detailed study of Smith's contribution, but for a review of the current state and prospects of economic thought. In the course of that review he insisted that the historical method so much favoured by Leslie while it might supplement abstract analysis could never replace it. So again it is hardly surprising to find that when Jevons came to refer directly to Smith's method he declared it 'very wise of Adam Smith to attempt no subdivision, but to expound his mathematical theory (for I hold that his reasoning was really mathematical in nature) in conjunction with concrete applications and historical illustrations'.[44] Thus Jevons and Leslie, writing in the same decade, contrived to see the analytical and historical parts of Smith's work in almost precisely inverse order of importance, but both were equally prepared to exempt Smith from the harsh criticism which they directed against Ricardo and his followers.

On other aspects of Smith's system, Jevons's views have to be pieced together from scattered references, mainly in his posthumous *Principles of Economics*. There he dealt specifically with the paradox of value (to which there is only incidental reference in his *Theory of Political Economy*) and made the point that in the famous 'water and diamonds' passage Smith was using the term utility in its ordinary connotation of usefulness and not in the sense of desirability—a point which has also been stressed by modern commentators.[45] Jevons had high praise for the 'exquisite

[42] Leslie, *Essays*, 166.
[43] Cf. Dorothy Lampen Thomson, *Adam Smith's Daughters* (New York, Exposition Press, 1973).
[44] Jevons, 'The Future of Political Economy', *Principles*, 200–1.
[45] Cf. Hollander, 'The Role of Utility and Demand in *The Wealth of Nations*', *Essays on Adam Smith*, Part II, 315.

chapters' on division of labour in the *Wealth of Nations*, but condemned the distinction between productive and unproductive
labour as 'quite untenable' on the ground that 'all labour is
directed to the production of utility'.[46]

An economist who in 1871 had stated 'the somewhat novel
opinion, that *value depends entirely upon utility*'[47] could hardly
have taken any other view, but the limited extent to which Jevons's
ideas had penetrated English economic thinking in 1876 is demonstrated by Bagehot in the most closely argued of the several pieces
he wrote on Smith, 'Adam Smith and our Modern Economy'.[48]
In this Bagehot suggested that:

if we look at *The Wealth of Nations* as if it were a book of modern
Political Economy, we should ask four questions about it.

(1) What, by its teaching, is the cause which makes one thing
exchange for more or less of other things?

(2) What are the laws under which that cause acts in producing
these things?—the full reply to which gives the laws of population
and growth of capital.

(3) If it turns out (as of course it does) that these things are produced by the co-operation of many people, what settles the
share of each of those people in those things, or in their proceeds?
The answer to this question gives what are called the laws of
distribution.

(4) If this co-operation costs something (as of course it does), like
all other co-operations, who is to pay that cost, and how is it to
be levied? The reply to this inquiry is the theory of taxation.[49]

Bagehot in fact attempted to answer only the first of these
questions. In the course of forty pages on the subject he referred
once to Jevons's definition of a market, but not at all to utility
concepts or their absence in Smith's theory. Bagehot's final
conclusion was that:

although . . . Adam Smith had the merit of teaching the world that the
exchangeable value of commodities is proportioned to the cost of their
production, his analysis of that cost was so very defective as to throw
that part of Political Economy into great confusion for many years,
and as quite to prevent his teaching being used as an authority upon
it now.[50]

In this final point at least Bagehot concurred with Cliffe Leslie

[46] Jevons, *Principles*, 87. [47] Id., *Theory of Political Economy* (1871), 2.
[48] Essay III in his *Economic Studies* (1879).
[49] Bagehot, *Economic Studies*, 131. [50] Ibid. 169.

and Jevons. The fifty years which had seen the policy message of the *Wealth of Nations* converted from a desideratum into an accepted truth and an accomplished fact had also seen Smith's economic analysis converted from the foundation of current thinking to a set of ideas which, while they might command more respect than those of Ricardo, were generally admitted to belong to a past age. If there was as yet no unanimity as to what the foundation of a new political economy might be there was equally no doubt that it could no longer be the Smithian system.

III

Between the centenary of the *Wealth of Nations* and its sesquicentenary the perspective in which it was viewed underwent another change—in fact almost a reversal, reminiscent of one of those drawings of hollow squares which when stared at for a time seem to turn inside out. For while the economists of 1878 had lost faith in classical theory without having found what to put in its place, the economists of 1926 were for the most part secure in their acceptance of the neo-classical doctrines as developed by Marshall and supported by the great weight of his authority. On the side of policy, however, the certainties of 1876 had completely dissolved and there was no agreement as to what should be put in their place.

Perhaps for this very reason, the academic economists, who had rather played second fiddle to the politicians and public men at the centenary celebrations, were mainly to the fore in both Britain and America when the time came to celebrate the 150th anniversary in 1926. Indeed the occasion attracted little notice from the wider public, perhaps not surprisingly.

In Britain, the London School of Economics marked the occasion with a series of lectures given by members of its staff, as did the University of Chicago on the other side of the Atlantic.[51] From

[51] The full series of L.S.E. lectures comprised—Edwin Cannan on 'Adam Smith as an Economist'; Morris Ginsberg on 'Adam Smith's Ethical Theory'; T. E. Gregory on 'Adam Smith's relation to Currency Theory'; H. J. Laski on 'Adam Smith's relation to Political Thought'; Hugh Dalton on 'Adam Smith's relation to Public Finance'; F. W. Hirst on 'Adam Smith and English Fiscal Policy', and James Bonar 'The Tables Turned—A Lecture and Dialogue on Adam Smith and the Classical Economists'. Bonar's lecture was separately published in pamphlet form (London, 1926). The Chicago lectures, by J. M. Clark, Paul H. Douglas, Jacob Hollander, Glenn R. Morrow, Melchior Palyi, and Jacob Viner were published under the title *Adam Smith 1776–1926* (Chicago, Chicago University Press, 1928).

the point of view of economic theory the most important lectures in these two series were Edwin Cannan's 'Adam Smith as an Economist'[52] and Paul H. Douglas's 'Smith's Theory of Value and Distribution'.[53]

Cannan, who thirty years before had discovered and published the notes of Smith's 1763 Lectures on Justice and twenty-two years previously had published what has remained until now the standard edition of the *Wealth of Nations*, was then perhaps uniquely qualified to pronounce on his topic. Yet for an established authority the estimate which he gave of his subject's contribution to economic thought was remarkably low—remarkably though perhaps not surprisingly to those who are familiar with what Jacob Viner shrewdly characterised as Cannan's 'Tom Tulliver' approach to classical economics.[54]

According to Cannan, 'Very little of Adam Smith's scheme of economics has been left standing by subsequent inquirers. No one now holds his theory of value, his account of capital is seen to be hopelessly confused, and his theory of distribution is explained as an ill-assorted union between his own theory of prices and the physiocrats' fanciful Economic Table.' He was equally scathing with regard to Smith's classification of incomes and theory of taxation but did credit him with accomplishing 'three great things'.[55]

These turn out to be—first, the substitution of the idea of real income or produce for the accumulation of gold and silver as the end of economic activity; second, the development of the idea that 'wealth per head' is the significant variable rather than 'wealth in the aggregate, whatever that may be'; and third, the development of the idea that regard for one's own interest may be, in economic affairs, 'a laudable principle of action' which does not damage others under a system of free competition.

Cannan's list of Smith's positive contributions as an economist was thus not only short, but such as to suggest that Smith's power

[52] *Economica*, vol. vi (1926), 123–34.

[53] In *Adam Smith 1776–1926*, 77–115.

[54] Its sharpest critic, he is also one of the most complete of the posthumous conquests of the classical school, although his attachment to it reminds one of George Eliot's Tom Tulliver, who, it may be remembered, was 'very fond of birds, that is of throwing stones at them'—Viner, Review of E. Cannan, *A Review of Economic Theory* (London, King, 1929) *Economica*, vol. x (1930), 74–84.

[55] *Economica*, vol. vi (1926), 123.

of analysis was not much more than rudimentary. Paul Douglas's account of 'Smith's Theory of Value and Distribution' was considerably more sympathetic and indeed presented what until recently could be considered the standard interpretation of the theoretical core of the *Wealth of Nations*. Even so, Douglas began by asserting that:

the contributions of Adam Smith to the theory of value and distribution were not great, and in commemorating the publication of the *Wealth of Nations* it might seem to be the path of wisdom to pass these topics by in discreet silence and to reserve discussion instead for those subjects, such as the division of labour, where his realistic talents enabled him to appear at a better advantage.[56]

It is unnecessary to rehearse the details of Douglas's well known account of Smith's theory of value, with its emphasis on the rejection of utility by Smith and elucidation of the labour-embodied and labour-commanded theories. On the subject of distribution, Douglas agreed with Cannan that Smith 'interested himself primarily in the question of profits per cent., wages per head and rent per acre' and tended to view his ideas very much in this 'functional distribution' or 'factor pricing' context.

In this perhaps lies the clue to the low estimate which the economists of 1926 gave of Smith's theoretical work. For however true it may be that an embryonic notion of general equilibrium can be traced in Smith's account of competitive market mechanisms, no one would contend that his treatment of the determination of individual market price is other than sketchy. Given that neoclassical partial equilibrium analysis placed its main emphasis in that quarter, and that in America particularly Austrian influences had tended to undermine the Marshallian attachment to real cost ideas, it is only natural that from this perspective the Smithian contribution to the analysis of the market economy could be written down as 'not great'.

On the side of policy, however, Smith's performance earned an equally low mark from Cannan. According to him, 'Smith was wrong in supposing that the desire for individual gain would pull the industrial chariot safely along in the absence of harness.' He argued that this 'vitiated Smith's doctrine' and explained the failure of free trade in the international sphere, where no framework of legal regulation existed as compared to its relative success

[56] *Adam Smith 1776–1926*, 77.

in the internal sphere, where there was such a framework. Thus Smith 'failed to see that self-interest had been put in the shafts and harnessed by law and order, products of collective wisdom', in Cannan's opinion, but nevertheless this 'detracts little from the value of his exposition that it was a very good horse'.[57]

It was left to Jacob Viner to show in his famous paper 'Adam Smith and Laissez Faire' that 'the absence of harness' had never been one of Smith's assumptions. After a pentrating survey of the place of the system of natural liberty in both the *Theory of Moral Sentiments* and the *Wealth of Nations* which he modestly claimed to be 'familiar matter' Viner went on to say:

What is not so familiar, however, is the extent to which Smith acknowledged exceptions to the doctrine of a natural harmony in the economic order even when left to take its natural course. Smith himself never brought these together; but if this is done, they make a surprisingly comprehensive list and they demonstrate beyond dispute the existence of a wide divergence between the perfectly harmonious, completely beneficient natural order of the *Theory of Moral Sentiments* and the partial and limited harmony in the economic order of the *Wealth of Nations*.[58]

Having proved his point by an impressive assembly of instances from Smith's own writings, Viner concluded:

Adam Smith was not a doctrinaire advocate of laissez-faire. He saw a wide and elastic range of activity for government, and he was prepared to extend it even farther if government, by improving its standards of competence, honesty and public spirit, showed itself entitled to wider responsibilities.[59]

Viner provided an important correction of the stereotyped picture of Adam Smith as the high priest of non-intervention with free enterprise. Yet he certainly did not deny the significance of that 'strong presumption against government activity beyond its fundamental duties of protection against foreign foes and maintenance of justice' from which Smith started, nor would he have denied the immense practical influence of the stereotype which had grown from it. It was, however, precisely this practical influence which was finally fading at this time.

'We do not dance even yet to a new tune', wrote Keynes in another 1926 publication, *The End of Laissez-faire*. 'But a change

[57] *Economica*, vol. vi (1926), 134.   [58] *Adam Smith 1776–1926*, 134.
[59] Ibid. 154.

is in the air. We hear but indistinctly what were once the clearest and most distinguishable voices which have ever instructed political mankind. The orchestra of diverse instruments, the chorus of articulate sound, is receding at last into the distance.'[60]

Keynes's assertion that 'It is *not* a correct deduction from the principles of economics that enlightened self-interest always operates in the public interest' was not essentially different from what Cairnes had said on the same subject in 1870.[61] The real difference which the intervening years had made to the economists' approach is shown by the fact that Cairnes went on to say that 'as a practical rule, I hold *laissez-faire* to be incomparably the safer guide' whereas Keynes urged that the chief task of economists was to distinguish afresh the *Agenda* of government from the *Non-Agenda* but 'without Bentham's prior presumption that inter-ference is . . . "generally needless" and "generally pernicious"'.

Keynes in *The End of Laissez-faire* had succeeded in capturing the spirit of the times with his customary felicity. No one in 1926, the year of the General Strike, would have dared to assert the beneficence of free trade, external or internal, with the confident dogmatism of Robert Lowe fifty years earlier, but many had still to learn that there was no way back to the comfortable certainties of the era before 1914. Many others who appreciated this fact had no idea of what could or should be put in place of those certainties. They 'did not dance even yet to a new tune', but when Keynes went on, in the closing sections of his essay, to reflect on 'possible improvements in the technique of modern capitalism by the agency of collective action' he showed that he had already sketched out the main elements of the tune to which so many were to dance in years to come.[62]

IV

The half-century between 1926 and 1976 has probably seen more and greater changes in both the method and content of economic

[60] J. M. Keynes, *The End of Laissez-Faire*, *Collected Writings* (London, MacMillan, for the R.E.S., 1972), vol. ix, 272.

[61] Ibid. 288; and cf. Cairnes, 'Political Economy and Laissez-Faire', *Essays in Political Economy*, 250–1.

[62] For a fuller account of the problems of economic policy in this period, and of the work of Keynes—then without the widespread influence on public affairs which it later gained—see D. N. Winch, *Economics and Policy* (London, Hodder and Stoughton, 1969), Part II.

analysis than did the whole century and a half which went before—
and these changes reflect, in part at least, equally great changes in
the circumstances of economic life. So it is hardly surprising that
Smith's contribution should be seen today in a new perspective;
what is surprising is that economists today should be finding more
of value in that contribution than did their predecessors of fifty
and even a hundred years ago. But there can be no denying that
such is the case, for the evidence is abundant—in the other papers
presented at this conference, in the volume of essays published in
conjunction with the bicentenary edition of Smith's works, and in
the numerous other works on and relating to Smith which have
appeared in recent years.

What is the reason for this remarkable revival and extension of
interest in Smith's ideas? It can, I think, be at least partly explained by the very nature of the change in perspective which has
occurred; for the standpoint from which the majority of economists
today are accustomed to view Smith's contribution is that of the
economics of growth and development. Seen from there, it
naturally appears more sensible and significant than when it is
viewed from the angle of a static theory of value and distribution
of the neo-classical type.

The striking point which emerges here is how very recently the
position from which we are now accustomed to judge Smith's
contribution has been reached. It was really only after the appearance of Professor Hla Myint's pioneer article on 'The Welfare
Significance of Productive Labour' in the *Review of Economic
Studies* in 1943 and his *Theories of Welfare Economics* in 1948 that
economists generally began to see Adam Smith in this light. The
lack of emphasis on growth in the thinking of 1926 can perhaps be
explained in terms of the dominance of the neo-classical approach
at that time; but the same emphasis is also notably lacking in
earlier appraisals of Smith. Bagehot in 1876 had noted:

in this very science of Political Economy, the first writers endeavoured
to deal in a single science with all the causes . . . which, as they would
have said 'made nations rich or poor' . . . But considered in this simple
and practical way, the science of Political Economy becomes useless,
because of its immense extent.[63]

Slight and dismissive as it is, this is the only direct reference to the

[63] Bagehot, 'The Preliminary of Political Economy', *Economic Studies*,
98–9.

treatment of economic growth in classical work which I have been able to find in the literature of 1876. Nor does the theme of growth figure prominently in 1826, although this may be because the writers of that day were still too much 'inside' the Smithian approach to select out this element for comment.

By no means all of what has recently been written about Smith's economics is concerned with its growth aspects, however. There have been significant re-interpretations of the utility aspects of his theory of value, and notable re-assessments of what can perhaps only be described as aspects of his political economy—the treatment of public goods in the *Wealth of Nations*, for example, and more broadly the relations between the views of the individual in society which Smith took in the *Wealth of Nations* and in the *Theory of Moral Sentiments*, now seen afresh as two parts of one system.[64]

Some of this represents a very valuable effort to set Smith's work properly into the context of eighteenth century ideas, events, and institutions; but some of it can also be seen as symptomatic of another shift in viewpoint, producing another new perspective on Smith's contribution. Many economists today are disenchanted about the prospects and results of economic growth, and many are likewise dubious or defensive about the long-vaunted idea of economics as a science, positive and value free. It is little wonder that such authors can find fresh interest in a system of thought which placed economic problems firmly in the context of ethics and jurisprudence and which was informed throughout by a concept of justice. This may well prove to be the aspect of Smith's ideas which the next generation of economists will see as vital.

Each period, indeed, has tended and will tend to see Smith's contribution in its own way and to evaluate it accordingly. Certainly also each one has tended and will tend to see the treatment of those problems and theories in which it has most interest as constituting the most significant part of Smith's work. There is a good deal of truth in Jacob Viner's typically astringent comment

---

[64] e.g. M. Bowley, *Studies in the History of Economic Theory before 1870* (London, MacMillan, 1973), especially Parts III and IV; S. Hollander, *The Economics of Adam Smith* (Toronto, University of Toronto Press, 1973), G. J. Stigler, 'Smith's Travels on the Ship of State', A. Peacock, 'The Treatment of the Principles of Public Finance in *The Wealth of Nations*', in *Essays on Adam Smith*, 237–46, 553–67. E. G. West, 'Adam Smith's Economics of Politics', *Carleton Economic Papers* (forthcoming in *History of Political Economy*, vol. viii, 1976).

that 'traces of every conceivable sort of doctrine can be found in that most catholic book, and an economist must have peculiar theories indeed who cannot quote from *The Wealth of Nations* to support his special purposes'.[65]

Is this the only reason why successive generations have continued to find something of value in Smith's contribution, from whatever angle it is viewed? Is this why the *Wealth of Nations* continues to form 'part of an extended present'?[66] Surely there is more to it than this. I am inclined to think that the perennial appeal of the *Wealth of Nations* rests not only on the wealth of ideas which it contains, even though it may be that 'there is scarcely any economic truth now known of which he [Smith] did not get some glimpse'.[67] Something also must be credited to Smith's realism and understanding of his fellow-men—in fact, to his possession of those virtues of humanity and self-command on which he placed so high a value.[68] In the words which Edmund Burke used to Smith himself in commenting on the TMS:

A theory like yours founded on the nature of man, which is always the same, will last, when those that are founded on his opinions, which are always changing, will and must be forgotten.[69]

COMMENT

by D. P. O'Brien*

Professor Black has given us an excellent survey, with characteristic lucidity and scholarship, of the changing historical perspective on Adam Smith. This is a tremendously important theme with implications for the entire history of economic thought. What I would like to do, very briefly, is to enlarge a little upon this theme

[65] Viner, op. cit. 126.

[66] K. E. Boulding, 'After Samuelson, who needs Adam Smith?', *History of Political Economy* vol. vii, No. 2 (Fall, 1971), 231.

[67] Marshall, *Principles of Economics*, App. B, §3 (9th ed., London, MacMillan, for the R.E.S.) vol. i, 757.

[68] Cf. D. D. Raphael, 'The Impartial Spectator' *Essays on Adam Smith*, Part I, 89.

[69] Letter 38, addressed to Adam Smith, dated 10 September, 1759. Quoted in C. R. Fay, *The World of Adam Smith* (Cambridge, Heffer, 1960), 9.

* University of Durham.

by indicating some of the specific ways in which perspective changes.

Firstly and most obviously the subject matter of economics, the central focus of the attention of economists at any particular time, is a changing thing. It is not I think profitable, particularly at this time, to discuss whether what is involved in a change of focus is a Khunian 'paradigm shift'. But every economist with any knowledge of the wider literature of economics will recognize the truth of this assertion. Historians of economic thought themselves have to be trained as economists primarily rather than as historians and so the changes of focus of the subject Economics affect their training, their mental conditioning, and hence their view of their subject. A striking instance of this, in relation to Adam Smith, is the way in which economists rediscovered economic growth after World War II and it became an important part of the literature. Professor Myint had already shown that Adam Smith's great work was about economic growth;[1] but his important message, well formulated though it was, might have fallen on much less receptive ears but for the change of focus which the subject itself had experienced.

Secondly, as a subset of changes in the subject, are changes in technique. No one can doubt that what has occurred during the last fifteen years has been a major change in the technique of economists and in the standards of mathematical familiarity (if not elegance) which they are required to reach. Virtually all economists now have a reading knowledge of mathematics (and what might be loosely called a 'reproductive knowledge') even if their manipulative skills are not of a particularly high order. This in turn has influenced the treatment which has been accorded to the history of economics. Sometimes the influence has not always been a happy one. But the formalization of Smith's growth model by Thweatt and (especially) Barkhai[2] has certainly been influential as have some of the mathematical models of Ricardo.[3] Of course some

[1] H. Myint, 'The Classical View of the Economic Problem', *Economica* N.S. Vol. 13 (1946), 119–30.

[2] W. O. Thweatt, 'A Diagrammatic Presentation of Adam Smith's Growth Model', *Social Research* vol. 24 (1957), 227–30; H. Barkai, 'A Formal Outline of a Smithian Growth Model', *Quarterly Journal of Economics* vol. 88 (1969), 396–414.

[3] L. Pasinetti, 'A Mathematical Formulation of the Ricardian System', *Review of Economic Studies* vol. 27 (1960), 78–98; H. Brems, 'An Attempt at a

corrective to the perspective given by this formalisation is required
—and Professor Spengler's contribution here is particularly note-
worthy.[4] But even if corrective is required the change in the focus
of historians of economic thought is undeniable.

Thirdly, and it is gratifying to be able to record this, research
in the history of economic thought has itself produced changes of
focus and made certain views no longer tenable. Decent scholarly
work in the history of economic thought does have the great
advantage of cutting the feet from underneath the caricatures of the
subject which are used for propagandist purposes. The carica-
turists are really of two kinds. There are those who caricature so
as to exalt their theoretical system—Marx, Bohm-Bawerk, and
Keynes come into this category—and those who caricature for
the easy purposes of reader appeal. Recent work on Poverty and
the Industrial Revolution comes into this category. Of course the
propagandists and the caricaturists are not necessarily deterred
from their efforts by the existence of scholarly work in the history
of economic thought. There is, after all, the income from the
public library market to consider. But at least their impact is very
considerably lessened by the existence of a body of literature
which does, I think fairly and objectively, evaluate the history of
economic thought. But the very process of the development of this
literature produces changes of focus. The gap between the view
of Ricardo advanced by J. H. Hollander[5] in the early years of this
century and the now widely accepted view stemming in particular
from the work of Professors Stigler[6] and Blaug,[7] is enormous.
(Incidentally it is, I believe, a tribute to Ricardo that it took better
economists to make better sense of him.) Scholarly work has also
changed our view of Adam Smith. Perhaps the outstanding contribution of the last generation of scholars was that by Jacob Viner.[8]
In recent times there has been a most important contribution

Rigorous Restatement of Ricardo's Long-Run Equilibrium' *Canadian Journal of Economics* vol. 26 (1960), 74–86.

[4] J. J. Spengler, 'Adam Smith's Theory of Economic Growth' Parts I–II *Southern Economic Journal* vol. 25 (1959), 397–415; vol. 26 (1959), 1–12.

[5] J. H. Hollander, *David Ricardo. A Centenary Estimate* (Baltimore 1910).

[6] G. J. Stigler, 'The Ricardian Theory of Value and Distribution' *Journal of Political Economy* vol. 60 (1952), 187–207.

[7] M. Blaug, *Ricardian Economics* (New Haven 1958).

[8] J. Viner, 'Adam Smith and Laisser Faire', *Journal of Political Economy* vol. 35 (1927), 198–232 reprinted in *The Long View and the Short* (Glencoe, Illinois, 1958).

from Warren Samuels[9] and most recently of all we have had Professor Hollander's weighty book.[10] These contributions to Smith scholarship help to correct not only the deliberate carica-turists but also the *simpliste* representation of Smith which the radical right like Robert Lowe, to whom Professor Black referred, often purveys. It also helps to correct the views advanced by those with very *subtle* minds, who over-simplify for a particular public occasion, like George Warde Norman who was also quoted. It also offers some check on Smith's 'good press' which stems in part from Viner's well known remark that it is a strange economist who cannot find support for his views in the *Wealth of Nations*.

Fourthly, there are in fact two distinct sources of writings in the history of economic thought. On the one hand there are books which are designedly written as works in the history of economic thought—and these, as Schumpeter[11] and Viner[12] showed, can themselves be great books. On the other hand there is a less obvious but certainly no less important source—criticism. For it is a fact that, for a certain kind of creative mind, criticism of previous work is itself a method of working. Schumpeter has pointed to this in the case of Marx;[13] but it is even more true of Ricardo. Another, and perhaps less obvious, example is that of Irving Fisher. The owners of these creative minds may, as in the case of Ricardo, become the leaders in their subject. If this occurs they influence the development of the history of economic thought in two ways. On the one hand their personal prestige causes other writers to take note of their evaluation of previous economists; this works quickly, and indeed in the case of Ricardo it worked very quickly indeed. Ricardo's evaluation of Adam Smith, especially on the subject of value, rent, and colonies was greatly influential though I would argue that we must not over-rate the extent to which McCulloch, in particular, regarded Smith's work as 'vitiated' even in the 1820's. For the Ricardian analyses are treated by McCulloch in his Notes to the *Wealth of Nations* as essentially *glosses* on the fundamental *basis* provided by Smith. The other method by which

9 W. Samuels, *The Classical Theory of Economic Policy* (Cleveland, Ohio, 1966).

10 S. Hollander, *The Economics of Adam Smith* (London 1973).

11 J. A. Schumpeter, *History of Economic Analysis* (New York 1954).

12 J. Viner, *Studies in the Theory of International Trade* (London 1937).

13 Schumpeter, *History*, 390. See also the same author's *Ten Great Economists* (London 1952), 26.

the owners of critically creative minds exercise their influence is slower but it is still effective. It is the influence exercised by these economists upon courses which train future economists and thus future historians of economic thought.

Finally there are what might be termed 'raids' by those who are not primarily (or even secondarily) historians of economic thought but economists with high (and admired) levels of technique, into the history of economic thought. Sometimes these are futile and fatuous. But occasionally the whole history of economic thought approach may be lastingly changed. Two instances which come to mind are Baumol's treatment of Classical Dynamics,[14] and Kaldor's treatment of Classical Distribution.[15]

For all these reasons, history of economic thought does not offer a fixed and unchanging view of the work of Smith or of other previous economists. To put the changes of view in perspective however, let it be said at once that total obsolescence does not affect the best work of any particular generation of historians of economic thought. Despite the harsh things which are said about Cannan, especially his 1926 contribution to which Professor Black referred, historians of economic thought can gain a great deal of illumination—sometimes indeed, even exhilaration—from a book more than three quarters of a century old; Cannan's *Production and Distribution*.[16] Indeed, until 1976, it was Cannan's edition of the *Wealth of Nations* which was exclusively used by every serious scholar. But there is a big gap between Cannan and J. H. Hollander. So although the highpoints remain the perspective does change: and it is this very fact which helps to make history of economic thought a living, continuing, and perennially fascinating subject.

COMMENT

by Donald Winch*

I find myself so much in sympathy with Professor Black's choice of theme, and his priorities in dealing with it, that were I to follow

---

[14] W. J. Baumol, *Economic Dynamics* (2nd edition New York 1959), chapter 2.
[15] N. Kaldor, *Essays on Value and Distribution* (London 1960).
[16] E. Cannan, *A History of the Theories of Production and Distribution in English Political Economy from 1776 to 1848* (London 1893).

---

* University of Sussex.

strictly in his footsteps it would only be to add a footnote here and there. Thus it occurred to me that I might expand a little on his treatment of the divergent appeals made to Smith's authority, especially during the formative period of what we now call classical political economy. I could, for example, draw attention to the appeals made by Malthus and Sismondi in their attempts to mount an opposition to various aspects of Ricardian orthodoxy. But this would entail showing why, in spite of the obvious fact that Smith remained an alternative authority, the heterodox claimants to his mantle were so signally unsuccessful in establishing their case, regardless of whether it was based on an accurate assessment of Smith's own methods and conclusions. Attention would thereby be shifted towards Ricardo and away from the *Wealth of Nations*, with the added risk of endorsing an already too prevalent view of Smith among economists, namely that he is best interpreted as some kind of muddled progenitor of an enterprise that only achieved clarity and fruition in the work of Ricardo, John Stuart Mill, and Marx.

If we are interested in establishing a less proleptic perspective on Smith, it may be helpful to entertain a quite different view of what occurred during the crucial transitional period marked out, say, by the publication of the fifth edition of the *Wealth of Nations* in 1789 and Ricardo's death in 1823. For it was during this period, in the aftermath of the French Revolution, and as a result of a series of problems connected with the Napoleonic Wars—rising food prices, growing population, fears of monetary disorder, heavy taxation, and increased public debt—that it became acceptable to conduct serious discussion of economic issues in a manner and form that was quite different from the example set by Smith. Ricardo's *Principles* epitomized the new style to followers and opponents alike, but perhaps he was only its most extreme practitioner rather than its originator; his opponents may have had more in common with him than with the father figure to whom they occasionally turned for authority.

Some years ago now, Professor Alec Macfie drew our attention to various discontinuities between the Scottish and English traditions of economic thought, partly by emphasizing those changes taking place during this period which centre on the Benthamite version of utilitarianism.[1] Can one go further and suggest that there

[1] A. L. Macfie, 'The Scottish Tradition in Economic Thought', in *The

are no obvious candidates—Scottish, French, or English—for the role of economic successor to the author of the *Wealth of Nations*? For one reason or another, Say, Sismondi, and Lauderdale do not seem capable of filling the bill, while Millar and Dugald Stewart have some of the qualifications for doing so, but only if one is prepared to overlook their lack of any sustained interest in political economy.

Or take the case of Malthus—English true, but no Benthamite. In spite of what Keynes might say about the methodological differences between Ricardo and Malthus, it was Malthus himself who, in his first *Essay on Population* published in 1798, introduced a quasi-mathematical approach to one of the questions that was later to become a central matter of concern to classical political economy. It may also be revealing to consider Edmund Burke, whose political and economic affinities with Smith have been the subject of several learned accounts. Burke had little in common with later generations of political economists, but neither can he be said to have spoken Smith's philosophical language when he made his intemperate defence of economic liberty in *Thoughts and Details on Scarcity*, a pamphlet written only five years after Smith's death. In their different ways, of course, Malthus and Burke are both classic post- (or counter-) revolutionary authors, but this does not license us to minimize the extent of the changes that took place not long after Smith had passed from the scene—changes which gave a new kind of urgency to certain public issues, and encouraged a narrower and more dogmatic application of the tools of reason to economic argument.

The relevance to our present deliberations of what I am trying to suggest in these tentative remarks may become clearer if I pose two more, intentionally provocative, questions. If there was a major change of emphasis and a narrowing in the scope of the science of political economy soon after Smith's death, can economists assume quite so confidently, as they appear to be doing this bicentennial year, that they are his rightful, if not sole, heirs? If, according to modern taste, Ricardo is more of an economists' economist than Smith, are today's economists the most natural celebrants of the *Wealth of Nations*? It may be significant that in 1876 even the politician Sir Robert Lowe had to Ricardianise

Individual in Society: Papers on Adam Smith (Allen and Unwin, London, 1967).

Smith in order to praise him—a tactic criticized by Thorold Rogers and (as Professor Black has indicated) Cliffe Leslie, both of whom wished to claim Smith as a relevant ancestor for their own brand of historical and inductive economics. I mention this point without wishing to endorse the view that it is any more valid to depict Smith as the founder of historical economics. From my point of view, this may only be yet another attempt to impose nineteenth century perspectives on what remains, quintessentially, a work of the eighteenth century.

Let me complete this irreverent train of thought by returning to an earlier assessment of Smith, one which clearly belongs to Scotland and to the eighteenth century. Three years after Smith's death, Dugald Stewart wrote what is still one of the most authoritative accounts of Smith's life and writings, though it is consonant with my earlier point that he later found it necessary to explain that he had been unduly influenced in writing it by the conservative mood created by the French Revolution. Stewart may also have been answering a sneer published in *The Times* in 1790 to the effect that Smith had 'converted the chair of Moral Philosophy into a professorship of trade and finance'—a fact which was crudely attributed to Smith's residence in Glasgow, 'a great commercial town'—when he set out to show the connection between Smith's 'system of commercial politics, and those speculations of his earlier years, in which he aimed more professedly at the advancement of human improvement and happiness'. For as Stewart concluded, rather primly: 'It is this view of Political Economy that can alone render it interesting to the moralist, and can dignify calculations of profit and loss in the eye of the philosopher' (Stewart, IV. 12). Stewart's corrective is still relevant if it reminds us that the *Wealth of Nations* was successful not simply as a work on 'trade and finance', but as the most striking attempt to sustain a peculiarly Scottish line of philosophical and historical inquiry into one of the most important emerging features of civilized society, namely the spreading network of commercial relationships, with all its consequences for the questions examined by traditional moral and political discourse. In this respect the *Wealth of Nations* can be said to mark the triumphant culmination of an eighteenth century enterprise, as much as the beginning of nineteenth and twentieth century economics. It can certainly do no harm to check hubris by reminding economists that, apart from his additions and corrections to later editions of the *Wealth of Nations*, after 1776 Smith published no further work on political economy— not even a single reply to his critics, few though they were. On the other hand, he did return to the *Theory of Moral Sentiments*, and we know that, given time, his next task was to have been the completion of his 'account of the general principles of law and government' (TMS VII. iv. 37).

Let me close with a related observation, which can most tactfully be introduced by rephrasing the comment by Jevons on the 1876 festivities cited by Professor Black. Jevons said that 'the statesmen mostly had it their own way, and the company appeared to care little what mere literary economists thought about Adam Smith'. Since Professors Black, O'Brien, and myself are, so to speak, the only accredited antiquarians billed to speak at this conference— leaving aside the 'proper' historians who spoke at the first session —it occurred to me, perhaps a little ungraciously, that we might echo Jevons by replacing 'statesmen' by 'economists', and 'literary economists' by 'historians of economic thought'. However, in view of Professor O'Brien's persuasive argument to the effect that we mere historians have a valuable corrective part to play, I concluded that my comment might be thought to embody an awkward mixture of presumption and undue pessimism. Nevertheless, I am a little less optimistic than Professor O'Brien appears to be in thinking that Gresham's Law operates very effectively in these matters to ensure that good scholarship drives out bad propaganda and caricature.

The record of shifting perspectives outlined by Professor Black ought to be sobering to any economist about to embark on yet another modern reconstruction of Smith's position on this or that sub-division of modern economics, particularly if he is anxious to present it as an interpretation of what Smith 'really meant'. Economists have not always been the most reliable or consistent interpreters of their own past, and their whiggish habits have perhaps done more damage to Smith than many later figures in the pantheon. The history of Smith scholarship and the history of economists' views on Smith have frequently lived entirely separate lives. Professor Black's remarks on Edwin Cannan are a good illustration of this state of affairs. For here was one of the leading Smith scholars of his generation, who, when he wrote on Smith as an economist, was guilty of being both perfunctory and patronizing.

Consider also the Chicago sesquicentennial volume. Paul Douglas's attempt to show how much Smith's theory of value 'almost inevitably gave rise' to theories of exploitation may have been interesting to economists at the time, but there is no doubt in my mind as to which of those essays has best stood the test of fifty years of discussion, namely Jacob Viner's scholarly contribution on 'Adam Smith and Laissez Faire'.[2] As an ex-Viner pupil— a privilege I share with Professor Black—I may be guilty of personal bias here, though I believe the judgement could be supported by the more objective evidence provided by the number of citations of the Viner article in the new volume of celebratory *Essays on Adam Smith*. Ideally, of course, we all ought to be more like Viner—as good as economists as we aspire to be as scholars. While this may be a counsel of perfection, one thing on which we can agree is that when we have all had our say this year, at this conference and elsewhere, the most important monument to the bicentenary of the *Wealth of Nations* will be that constructed so patiently by the scholars who have worked on the Glasgow edition of Smith's complete works. This alone should silence ungrateful thoughts by holding out the prospect of uniting what have all too often been disparate enterprises.

[2] Jacob Viner, 'Adam Smith and Laisser Faire' in *Adam Smith 1776–1926: Lectures to Commemorate the Sesqui-Centennial of the Publication of the Wealth of Nations* (Chicago, 1928, Kelley, New York, 1966).

3

Sympathy and Self-Interest

BY THOMAS WILSON*

I. CONFLICT OR CONSISTENCY?

'SELF-INTEREST' is an obvious topic for any discussion of the views of Adam Smith or for any appraisal of an economic system based on private ownership, free enterprise and competition. 'Sympathy' is less obviously relevant. Whereas the pursuit of 'self-interest' is bound to be a central theme in any discussion of individualism, 'sympathy' may not appear to be so—not, at least, at first sight. For 'sympathy' is more likely to suggest a different tradition and a different view of human nature and human society. This, I think, is the initial response that the two words—'sympathy' and 'self-interest'—might be expected to evoke. It is the obvious response; but it may not be the right one. Clearly we must not overlook the fact that Adam Smith, for his part, had a great deal to say about 'sympathy'. 'Sympathy' is indeed an integral part of his moral theory. It is the opening theme of the *Theory of Moral Sentiments*:

> How selfish soever man may be supposed, there are evidently some principles in his nature, which interest him in the fortunes of others, and render their happiness necessary to him, though he derives nothing from it, except the pleasure of seeing it. (TMS I. i. i. i.)

Smith's use of the term 'sympathy' calls for a word of explanation. 'To sympathize' may mean to feel pity for those who are the victims of ill-fortune or ill-usage. That is obvious enough. But the term has a wider sense. To quote once more from Smith:

> Pity and compassion are words appropriated to signify our fellow-

* Adam Smith Professor of Political Economy in the University of Glasgow. The author is indebted to Professor David Raphael, Imperial College of Science and Technology and to Mr. A. S. Skinner and Mr. Malcolm MacLennan of the University of Glasgow for comments on this paper. He is solely responsible for any errors it may contain.

feeling with the sorrow of others. Sympathy, though its meaning was, perhaps, originally the same, may now, however, without much impropriety, be made use of to denote our fellow-feeling with any passion whatever. (TMS I. i. 1. 5.)

'To sympathize' is to put oneself in another's shoes. It is to share by imagination in the feelings of another person and these feelings may be occasioned by good fortune as well as by bad. 'To sympathize' may even mean to share in the pleasure another person derives from his own personal appearance. To quote again, this time from David Hume:

Broad shoulders, a lank belly, firm joints, taper legs; all these are beautiful in our species, because they are signs of form and vigour, which being advantages we naturally sympathise with, they convey to the beholder a share of that satisfaction they produce in the possessor. (*Treatise* III. v.)

Sympathy plays an essential part in Smith's account of the way in which moral judgements are formed. For it is the act of imaginative sympathy that allows a person not only to understand the position of other people but also to view his own conduct through other eyes. Although Smith is careful not to identify morality with a mere respect for public opinion, he holds that it is the desire for approbation from our fellows that fosters our capacity for detached judgement. Thus, to use his own imagery, we learn to observe our own behaviour as it might be seen by an imaginary spectator who is at once impartial and well-informed with regard to our motives. Smith's individualism is therefore very different from that of, say, James Mill.[1]

As we have seen, sympathy can be inspired in many ways and expressed in different forms. In some circumstances it may lead to unselfishness and for this Smith had the highest praise; remarking

. . . that to feel much for others, and little for ourselves, . . . to restrain

---

[1] A. L. Macfie, *The Individual in Society* (George Allen and Unwin, London, 1967), ch. 3; T. D. Campbell, *Adam Smith's Science of Morals* (George Allen and Unwin, 1971); 'Scientific Explanation and Ethical Justification in the *Moral Sentiments*' by T. D. Campbell and 'The Impartial Spectator' by D. D. Raphael, both papers in *Essays on Adam Smith*; Dorothy Emmett, *Rules, Roles and Relations* (Macmillan, 1966), 71–74; Richard B. Brendt, *Ethical Theory* (Prentice Hall, 1959), 173–6.

our selfish, and to indulge our benevolent affections, constitutes the perfection of human nature: and can alone produce among mankind that harmony of sentiments and passions in which subsists their whole grace and propriety. (TMS I. i. 5. 5.)

The view presented in passages such as this may seem to be in sharp contrast with that traditionally associated with Smith. Let us recall some familiar sentences from the WN which express so clearly his honesty and realism, his contempt for self-deception and cant.

In almost every other race of animals each individual, when it is grown up to maturity, is entirely independent, and in the natural state has occasion for the assistance of no other living creature. But man has almost constant occasion for the help of his brethren, and it is in vain for him to expect it from their benevolence only. He will be more likely to prevail if he can interest their self-love in his favour, and show them that it is for their own advantage to do for him what he requires of them . . . It is not from the benevolence of the butcher, the brewer, or the baker, that we expect our dinner, but from their regard to their own interest. We address ourselves, not to their humanity, but to their self-love, and never talk to them of our own necessities, but of their advantage. (WN I. ii. 2.)

This is the voice we all recognize. It sounds like a different voice from that of the author of the passages I have quoted from, and it is natural to ask whether there is not in fact a difference, indeed a conflict, between the view expressed in these two books. Professor Macfie has examined this possibility and dismissed it.[2] That there are differences is, of course, the case. In his famous essay, 'Smith and Laisser Faire', Jacob Viner referred to the attention these differences have received in Germany where they 'have coined a pretty term, *Das Adam Smith Problem*, to denote the failure to understand either which results from the attempt to use the one in the interpretation of the other'.[3]

It would, however, be an error to suppose that the theme of the TMS is 'sympathy' and that of the WN 'self-interest'. On the contrary, it is in the TMS that an 'Invisible Hand' is first

---

[2] 'Adam Smith's *Moral Sentiments* as Foundation for his *Wealth of Nations*', in *The Individual in Society*.

[3] J. Viner, Essay V in Adam Smith, 1776–1926; *Lectures to Commemorate the Sesqui-Centennial of the Publication of the Wealth of Nations* (Chicago, 1928, Kelley, New York, 1966), 120.

mentioned—Smith's metaphorical way of describing how the self-interested activities of countless individuals seemed to promote an outcome intended by none but beneficial to all. Far from suggesting that the TMS lays less emphasis on self-interest than the WN, Viner's contention was to the opposite effect. The WN is a more empirical and less metaphysical book than the TMS. Although a great deal is said in the WN about the socially beneficial outcome to be derived from the pursuit of self-interest, there are also many qualifications and exceptions, and attention is properly paid to the identification of those circumstances in which the pursuit of self-interest may, in fact, be socially harmful or, at best, socially inadequate. It is true that there is not much explicit reference to sympathy in the WN; but it is also true that the claims made for the Invisible Hand are significantly qualified.

If, then, there is really any inconsistency between what Smith said about 'self-interest' and what he said about 'sympathy', this inconsistency must lie *within* the contents of the TMS itself and, to a lesser extent, *within* those of the WN. But there may, in fact, be no such inconsistency and my first task will be to consider this question. My purpose in doing so will not be only, or even mainly, to discuss an academic point about the history of thought. There is a more practical and more contemporary reason for directing our attention to these matters. For it is not merely that the views of Adam Smith have often been misunderstood. It is undoubtedly the case that the market economy which he analysed and admired has also been misunderstood and continues to be so. The perpetuation of much public misunderstanding about this important social mechanism is—to say the least of it—a serious matter. We shall, therefore, be obliged to direct our attention to some basic problems of communication and control and to consider their implications for the pursuit of self-interest in the conduct of production and exchange. In doing so we shall find that the problems encountered in this connection are not in fact peculiar to private enterprise but are also met, though in a somewhat different form, in countries where much more emphasis is placed on planning by the state. That is now our first task. Our second task will be to explore the ways in which sympathy—in some sense of that term —can find practical expression and, in doing so, we shall, of course, extend the analysis much further than it was taken by Smith two centuries ago. For we shall have to devote at least some attention to what is loosely described as the 'welfare state'. In our cumbersome modern jargon, 'sympathy' implies interdependence in utility functions. To what extent, then, does the recognition of such interdependence in itself allow economists to say significantly more about the welfare state than it is possible to say within the traditional boundaries of Paretian welfare economics? If the answer is disappointing, how should we proceed? My final task will be to discuss the link between sympathy and respect for the individual. We shall see that moral judgements derived from sympathy can provide a basis not only for the welfare state but also a firm foundation for consumers' sovereignty and, more generally, for a wide measure of freedom in the conduct of economic affairs. It is often assumed that egotism is the basis of individualism; but individualism may also be founded on sympathy.

The first point to be made is a semantic one. For the charge of inconsistency is to be explained partly by the ambiguity of the term 'sympathy'. It must be stressed once more that in Smith's usage 'sympathy' is not just another word for 'pity' or 'compassion' as motives for action. It means rather the capacity for fellow-feeling and is part of his explanation of the manner in which moral judgements are formed. The objectivity thus attained may, of course, lead to generous actions with personal advantage sacrificed for the benefit of other people. The Impartial Spectator—like Smith himself—must be deemed to approve highly of actions of this kind. Smith also believed, however, that there were circumstances in which the Impartial Spectator would sanction the pursuit of personal advantage. For he was not prepared to regard the pursuit of personal advantage as being in itself inherently immoral.

Secondly, Smith's concern with results as well as motives led him to recognize that all may gain from activities in which the various participants are guided only by self-interest. For it is a matter of empirical observation that both sides may benefit from a freely negotiated bargain and it is quite wrong to suppose—as is so often done today—that when someone gains, then someone else must lose. Economic activity is not a zero-sum game, although there may be a deeply rooted inclination, especially in Britain, to suppose that this is so. Nor is this realistic recognition of a possible harmony of interests so tainted with cynicism as to deserve the furious condemnation of moralistic commentators who appear to be interested only in motives and to be bored by results. What is surely far more dangerous is the tendency to ignore the possible community of interests and thus to create a cult of confrontation for this entails what are highly dangerous implications for the conduct of both domestic and international affairs.

Although Smith's defence of the pursuit of self-interest was qualified at many points, it must be conceded that there are in-cautious paragraphs in which he seems to have claimed too much. For he wrote in a bold style and never sought to confine himself to a demure and cautious prose. The metaphor of the Invisible Hand—though used by Smith on only a very few occasions—was particularly unfortunate for it laid him open to easy attack and to ill-considered ridicule as the Dr. Pangloss of the early capitalist system. But it is only fair to observe that his is by no means the only theory that seems to depend for a happy outcome upon the protection of an Invisible Hand of one kind or another. Perhaps the most important contemporary example is the claim that the leaders of a victorious Communist party—restrained presumably by some Invisible Hand—can be relied upon not to abuse their dictatorial power as other non-Marxist dictators might be expected to do. Or consider the view that political freedom should be sacri-ficed for the sake of greater equality on the assumption that inequality of power will not, in due course, be reflected in inequality of income. The fact is that Marx was far less cautious in what he had to say about post-revolutionary society than was Adam Smith in what he, for his part, had to say directly or by implication about the working of the Invisible Hand in the WN.

II. SELF-INTEREST, COMMUNICATION, AND CONTROL

May we then accept the conclusion that the pursuit of self-interest may have socially beneficial results, though this will not always be so? The competitive market may then seem to deserve the follow-ing muted and qualified blessing pronounced by Alfred Marshall:

. . . in a world in which all men were perfectly virtuous competition would be out of place . . . But in the responsible conduct of affairs, it is worse than folly to ignore the imperfections which still cling to human nature.[4]

---

[4] *Principles of Economics* (8th edn., Macmillan, London, 1930), 9.

But it will not do to leave the matter there. It will not do because—somewhat surprisingly—Marshall's contention leaves out of account the immensely important and difficult problems of communication and control with which, elsewhere in his writings, Marshall was, of course, so much concerned. Production should indeed be production 'for use'; but if that rather obvious requirement is to be met, there must be some reasonably satisfactory method of ascertaining the wants of the final users, whether of private individuals or of private organizations or, for that matter, of the public authorities. There must be some way of presenting these users with the possibility of making a rational choice among the available alternatives. In a modern economy with a highly elaborate division of labour, this problem of communication becomes correspondingly complicated and involves a long series of intermediate stages. Even in the eighteenth century, Smith was much impressed by the complexity of the economic system and emphasized again and again the extent to which everyone is dependent upon the activities of other people. A satisfactory solution was not to be found in blind adherence to customary behaviour or in the conservative acceptance of the regulations of the mercantilist state. A social mechanism of some kind was needed to perform this task but it should be one that would provide communication and control without smothering the preferences of the consumers. Nor must the creative activities of imaginative individuals be restrained by regulatory mediocrity, for no-one can tell in advance what these creative individuals are capable of achieving. There should be freedom of action with competition providing both a stimulus and a test of success. The social mechanism required for this purpose was indeed in existence. It was not one that had been created by conscious effort but rather one that had come into being from the natural human propensity to truck, barter, and exchange. This social mechanism—the market—could not do everything that was required, as Smith was well aware; but it was nevertheless a mechanism of extraordinary efficiency. There was no other mechanism at that time which would have been capable of achieving anything like as much.

If, however, people are to behave intelligently and effectively in the market, they must have limited objectives. For it is simply not possible for each of us to ascertain all the social implications of every act and to shape our behaviour accordingly. The point has been made frequently enough that the effective range of personal benevolence is limited with its force dropping sharply outside a restricted circle of relatives and acquaintances. But it is not merely benevolence but also knowledge that has a narrow range. The various agents in economic life are obliged, in the nature of the case, to economize in the use of information and to do the best they can with what is available to them. If every consumer, every worker, and every manager were to try to take into account all the potentially far-reaching consequences of their individual actions, the result would be bewilderment and confusion with action paralysed by unending iteration. This is a fact that must always be kept in mind in assessing the claim that firms should be run with a wide range of broad social objectives in mind as well as their usual commercial objectives. To accept this view uncritically could blur the edges of responsibility. The point has been clearly put by an economist who is the chairman of a large British company:

If the profit and loss account is supplemented by other imprecise and conflicting objectives, good management will be jeopardised . . . If we try to look after everything we shall get into a great muddle.

He goes on to concede that firms may sometimes be required, and quite properly required, to depart from the course indicated by commercial considerations; but there should then be:

specific interventions or encouragements, administered in accordance with rules which are as precise as possible. And inability to frame precise rules must be a quite powerful argument for abstaining from intervention.[5]

The pursuit of self-interest in economic affairs now begins to appear in a somewhat different light. It is not simply a question of accepting, as a fact of life, that people are often self-interested and of seeking to identify and, if possible, to establish those social arrangements which will allow their self-interested pursuits to contribute to the common good. This is, as we have seen, an important aspect of the matter but there is now more to be said. If scarce but diverse resources are to be used effectively in satisfying a multiplicity of wants, it is positively desirable that the economic agents should pursue limited objectives.

[5] Arthur Knight, *Private Enterprise and Public Intervention* (George Allen and Unwin, London, 1974), 201–03.

It has often been pointed out that the pursuit of self-interest need not imply selfishness. Marshall, himself, was clear on this point. The ultimate objectives of the person concerned may be strongly altruistic, and self-interest is really a confusing expression for limited self-chosen objectives which may be selfish or unselfish or some combination of both. It does not follow, however, that in the ordinary business of production and exchange, a person ought to sacrifice whatever interests he is seeking to advance in favour of those of the other party to each bargain. The matter was put as follows by Philip Wicksteed:

What makes . . . an economic transaction is that I am not considering you except as a link in the chain, or considering your desires except as the means by which I may gratify those of someone else— not necessarily myself. The economic relation does not exclude from my mind everyone but me, it potentially includes every one but you.[6]

Or again:

. . . the note of a business transaction between A and B is not that A's *ego* alone is consciously in his mind, but that, however many the *alteri* are, B is not one of them; and B, in like manner, whether he is thinking only of his own *ego* or of innumerable *alteri*, is not thinking of A.[7]

Thus he concludes that:

The specific characteristic of an economic relation is not its 'egoism' but its 'non-tuism'.[8]

'Non-tuism' is necessary if the market is to work satisfactorily just as 'non-tuism' is necessary for a decent game of football or of chess. Without 'non-tuism' the game will be spoiled.[9]

Admittedly it may be objected that, however plausible this

[6] *The Commonsense of Political Economy*, ed. Robbins (London, George Routledge, 1933), i. 174.
[7] Op. cit. i. 179.   [8] Op. cit. i. 180.
[9] It may be felt that Wicksteed presents this argument in an unnecessarily exaggerated way. Could A not make some allowance for B's interests and B for A's? The question is a reasonable one if we are really thinking of the relationships between two or three individuals; but the point is that A's actions impinge on large numbers of B's and *vice versa*. Wicksteed was probably unwise to express his point in terms of an example which by its nature obscures the crux of the problem—the multiplicity of actors, the complexity of their relationships and the paucity of information. Hochman and Rogers are, I think, open to similar criticism with their example of Mutt and Jeff: 'Pareto Optimal Redistribution', *American Economic Review* (1969).

justification of the pursuit of self-interest, in practice the attitude adopted in the market will foster selfishness and give the impression of sanctioning it—mistakenly perhaps, but strongly nevertheless. I am myself inclined to the view that this point is by no means without substance. We must, however, go on to ask whether there is any alternative form of economic organization that can avoid tensions of this kind. If the market were to be abolished, economic affairs would have to be controlled by plans. We can rely on the price system or on plans or, more probably, on some combination of the two; but there is no third method which would perform the functions of communication and control without the use of either the price system or a bureaucracy. The belief that there is a third method that would somehow manifest itself was cherished by what, only yesterday, was described as the New Left; but this is economic mysticism unsupported by logic or experience?[10] Let us then envisage, if we can, a fully planned economy with no markets at all. Even in an economy of this kind there must be decentralization, and economic objectives must be set before the multitude of economic agents—objectives that are clear, meaningful and necessarily limited in scope. The worker will be told that his social function is to perform a certain task in the production of some commodity and will be given some target by which this performance can be judged. The manager of the enterprise will seek to fulfil its specified plan whether expressed in tons or litres or whatever, and will be expected to do so with the least possible use of scarce resources. His attitude to those who supply him with inputs, whether inside the enterprise or outside it, must be that of 'non-tuism'. He has his own job to do and it is in the performance of this task that his obligation lies. The arrangements might be such that the fulfilment of a plan, or its over-fulfilment, brought no more reward than the satisfaction of knowing that a socially desirable task has been satisfactorily fulfilled; but, of course, there are likely to be other rewards as well which appeal directly to more selfish motives. These rewards may take the form of medals or other honours, but may also take the form of extra material benefits. This has long been the case in Russia.

We began by envisaging a fully planned economy with no market: but in practice the Communist economies use markets as

---

[10] Thomas Nagel, *Altruism, Morality and Economic Theory*, ed. E. S. Phelps (Russell Sage Foundation, New York, 1975), 63 ff.

well as plans and it is a familiar fact that their use of markets and of market criteria has tended to increase. This tendency has been related to changing views about the best way of assessing the relative performance of different enterprises. We may note the partial shift of emphasis away from the fulfilment of plans expressed in physical units to estimates in monetary terms of outputs and of costs and even to the limited use of profits both as an indicator of success and as a means of rewarding this success. As in the West, the enterprise must be run on the basis of 'non-tuism'. The same conclusion can be seen to hold if we turn our attention to the markets for consumer goods in the Communist countries. After Russia's early and disastrous experiment with War Communism, these goods have been distributed through markets in exchange for money. But no one expects the housewife to be indifferent to prices or quality or the regularity of supplies merely from a regard for those who are responsible for running the shops. As a matter of empirical fact, she can be supposed to do the best she can for her family and no one presumably would suggest that she is under a moral obligation to consider in the same way either the welfare of the shop and its employees or the long chain of suppliers who provide the goods she buys. In short, 'non-tuism' is the rule for such behaviour in Russia as well as in the West.

Let us now return to Smith and the market economy as he saw it. The pursuit of limited objectives by a multitude of economic agents could produce socially desirable results even if this social outcome had not been explicitly formulated as a conscious social objective. This *could* happen, but would not do so unless their activities took place within an appropriate social framework. If Smith emphasized the market, he also emphasized the need for a system of justice without which neither the market nor, indeed, society itself could exist. There must be rules of the game enforced by law, but this was not all. Consider, for example, the famous passage where competition is compared to a race in which each person:

. . . may run as hard as he can, and strain every nerve and muscle, in order to outstrip all his competitors. But if he should justle or throw down any of them, the indulgence of the spectators is entirely at an end. It is a violation of fair play, which they cannot admit of. (TMS II. ii. 2. 1.)

The sanction for tripping another runner may be legal punishment, but it may also be the powerful sanction of public disapproba-
tion when there has been a breach of some understanding of what
constitutes good behaviour. But Smith does not even leave the
matter there. He is not to be regarded as a utilitarian with a
philosophy of enlightened self-interest. For a person may, in his
view, be restrained from adopting, say, some dishonest business
practice even if there is no danger of being found out and therefore no danger of incurring the sanction either of legal punishment
or of public disapproval. He may be restrained by his desire to be
'praiseworthy', not just to be 'praised'. He should take into account,
and often will take into account, the imagined disapproval of an
Impartial Spectator, 'the arbiter of conduct', 'the man within the
breast'. He may be influenced not only by justice, with its rules
that resemble the rules of grammar, but also by 'beneficence',
which should be taken to mean not just personal kindliness but
also a heightened awareness of social obligation (TMS III. 6. 11).

The question then is how far a firm can properly be expected to
look beyond the profit-and-loss account. Let us consider the
highly topical issue of pollution. Some firms may be quite prepared
to meet the costs involved in preventing pollution but they fear
competition from rivals who would not do so. Thus Government
may need to intervene.[11] May I add that this state intervention can
probably be exercised most effectively through the price system
itself by the use of tax or subsidy? May I also add that the need
for specific state intervention is not to be attributed simply to the
market or the private ownership of capital? For pollution is a
serious problem in Soviet Russia as well as in the West.[12]

The harm caused by pollution has long been perceived but its
seriousness has been recognized much more widely in recent years
than in the past. It may be that in the future firms will be prepared
voluntarily to take more care. In economic jargon, the border-line
between 'internalities' and 'externalities' is not precisely or permanently drawn. This must be conceded. But efficient manage-

[11] Assar Lindbeck, *The Political Economy of the New Left* (Harper Row,
London, 1971); see also A. Nove, 'Market Socialism and its Critics', *Soviet
Studies* (July, 1972).

[12] Nor is it simply the consequence of devolving authority to the management
of the individual enterprise. For decisions about investment, which have so
direct a bearing on pollution, are taken at a higher level in the hierarchy of
power in Soviet Russia.

ment will suffer if too much is transferred to the internal zone. It is still the case that we must not expect firms to take too many broad considerations into account for this would entail an excessive sacrifice of coherent objectives and a weakening of managerial efficiency.

Let us now move on to a different point: the need for competition. The socially beneficial outcome that may follow from the pursuit of limited objectives requires a reasonably competitive market.[13] The so-called 'perfect competition' of static theory is not required and is, in any case, a somewhat dubious concept; but effective dynamic competition is another matter. Smith saw this very clearly:

> Monopoly, besides, is a great enemy to good management, which can never be universally established, but in consequence of that free and universal competition which forces everyone to have recourse to it for the sake of self-defence. (WN I. xi. b. 5.)

His remarks about the propensity to adopt restrictive practices are no less forthright, and are, indeed, too well known to call for quotation. The market should be competitive but if this condition is to be fulfilled, intervention by the state may be required. That this is so is now generally accepted as far as private industry is concerned, although it is still often maintained, with doubtful logic, that public ownership justifies and even requires monopolistic power. In private industry competition is strong and effective, especially when there is competition from imports. It is the labour market that poses by far the most serious problem and the obstacles in the way of breaking up these monopolies or of controlling their power are only too familiar. This is, however, the subject of other papers and I shall say no more about it.

III. SELF-INTEREST IN THE MANAGEMENT OF PUBLIC AFFAIRS

Let me rather turn to the pursuit of self-interest by the agencies of the state itself. It is easy to fall into the habit of supposing that state action is determined and guided by a single will—a will that is beneficent, impartial, wise and exceedingly well-informed, as

---

[13] Thus we see how two of the main themes of the WN fit together: the theme of *competition* and the theme of *co-operation* between large numbers of economic agents as a consequence of the division of labour. There is no antagonism between these themes: on the contrary it is by means of the competitive market that effective co-operation is achieved.

though the state were the Invisible Hand made manifest. In fact the state itself consists of many organizations with many subdivisions, each engaged in the pursuit of its own limited objectives. Let us reflect, then, upon the position of a middle-grade official in central or local government. Both his group loyalty and his personal interest will lead him to work for the expansion of the particular section or division in which he finds himself. This expansion may cost public money and he may well be prepared to accept the view that high taxation is harmful. But what can he do? The economies he can achieve will make little significant difference to the taxpayer and may only provide more public money to be spent by his professional rivals. This, of course, is a version of the free-rider theory. It is a theory that should certainly be extended to the running of public departments. I have taken as an example a middle-grade official and the free-rider argument ought to be less applicable at higher levels of responsibility. The fact remains that it is the primary concern of every spending department to advance the interests for which it is responsible. Any minister who fails to play this game and tries to take a wider view must be prepared to risk serious damage to his own political career. For a strongly departmental approach is one of the most deeply engrained characteristics of Whitehall, and presumably of all centres of Government. Naturally the Treasury must take a broader view and the Cabinet, for its part, should try to do so. But the Cabinet will include among its members some of the toughest bargainers among the spending ministers, and the pressure of a national crisis may be needed in order to check for a time the further extension of departmental empires, even with a strong Prime Minister and a strong Chancellor. Thus it is not only in industry that the pursuit of limited objectives may sometimes lead to socially harmful consequences. For harm may be done within the Government machine itself, at both the central and the local level. Nor should we suppose that this is merely a feature of democratic Government. Departmentalism is also a feature of Communist Government and is, of course, one of the reasons why inflationary gaps persist even in economies as fully planned as that of the Soviet Union.[14]

---

[14] This point is further developed in the Fifth Keynes Lecture to the British Academy delivered on 29th October, 1975: T. Wilson, *The Political Economy of Inflation* (Oxford University Press, 1976).

Some of Smith's general remarks about orders and societies within the nation might well be applied today to Government departments. I quote from the TMS:

Every independent state is divided into many different orders and societies, each of which has its own particular powers, privileges, and immunities. Every individual is naturally more attached to his own particular order or society than to any other. His own interest, his own vanity, the interest and vanity of many of his friends and companions, are commonly a good deal connected with it; he is ambitious to extend its privileges and immunities—he is zealous to defend them against the encroachments of every other order or society. (TMS VI. ii. 2. 7.)

With these sentences before us, it is apparent that the use of the term 'self-interest' may mislead because it suggests the pursuit by an individual of his personal interest, whether ultimately selfish or altruistic, and this may obscure the importance of loyalty to an organization be it a firm, an industry, a trade union, a charity or a government department. It may be less confusing, in this more general context, to refer to 'the pursuit of limited objectives'. There is a further point of some importance that must be added. It may seem natural to suppose that when a person identifies himself with an organization of this kind and takes as his limited objective the furtherance of *its* interests, he is more likely to behave in a socially beneficial way than he would be doing if his limited objective was his own welfare or that of his family or immediate friends. No doubt it is easy to envisage circumstances in which this would indeed be so but there can also be circumstances when the opposite is the case. For these organizations may be bargaining units large enough to exercise monopolistic power in the market or may be political units that can powerfully affect the level of taxation and the disbursement of public money. In so far as it is true that the pursuit of limited objectives is likely to be most socially beneficial when disciplined by competitive pressures, it follows that the 'non-tuism' of smaller groups is more likely to be beneficial than that of large ones. Social welfare requires that these larger groups should take a broader view and, fortunately, it is easier for them to do so. Misplaced 'non-tuism'—non-tuism in the wrong contexts—is, however, a dangerous fact of life that should not be ignored.

I have been touching here on a problem that still receives

surprisingly little attention in economic literature. For we have been slow in the West to adjust our emphasis to allow for the vast increase in the activities of the state. Before the turn of the century, total public expenditure of all kinds came to about ten per cent of the gross national product of this country. Today the figure is well over half and is about a half in a good many other countries. The change of scale reflects a vast enlargement of function. In this situation economists now need to devote far more of their attention to the operation of the political machine itself.[15]

IV. SYMPATHY AND THE WELFARE STATE

May I now turn to our second topic? I have been concerned in the previous section with the pursuit of self-interest in the sense of 'non-tuism'. It is time to direct our attention once more to sympathy. As we have seen sympathy is sometimes taken, quite simply and directly, to mean pity or compassion. Alternatively we can retain Smith's meaning, use the term to explain how moral judgements are formed and then direct our attention to the means for giving effect to a variety of motives. It is, of course, the humanitarian motives with which we are concerned in this section and these can find traditional expression in the form of voluntary transfers made through private channels for the benefit of other people. There is, however, another mode for their expression and this is by giving support to certain kinds of public policy. The tax structure is an obvious example and would be relevant even if the proceeds were to be used to finance only public goods in the strict sense: defence, administration and the like. But, of course, the state also follows policies designed to assist the less fortunate members of society by the provision of benefits in cash or in kind. These are usually described as the policies of the 'welfare state' and I am going to use that somewhat loose expression for reasons of convenience. I shall do so although there is such an immense amount of scope for variation in the coverage of social benefits: in the conditions attached, in the scale of their provision and in the manner of financing them. The term 'welfare state' is also confusing because it tends to foster the mistaken view that it is wholly, or mainly, from measures of this kind that improvements in the

---

[15] James M. Buchanan, *The Limits of Liberty* (University of Chicago Press, 1975).

standard of living of the masses are derived to the neglect of the fact that the basic contribution comes from production organized on the basis of 'non-tuism'. With these reservations I shall use the term 'welfare state', and I shall regard support for the welfare state—in some broad sense of that term—as one of the ways in which humane motives can be translated into action. For, in part, the welfare state can be taken to imply some measure of vertical redistribution. Of course, a regard for others is only one of the sources from which such support may be derived. It may also come—and come very largely—from the prudential self-interest of those who want these safeguards for themselves in face of the risks they must expect to encounter. There is, however, a different reason for objecting to the term 'benevolence' as too narrow a base. For 'benevolent actions' would seem to imply that those who surrender part of their income for the benefit of others had a full *right* to the receipt of that income. This assumption does not adequately match our modern temper. The social transfers may rather be regarded by both donors and recipients as a way of providing some correction of an initial distribution that is thought to be unfair. It may therefore be better to refer both to 'benevolence' and to 'a desire for greater fairness'. What, however, is the role of the economist in the discussion of these matters?

Those who are unfamiliar with academic economics might reasonably suppose that the welfare state is one of the topics with which theoretical welfare economics is concerned. This is so only to a very limited extent. In its traditional Paretian form, welfare economics was inhibited for certain familiar reasons: first, there was the desire to avoid interpersonal comparisons which are so hard to verify and, secondly, there was a scientific concern to avoid value judgements. There was also a third reason. This was the assumption, relaxed in recent years, that utility functions are independent—an assumption which excludes both compassion and envy. The significance of this assumption is seen in the familiar ruling that situation B should be preferred to situation A if at least one person is better off in situation B and no one is worse off. No doubt the term 'better off' could be so interpreted as to ensure that the statement is always valid in a purely formal sense. Let me, therefore, sharpen the issue by rephrasing: situation B is better than situation A if, in the second situation, at least one person has been able to dispose of more goods and services for his own personal use and no one else has less. In this formulation the utility functions are clearly independent. Each person is assumed implicitly to be concerned only with his own supply of goods and services and is indifferent to that of others. There is no social conscience and no feeling of relative social deprivation.

When we make the more realistic assumption that utility functions are interdependent, account must be taken not only of compassion but also of jealousy. In the TMS, the utility functions, in modern jargon, are *very* interdependent. Smith's consumer is not content to eat with his eyes fixed on his own plate. He is greatly interested in what other people are getting because this is an indicator of his place in society. Smith had in fact a lot to say on this subject and it aroused his sense of satire:

> And thus, place, that great object which divides the wives of aldermen, is the end of half the labours of human life. (TMS I. iii. 2. 8.)

Ambition, the demonstration effect, envy, a sense of injustice— these are all aspects of interdependence. Our concern, however, is with that aspect of interdependence which is described by such terms as compassion, benevolence, a sense of fairness. This means that a person's satisfaction depends not only upon his own income but also upon an assurance that the needs of other people are also being reasonably satisfied. It means that his welfare may in some circumstances be increased by taking less himself in order to allow others to have more. Thus, in a well-known article, Professors Hochman and Rogers have thrust aside the assumption that 'redistribution yields no benefits to the parties who finance it, so that from this viewpoint it imposes a dead loss.'[16]

Let us then consider the proposition that interdependence in utility functions—or sympathy—provides a basis for supporting compulsory transfers by the state and can do so without its being necessary to break through the usual Paretian boundary into the territory of interpersonal comparisons and value judgements. To quote again from the same article by Hochman and Rogers:

> . . . redistributive activities can be justified without interpersonal comparisons, provided that utility interdependence is recognised and taken into account in formulating social policy.

This is a bold claim. Can it be sustained? First of all, it is hard to

[16] Harold Hochman and James D. Rogers, 'Pareto Optimal Redistribution', *American Economic Review* (1969).

see how interpersonal comparisons can be avoided even if the transfers are voluntary. For interdependent utility functions necessarily imply interpersonal comparisons even if these are made only by individuals who may then be prepared to make such transfers willingly to other people. This line of reasoning therefore leads naturally enough to an explanation of voluntary transfers made through charities and the like. To non-economists it may seem that economists have made unduly heavy weather of getting thus far! Moreover this reasoning would support transfers administered by the mechanism of the state, if made on a voluntary basis. The real question is the justification for transfers that are compulsory. Compulsion is the crux. For it is not then possible simply to leave individuals to make their own personal interpersonal comparisons and to apply their own value judgements as they wish. Some general basis for action is required. The justification for compulsion that is frequently offered rests on the need to remove the fear of 'free-riders': that is to say, the fear that what some freely contribute may not be fairly matched by what others will freely give so that the burden is inequitably shared. This fear, or this lack of a mutual understanding, may inhibit the making of transfers even by those whose outlook is strongly sympathetic. If those concerned form only a small group, then the fear of free-riders may be dispelled by voluntary agreement, but it is a different matter when this group is large, as Professor Mancur Olson has explained in his discussion of this matter in a wider context.[17]

An official ruling may then be necessary to get everyone into line and such compulsion *may* be willingly accepted. This argument appears to be valid up to a point; but we must surely recognize that the sums to be transferred may still be severely restricted if we really accept the condition that everyone who pays the levy must be entirely willing to do so on the assumption that others, in similar circumstances, are doing the same. If the support for the necessary taxation must be unanimous, even one mean person can exercise a veto.[18] For if his view is disregarded, then an interpersonal comparison of utility has in fact been made by an outside authority—in this case the state—and a value judgement imposed.

[17] *The Logic of Collective Action* (Harvard, 1965).
[18] Knut Wicksell, 'A New Principle of Just Taxation', reprinted in *Classics in the Theory of Public Finance*, edited by Richard A. Musgrave and Alan T. Peacock (Macmillan, London, 1967).

In its turn this line of reasoning is, however, open to the destructive criticism that it takes the initial distribution of income for granted and allows it to be altered only to the extent that every loser will consent to its alteration. But there is no obvious reason why the initial distribution should be viewed in this light. In short, we still lack adequate criteria for dealing with distribution—whether for changing it or maintaining it.

The attempts to find a justification for compulsory transfers on the basis of interdependent utility functions alone does not therefore carry us far—so long as we remain within the Paretian boundary. If we jump that boundary we are confronted with the familiar difficulties of interpersonal comparisons, value judgements and so on, and it may be objected that we have now entered the territory of the moral philosophers where scientific economists are no better than trespassers. But we can refuse to be over-intimidated by these professional barriers. After all these questions of distribution raise many technical issues that are undeniably economic and these technical issues are so intertwined with other issues that the economist cannot properly stand aside. He may perhaps wish to confine himself to the construction of welfare simulation models. He must certainly be careful not to disguise his moral and political values as 'science'. This is an old danger and a familiar one. There is another danger. It is that we shall waste time in trying to formulate what is sometimes described as the *optimum optimorum* or a 'fully ordered social system'—and that is describing with might and main! To leave the Paretian territory does not mean that we are licensed to indulge in every kind of Utopian silliness whatever the camouflage of pedantic terminology.

V. SYMPATHY AND INDIVIDUALISM

We have now reached this position. The pursuit of self-interest—or 'non-tuism'—should properly govern the relationships of production and exchange and sympathy should, in its turn, find expression not only through private charity but through the mechanism of the welfare state. This, however, is not the end of the story. I now turn to my final topic which is the link between sympathy and individualism or, if you prefer it, between sympathy and permissiveness. There is, I think, a real danger nowadays of adopting an unduly narrow interpretation of what is implied by sympathy. Our modern habits of thought are such that we may simply identify sympathy with compassion for those less well-off than ourselves and suppose that the expression of sympathy is to be seen only in the making of transfers for their benefit or in the adjustment in some other ways of the distribution of income and wealth. But sympathy entails more than this—even if 'sympathy' is loosely identified with compassion or pity according to common modern usage. For even in this sense of the term, sympathy should also entail a respect for individuality and require some firm insistence on the importance of freedom. It is, however, helpful at this stage to recall once more the manner in which Smith interpreted 'sympathy'. As we have seen sympathy was part of his explanation of the *manner* in which moral judgements were formed and these judgements might take a variety of forms and express a variety of motives. Nevertheless the interpretation of sympathy as an imaginative act, the emphasis on fellow-feeling and the imagery of the impartial Spectator could be expected to lead to moral judgements in favour of liberty. If we succeed in sharing by imagination in the feelings of another person, it is only to be expected that we shall respect his attitude and his preferences more fully and seek to protect him from undue interference. If a somewhat broad use of the term may be permitted at this stage, I should wish to maintain that 'sympathy' therefore necessarily involves a respect for individuality and conveys an ability to share in the sense of frustration that a person must feel when his preferences are disregarded and their expression baulked by an entanglement of official restrictions and controls. To employ a modern term, sympathy leads to some degree of commitment to 'permissiveness'. By permissiveness I mean freedom for the individual to dispose of his income as he likes, to work where he likes and to choose the job he likes.[19] It goes without saying that his range of choice will be limited by practical possibilities, but this range may be further restricted by the commands of the state. Of course permissiveness may have to be so restricted in certain respects in economic affairs as in other aspects of life. But sympathy requires that there should be a bias in favour of liberty. Persons are not to

---

[19] I developed this line of argument about permissiveness in an article in *New Society*, dated February 15, 1968, entitled 'The Contradictions in Our Attitudes to Freedom'. This theme was further developed by Sam Brittan in his book, *Capitalism and the Permissive Society* (Macmillan, London, 1973).

be treated as passive objects in delineating the scope of official policies, even when these policies are benign in their objectives. Sympathy calls for a much deeper regard for the individual and a profound respect of his freedom to shape his own life in his own way—and to make his own mistakes. It means that people should be treated as responsible beings and the exercise of responsibility requires liberty of action. Sympathy and individualism are not therefore at opposite poles. Sympathy can be the basis for individualism.

Sympathy, therefore, affects our attitude to the state in two ways. It endorses and indeed clearly requires the adoption of policies designed to provide assistance and protection and to compensate, where possible, for the ill-effects on distribution both of inheritance and of productive activities that are conducted, as they must be, on the basis of 'non-tuism'. In this and in other respects, action by the state can be an effective channel for the expression of sympathy. But sympathy also requires us to place reasonable limits on state action in order to ensure that individuality is not stunted and smothered by a dense undergrowth of official activity. What is then both particularly interesting and troublesome is the possibility of a conflict, and quite a serious conflict, between these two lines of policy, both based, at least in part, on sympathy. Let us investigate this possibility.

Even if agreement is reached about the *general direction* in which economic justice would seem to point—and that is a large assumption—something much more definite and concrete is required for the formulation of policy. Suppose there to be general support for social security payments that embody some measure of vertical redistribution. The precise form of these measures must still be decided and the scale of contributions and benefits must be determined. The whole problem of quantification has still to be resolved. Consider, for example, the I.L.O. Convention No. 128 of 1952 which laid it down that the minimum income for a man and wife should be about two-fifths of average earnings. Why two-fifths? Why not more or less? It is no part of my purpose to suggest that 'two-fifths' was in some sense wrong, nor to deny that such figures are bound to be partly arbitrary. My purpose is rather to give an example of the need to move such general principles. Pigou's utilitarianism or Rawls' difference principle point in a general direction and this is helpful; but it is by no means enough. At some point someone must quantify and specify the precise form that a policy is to take and it is then, I suggest, that disagreements may be particularly sharp. Most people would presumably agree that there should be welfare services of some kind. The real questions at dispute will usually relate to the types of policy to be chosen, the scale on which benefits should be provided and the manner in which they should be financed.

How, then, can these practical decisions be reached? There has been much discussion of the ways in which the structure of public policy might be built up, brick by brick, from the preferences of individuals as expressed through their votes. Thus it is sometimes supposed that the Government could ascertain the views of those who wished to make transfers in favour of those less well off. This approach is unconvincing. First we must recognize that a clear majority in favour of some course of action may be unattainable when there are more than two alternatives. This is the Condorcet paradox to which Professor Arrow drew attention in his famous book.[20] Even if this difficulty was not, in fact, encountered, it would still be wrong to imply that politicians and civil servants are no more than agents of the electorate which will issue its instructions regarding every particular issue through an unending succession of referenda. Representative Government does not work like this. Members of Parliament are representatives, not delegates. Elections are fought on a variety of issues and public opinion normally exerts its pressure only fitfully with regard to any single issue. For the business of Government is often technical and complex and public opinion, even if fully consulted, would prove to be inadequately informed. This would be found to be so even if attention were confined to the social transfers of the welfare state, notwithstanding the fact that these transfers affect the personal lives of many people.[21] Presumably public opinion is still

[20] *Social Change and Individual Values* (John Wiley & Sons, 1951).

[21] A good example was afforded by the view widely held and frequently expressed that state pensions were being eroded by inflation because these pensions were believed to be fixed in money terms. In fact pensions were raised roughly in line with average earnings when each review took place with the result that the real value of official pensions has increased substantially in Britain as in many other countries over the inflationary post-war period. Such increases took place in Britain long before there was any official commitment to index pensions. The real value of pensions has, however, been eroded *between* review periods especially when the pace of inflation has accelerated. That is the real point. These developments in a number of countries have been examined in *Pensions, Inflation and Growth* (Heinemann, 1974).

less informed about other branches of policy. This is not surprising. The division of labour on which much stress is laid, is not confined to industry. Limitations of knowledge and problems of communication are encountered not only in industry but in the conduct of public affairs. To rely upon state action backed by compulsion is to accept a substantial measure of paternalism. It is true that this paternalistic action will be influenced in varying degree by public opinion and in some circumstances it is public opinion that will in fact be decisive. But it is a familiar fact that much official action is not under the effective control of the electorate or even of Parliament. This is a familiar enough aspect of political life, and this is so not only in Britain but in other countries as well. As economists we should perhaps pay attention to the plea made by John Plamenatz[22] and take more fully into account the way in which representative Government operates. For it will not do to assume that the views of the electorate can be obtained and used to determine official action with much degree of precision on a wide variety of issues. It is not only that the views of a substantial minority may be overborne—though that is important. The policies adopted may not even reflect the views of the majority partly because the majority may not hold views that are sufficiently well formulated to be the basis of policy. In saying this it is far from my intention to imply that these large issues are determined in a rational if undemocratic fashion by what it is now customary to describe as an all-powerful group of faceless bureaucrats. If one talks to senior officials, they are likely to emphasise the extent to which their scope for action is narrowly limited, partly by decisions taken in the past. The final outcome results from a whole series of incremental measures and the difficulty of foreseeing and controlling this outcome is particularly difficult when public expenditure absorbs a very large proportion of resources.

To say that Government action—benevolent Government action—must be partly paternalistic is not to assert that, on balance, such action should always be condemned. Smith, himself, was a firm believer in the benefits the state could contribute in appropriate fields of activity. But he would, we may reasonably infer, have endorsed Keynes's famous observation that:

The important thing for Government is not to do things which

<hr>

[22] *Democracy and Illusion* (Longmans, London, 1973).

individuals are doing already, and to do them a little better or a little worse; but to do those things which at present are not done at all.[23]

The question is, of course, how to determine what fields of activity the state should enter, what form its policies should take, and the extent to which these policies should absorb resources at the expense of private activities. The state must provide public goods. This is one of its roles and one that was clearly recognized by both Hume and Smith. But the scale on which these should be provided has to be decided. The state may also modify the distribution of income by its choice of a tax structure for the financing of these public goods. The more controversial question is then how progressive this tax structure should be. Presumably the vast majority of people today would support the view that the state should not only provide public goods but should make transfer payments in order to prevent anyone from falling into destitution; but controversy may begin when these transfers are carried beyond this point in order to make more substantial changes in the distribution of income. Moreover, the activities of the modern state go far beyond the provision of public goods and the modification of the vertical distribution of income. Public expenditure is also designed to provide merit goods and to provide transfers on a scale that cannot be explained adequately as vertical redistribution. These public services lie outside the agenda proposed by Keynes in the passage I have quoted for the state is carrying out many functions that can be and have been performed privately. Even so it does not follow that such services are therefore to be condemned out of hand but it should be possible to demonstrate that the state can do the job so very much better in particular cases as to outweigh the inherent disadvantages of paternalism. A special onus of proof must rest with those who propose policies that will restrict the individual.[24] Apart from any question of efficiency, there may be a strong desire for greater equality in the distribution of some services—such as the health service—than there is for equality in the distribution of income as a whole. This is the demand for what has been described by Tobin as 'specific

---

[23] J. M. Keynes, *Essays in Persuasion* (Rupert Hart-Davis, London, 1952), 317.

[24] It is natural at this stage to refer to John Rawls's principle of equal liberty for all. But I do not think I understand sufficiently the implications of his 'lexical ordering' to know whether the balancing of moral considerations to which I refer in the text would be acceptable to him.

equality'.[25] Within limits such measures may be defended; the point to be stressed is simply that a convincing defence is required. If specific equality is to be carried to the point of compulsory uniformity, then a convincing defence may be difficult.

We must, then, accept the conclusion that welfare policies even when based on disinterested sympathy may conflict with the respect for individualism and the inclination towards permissiveness that may also be founded on sympathy. It does not follow, of course, that there will always be a conflict. In particular we must remember that paternalism in one field may widen the range of choice before the individual in other respects at a later stage. Compulsory education is the obvious example. There is a quite different possibility that must not be overlooked. This is that the requirements of sympathy may be sacrificed under both headings at once. This may indeed be the consequence of an undue extension of paternalistic policies. For such policies may not only restrict freedom of choice and thus disregard the respect for the individual that sympathy enjoins; but may also entail a claim on resources so extravagant as to curtail the provision that can be made for those really in need.

Such dangers can, of course, be greatly reduced if care is taken to ensure that welfare policies are so designed as to interfere as little as may be with individual freedom and responsibility. But this is only likely to happen if it is generally accepted that individual freedom and responsibility are important and a number of relevant tests are applied. To what extent does a particular measure help those really in need? Is it adequate for this purpose? Is the scope of the policy so extended that it provides assistance to those who could well help themselves? If so, on what grounds can the policy be justified? What resources are required to administer it? What effects of a more general kind is it likely to have on economic growth? Simple questions, it may be said, but it can scarcely be doubted that these questions, if seriously pressed and honestly answered could have important implications for public policy in Britain. I shall mention only one obvious example and that is our traditional method of subsidizing the rents of local authority houses.

[25] James Tobin, 'On Limiting the Domain of Inequality', *Journal of Law and Economics* (October 1970). Reprinted in *Economic Justice*, edited by E. S. Phelps (Penguin Books, Harmondsworth, 1973).

The particular aspect of public affairs that calls for criticism varies from generation to generation. In Smith's own day it seemed to him that the restrictions of the mercantilist state were often an impertinent infringement of personal liberty and a barrier to economic efficiency. During the nineteenth century and part of the present century, the critic could be led by sympathy to direct very proper criticism against the evil consequences of an excessive attachment to *laissez-faire* and to plead for an extension of the activities of the state partly on grounds of humanity. My own assessment of the facts and my own value judgements lead me to believe that the emphasis today needs to be changed again. The scope of the state's activities now needs to be curtailed and that of the market correspondingly enlarged. If the state did less, it might do its job more efficiently and what it did could be subjected more readily to democratic political control. If more were left to the market, democratic control in a different sense would be strengthened for it should never be forgotten that a vast range of personal preferences can be given democratic expression through the market in a way that is quite impracticable through even the most democratic political machine. Moreover the market has the immense merit of not suppressing the preferences of the minority.

A change in the respective roles of the market and the state is in my view badly required but it is not one that will be easily achieved. Of the many difficulties I shall mention only one and that is the failure to understand the nature of the price system, a failure that is still widespread two centuries after the publication of the WN. This is one of the reasons—and it is surely an important one—for believing that much of Smith's economic philosophy retains its force and relevance today.

COMMENT

by R. S. Downie*

Professor Wilson shares with Adam Smith and most other economists the assumption that self-interest is the basis of a free market economy. Wishing to provide a moral defence of a free market Professor Wilson's strategy is to emphasize the importance of the

* University of Glasgow.

less discussed side to Adam Smith's thinking—his use of the concept of sympathy. Like Professor Wilson I think that a free market economy can be morally justified, but I differ from him in what I consider to be the best way of showing this. In particular, I shall draw attention to some important obscurities in the thesis that self-interest is the basis of the market, and then I shall indicate my reservations about the use which Professor Wilson makes of the concept of sympathy.

I

SELF-INTEREST

There are two ambiguities which confuse discussions of the concept of 'interest'. Firstly, there is a distinction between a psychological or descriptive sense, and a normative sense. When we are using the term in the former sense we are concerned with what people actually want to have, but in the latter sense we are concerned with what they ought to have, whether or not they actually want to have it. Secondly, 'interest', particularly as the term occurs in the expression 'self-interest', can refer either to an *end* which someone is pursuing, or to a *motive* for pursuing an end. Thus, we can ask someone what his interests are, or what ends he is pursuing; but we can also say that in pursuing an end (which may be the good of himself or of another person) he acted out of the motive of self-interest. It is worth noting here that whereas 'interest' can be either an end pursued or a motive for pursuing an end, 'benevolence' can only be a motive for pursuing an end and cannot itself be an end. Finally, it is worthwhile stressing (as Professor Wilson does) that to say of someone either that he is pursuing self-interest as an end or acting from it as a motive is not necessarily to say that he is being selfish.

The concept of 'self' in 'self-interest' is also ambiguous, and these ambiguities will obviously affect views as to what the interest of the self consists in. Corresponding to the psychological and normative senses of 'interest' we find psychological and normative senses of 'self', the latter often marked out in the expression 'true or real self'. Moreover, we find that differing views on the nature of the true self affect ways of drawing the distinction between self and others. Thus, thinkers such as Plato or Hegel, who regard the true or real self as social in nature, tend to blur the distinction between self and others, whereas a thinker such as Adam Smith who is presupposing a framework of individualism, tends to operate with a sharp distinction between the interests of one self and the interests of other selves; and it is in such a context that we find the contrast between the motives of self-interest and benevolence has most point.

II

SELF-INTEREST AND THE MARKET

Is Adam Smith correct in claiming that the butcher (or any trader) serves us out of self-interest rather than benevolence? The answer depends on whether we interpret the claim as an empirical or as a conceptual one. Interpreted as an empirical generalization, about the reasons for which actual traders act on specific occasions, it certainly cannot be known to be true since it is notoriously difficult to know what people's motives really are, and it may in fact be contingently false, since some traders may well on some occasions act out of benevolence, or a desire to provide a service to their customers. Interpreted conceptually, the claim concerns the motive of the butcher *qua* butcher, and it is to the effect that whatever the actual motives, if any, of Mr. X and Mr. Y who happen to be butchers, the motive of butchers as such is necessarily self-interest in the form of the maximum profit obtainable. But it is false—indeed, necessarily false—that the butcher *qua* butcher is aiming at maximum profit. Rather, the defining aim of the butcher is the carving, mincing, and otherwise dispensing of meat, and a good butcher is one who does these things well, not necessarily one who makes a profit. In a similar way, the doctor *qua* doctor aims at curing his patients, and one doctor is better than another in respect of his skill in attaining this end, rather than that of high fees (cf. Plato, *Republic* 346).

It might be objected that a trader is also a business man, and as such must make a profit. But while this is true it says nothing peculiar to the market, for the professional man also makes a profit in the form of his fee or salary, and so must anyone who earns his living. The difference between the business side to being a trader and the business side to being in a profession lies in the fact that the former is marked by a competitiveness from which the latter is (mainly) immune, rather than in any necessary connection between being a trader and being self-interested. It seems to me, then, that the claim that self-interest is the basis of the market is on one interpretation contingently false, on another necessarily false, and on a third trivially true.

III

THE MARKET AND MORAL CORRUPTION

It might be pointed out that in comparing the trader with the professional man I have uncovered the real moral infection of the market—competitiveness. For, while competitiveness is not the same as self-interestedness (and may sometimes be destructive of it), it is nevertheless a bad quality both in itself and in its tendency to smother other morally good qualities. But the competitiveness of the market need not corrupt a man, or his society, for the reason that any person is more than a trader. He will have motives of many different sorts, generated by the many aims which he can have quite unconnected with the market, such as the enjoyment of family life, the appreciation of music, participation in sport, etc. Generalizing, we can say that a unitary human consciousness is a focus for many interests, of which the market will be only one. To use the language of sociology, a man has many roles of which that of trader is one and, more important, the man as such logically cannot be reduced to the sum total of his roles, far less to one of them. Now, insofar as we are speaking of a person who is *inter alia* a trader or a business man, there is no reason to think that the standard range of moral qualities—honesty, conscientiousness, courtesy, for example—will not be shown in economic relationships as in any other sort of human relationship.

Moreover, there is a positive safeguard against the supposed corruption caused by the competitiveness and desire for profit to be found in the market: an economic relation is also by its very nature a juridical relation to the extent that it constitutes a 'contract' defining the rights and duties of the parties. In other words, as Adam Smith was himself aware, a *purely* economic relation is an abstraction; all economic relations are integrated with juridical relations and the self-seeking of the parties is thereby limited.

There is another moral quality which a free market economy possesses, an important one in that it affects the whole moral atmosphere of a society. Let us agree with Adam Smith that human beings, while they may be sympathetic to each other, are also, and perhaps mainly, self-seeking—they have, in Hume's phrase, a 'limited generosity'. This tendency to pursue self-interest to the possible detriment of others will show itself in employment in such forms as laziness or greed for excessive profit. No doubt self-discipline is the morally best cure, but if a man will not discipline himself, there are in the end only two other forms of discipline: the market or an elaborate bureaucracy which must in the last resort be supported by the police. On the other hand, granted that a free market economy is compatible with social safety-nets such as unemployment benefits, social security payments, and so on (although, of course, whether or not it is compatible with these needs argument), it seems a reasonable moral preference to opt for its discipline rather than that of the police-state. To put it another way, the discipline of the 'invisible hand' simply ensures that I as a trader cannot benefit myself without at the same time, and to a varying extent, benefiting others, whereas the discipline of the police-state, in itself harsh, is not necessarily directed in the end to my interest at all.

So far I have been discussing the morality of a free market economy mainly from the point of view of the trader, but consider it next from the point of view of the consumer. Critics of Adam Smith point to his hedonistic and individualistic conception of the self. They can argue that a free market gradually but inevitably generates inordinate desires for its goods, and that this is morally corrupting because eventually no one has a conception of himself other than in hedonistic terms, as a consumer. While it may be unfortunate, the criticism runs, that some people in a free market cannot get what they want, it is more unfortunate that in the end they want only what they get. This type of criticism can be levelled with some justice at Adam Smith because the psychological and normative conceptions of the self run together in him, to the extent that he sees the good of the self as consisting simply in the satisfaction of its psychological desires ('interests').

There is, however, another aspect to Adam Smith's view of the self, implicit in his account of what has come to be known as 'alienation', but not fully understood until it was developed in the liberal-democratic tradition from Kant to J. S. Mill: that essential to the self is free choice. Insofar as a person is prevented, either by the might of the State or by its paternalism, from exercising his 'rational will' his humanity will atrophy. Indeed, the criticism, that the supporters of a free market economy trivialize human life by encouraging a consumer conception of the self and its interests, can in fact be levelled with more justice at the supporters of an authoritarian collectivist market, or even of a developed form of welfare state: in removing from the individual his responsibility for his own and his family's health, future security, old age, education, they remove from the scope of his own will those matters which ought to be of deepest concern to him, and his area for choice will as a result be restricted to that of the trivialities or luxuries of life.

IV

THE INTEREST OF THE COMMUNITY

The criticism considered in the previous section—that a free market economy tends to corrupt a person by encouraging him to adopt a purely consumer conception of himself—has social as well as individual applicability. If we take seriously social problems such as that of pollution, to which Professor Wilson refers, we are necessarily operating with hazy conceptions of a *public* interest (in the normative sense of 'interest') and of a continuing community. The point here is not that a government may impose some conception of intrinsic good with no relation to what individuals within a society actually want, but rather that it must develop the implications of what people at a given time actually want in order to elicit an enlightened conception of what in the long run they will want. Now, whereas Adam Smith himself may have held that there should be public policy over matters such as defence or education, the tradition of individualism and hedonism of which he was the outstanding figure cannot easily accommodate the idea of the interest (in the normative sense) of a continuing community.

It might be replied that the concept of sympathy, essential to Adam Smith's view of man, can give us the theoretical basis for the idea of the (non-hedonistic) interests of a continuing community. The fundamental weakness of the concept of sympathy for this task, however, is that it remains a matter of *psychological* reaction; and whereas as a matter of psychological reaction sympathy may have certain uses in socializing human beings it presupposes a prior rational moral *judgement*. And it is particularly important to distinguish emotional reaction from moral judgement in an international economic context where we are dealing with people whose feelings and purposes may be hard for us to understand. This crudely stated criticism of Adam Smith remains valid in the end, I believe, even after we have taken into account the complex and interesting views which he has on sympathy.

COMMENT

by Mancur Olson*

I

Of the several aspects of Professor Wilson's paper that would repay discussion, the most important, I believe, is his emphasis on 'the pursuit of limited objectives'. Professor Wilson argues that every individual must be constrained by his limited knowledge of all the possible consequences of alternative courses of action. This limited knowledge and the normal difficulties of communication and control in large firms and government departments make it obvious that the individuals and organizations in any society must pursue a limited set of goals. This holds true whatever the system of social organization and even if people have highly altruistic attitudes toward family and associates and a strong general sympathy for fellow human beings.

One of the consequences of the limited objectives of individuals is that they place the welfare of the groups with which they are most closely associated above those with which they have less connection. Thus, as we have heard from Wilson's quotation from the *Theory of Moral Sentiments*, 'every individual is naturally more attached to his own particular order or society than any other' and is 'ambitious to extend its privileges and immunities'. It follows that we should expect those who staff a government department to favour it over other groups or institutions. Given also the difficulties of communication and control in large organizations, and the limited knowledge of the consequences of a department's

* University of Maryland. I am most grateful to Sir Alec Cairncross and John S. Fleming for a number of helpful criticisms, but they are not of course responsible for any of the shortcomings of my argument. The National Science Foundation and Resources for the Future have provided invaluable support for my research.

policies, there are limits to the extent to which a government department can be a disinterested and efficient organizer of economic life.

Though Professor Wilson points out that there may also be loyalty to trade unions, industries, charities, and firms, he gives most attention to government departments. It may be useful to look at some other types of organisations from the same perspective from which Wilson looked at government departments or agencies. From this perspective we shall be able to see a possible explanation of some puzzling variations in the rates of growth of the economically developed democracies. These pages will accordingly attempt to develop a model that helps to explain the prevalence of common interest organizations with monopoly power and political clout in different countries and different periods. It will then attempt to assess the effect of different levels of common interest organization on the rate of economic growth.

II

The need for a new perspective on the determinants of the rate of economic growth is evident from two sets of facts that are not adequately explained by conventional analyses of economic growth. The first is the unexpectedly high rates of growth of nations that have been ravaged in war, occupied, and even defeated.

The second set of anomalous facts is found in the economic history of Great Britain. From sometime in the middle of the eighteenth century until sometime in the mid-nineteenth century, Great Britain seems to have had the fastest rate of growth of per capita income of any country in the world. This well known period of growth is of course usually—and to my mind aptly—called the 'industrial revolution'. Paradoxically, the same country that for a considerable time led all other countries in the rate of economic growth, and which indeed invented the sustained growth of per capita income, has for at least two generations normally had a slower growth of income than any other major developed country.

It will be argued here that to explain the foregoing anomalies we must take account of the role of organized interest groups or associations as well as the variables customarily included in an economic analysis. To understand these groups—trade unions, professional associations, farmers' organizations, lobbying groups, trade associations, informal price-fixers, and formal cartels—we must in turn have an adequate model or conception of their formation and functioning. If we have a more general model of such organisations we can better accommodate Professor Wilson's emphasis on 'limited objectives' and Adam Smith's precious but scattered insights on what makes it possible for a group to organize to serve its interests monopolistically or politically.[1]

Any appropriate general model must spell out the implications of a fundamental common feature of all of the kinds of organizations in the foregoing list: the fact that, whatever else they may do, each and every one provides some service to everyone in some group. If a union wins higher wages the higher wages go to every worker in some category; if a cartel raises the price of some good, every firm selling that good in the relevant market enjoys the higher price; if a farm organization or other lobbying group obtains legislation favourable to some group, everyone in that group can benefit from it. In other words, each of the types of associations provides what the economist must define as a 'public good': a good which goes to everyone in some group if it goes to anyone in that group. Though the phrase 'public good' is in many discussions applied mainly to certain goods provided by governments, such as pollution control, national defence, and law and order, there can be no doubt that most of the outputs of organized interest groups in the private sector are analytically identical to most of those of governments: neither governments nor organizations of interest groups in the private sector are able to exclude those in the relevant group from some or all of their services.

In 1965 I pointed out, in a book that Professor Wilson generously cited,[2] that organizations in the private sector designed to further the common interests of large groups of people are like governments

---

[1] Smith was extraordinarily sensitive to the varying capacities of different groups to organize to obtain the advantages of monopoly, whether through concerted action in the market or by exerting pressure on governments. Among the factors influencing the acquisition of this power, Smith mentioned location and the degree of dispersal (WN I. x. c. 22–3); group size (WN I. x. c. 61) and prior governmental regulation (WN I. x. c. 27, 28). These portions of Smith's work support the interpretation of his view of politics offered by A. W. Coats in 'Adam Smith's Conception of Self-Interest in Economic and Political Affairs', *History of Political Economy* (1975), 132–6.

[2] *The Logic of Collective Action* (Cambridge, Massachusetts, Harvard University Press, 1965, 1971).

in that they cannot normally sell their basic services in a market, that is, rely on purely voluntary dues or contributions for support. If such associations are to operate for any length of time at a significant scale, they must either use some overt or covert form of coercion or else somehow offer some benefit in addition to a public good, which other benefit can be withheld from those who do not join and thereby provide an incentive for paying dues.

The single most important type of organized interest group in the private sector is the labour union and it is well known that most strong unions in the developed countries enjoy some form of union shop, closed shop, agency shop, or other formal or informal arrangement which makes it costly or hazardous or simply impossible to get employment in certain establishments or occupations without paying dues to the union.

In the United States, at least, the next largest organization working for the common interests of a group are the farm organizations, and they have financed themselves primarily by 'checking off' the dues for the farm organizations from the patronage dividends or rebates of farm cooperatives and mutual insurance companies, by allowing members favoured access to the services of agricultural extension services, or by providing social events attractive to farm families spread out over sparsely settled rural areas.

The next largest interest groups, the professional associations, have used both types of methods to get members: coercion (the 'closed bar') and offers of 'private good' benefits (professional journals, mutual insurance, testimony in malpractice suits, cheap group air fares, etc.). Organizations that represent relatively small groups of prosperous firms or individuals, such as trade associations, may be able to get by with providing only the public good they offer their clients, because each firm may get so large a share of the common benefit provided by the organization that it pays some firm to contribute enough to make sure the organization can function.

Professor Wilson called our attention to that aspect of the *Theory of Moral Sentiments* which emphasizes each individual's sympathy to his own group or order. This partiality, and the inevitability of 'limited interests' that Wilson himself pointed out, make it overwhelmingly likely that the organized interest groups we have been discussing will use whatever monopoly power or political influence they have in a selfish way. Even if the members of the group were not self-interested, their greater sympathy with their own group order, and the inevitability of limited objectives, would still make the organized interest serve the selfish interests of its group to a considerable extent.

III

The argument outlined in the previous section has several implications for the pattern of organization of interest groups in democratic societies. One implication is that the largest and most scattered interests will presumably never be able to organize on a mass basis. Such groups as consumers, taxpayers, and the poor certainly have important common interests and would benefit substantially if there were effective mass organizations working on their behalf. But it is hard to see how any organizer or political entrepreneur could (unless he had substantial assistance from the government) manage to coerce most consumers, taxpayers, or poor people; in addition to being so numerous, these groups do not assemble at any one spot, the way the workers at a mine or factory do, and this means that nothing resembling the picket line would be feasible even if most people wanted it and the government would tolerate it. Nor does it seem possible to think of a way of getting enough resources in the private sector to induce the great mass of consumers, taxpayers, or poor people to participate substantially in collective action in their group interests. Thus it seems reasonable to conclude that it isn't just an accident that there aren't mass contributions to consumer or taxpayer or poverty organizations in any of the economically developed democracies: this reflects the underlying logic of the situation and isn't likely to change.

A second implication of the model in the previous section is that even those large groups that can be organized into effective voluntary associations aren't usually so organized until some time after the common interests emerge. The organization of a labour union, for example, may wait until there is a jump in the demand for the relevant type of labour (in the United States, World Wars I and II, and especially the latter, were leading periods of union growth) so that scabs will be hard to find and employers would lose a great deal from a strike. In some cases when the other conditions are right, organization may fail for lack of imaginative leadership.

The part of this intellectual structure that needs to be built next is the one which will encompass the effect of organized interest groups on economic growth, or more precisely, the effect of organized interest groups on the producer rather than the consumer side. This is happily a relatively easy part of the argument to construct, since the effect of such groups on economic growth (as it is conventionally measured) is surely overwhelmingly negative. In saying this there is no attempt to deny that these organized producer interest groups serve useful functions. They will, for example, make political life more pluralistic and this may help to protect democratic institutions. Labour unions, moreover, surely perform a valued function in making employees feel more secure and less subordinate to their supervisors. Many other contributions of such organizations could of course also be cited, but this wouldn't help us explain international and inter-temporal differences in the rate of economic growth.

One reason why the effect of organized groups on the producer side on economic growth is overwhelmingly negative is that these groups systematically have an incentive to keep out new entrants to their industry or occupation. Since rapid economic growth requires reallocations of labour and other resources as technologies, tastes, and resource availabilities change, such barriers to entry will not only make the national income lower on a one-time basis when they are first imposed, but will also reduce the rate of economic growth over the longer run by limiting the flow of resources into whatever industries and occupations should be expanding most rapidly. Organized interest groups on the producer side also often have an incentive to block or delay the innovations that are the single most important source of economic growth. When producer groups demand favourable legislation from government, this also will in most cases lower the rate of growth.

Great as the tendency for organized producers to reduce the growth rate is, it is important to emphasize one especially important class of cases where this will not happen. That is when the organized producer group is so large or so strategically placed that its members would get a significant share of the benefits of whatever increase in efficiency results from a policy. If a union, for example, contains such a large proportion of the population that its own members would get much of the benefit of the lower prices for consumers that result from increased efficiency, then it will have a reason to reconsider any practices it has that make the economy less efficient. Similarly, if a large industrial union counts among its members those skill groups whose wages could be increased with a new technology as well as those workers who would be displaced by it, then it may allow the new technology to be used. This consideration partly explains why craft unions representing narrowly defined skill groups, such as railroad firemen, will often be more adamant in resisting new technologies or demanding featherbedding than large and diverse industrial unions.

IV

One implication of my argument is that countries whose common-interest organizations have been destroyed or damaged by totalitarian repression, foreign occupation, or defeat in war should be expected to grow far faster than casual observers of the physical and institutional destruction would expect. And this, as we saw, is just what happened after World War II.

It also follows that the longer the period in which a country has had a modern industrial pattern of common interests and at the same time democratic freedom of organization without upheaval or invasion, the greater the extent to which its growth rate will be slowed by organized interests. This explains why Great Britain, which has the longest experience of industrialization of any country, centuries of success in resisting invasion that might have damaged or destroyed its evolving organizational life, and extraordinary success in avoiding any dictatorship, revolution, or other interruption of stability that would have disturbed its common-interest organizations or the pattern of public policies they have won from a democratic government, has in this century normally had a slower rate of growth than most other developed countries. This explanation of the contemporary British growth performance (unlike some others) is not contradicted by the fact that for nearly a century Britain was normally the country with the fastest rate of economic growth. Britain also has the dense and powerful network of common-interest organizations that the argument developed here would lead us to expect in a country with such a record of military invulnerability and democratic stability.

If the argument that has been presented here is correct, another country that should reveal many of the same symptoms as Great Britain, though in less striking form, is the United States. Though its experience of industrialization is decidedly shorter than that of Britain, it still is longer than that of virtually every other country. And the United States also, with the single exception of its gigantic civil war, has an exceptional record of democratic stability and immunity from invasion. It also is described as a land of 'joiners' and powerful pressure groups. And, as the argument here would predict, it has had a relatively slow growth rate.

Some might suppose that the higher rates of growth that Sweden has lately obtained contradict the idea outlined here, since it has also enjoyed democratic political stability and freedom from invasion for the whole of the period since it began to industrialize. As a country that industrialized much later than Britain (and than the United States and various Continental countries) Sweden has not only had somewhat less time to develop institutional arthritis, but also organized its interest groups under different conditions. As a small country, and one that could observe the institutional examples of countries that industrialized earlier, Sweden somehow happened to acquire unusually centralized common-interest associations. And the centralized Swedish labour unions, at least, behave in a way consistent with one of the arguments developed above. They note that their own members get a large proportion of the benefits of a more efficient economy and often choose labour policies which speed up the rate of economic growth.

If the argument here is correct, there is a most disturbing 'contradiction' in the evolution of the developed democracies. This is not the contradiction of which Marx wrote, but rather a tension between the desire for democratic stability and peace, on the one hand, and the desire for a more dynamic economy, on the other. Even for those who, like this writer, are so intensely devoted to the democratic freedoms that they have no doubt they would opt for retaining them even if the cost were forgoing all growth, this is not a happy prospect. It would take too long now to go into various methods that could be used to countervail, offset, and occasionally even weaken common-interest organizations, but the case for more thinking and research about these questions seems clear.

4

The Market and the State

BY ALEXANDER CAIRNCROSS*

MODERN economics can be said to have begun with the discovery of the market. Although the term 'market economy' had yet to be invented its essential features were outlined in the *Wealth of Nations* which provided us with the first coherent model of an economic system and analysed the role of the market within such a system. Since the days of Adam Smith economists have debated the strength and limitations of market forces and have rejoiced in their superior understanding of these forces.

The state, by contrast, needed no such discovery. Its operations were only too visible and were the subject of constant political debate. It was never argued that the state could be wholly replaced by the market and Adam Smith himself laid stress on the positive functions of the state, e.g. in maintaining order, dispensing justice, providing free compulsory education, and abolishing positions of privilege and monopoly. The criteria he suggested for state activity could be used to justify an extensive programme under modern conditions, however slight the programme he approved in his own time. What he reacted against were the ideas he dismissed as 'mercantilist' which took for granted the need to make use of political power in order to achieve economic ends.

The retreat from mercantilism into *laissez-faire* in the course of the 19th century at no time led the state to forswear the use of political power and rely entirely on market forces: the state did not wither away although it came much nearer to doing so than under subsequent régimes that have set themselves that objective. The market was allowed more scope and freedom but the state still determined the framework of law and regulation under which private initiative could be exercised to meet market requirements.

* Sir Alexander Cairncross, Chancellor of the University of Glasgow, and Master of St. Peter's College, Oxford.

The pendulum has since swung the other way and we are back to a managed economy in which the role of the state is steadily expanding while market forces operate within increasingly severe restraints and are viewed with growing distrust. Economists have played an important part in this reversal by providing a critique of the market that lays stress on its inadequacies.

Very often this critique is highly unbalanced. Theoretical models of a market economy bring out various ways in which it is likely to operate in conflict with broad social objectives. We are left to conclude without further argument that this establishes the case for government intervention to resolve the conflict. But of course it does nothing of the kind. As every economist knows, arguments about policy can only proceed sensibly in terms of alternatives. If the alternative involves government intervention we need a supplementary model of the way in which governments operate and a supplementary analysis of the conflicts which may arise between the proclaimed objects of governments and the actual outcome of their operations. Too often we are offered over-simplified models either of market economies or of government operations that do justice to neither and emphasize comparatively minor aspects of each. Either an ideal government is invoked to remedy some weakness of the market or market forces are idealized in order to bring out some weakness of government. This is no way to come to a judgement between the two.

There is also a strong tendency to oppose the state and the market as if they were all-or-none alternatives. We have the enthusiasts for a market economy in which intervention by the government seems to have no place; and we have the enthusiasts for comprehensive planning in which no provision is made for the operations of the market. It is difficult to square these ideological positions with the observed trends towards greater intervention in economies relying primarily on the market and towards carving out a place for market forces in economies priding themselves on the achievements of government planning. The truth is, as many economists have insisted, that if the state is to set about planning intelligently it needs indicators of social priorities and that, as a first approximation, market prices are difficult to improve upon. To allocate resources without a pricing mechanism is a complex and wasteful task; and to devise a pricing mechanism that accords with social values and allows citizens to express those values freely is almost impossible without a market that registers their choices. Similarly, an economy without a governmental framework is a prescription for anarchy. Nobody would seriously propose that the state should refrain from all intervention in the market or, if they did, would be able to explain how it could be arranged when the state already *is* the market for a quarter or more of national output.

The only sensible question worth pursuing is the division of labour between the state and the market. For what purposes should market forces be allowed free rein and for what purposes should the state try to regulate or short-circuit them? Are there grounds for expecting that as time moves on, the thrust of market forces will be less powerful or less socially beneficial? Or are there grounds on the other hand for discouraging state intervention because it is increasingly likely to be misdirected, or to cause the market to function less satisfactorily, or to have unfortunate side-effects in the bureaucratic apparatus created, or to transfer or concentrate political power in undesirable ways?

I

If we are to form a view of how these issues would appear to Adam Smith returning like Rip van Winkle to a different society we have to start from the changing functions of the state and the increasing importance attached to objectives of economic policy that the market cannot fulfil.

(a) *Equality*

One such objective is the promotion of greater economic equality. Historically, the most direct challenge to a system relying on uncontrolled market forces came from those who saw no virtue in the resulting distribution of income. The Marxists in particular pointed out that market forces reflected class structure and that class structure had its own dynamic and would control, and if necessary over-ride, the market in apportioning rewards for economic services. Other economists were bound to agree that, however efficient or indeed indispensable the market in allocating resources to meet consumer demand, the existing pattern of demand was not necessarily in keeping with social justice. Since rich and poor did not compete on equal terms even under so-called 'perfect' competition, the verdict of the market could not be final. Progressive taxation and the welfare state have turned the flank of this line of criticism, although not completely or without cost, since income transfers beyond a certain level react back on the functioning of the market. But once the state is prepared to set aside the verdict of market forces on income distribution it is unlikely to rest content with income transfers. Experience in all countries points to an increasing willingness to operate simultaneously through prices with a view to shielding lower income groups from the consequences of adverse market trends: through control of rents, subsidies on foodstuffs, differential fares, and so on. The consequences of these market entanglements are usually less obvious but almost invariably less happy than those of direct income transfers.

(b) *Full Employment*

A second macro-economic objective that has brought about an extension of state intervention is full employment. This is not an altogether new objective any more than re-distribution of income. To the mercantilists it presented itself as 'setting the poor to work'. Their concern, however, was with a semi-permanent residue of underemployed workers or with the aftermath of war and demobilization. The modern problem is seen more as one of economic stability at a high level. It springs from acceptance of the Keynesian thesis that the market system is not self-regulating and that the price adjustments that keep a commodity market in balance may be powerless to restore full employment in an economy where effective demand fluctuates.

It is of course true that the Keynesian analysis does not by itself require active intervention by the state. If it were possible, for example, to secure continuous full employment by the exercise of monetary policy alone, responsibility for pursuing the appropriate policy could be devolved on an independent central bank armed with all the necessary powers. But this reflection does not take us very far. In the first place, any one objective of public policy, so long as it is not in serious conflict with other objectives and is fairly easy to interpret can be hived off and surrendered to some quasi-independent body. This does not make it any the less an exercise of political power. But, secondly, full employment does not answer to the description given: all the major objectives of economic policy are intertwined and the emphasis and priority to be given to each calls for constant reinterpretation. Any central bank would have to ask itself like any government: how full is full employment? how urgent is it to restore employment to some previous level when demand at home or, still more, abroad weakens? how is employment policy to be reconciled with the danger of inflation or an external deficit? and so on. In any event, how in 1976 can one separate monetary from fiscal policy? Once the budget becomes so large an element in the economy that the budget surplus or deficit dominates all other sectoral surpluses or deficits, changes in the money supply are either dictated by the budget or can be held within narrower limits only by what may have to be wide fluctuations in interest rates that have disastrous consequences for financial markets. The idea that monetary policy could control the level of employment whatever the fiscal stance adopted by the government is too preposterous to pursue.

It remains true that the use of monetary and fiscal policy to promote economic stability need not involve the state in detailed intervention in the market. But just as distributional considerations lead to various forms of price control, so employment considerations are cited in justification of measures to help this industry or that, to keep particular firms or projects in being, and to continue over-manning in nationalized industries. The more old-fashioned approach of public works, the maintenance of a 'shelf' of projects to be brought down and put into effect in a depression, and the support of specially devised local authority schemes to employ more labour in areas of high unemployment also reflects lack of faith in orthodox reliance on monetary and fiscal policy alone. It is indeed almost inevitable that if the state is itself the employer of one-quarter of the working population it should exert itself directly to stabilize employment rather than work on itself through financial channels.

(c) *Inflation*

A third macro-economic objective that has greatly extended the role of the state is the avoidance of inflation. Here again the objective is not one that can be attained by leaving things to market forces so long at least as the two objectives we have just discussed continue to be pursued. It may be true that there was very little inflation in the nineteenth century except when the government was generating it and that market forces do not necessarily operate so as to give rise to inflation. But in a world in which political power rests with wage- and salary-earners, that power can hardly fail to be used in order to re-distribute income and maintain employment. The budgetary struggle over distribution is carried over into the labour market; and full employment, by reinforcing the bargaining power of labour, turns the struggle in the labour market into outright inflation.

Economic systems develop their own defence mechanisms when the pressure put on them rises dangerously. Inflation and external deficits are the defence mechanisms of a market economy when claims are created in excess of what the system can deliver. Unemployment was an earlier and harsher defence mechanism since it ensured that excessive claims would not be made. Even if it were beyond dispute that unemployment would still function to moderate wage claims it is doubtful whether governments that enlist the defence mechanism of unemployment to achieve their aims can hope to continue in power in a fully democratic society. Hence the effort to find some alternative means of regulating wages and prices without altogether superseding market forces. But whereas with distribution of income and economic stabilisation there are policy instruments that do not require detailed intervention in the market it is not at all clear that anti-inflationary incomes policies can be devised that avoid the need to intervene extensively.

(d) *Balance of Payments*

Another objective of policy that has had a powerful influence on the activities of the state is the preservation of external balance. It is not a new objective and Adam Smith for one would have thought it misguided. He, and still more David Hume, saw no reason why the balance of payments should not look after itself. But countries in deficit or believing themselves to be constrained by their balance of payments have rarely been willing to trust market forces to rid them of the deficit or free them from constraint. Even when they have opted for a floating rate of exchange, or more commonly been obliged to acquiesce in floating, they have continued to justify a wide variety of controls by real or supposed balance of payments difficulties. Sometimes these controls have been primarily over capital movements or have applied to a broad range of imports or exports so as to act as a kind of ersatz depreciation. But very often they have involved outright protection or subsidy to specific industries expected to show large balance of payments gains. The more the state has felt itself obliged by its international commitments to give up overt protection to such industries the more ingenuity it has shown in devising alternative forms of support (including 'non-tariff barriers') that keep to the letter but not the spirit of its undertakings. Such support may be purely protective and have nothing to do with the balance of payments but even when this is so balance of payments considerations are likely to be urged in extenuation.

(e) *Economic Growth*

Efforts by the state to accelerate economic growth fall into the same general category. There can be no presumption that market forces 'left to themselves' (if one can give meaning to such a concept) will generate either the maximum or a socially acceptable rate of growth. Once the rate of growth becomes a matter of public concern the state cannot avoid taking an interest in it and trying to bring it more into line either with what it judges to be the economy's true potential or with what the public would find acceptable.

Unfortunately there is simply no way of telling what ought to be done in fulfilment of either of these objectives. We know very little about the forces governing the rate of growth and still less about how to make them operate more powerfully. There is no simple or certain way of establishing the maximum growth rate of which a country is capable or of finding out what rate or rates would be socially acceptable. We cannot be sure that the efforts of the state to accelerate growth will have a significant effect or that they will necessarily be beneficial in the long run. So we are in an area of almost total uncertainty in which economists have expressed themselves for thirty years with unbecoming assurance and have had to unsay in one decade a large proportion of what they said in the previous one.

Nevertheless the stakes are high and the incentive to act correspondingly powerful. Advised or not advised by economists, heedful or not of their advice, governments believe that they can influence growth and have adopted a wide variety of measures in this belief, ranging from increased public investment to tariff protection, university expansion, indicative planning, investment grants or allowances, free trade areas, etc., etc. Whether all of these taken together have been of more than minor importance in comparison with market forces operating in a world of almost continuous full employment is a very open question.

More recently, growth theory and growth programmes have begun to lay more stress on science and technology. But the rate of technical change is very much a matter of the speed of diffusion or what is nowadays called 'technological transfer'; and anyone reared on Marshall or still more on Schumpeter does not need to be told that this is what competition in the market is all about. Once it is taken on board that innovation and growth or development are opposite sides of the same penny the role of the state in promoting growth will need thorough re-examination.

(f) *The Growing Importance of the Budget*

There are several other macro-economic objectives such as regional policy which it would be possible to enumerate and analyse and which call for some form of intervention by the state. These would be further examples of the emergence in modern times of more ambitious policy goals that can be realized only through collective action. The more importance is attached to such goals the greater is bound to be the emphasis on centralized control over market forces or their supersession by direct action by the state. But it is not *indispensable* to the fulfilment of any of the macro-economic goals (except perhaps incomes policy) that the state should engage in direct intervention in the market: in principle, it would be possible to proceed by way of strengthening or weakening existing incentives and by way of adding to or taking from existing incomes without suspending the freedom of buyers and sellers to react to market forces as thus modified. There is, for example, nothing intrinsic to the objectives that makes them incapable of attainment without a change in the border between the public and private sectors. It is not even beyond dispute that an expansion in the public sector would make any of them more likely to be attained. What logic and experience alike suggest is that all of them give rise to an increase in the importance of the budget and that the main instruments of macro-economic policy are, of necessity, budgetary instruments. Economic management in pursuit of collective goals leads not only to increased centralization but to increased centralization in the

Treasury. Where this is not so it either reflects a disinclination to rely on market forces or an effort to speed up structural changes by long-term planning backed by controls that are not primarily financial.

II

This brings us to a second set of reasons for setting aside the verdict of the market.

(a) *Market Imperfections*

It is not merely that there are some broad collective purposes that the market cannot be relied upon to serve but that it may fail to function as it should in the allocation of resources. Economists have drawn up a long list of market imperfections and failings. There are market imperfections associated with monopoly or monopolistic competition: with ignorance and inadequate knowledge of market options: with externalities of all kinds and consequent divergencies between private and social costs and benefits: with exposure to risk and uncertainty, particularly in relation to innovation: and with decisions between present and future, where the response to current prices may be perverse and calculated to lead to prices in future which, if foreseen, would provoke an opposite response. The implications of each of these would suffice for a lengthy discourse and the success of the state in seeking to correct each limitation could give rise to endless debate. We cannot avoid asking ourselves, however, how seriously to take them and how radically, in their totality, they alter the reliance that should be placed by a modern state on market forces.

(b) *Wartime Controls*

An example will show that they have to be taken very seriously indeed. Suppose that a country is obliged to defend itself against military attack and has to mobilize for war. No juggling with public expenditure and bidding for resources in the market is likely to be as effective or as quick in creating the sinews of war as the use of compulsion and conscription to short-circuit the market and build up the armed forces in the form and on the scale that the government thinks appropriate. Who else but the government can hope to fathom the mind of the government or grasp the necessities that war will impose? Market prices and rates of pay are most unlikely to convey the priorities in governmental strategy or to effect a transfer of men and materials to wartime employment at the rate required. The system of market prices is not designed to promote a comprehensive reallocation of resources from peace to war or vice versa.

(c) *Development Plans*

The same logic applies to a less developed country where the structural upheavals required may make market prices a poor guide to the adjustments necessary. The indivisibilities, discontinuities, and externalities that are so prominent in such countries make the price-mechanism a less satisfactory instrument for regulating economic activitity. Where the prime aim of economic effort is the satisfaction of the conflicting wants of a multitude of consumers the market can contribute powerfully to that objective by securing the necessary marginal adjustments. But when the adjustments are no longer marginal and the pattern of supply and demand has to be radically and quickly transformed in pursuit of some over-riding task such as industrialization, it may be difficult to use ordinary market mechanisms in order to reconcile the priorities flowing from such a task with the preferences of consumers. Direct controls, over-riding the price-mechanism, may be required to bring outputs promptly into line with the plans of the authorities. The larger the adjustments to be made, the less the time in which they are required, and the lower the elasticities of response to price changes, the greater is the temptation to resort to compulsion in order to avoid violent fluctuations in price. Apart from the abuses to which compulsion lends itself, there is a danger that the state may seek to avoid making any change in price and rely exclusively on administrative measures without the supplementary, and in the long run indispensable, pressure that the market could provide.

(d) *Floating Exchange Rates*

A further example is provided by fluctuations in exchange rates. Here, obviously enough, professional opinion has moved strongly against administrative control and in favour of allowing market forces free play. But there is the same risk of wide, and eventually perverse, fluctuations in price because of low short-term elastici-

ties. The swing in exchange rates may be so violent that it thwarts
the very approach to a new balance between receipts and payments
which it is its function to promote. The danger is then of an insistence on exclusive reliance on fluctuating exchange rates without
any dampening of the fluctuations out of reserves of foreign exchange or by administrative measures to reinforce market pressure.

In all such cases one can of course pooh-pooh the case for
direct action by the state by denigrating all forms of official
intervention in the market. Those who run a war economy or
make plans for developing countries or intervene to stabilize
exchange rates are bound to make major blunders from time to
time and when they do their mistakes are likely to be blazoned
abroad. But if every argument for state intervention is met by a
sweeping attack on ministerial and bureaucratic folly as the
necessary concomitant of such intervention there is not much
point in pursuing the argument. It is just as one-sided to exclude
the possibility of improving on the market as it is to think it enough
to show that the market is not altogether perfect.

(e) *The Problem of Monopoly*

Of all forms of market failure most importance has been
attached traditionally to monopoly. In the *Wealth of Nations*
restrictive practices are strongly criticized but treated largely in
terms of agreements between merchants or employers. Nowadays the emphasis is more likely to be on the powers enjoyed
by multi-national companies or trade unions: powers which
Adam Smith could hardly have foreseen.

Where monopoly is rooted in collusion between a group of
producers and consumers with a view to exploiting their collective
hold on the market the matter is in principle straightforward.
Action in restraint of trade can be made illegal. But what if a firm
simply grows into a position of monopoly? Or if it straddles the
globe so that only part of its activities are within the jurisdiction
of any one government? What remedies has the state for abuses
of market power in those not uncommon situations? An even more
difficult problem is posed by collective bargaining agreements
between employers and employed that necessarily reflect the
exercise of monopoly power. How can that power be qualified
without prejudice to either side? And if it is not qualified how is
it possible to avoid an ineradicable inflationary bias that is far

more damaging to the economy than any sectional gains levied by the most powerful bargainers in the labour market?

These are not questions to which any short or easy answers can be given. The dilemmas remain. What starts out as the protection of the weak becomes the prop of the strong. Bigness may bring efficiency; but it also brings market power and release from competitive pressure. Monopolies may be broken up; but the parts cannot be made to compete with one another. Freedom to compete can degenerate into freedom to conceal collusion or take over competitors; the enterprise that the market is supposed to harness may take perverse forms. Above all, positions of privilege may rest on political as much as economic power and be as firmly entrenched in the state as in the market.

There may be an even greater danger. There can be no guarantee that the market environment will always make for decentralization in competing units of limited size. A variety of circumstances —modern technology, improved communications, the advantages of marketing in bulk, the greater ease and cheapness of access to finance—may tell in favour of large concerns. The government may have its own reasons for favouring large units over which it can exercise more immediate influence. In those circumstances what is to be done if business becomes increasingly concentrated in a small number of large units? In the United Kingdom the 100 largest firms in manufacturing, which produced 15 per cent of total output before the First World War, were producing nearly half by 1960 and may reach two-thirds by 1989. If this is what market forces produce what is the state to do? Suppose, for the sake of argument, that the trend owed nothing to active encouragement by the state and was sufficiently established to persist in the face of strong discouragement. In what sense would it be possible to oppose the state to the market and insist on the superiority of a decentralized system responding to market indicators over a system of direct operation by the state? Is there any reason why manufacturing industry should not go the way of postal services, the railways, and the power stations?

If the question were one to be answered exclusively in terms of economic efficiency the answer must surely be: in principle, no. The scale of operations consistent with efficiency may grow until there is a plain choice between a private and public monopoly and the substitution of a state holding for the stake held by private investors may do little to change the mode of conduct of the business. The mere change of ownership would not by itself limit or transform the role of the market. It would reflect the decay of the market and the fading out of competitive influences. Whatever remained of these influences might be allowed to continue.

The question can be put in those terms, however, only if one abstracts from the characteristic features of public ownership. The state is not simply a new kind of shareholder but a shareholder with very special powers and preoccupations that do not always march with business efficiency. It is to some extent in the same position in relation to public enterprises as any large business is in relation to its subsidiaries. That is, it can leave them to run themselves or furnish them with rules and targets (and, on cause shown, additional finance) or maintain control directly. It can let them be guided by their own judgement of the market or impose its own judgement or it can require them to pursue policies that are essentially non-commercial and do not spring from market considerations. It is this last possibility that, *in principle*, distinguishes the economic activities of government. So long as the growth of business units leaves them as responsive as before to market influences, even if they come to possess more market power, that growth does not detract from the potentialities of the market as a guide to decision-making. But if the internalizing of decisions through growth reinforces non-commercial influences on those decisions then the displacement of small firms by large is a vote against the market and in favour of the state. To put the point more concretely: big business is still business when guided by considerations of profit; but public enterprise is likely to have to marry political and commercial considerations. If commercial considerations are diluted by political, the result can hardly be as satisfactory from the limited point of view of economic efficiency; and the question then becomes how far dilution should go? What are the political purposes that are served by state ownership that warrant a sacrifice in efficiency? Could not such purposes be equally well served by the use of state control in order to regulate the functioning of the market?

It may be objected that all this presupposes that there is a market to be regulated. But this seems inconsistent with the initial postulate of growing industrial concentration and a trend towards monopoly. The existence of large firms each able to dominate its own market is quite compatible, however, with the threat of keen competition between them since each may be capable of entering some at least of the markets supplied by other large firms. Potential rivalry can be as powerful a factor as actual in maintaining industrial efficiency. Moreover large private firms show a great deal more flexibility in adapting their structure and activities to changes in market conditions than public enterprises do. If they engage in take-over activities they also sell off or shut down.

As firms grow in size and acquire increasing monopoly power they tend to exhibit more and more of the characteristics of state undertakings. They exert more social and political pressure and are themselves subject increasingly to such pressure. Their objectives of policy become more complex and diluted by considerations of social acceptability so that their pursuit of efficiency is less single-minded. But so long as they are in private hands they can establish their own priorities within the limits of the slack available to them and are simultaneously free to make their own arrangements within the limits set by the state. These limits may be wide and extremely general or they may be narrow and specific to the point that the state exercises more control than if it were the actual owner of the businsss.

(f) *The Market as a Decentralising Agency*

The monopoly case is rather fundamental because it brings us back to the *raison d'être* of the market. The state cannot organize the economy on the basis of simple directions, any more than any army can be successfully controlled by orders of the day. There has to be co-operation based on accepted rules of behaviour, as Adam Smith repeatedly emphasized and there have to be incentives that are sufficiently powerful to get the job done. The incentives in turn must either be of the kind that makes an army fight, i.e. calculated to secure co-operation in a common endeavour, or they must take the form of rewards and punishments for individual acts. These cannot be prescribed by the state, just as directions cannot be given, because of the complexity of the economic system. But if they are left to the market in which bargains are struck to the mutual advantage of both sides, the market can graduate the incentives to what is required and provide indicators of action that allow control to be decentralized.

Decentralization, however, is limited by economies of scale. If economic activity is broken down too far and made a matter of individual bargaining it cannot be as efficient as it would be in units large enough to take advantage of those economies. For the sake of efficiency there has to be some submission to central direction. The greater the economies of scale and the economic virtues of size, the more the scope for central direction. Thus arguments about the state and the market are arguments quite as much about centralization and decentralization as about the intrusion or exclusion of political influences.

(g) *The International Market*

The forces of decentralization are reinforced by the international character of the market as opposed to the national character of the state. So long as the domestic market is open to competitive influences from outside, a limit is set to monopoly powers of all kinds: whether exercised by groups of producers or groups of workers, whole industries or individual firms. It was this aspect of international trade that particularly appealed to Adam Smith. He developed the argument elaborated later by Ricardo that free access to the international market, whether as exporter or importer, was calculated to improve the efficiency of an economy and encourage its growth. The enlargement of the market was doubly advantageous because it made the economy more competitive and at the same time opened up new opportunities of specialization on the basis of comparative advantage. The mutual benefits that both sides enjoyed from the pursuit of these opportunities were an illustration of his basic thesis of the harmony of opposed interests in all market transactions. The older, mercantilist, view with its emphasis on confrontation and a clash of interests encouraged interference by governments which ran the risk of provoking trade wars while unrestricted trade tended to promote friendly and peaceable relations. Cobden and others in the 19th century were so impressed by this argument that they gave priority to free trade even over the abolition of slavery and supported the Southern States in the American Civil War for that reason. Much later it was possible for a major political party to defend simultaneously international free trade and a highly interventionist domestic policy such as the nationalization of all the means of production. Later still it was possible to advocate a Common

Market free from tariff barriers in countries dedicated to various forms of *étatisme* and other active industrial policies that inevitably affected, and were usually designed to affect, the competitive position of major industries. Intervention, driven out at the door, came in again at the window.

We need not pursue these apparent inconsistencies or trouble to ask whether the international market is totally different from the domestic. That it is different is evident if only because there is at least one other government involved in every international transaction and the degree of control that can be exercised reflects this fact. There is also the fact that domestic transactions automatically balance while external transactions do not, and that governments may have cause to regret an enlargement of their business with other countries in a way they can have no reason for regretting domestic expansion so long as it is non-inflationary. The international market may encourage the channelling of resources along blind alleys or delay investments necessary to eventual development and encourage investments that are of immediate advantage but involve a high negative yield for the economy at a later stage. The state *may* be more far-sighted or more willing to make the investments that long-term development requires or able to act on a broader front to secure results that a fragmented market would fail to deliver. We have also to recognise that the international market is the domain of the really large firm which may combine a competitive spirit with unmistakable monopoly powers. Like the domestic market the international market tends to favour those already in possession of resources as against those with only limited options, the rich against the poor. Yet on the other hand the international influences which tend to flood in behind trade and investment and to be inseparable from them are likely to be the major factor in successful development.

III

Let us now look at matters the other way round and ask ourselves not what is wrong with the market but what is wrong with the state? We live in a world of increasing centralization in which there is a profound belief in planning and control from the highest motives. This of itself politicizes economic decisions of all kinds and puts pressure on the state to expand its functions, its powers, and its machinery of control without much regard to the cumulative effect of the complex machinery so created. The technostructure of which Galbraith complains is the result of bending the economic system to political demands rather than a means of bending consumers to the will of big business outside and inside government.

Willingness to turn to the state as the agent of social planning and control is reinforced by the change in the balance of political power. Those who exercised political power in the past—the agricultural interest apart—had usually relatively little to fear from the operations of the market and much to resent in the operations of the state. Possessing wealth, they could profit from the cheapness that the market ensured. In safe jobs, they had little reason to fear unemployment. For them, market forces were on the side of peace and prosperity, rewarding the diligent and the enterprising when diligence and enterprise were indispensable to the survival of a hard-pressed economy. But as political power moves from the old to the young, from the capitalist to the manual worker, it is the state not the market that is seen as delivering the goods. The possessors of power are not, as a rule, those whom the market has blessed nor are they content to abide by its verdict. They are willing to use the state, as other social classes have done before them, for the achievement of ever more ambitious targets in furtherance of their own ends. In doing so they are not content merely to see different parameters set for market forces but prefer the creation of fresh organizations under state auspices visibly and directly responding to specific social needs.

(a) *Overloading of the State Machine*

The net effect of the change in intellectual climate and social pressures is to overload the state machine and to overload it unnecessarily. Additional, often conflicting, responsibilities are thrust on it without enough thought being given to the consequences of the overload: bureaucracy, inefficiency, and waste, frustration and the consequent danger of corruption, disregard for regulations and later for the law, contempt ultimately for the business of politics and for the state itself. There is a need for devices that allow the state to devolve some of its responsibilities: for agencies that can be made to function to the public advantage without detailed supervision by the state: for ways of securing the broad results desired through voluntary effort with a minimum of state participation: in a word, for reviving the use of the market.

What scope is there for enlarging the use of the market within the general objectives we associate with the welfare state? We have seen one such enlargement in the past few years with the move from fixed to floating rates of exchange. But the international sector (if one could isolate international influences within a single sector) is a law unto itself and requires separate treatment. Confining ourselves for present purposes to the public sector we can detect a limited number of possible openings.

(b) *Free Public Services*

For example, we have the large range of services provided free by the state and absolved from market tests of priority (on the demand side at least). It is not at all obvious why this range of services should be picked out and why it should be so readily accepted that services should either be provided free or at full cost. (Housing is one of the few exceptions.) The effect is usually to increase demand to the point at which the kind of service offered is diluted in order to keep down the bill. At the same time competitive services that maintain higher standards (or purport to do so) are provided privately but efforts are often made by the state to put obstacles in the way of such provision. This polarization of services between free and full cost and polarization of customers between those content to queue and avoid payment and those willing to pay and avoid queuing seems neither necessary nor efficient. Yet in one direction after another the government in Britain seems determined to put an end to intermediate solutions. Even in the case of housing, where the economic consequences of abolishing rent would be so dramatic that it is hardly necessary to explain why that situation has still not quite been reached, there is a polarization between council tenants and owner-occupiers that is perhaps the most important single line of division in British politics.

The bill for the wide range of services involved is a large one and rather arbitrary judgements have to be made on the size of the bill that can be afforded. One can understand the logic of the situation where the consumer is offered no choice, as with army uniforms, and either is required to take what he is given or, if a charge were levied, would be obliged to make a compulsory purchase. This applies to defence services where the taxpayer has to accept what is voted by his representatives and there is no other way of settling the matter. But what of health, education, pensions, etc.? The state does not deprive consumers of all choice since it permits a parallel market to exist side by side with its own administered supply. But why should the official supply be at zero price when other necessities like bread and butter or housing are not? The combination of zero pricing and a limited allocation of funds means that the free services have to be rationed without ration cards and the rationing process is bound to be arbitrary and difficult. Perhaps some minimum charge to the beneficiaries would still be preferable to present arrangements even if the charge had to be waived for large numbers of consumers with limited means.

(c) *Commercial Services*

Where services provided by the state or a public undertaking are charged for, as in the nationalized industries, familiar issues of pricing policy arise. There is no need to recapitulate the controversies associated with those issues. But there is another deeper problem arising out of the statutory monopoly that nationalized industries usually enjoy. In a competitive market or even where there is a private monopoly it is possible to improve the services provided by creating a new organization superior to those existing or, after a successful take-over bid, by a reorganization of the resources employed. But a statutory monopoly is beyond such influence. There is no way in which a thrusting and imaginative outsider can back his claim to be able to improve on the *status quo* and every reason why the existing organization should seek the quiet life to which good monopolists traditionally aspire. How is the public sector to devise the counterpart of a take-over bid, or even the threat of one? How can it ensure that public undertakings undergo the drastic surgery that exposure to competition in a free market would undoubtedly call for?

Part of the answer lies in the willingness of the state to qualify the monopoly powers it has assumed through nationalization. The question at issue from this point of view is whether the state is prepared to permit various forms of choice to continue. Does the Ministry of Defence insist on taking over the manufacture of armaments or is it prepared to buy equipment from private firms?

Does the state insist on exclusive operation of all coal mines and steel mills or will it permit competition from mines and steel mills in private hands? Does the Post Office prohibit the organization of private postal services? Could new coal mines be sunk with private capital? Are consumers of coal free to place orders for imports from abroad or are they free only to purchase imported oil? Do any of the nationalized industries so organize themselves as to promote competition between the constituent parts? What, in short, is the importance that the state attaches, once it attains a position of monopoly, to the continued exercise of choice and the continual risk of supersession? What does it do to ensure that the range of services between which consumers can choose is at least as great as efficiency requires?

CONCLUSION

The load on the modern state has increased steadily, continues to increase, and in the opinion of many ought to be diminished. But the increased load does not in the main reflect ideological antipathy to reliance on market forces. It is much more the outcome of new and wider ambitions for social control: fear of unemployment on the one hand and inflation on the other, a more egalitarian temper, concern for social justice, for the environment, and for human needs for which the market does not cater, the trend towards industrial concentration and larger business units. These have caused the budget to expand, the relative importance of the private consumer to shrink, the totality of social organization to grow, and far more of this formidable total to devolve on public authorities. All this adds ineluctably to the importance of organizational as opposed to market instruments of economic co-ordination and inflates the role of the state as the centre-piece of social organization. But in most industrial countries the private sector is still far greater in size than the public sector and the market remains indispensable to the functioning of the economy, whether as an agency for the co-ordination of activities in the private sector or as the meeting place of private consumers and public authorities. Even as a network of dealings within the public sector itself, the market retains its usefulness and significance although various normal responses to market changes can then no longer appear. What requires thought is how more use could be made of the market in order to relieve the overload on the state, perhaps at the cost of some slight derogation from the prime objectives of state intervention.

This is essentially a question of organization. It is not just a matter of changing the boundary between the public and the private sector or of giving the consumer more freedom of choice. It is also a matter of how the public sector should be organized; how competition within it can be re-created; how the decision-taking units in each part of the public sector can be re-structured from time to time without take-overs, bankruptcies, and the machinery for reorganization used in the private sector. It is a matter also of the limits within which the private sector should be asked to operate. These limits could be drawn in such a way by high taxation, government regulation, or administrative order, as to make the line between the private and the public sector an irrelevance and for this reason alone most of the argument about nationalization that continues even in 1976 is itself irrelevant. But the limits could also be drawn in a way that enlarged the scope for private enterprise at the same time as wider social interests were more securely guaranteed. This would be so if restrictive practices by management or workers were effectively outlawed. It would also be so if the state found means to prevent the use of economic power to enforce claims conceived in the interests of limited groups whether of workers or their employers.

The danger of overloading the state is least in a static world since routine and overload rarely go together. If there were no need for concern about growth it might be possible to heap more duties on the state without undesirable consequences. But in a dynamic world it is otherwise. The managerial burden of responding to change readily becomes excessive and the need to use market forces and indicators in order to relieve the burden mounts correspondingly. It is the great virtue of the market that it provides a testing-ground for responses to new influences, for eliciting and trying out alternatives and demonstrating which new ideas have greatest survival value. It can also provide a measure of managerial performance and a test of the survival value of managements. When the market is allowed to decay this selective function is endangered. In the absence of a market, committees have to take its place in the adjudication of known alternatives, in providing a stimulus to the devising of new ideas, and in judging managerial capabilities. Committees have their virtues; but they are usually a poor substitute for a market.

It was the experimental character of market responses that Adam Smith stressed most heavily: the efforts of every man to improve himself by offering the consumer a better deal. It was the shortcomings of the state in its efforts to encourage development and improvement that disposed him to scepticism of its pretensions. No doubt he overstated his case. The focus of the market is too narrow; the choices that consumers and producers make are governed by a far greater number of variables than the state can take into account. What a man buys does not tell us what he wants from life; what he is able to sell is only to a small extent the fruit of his unaided efforts. There is in the background the society in which his wants and his efforts take shape, the facilities and opportunities, the social capital and the social pressures that condition his behaviour. We are more conscious perhaps than Adam Smith of the need to see the market within a social framework and of the ways in which the state can usefully rig the market without destroying its thrust. We are certainly far more willing to concede a larger role for state activities of all kinds. But it is a nice question whether this is because we can lay claim, after two centuries, to any deeper insight into the forces determining the wealth of nations or whether more obvious forces have not played the larger part: the spread of democratic ideals, increasing affluence, the growth of knowledge, and a centralizing technology that delivers us over to the bureaucrat.

5

The Diffusion of Development

BY W. ARTHUR LEWIS*

I

SEEKING a topic for this paper[1] I at first toyed with a suggestion that it be: what we know about development that Adam Smith did not know. However, this fantasy did not last long. For one thing it would propel me into the 'What Adam Smith Really Meant' industry, where I have only comparative disadvantage. And for another, I am not certain that we know more that matters about development than Adam Smith already knew. So I have settled for a less hazardous exercise.

The question I wish to probe is why the Industrial Revolution has taken so long to become a universal phenomenon. By 1830 the main lines of industrial and agricultural advance were already demonstrating themselves in Britain, France, and the United States. Why has it taken a century and a half for every country in the world to be practising these principles?

Before answering the question, I must first defend it. To the historian of cultural diffusion, it is an absurd question. Why did it take a century and a half for a major cultural innovation to spread across the world? This process has in the past normally taken centuries; one should ask rather how come this thing has happened in so short a time, if it has indeed happened. I sympathize with this reaction, since this is my basic approach to understanding the history of the human race. My defence against the diffusionists rests partly on the explosion of communications since 1830, which has speeded up cultural diffusion, and partly on the fact that changes which were already in process in the second half of the

* Sir Arthur Lewis, Woodrow Wilson School of Public and International Affairs, Princeton University.

[1] There is considerable overlap with my forthcoming book, *Growth and Fluctuations 1870–1913* (London, Allen and Unwin). All references to world trade and the terms of trade are documented there.

nineteenth century seem to have slowed down in the first half of the twentieth century. I shall return to this later.

The question must also be defended against those who deny that the industrial and agricultural revolution is already a universal phenomenon. I will cede a little ground, but not much. I shall not rely on 2·5 to 3 per cent *per capita* annual growth rate of the Third World since the Second World War which is unprecedented in human history, and which was certainly not foreseen by anyone in 1950. Instead I shall take the proportion of the population in agriculture, a measure of economic change which was already familiar to Adam Smith. No test can tell us whether any country will continue to sustain economic growth in the future, but a country which has got the proportion of its labour force in agriculture down from 70 to 80 per cent to less than 50 per cent has certainly sustained a lot of growth in its past even when one discounts for disguised unemployment in the towns. In 1830 only one country has passed this 50 per cent test, namely Great Britain. By 1913 you must add most of Western Europe, the U.S.A., Canada, Australasia, Argentina, and Chile. By 1939 most of Europe is in, but not quite all; half a dozen Latin American countries, and Japan. By 1970 all of Europe and practically all of Latin America. In that year 61 countries had less than 50 per cent in agriculture, including 17 in Latin America, 8 in Asia, and 5 in Africa.[2] Every decade adds another 5 or so countries to the list. However, my purpose is not to predict, but only to ask why it took a century and a half for this list to grow from 1 to 61.

II

The industrialization of the pioneers in the first half of the nineteenth century presented two opportunities to the rest of the world —the opportunity to follow their example, and the opportunity to trade. Example was much the more important of these two, since trade was small.

The example was easy to follow. The Industrial Revolution started from new technologies in making textiles, mining coal,

---

[2] In Latin America: Argentina, Brazil, Chile, Colombia, Costa Rica, Cuba, El Salvador, Mexico, Panama, Paraguay, Peru, Puerto Rico, Surinam, Uruguay, Venezuela, British West Indies, French West Indies. In Asia: Ceylon, Japan, North Korea, Iran, Malaysia, Philippines, Seychelles, Syria. In Africa: Algeria, Libya, Mauritius, South Africa, Tunisia.

smelting pig iron, and using steam. The new ideas were ingenious but simple, and easy to apply. The capital requirement was remarkably small, except for the cost of building railways, which could be had on loan. At first the new machines were used at home, or in small workshops, and even when the new technology moved into factories the additional expense was small, since factories were not in those days built for the glorification of architects or the enrichment of construction unions. There were no great economies of scale, so the skills required for managing a factory or workshop were well within the competence and experience of what we now call the third world. The technology was available to any country that wanted it, despite feeble British efforts to restrict the export of machinery (which were over by 1850), and Englishmen and Frenchmen were willing to travel to the ends of the earth to set up and operate the new mills.

Example was reinforced by 'backwash'. Any country which neglected to revolutionize its own textile and iron industries would soon see them eliminated by a flood of cheap British imports. This spur affected even Germany, France, and the United States, which did not free themselves from dependence on British textiles until the middle of the nineteenth century, or from dependence on British iron until the 1880s. Marx dramatized the destruction of Indian spinning by British imports during the first half of the nineteenth century, but the sequel is often forgotten. India built its first modern textile mill in 1853, and by the end of the century was not only self-sufficient in the cheaper cottons, but also had driven British yarn out of many Far Eastern markets. (British yarn exports peaked in 1884.) Sweden was not so lucky. In the eighteenth century its irons smelted with charcoal were known all over Europe. Since Sweden lacked coal, British iron killed this trade, except for wrought iron of the highest quality, and Swedish smelting could not revive until the progress of heat economies made it economic to import coal. Russian iron illustrates the good side of the backwash; rich in both coal and iron, Russia became by 1913 already the fifth largest iron producer in the world.

Although the techniques and capital requirements of the revolution were no obstacle, its fruits would be enjoyed first by those countries which already had an industrial sector that could be revolutionized. There had to be a market. As Adam Smith already knew, the size of this market would depend in the first place on agricultural productivity, since there can be no industry without a surplus of food and raw materials to feed the industrial population—unless industry is going to live by exporting its produce and importing food and raw materials. In this sense the countries most ready to follow the example of the pioneers were those which were already experiencing the agricultural revolution as well, and which therefore already had large industrial sectors. These were the countries of western Europe, especially Germany and north-west Europe, which by the end of the nineteenth century were going along with their own industrial and agricultural momentum.

Agricultural productivity was still low in central, east, and southern Europe, but there was some industry. In countries where landowners take half the farmers' output in rents and taxes one can have sizeable secondary and tertiary sectors despite low agricultural productivity; but low output per man is still a constraint. We can get some idea of the hierarchy by comparing the proportions of the industrial population around 1911: Germany 0·41, Italy 0·26, Hungary 0·17, Japan 0·16, India 0·12, Roumania 0·08.

But the size of the market was not the only limitation, even in Europe. Another problem from 1870 onwards was the agricultural backwash. As American grain came pouring into Europe, not only were the farmers depressed, but eastern Europe was deprived of a possibility of trade. International trade was growing quite rapidly before the First World War. In value terms the growth rate of world trade between 1883 and 1913 was 3·4 per cent per annum, whereas eastern and southern Europe achieved only 2·6 per cent per annum. This was the lowest of the regional growth rates, comparing adversely with north-west Europe 3·5, the tropical countries 3·6, and the overseas countries of recent settlement 4·3. If eastern Europe had not been crowded out of the rapidly expanding international trade in agricultural products its industrial growth would have been more vigorous.

'Crowded out' is of course not the right phrase; 'allowed itself to be crowded out' would be a better description. For, in industry as in agriculture, the basic constraint on the response of the southern and eastern Europeans to the revolutionary techniques was the backwardness of their societies. Their small farmers, burdened with debt, taxes, and rents, lacked incentive to increase their yields, since higher yields would lead to higher exactions; and their great landowners, unlike the Junkers of Prussia or some of the British gentry, still regarded their lands as a base for political power and economic tribute rather than as a factor of production capable of being coaxed into higher productivity. The political atmosphere was also inappropriate. Industrialization required governmental activity of various kinds, including borrowing for railway construction, some tariff protection, modern company legislation, abolition of taxes and restrictions on the mobility of labour, and so on. Instead these governments continued until 1913 to be dominated by backward landed aristocracies, hostile in spirit to industrialization, which menaced their political power and threatened to bid away their labour force. Indeed, the problem posed by the more backward parts of Europe is not why they progressed so slowly, but why the landed aristocracy gave in so easily in western Europe to a rising industrial class which was going to rob it of both rents and power.

One must avoid putting all the backward countries of Europe in one boat since they differed considerably among themselves, with their industrial populations ranging from 8 to 25 per cent of the labour force. Most of them had started to move by the end of the nineteenth century. But even when governments began to interest themselves in industrialization, which was frequently for military reasons, their interests tended to be limited to parts of their territories. Eastern Europe was a land of empires, where ruling nationalities imposed their will on numerous subject peoples, differing in language, culture, or religion. When the Russian Government began to promote industrialization, it did not remember its Polish provinces. The subject peoples of Russia, Austria-Hungary, Serbia, or Turkey were not forbidden to industrialize, but neither was anything done to help them. If they possessed a vigorous mercantile tradition, as in Bohemia, they could make progress on their own; but mostly they were just as much suppressed by their own backward landed aristocracy as by the imperial power itself.

The deadly hand of imperialism was of course not limited to the backward parts of Europe. India's agricultural productivity was one of the lowest in the world, but partly because of its inequitable income distribution, it had a large handicraft sector, including about 10 per cent of the labour force. Large-scale industrial output was growing rapidly at the end of the century (by about 5 per cent per annum) but still occupied only 1 per cent of the labour force. Textiles and jute were racing ahead, with large export components. The weak spot was in iron and steel, and the main cause of this weakness was the hostility of the British Government. Government policy was very important in iron and steel because the Government was the largest buyer—for its programme of railway construction, irrigation facilities, public buildings, ordnance factories, and so on. Until 1875 the Indian Government bought its industrial supplies only in Britain, so Indian manufacturers stood no chance. The policy was thereafter gradually eroded, but the final restrictions on Indian Government purchase of Indian manufactures did not disappear until 1914. Thus when an English group built the first modern blast furnace in India in 1875, it was important to get Indian Government contracts, and the company sought a long-term understanding. The Government would not co-operate. It bought a little iron from the company from time to time, but not enough to keep the factory going. When Lord Ripon became Governor General in 1880 he bought the plant and wanted to develop it as a government enterprise, but the Government in London would not allow him to do so.[3] It took thirty years for London to abandon this policy, and agree to give the Tata brothers the contract which became the basis of their plant in 1912.

III

I have said that there were two options; one to reconstruct on the new lines an already existing industrial sector; the other to develop by exporting food and raw materials to the expanding industrial nations. The latter could also be a route to industrialization since exports would pay for infrastructure and human capital, and would generate a demand for industrial products which through import substitution would start off industrial growth.

This option had two snags. The first was that the industrial nations were not all that dependent on food and raw materials from abroad. The raw materials of the industrial revolution were coal, iron ore, cotton, and wool, and the leading foodstuff was wheat. Taking the U.S.A. and Western Europe together, the

---

[3] The story is told in detail by S. K. Sen, *Studies in Industrial Policy and Development of India 1858–1914* (Calcutta, Progressive Publishers Ltd, 1964).

industrial nations were practically self-sufficient in the leading raw materials, except for wool. The idea that it was the raw materials of the third world that made the industrial revolution is a myth. As late as the year 1883, for which the figures have been collected, Britain, France, Germany, and the United States together were taking only one-third of their imports from the rest of the world, excluding themselves and Europe; it came only to $1·4 billion dollars, or about one and a half dollars per head of the rest of the world's population. To be sure the demand was growing rapidly for those days; industrial production in these four countries was growing by about 3·4 per cent per annum, and world trade in primary products about 90 per cent as fast. But it was a very small tail to be wagging such a large dog.

The other snag was that the effect of exporting primary products on the prospects of industrialization would depend on the terms of trade, and here there was not one option but two, one for the temperate world and one for the tropics.

I refer not to the commodity terms of trade but to the factoral terms of trade. The industrial nations had to pay for primary exports and the opportunity cost of producing them, and this was very different in the temperate and the tropical worlds.

We have to start from the fact that around say 1900 the yield of wheat in Britain, which was the biggest single source of European emigration, was 1,600 lb. per acre, as against the tropical yield of 750 lb. of grain, and that the Europeans also cultivated more acres per man. In the country to which most of the European emigrants went, namely the United States, agricultural output per man was even higher than in Europe, because of greater mechanization, and industrial productivity was also 50 to 100 per cent greater. The temperate settlements could attract and hold European emigrants, in competition with the United States, only by offering income levels higher than prevailed in north-west Europe. Since north-west Europe needed first their wool, and then after 1890 their frozen meat, and ultimately after 1900 their wheat, it had to pay for those commodities prices which would yield a higher than European standard of living.

The tropical situation was different. Any prices for tea or rubber or peanuts which offered a standard of living in excess of the 750 lb. of grain per acre level were an improvement. Farmers would consider devoting idle land or time to producing such crops;

and, as experience grew, would even, at somewhat higher prices, reduce their own subsistence production of food to specialize in commercial crops. But whether the small farmer reacted in this way or not, there was an unlimited supply of Indians and Chinese willing to travel to the ends of the earth to work on plantations for a shilling a day. This stream of migrants from Asia was as large as the stream from Europe. This set the level of tropical prices. In the 1880s the wage of a plantation labourer was one shilling a day, but the wage of a navvy in New South Wales was nine shillings a day. If tea had been a temperate instead of a tropical crop its price would have been perhaps five times as high as it actually was. And if wool had been a tropical instead of a temperate crop it would have been had for perhaps one-fifth of the ruling price. Adam Smith would have understood this arithmetic; what has clouded our understanding has been the neo-classical preoccupation with marginal utility and marginal productivity.

Given this difference in the factoral terms of trade, the opportunity which international trade presented to the temperate settlements was very different from the opportunity presented to the tropics. The temperate settlements were offered high income per head. From this would come immediately a large demand for manufactures, opportunities for import substitution, and rapid urbanization. Domestic saving per head would be large. Money would be available to spend on schools, at all levels, and soon these countries would have a substantial managerial and administrative élite of their own. They would thus create their own power centres, with money, education, and managerial capacity, independent of and somewhat hostile to the imperial power, such that Australia, New Zealand, and Canada had ceased to be colonies in any political sense long before they acquired formal rights of sovereignty. The factoral terms available to them offered them the opportunity for full development in every sense of the word.

The factoral terms available to the tropics, on the other hand, offered the opportunity to stay poor—at any rate until such time as the labour reservoirs of India and China might be exhausted. A farmer in Nigeria might tend his peanuts with as much diligence and skill as a farmer in Australia tended his sheep, but the return would be very different. The just price, to use the medieval term, would reward equal competence with equal earnings. But the market price gave the Nigerian for his peanuts a 750 lb. of grain per acre level of living, and the Australian for his wool a 1,600 lb. per acre level of living, not because of what they did, nor because of marginal utilities or productivities in peanuts or wool, but because these were the respective amounts of food which their cousins could produce on the family farms. This is the fundamental sense in which the leaders of the less developed world denounce the current international economic order as unjust, namely that the factoral terms of trade are based on opportunity cost and not on the principle of equal pay for equal work. And of course nobody understood the mechanism better than the working classes in the temperate settlements themselves, and in the U.S.A. They were always adamant against Indian or Chinese emigration into their countries because they realized that, if unchecked, it must drive wages down close to Indian and Chinese levels.

The temperate settlements for the most part seized their opportunity. Though continuing to rely on exporting food and agricultural raw materials, they rapidly created their own industrial bases, and were, in this respect, as industrialized and urbanized as western Europe. One index of this is the value added in manufacturing and mining, not per worker, but per inhabitant.[4] If we take the American figure as 100, the 1913 index ranges all the way down to 1 for India, past such figures as 6 for Japan or 50 for Sweden. The three top temperate settlements, Canada, Australia, and New Zealand, ran 84, 75, and 66 respectively, in the same class with the three top Europeans, the U.K., Belgium, and Germany, which ran 90, 73, and 64. It is possible to grow rich by exporting agricultural products, when their prices yield a higher than European standard of living. The anomaly is Argentina, also a rich country in 1913, and as urbanized as north-west Europe, but whose index was only 23, competing with that of Italy. Argentina confirms the point we have already made about the relevance of Government policy to industrialization. Its politics were dominated by landowners and capitalists interested in the export trade, who were hostile to industrialization. It is fashionable to blame British interests, but British interests could not prevent industrialization in Canada or Australasia where they were even more fully entrenched. The essential difference

---

[4] Based on the data in League of Nations, *Industrialisation and Foreign Trade* (Geneva, 1945).

in Argentina was that the *Argentinian* interests who manipulated political power tolerated nothing that might stand in their way.

The tropical countries also responded quite well to their much more limited opportunity. Like Canada and Argentina, they had to wait until the transport revolution reached them, in the forms of finance for railway building, and of a two-thirds reduction in ocean freights, both of which come effectively only in the last quarter of the nineteenth century. Thereafter the volume of tropical exports grew as rapidly as west European industrial production, so until the First World War the two engines of growth had the same speed. The tropical countries also built themselves infrastructure, ports, secondary schools, urban water supplies, and roads, and above all began to sprout a modern managerial and administrative élite, which is the first step to modernization. Since they both continued to feed themselves and doubled their exports every 20 years, we know that real output per head was growing, and in some, like Ceylon or Ghana or Colombia, must have been growing as fast as in western Europe—say at 1·5 per cent a year. If you ask how could all this have been happening despite my dirge about the terms of trade the answer is of course that they were using idle resources of both time and land and were therefore adding to output, whatever the terms of trade. Adam Smith would have understood this too, as Professor Myint has reminded us. But though output per head was rising, it was growing from a much smaller basis, and the special relevance of the factoral terms of trade is that their low level did not allow for any large consumption of manufactures or for any major accumulation of savings.

Still, all these countries could have done better. We have already used one test of performance, namely the ratio of the industrial population to the labour force at around the year 1911. Population censuses were not in those days standardized, so figures are not strictly comparable; they are merely suggestions. One does not expect the tropical countries to have reached the 32 per cent of France, or even the 21 per cent of Austria, but the 16 per cent of Japan is not an unreasonable standard, considering how recently Japan had emerged into the world market. By comparison Mexico's 12 per cent, Egypt's 11 per cent, and Brazil's 1920 figure of 13 per cent are poor performances, though on the same level as such backward European performances as Spain's 14 per cent, or the 1921 figures of Yugoslavia and Poland which were 11 and 9 per cent respectively. India's 1911 figure of 12 per cent looks very respectable in this company, but is rather misleading since most of these are very low productivity handicraft workers; factory industry absorbed only 1 per cent of India's labour force. Indonesia's 1905 figure of 4 per cent must have been typical of a great many countries.

There was some manufacturing everywhere, in industries which are market-related like food-processing, furniture, and some building materials. The 'frontier' industry, testing competitive power, was cotton manufacture, especially of cheaper and medium yarns and fabrics. Among the countries moving up to self-sufficiency in cottons by 1913 were India, Brazil, Colombia, Mexico, and Ceylon. At the other end possibly the oddest case is Egypt, in 1913 one of the more prosperous tropical countries, which nevertheless failed to produce a single industrialist from its rich landowning and merchant classes. It is true that Lord Cromer, on instructions from London, imposed from 1901 excise duties on local manufacture equal to customs duties on imports, as the British had also done in India. But the Indian case also shows that cotton manufacturing could be competitive at low wages without protection, so this is not an adequate explanation. Neither does it apply to Venezuela, Peru, or Thailand, which were equally deficient in industrial initiatives.

Brazil was doing well in cotton manufacture. What handicapped that country's industrial development was lack of coking coal, which prevented it from using its iron ore deposits as a basis for a large iron and steel industry. Nowadays one can base an iron industry on imported coal; but in those days the much greater requirement of coal per ton of iron made that proposition uneconomic. One can also import iron or steel for fabrication into metalwares and machines, but if this has only a local market, it is confined to the types of commodities that can be produced economically on a small scale. Japan had enough coal of its own to start modern metal production well before 1913. We cannot expect as much from other beginners who lacked the basic materials.

But when all is said in extenuation, including the smallness of the agricultural surplus, a failure of will remained. The tropical countries and the backward countries of Europe shared a common obstacle: reactionary landed aristocracies more interested in tribute than in growth; vested interests more interested in cheap imports than in industrialization; governments steeped in *laissez-faire* or positively hostile to domestic manufacturing for reasons of imperial power or agricultural domination. To break this constraint they would have to evolve a modernizing élite, including both a professional and a managerial middle class, and also an industrial bourgeoisie. To their credit it must be said that they were all moving in this direction at the beginning of the twentieth century; though in the colonial countries the colour bar limited the opportunity of talented people to obtain administrative experience and other advanced skills, and therefore constrained productive capacity.

Then came a major setback, the period between 1914 and 1950, containing the First World War, the adverse 1920s, the great depression of the 1930s and finally the Second World War and its aftermath—some three and a half decades of economic disaster for tropical countries. The First World War and the political and economic dislocation which lasted into the middle 1920s reduced the growth rate of the European economy, and turned the commodity terms of trade against the tropics.[5] Taking 1913 as 100, the average of these terms of trade in the 1920s was 91, falling to 62 during the 1930s. This brought economic development in the tropics almost to a standstill. India's is the most spectacular case. Indian output per head seems to have been growing at about 1 per cent per annum over the twenty years before the First World War. After the war Indian output per head stagnated until about 1950.

Also at this time another phenomenon began to manifest itself which would become increasingly costly after the Second World War, namely the rise in the rate of natural increase of the population, which averaged less than 1 per cent per annum for the tropics as a whole in 1900, and now exceeds 2·5 per cent.

A rise in the rate of natural increase always sets people moving in the countryside. If they are farmers, the increase in family size threatens the integrity of the family farm, which may have to be broken up in succeeding generations. If they are landless labourers

[5] These are the terms of trade of tropical agricultural exports in terms of manufactures; W. A. Lewis, *Aspects of Tropical Trade 1853–1865* (Wicksell Lectures, Almquist, Stockholm, 1969).

they face either unemployment or reduced real wages. Hence the normal response to population growth is for some younger family members to leave the village. If empty cultivable land is available they move toward it; if not, they move to the towns, or seek overseas outlets. Only if the towns are stagnant and external migration is impossible do the people stay where they are and turn to more and more intensive forms of cultivation, as Mrs. Boserup has described.[6]

In western Europe in the nineteenth century, population growth led to a vast migration from the countryside to the growing European towns, to the United States, and to the countries of temperate settlement. The whole movement coincided with rapid urbanization, since the temperate countries were rich, and were urbanizing even faster than western Europe. At the end of the nineteenth century the urban population was growing at the following annual percentage rates: France 1·0, England 1·8, Germany 2·5, Australia 3·5, U.S.A. 3·7, Canada 3·9, and Argentina 5·3. Urbanization is very expensive, but it was financed by the export of capital from countries with low to countries with high urbanization rates.

For the same reasons the rise in third world populations today is accompanied by a massive flight from the country, and very high urbanization rates, running in some countries as high as 6 per cent per annum. We economists have been coming up with special explanations, such as the gap between urban and rural wages and public services, the effect of the school curriculum in driving rural adolescents into the towns, the failure of industry to use labour-intensive technology, and so on. But the truth is that this is not a special phenomenon; it is just the repetition of a nineteenth-century occurrence.

It is, however, a setback to the growth of real output per head in the less developed countries. First, capital which could be used to raise output per head is used instead to support larger numbers. Here is a spectacular example. Twenty years ago I was involved in making a development plan for Trinidad. The population was then 750,000 and is now over a million, despite a very high emigration rate. Real national income has more than doubled. I guess that if the population had remained the same, the national

---

[6] Esther Boserup, *The Conditions of Agricultural Growth* (London, Allen and Unwin, 1965).

income would now be just as large or negligibly smaller—perhaps by 5 per cent. The principal sources of income would be of the same size—the oil industry, manufacturing, the sugar plantations. The medical services would be of the same size, and secondary and higher education. The primary schools would have fewer children, and perhaps (but not necessarily) fewer teachers. Otherwise the main sectors that would be smaller are small scale-agriculture, petty retailing, and domestic service, which contribute much more to numbers than to national income. And of course there would also be fewer unemployed.

Apart from being costly in capital and in income per head, population growth also creates difficult agricultural problems. Thanks to emigration, western Europe soon reached the stage where rural populations ceased to grow. But the third world has no outlet for emigration, and cannot manage the 8 to 10 per cent per annum rates of urbanization which would be needed to keep their rural populations constant. They therefore have to plan for their rural populations to continue to grow rapidly for the next several decades. Moreover, they need the bodies in agriculture. Germany could keep its agricultural population constant because the growth rates of population and of agricultural productivity were about the same; somewhat over 1 per cent per annum. But L.D.C. populations will grow faster than agricultural productivity, so they will need more farmers.

This problem is both unprecedented and difficult. Based on the European experience our agricultural economics texts tell us how to reduce the agricultural population absolutely, for industry's benefit. They do not tell us how to increase labour utilization per acre, which is what must happen in countries short of cultivable land. Such countries must expect continual difficulty with unemployment, both urban and rural, until they can bring down their rates of natural increase.

IV

In trying to understand the slow diffusion of the industrial revolution in the tropical countries I have been concentrating on the period since 1870, when cheap transport brought them within the world market system. Other historians take their explanations further back. The 'under-development' school attributes the poverty of the tropics rather to rape and disorganization inflicted by

Europeans over previous centuries, including the looting of India in the eighteenth century and the backwash effects of cheap British imports of iron and cotton in the first half of the nineteenth century; the effects of the Culture System in Java, the disorganization induced in East and West Africa by the slave trade, and so on. The historical record is certainly grim, but Occam's razor seems not inappropriate. It is conceptually possible that the failure to respond to new opportunities after 1870 was due to destructive activities in the eighteenth century, and one can doubtless cite particular cases. But some countries did much better than others after 1870, and the division is not between those who had earlier been raped and those who had not. The performance of countries is indeed influenced by their history, but a good past does not necessarily pre-determine a good future or a bad past a bad future. That some destruction persisted beyond 1870 and even to our own day is more to the point. The worst cases have been in those parts of Africa where the colonial government set out to get Africans to work for low wages in mines or on European farms. Every device was used, from conscription of labour for private employment in the French, Belgian and Portuguese territories, through curtailing the tribal lands, prohibiting cultivation of crash crops, or imposing taxes payable only by working for cash, which were the preferred measures in British East and Southern Africa. In such cases the economic life of African farmers was disrupted, without any prospect of participating in economic expansion. The 'Ethical Policy' of Java after 1870 had similar effects. But in the broad tropical conspectus of Asia, Africa, and Latin America these are the extreme cases. The prevailing crime after 1870 was neglect rather than destruction, and neglect must loom large in our understanding of retardation.

Another school sees the major constraint on tropical countries in their dependency on north-west Europe. The term has political overtones, but is meant in an economic sense, and therefore embraces both Latin American countries, which were not politically dependent, as well as third world countries which have since achieved political independence while retaining economic dependency. Actually, though the term is now used only with respect to poor countries, the idea originated in the overseas countries of temperate settlement, whose growth depended on and descended from their exports to Europe. The first to articulate it was the Canadian historian, Harold Innis, who in 1930 was writing about the importance of 'the staple' as an engine of growth.[7] He did not use the term 'engine of growth'; we owe that to Sir Denis Robertson in 1938.[8] Meanwhile already in 1933 Sir Ronald Walker was writing about Australia's dependency on world trade, and calculating the multiplier effects on the Australian economy of the contraction in trade;[9] followed by the New Zealander Harold Belshaw in 1939 who actually called his article 'Stabilisation in a Dependent Economy'.[10]

It is not surprising that the idea of economic dependency originated in the temperate settlements since it applied much more to them than it did to the tropical countries. It was their economies whose exports averaged $60 per head in 1913, in contrast with the tropical countries' average of $4 per head. Their relationship to the industrial countries was also symmetrical. I have already made the point that the industrial countries were more or less self-sufficient in food and raw materials at the beginning of the nineteenth century, and this continued right down to the last quarter of the century. But they then tied in to the countries of temperate settlement, for wool, meat, and wheat, and there also they put their major foreign investment. In this league the tropical countries were 'also ran', and of very peripheral economic significance to the industrial countries. They on the other hand depended on the industrial countries for their meagre trade. But it was not dependency that made them poor. If dependency made the temperate settlements among the richest countries in the world, why would it have made the tropics poor? It was, in the first place, the unfavourable factoral terms of trade that kept the tropics poor. Also their failure, unlike Australia, to use their increase in wealth as a basis for some industrialization. Some who failed owed this to their colonial status; but in truth, self-governing East and Central Europe and self-governing Latin America were just about as defective in this respect as the colonial states.

[7] H. A. Innis, *The Fur Trade in Canada* (Yale University Press, New Haven, 1930).

[8] D. H. Robertson, 'The Future of International Trade', *Economic Journal* (March 1938).

[9] E. Ronald Walker, *Australia in the World Depression* (London, King, 1933), chapter vi.

[10] H. Belshaw, 'Stabilisation in a Dependent Economy', *Economic Record* (Supplement April 1939).

The proposition that participation in world trade impoverishes a developing economy rests on two pillars; either on the measures used to get land or labour for European mines and plantations at the expense of peasant production; or else on the emergence of institutional or psychological factors which inhibit a society from developing its own entrepreneurial class, working with its own conceptions in ways peculiarly appropriate to its own circumstances. The list of such factors is still unfolding. One item would be the extent to which the complex of external wholesale trade, shipping, banking, and insurance fell into the hands of expatriates, who supported each other at the expense of potential domestic competitors, who therefore could not gain entrepreneurial experience, or earn the profits from which domestic savings might have been built up. Another item is the exclusion, through colour bars or otherwise, of domestic talent from administrative positions, public or private, whether in external trade or in domestic sectors. Associated with these items would be the implanting of an inferiority complex, with either genetic or cultural overtones; or at least a propensity for destructive criticism, rather than for constructive initiatives. Another item would be the accustoming of consumers to demanding foreign goods, a preference which reduces the export multiplier and therefore diminishes the potential gain from exporting. A similar item is failure to exploit the use of domestic raw materials in place of foreign raw materials. Also, failure to develop indigenous techniques of manufacturing. There is no disputing that any of these factors is potentially damaging. Newly developing countries have been adversely affected by one or more of them, whether in Europe, Asia, Africa, or Latin America: this is part of the penalty of not being the first with innovations. On the other hand, the actual experience of these countries was rather diverse, some doing much better and others much worse than the average. It is therefore clear that these institutional and psychological factors were not lethal; they could be offset by other positive factors, namely the gains from trade, the gains from using the new technology, and the strength and political effectiveness of nationalist forces supporting industrialization. Each case must be studied separately.

The situation has been transformed, since the Second World War, with nationalism coming to its peak. For during the 1950s and 1960s import substitution was pursued vigorously all over the Third World, speeding up a trend which had, of course, begun before the First World War. Import substitution, a vast expansion of public services, and exports of minerals have been the leading factors sustaining that continual passage of tropical countries below the 50 per cent ratio in agriculture to which I have referred. But import substitution is only a temporary phase, whose limits are reached quickly. As the term implies, it depends on the purchasing power generated by exports. Any factor which keeps the value of exports low—including poor terms of trade—diminishes the scope of import substitution.

v

Let me return to my starting-point. The industrial revolution in north-west Europe and the United States offered the rest of the world not one opportunity but two; an opportunity to follow the example by applying the new technology and new systems of organization in agriculture and industry; and an opportunity to trade. The opportunity to trade was substantial for temperate countries, but marginal for tropical countries. The fundamental weakness of the tropical countries was that they concentrated on the trade option instead of taking up the challenge to revolutionize their agricultural and industrial technologies. The development of the tropical countries does not have to depend on supplying materials to others. For they could, like those same others, develop by modernizing themselves.

The Europeans modernized themselves by changing their agriculture and their industry simultaneously. The fact that both happened together is important. The farm surplus both feeds the towns and also yields the farmers the income with which to purchase the industrial product. The obstacle to tropical development on these lines has been the failure to improve productivity in food. This is not due to wickedness on the part of imperial governments. The capitalists needed food for their Indian and Chinese plantation workers, and would have been glad to get it cheaply. The fact is that tropical soils are rather difficult to manage—they are baked by months of sunshine, then leached by torrential rains. Also, in the absence of a winter, which controls temperate pests and diseases, the enemies of tropical plants and animals multiply throughout the year. It will take massive research to lick these problems, and the institutions for this purpose have only recently been created.

If agricultural productivity is constant, one can expand the industrial sector only by exporting manufactures to pay for the food and raw materials which it consumes. This, therefore, was a further option open to the tropical countries. India opened it up in the late nineteenth century with exports of cotton and jute yarns and fabrics. But it is only during the 1960s that tropical exports of manufactures have become significant. They have been the fastest growing sector of tropical trade, averaging about 10 per cent per annum, and are already about 20 per cent of tropical exports. European economists have been telling the tropical countries for half a century that their comparative advantage lies in agriculture, but this seems not to be true. Anybody can learn the skills of manufacturing, and both capital and entrepreneurship are highly mobile. But agriculture depends on natural environment, and it is by no means obvious that the tropical environment is better suited to food production than the temperate environment. Generalizations are misleading. Some well watered parts of the tropics are potential Denmarks or New Zealands. On the other hand perhaps as many as 40 per cent of tropical farmers live in areas which are marginal to agriculture, because their rainfall is inadequate or too variable, especially in the Indian subcontinent, and on the fringes of the African deserts. Pending a major breakthrough in dry-farming which is not yet in sight, the agricultural prospects of such areas are bleak.

In any case, agricultural raw materials can no longer serve the tropical countries as an engine of growth. The 3 to 4 per cent per annum rise in demand for such commodities suited the leisurely development pace of the end of the nineteenth century. Nowadays economies grow much faster, but the growth rate of this particular trade has remained more or less the same. And since the tropical countries have been increasing their productive capacity, and opening up their hinterlands with better transport facilities, the terms of trade for such products relative to manufactures moved sharply downwards from the second half of the fifties, averaging in the 1960s as low as 85 per cent of 1913. If the tropics are to continue their 5 to 6 per cent growth rate, they must seek an engine with a faster pulse.

World trade in manufactures offers this opportunity. The

character of this trade has changed dramatically since the Second World War. For seventy years (1880 to 1950) the share of manufactures in world trade was constant at around 40 per cent, and this trade grew in volume at the same rate as the trade in primary products. But now the trade in manufactures grows twice as fast as the trade in primary products; and in a quarter of a century has risen from 40 to 60 per cent. The tropics cannot grow rapidly through international trade unless they capture their share of the trade in manufactures.

They are being helped in this by a structural change which is occurring in the advanced industrial countries themselves, namely the approaching end of dualism in their labour markets. Let me digress on this for a moment.

The continuation of near zero population growth and full employment brought tension to the labour markets of the advanced industrial countries in the 1950s and 1960s. These are still dual markets, in the sense that there are aristocratic jobs and poorly paid jobs. Rapid expansion of the aristocratic jobs was at the expense of the poorly paying sectors, where shortages developed. Countries ran short of bus conductors, police, agricultural workers, hotel and laundry workers, domestic staff, nurses, and other traditionally low-paid workers.

Three reactions follow. One is to mechanize and reorganize these low-paid sectors. Agriculture is mechanized; policemen are taken off the beat; offices are computerized; shops turn to self service; nurses acquire aides; household equipment releases more wives into the labour market, and so on. But if growth rates of 3 per cent per head and more persist, the relentless expansion of the higher-paid occupations continues to drain the low-paid sectors, and the shortages persist.

The next stage is emigration from the under-developed countries to meet these shortages—Indians, Pakistanis, and West Indians to Britain; Turks, Italians, and Yugoslavs to Germany; and into the Northern States of the U.S.A. blacks from the South, Puerto Ricans, Mexicans, and a flood of illegal emigrants. These emigrant flows have produced resistance everywhere from the aristocrats of the labour market, not primarily because of the threat to the higher wage levels, but for other reasons. One set of reasons has to do with pressure on other resources, above all on scarce housing, but also on places in schools, hospitals, and other public facilities. Another set is the antagonism spawned by cultural differences—language, religion, dress, eating habits, noise levels, and so on—exacerbated by race prejudice where race is involved, but almost as powerful even where there is no racial difference (e.g. the South Europeans in Western Europe). Hence already by 1970 powerful voices in Western Europe were calling for an end to emigration.

A third way of coping with the shortage of low-paid labour is to invest in manufacturing industry in low-wage countries, and import the product. This is a new departure, full of promise for the tropics. The purpose of nineteenth-century foreign investment was to facilitate the export of primary products. Indeed industrial countries went to great pains to shut out imports of manufactures from low-wage countries, and as Professor Balassa showed, even after the Kennedy round the tariffs of industrial countries on the kinds of manufactures imported from developing countries were much higher than the tariffs on goods they imported from each other. European and American investment in the developing countries to produce manufactures for European and American markets is a phenomenon of the second half of the twentieth century, responding in part to the drying up of the reservoirs of unskilled low-wage labour in the industrial countries which had persisted even over a century and a half of economic development.

Currently the tide is moving this way; the barriers to the export of manufactures from less developed countries are falling. If the industrial countries did not pursue this option, and did not let in low-wage emigrants, and continued to grow at 3 per cent per head, the dualism of their labour market would at last come to an end. All workers would be paid according to competence. Conceivably this would not affect profits adversely, but more probably it would, since the factors preventing aristocratic wages from rising even faster would have been removed.

From the standpoint of the less developed countries this option begins as another kind of dependency, adding low-wage exports of manufactures to low-wage exports of primary products. Even this is not to be despised, where rapid population growth has pushed unemployment beyond tolerable limits. Still, is there no way to break out of unfavourable factoral terms of trade? Simply to raise productivity in the exporting sectors (whether manufacturing or agriculture) does not do the trick, if exporters' wages remain tied to low-productivity in food; since export prices then fall *pari passu* with rising productivity. If tropical populations were small they could, in the present context, move out of agriculture into manufacturing, and raise their productivity and earnings to temperate levels. But since tropical populations are large and, thanks to population growth, will for decades be increasing in the agricultural sectors, there are only two ways of improving their factoral terms of trade—either to break the link between earnings from exports and productivity in food, or to raise productivity in food. The first of these is hardly likely on a world-wide basis; all commodity schemes so far have foundered on the rock that an income differential brings out more supplies; and the propensity of manufactures to move from low-wage centres to lower-wage centres has already been demonstrated. Ultimately the tropical world must complete its industrial revolution with a green revolution, on the original pattern. The option to grow by example has always been more important than the option to grow by trade.

COMMENT

by H. Myint*

According to Sir Arthur Lewis:

The industrial revolution in north-west Europe and the United States offered the rest of the world not one opportunity but two; ... to follow the example by applying the new technology and new systems of organization in agriculture and industry; and an opportunity to trade ... The fundamental weakness of the tropical countries was that they concentrated on the trade option.

Instead, they should have pursued a 'balanced-growth' policy of simultaneously expanding the output of their domestic agriculture and domestic industry so that the farm surplus could both feed the towns and yield the farmers the income with which to purchase the industrial product. This was the true 'example' set before them (p. 152). There is also a further reason why the tropical countries should concentrate on raising their productivity

* London School of Economics.

in food: this is the only method open to them to improve their factorial terms of trade and attain a satisfactory rate of growth. 'Simply to raise productivity in the exporting sectors (whether manufacturing or agriculture) does not do the trick, if exporters' wages remain tied to low-productivity in food; since export prices then fall *pari passu* with rising productivity' (pp. 155–56).

Professor Lewis's paper raises the fundamental question whether it is satisfactory for the purposes of economic analysis and policy to draw a sharp contrast between the opportunity for international trade and the opportunity for domestic economic development as though they were mutually exclusive alternatives. In this note, I hope to show that Adam Smith had much that is relevant to say on this question.

Smith was a free trader but he also appreciated the need to strengthen the domestic economic base at the early stages of economic development. Professor Lewis can derive support from Smith's dictum that:

When the capital of any country is not sufficient for all those three purposes, in proportion as a greater share of it is employed in agriculture, the greater will be the quantity of productive labour which it puts into motion within the country; as will likewise be the value which its employment adds to the annual produce of the land and labour of the society. After agriculture, the capital employed in manufactures puts into motion the greatest quantity of productive labour . . . that which is employed in the trade of exportation has the least effect of any of the three. (WN ed. Cannan (1930), i. 346; II. v. 19.)

Perhaps it is also salutary to remind the modern development economists that the doctrine of 'balanced growth', put forward as a great discovery during the nineteen-fifties, was something of a commonplace in Book III of the *Wealth of Nations*:

It is the surplus produce of the country only, or what is over and above the maintenance of the cultivators, that constitutes the subsistence of the town, which can therefore increase only with the increase of this surplus produce. (WN 356; III. i. 2.)

The town is a continual fair or market to which the inhabitants of the country resort, in order to exchange their rude for manufactured produce. It is this commerce which supplies the inhabitants of the town both with the materials of their work and the means of their subsistence. The quantity of their finished work which they sell to the inhabitants of the country necessarily regulates the quantity of the materials and provisions which they buy. Neither their employment nor subsistence, therefore, can augment but in proportion to the augmentation of the demand from the country for finished work; and this demand can augment only in proportion to the extension of improvement and cultivation. (WN 357–8; III. i. 4.)

While Smith appreciated the importance of domestic balanced growth, he put forward two good reasons to show that the extension of foreign trade and the promotion of domestic economic development are complementary rather than competitive. (i) The division of labour is limited by the extent of the market, and foreign trade, by enabling a country to overcome the narrowness of the home market, raises its productivity by promoting a greater degree of division of labour and specialization. Smith viewed this fundamental principle as operating at successive levels: at the level of the local markets within the manufacturing sector; at the intersectoral level between agriculture and manufacture; and finally at the level of international trade. Thus even a country like China, the size of whose home market Smith believed to be 'not inferior to the market of all the different countries of Europe put together', could still improve its productive powers through an extension of foreign trade (WN ii. 178–9; IV. ix. 41). (ii) Foreign trade serves as the medium through which new commodities and technologies are introduced to different countries.

Smith's understanding of the interrelation between foreign trade, domestic manufacturing, and domestic agriculture is illustrated by his analysis of the two different ways in which the manufactures 'fit for distant sale', i.e. the export market, have been introduced into a country:

Sometimes, they have been introduced . . . by the violent operation, if one may say so, of the particular merchants and undertakers, who established them in imitation of some foreign manufactures of the same kind. Such manufactures, therefore, are the offspring of foreign commerce . . .

At other times, manufactures for distant sale grow up naturally, and as it were of their own accord, by the gradual refinement of those household and coarser manufactures which must at all times be carried on even in the poorest and rudest countries. Such manufactures are generally employed upon the materials which the country produces, and they seem frequently to have been first refined and improved in such inland countries . . . at a considerable distance from the sea coast, and sometimes even from all water carriage . . . The manufacturers first supply the neighbourhood, and afterwards, as their work improves and refines, more distant markets. For though neither the rude produce, nor even the coarse manufacture, could, without the greatest difficulty, support the expense of a considerable land carriage, the refined and improved manufacture easily may . . . Such manufactures are the off-spring of agriculture. (WN i. 379, 380, 381; III. iii. 19, 20.)

If one accepts (as I do) Adam Smith's view of the mutual interaction between foreign trade and domestic economic development, Professor Lewis's antithesis between 'the trade option' and the option of domestic balanced growth seems to be overdrawn. It has contributed to a somewhat simplistic view both of the past experiences of the advanced countries and the present-day policy choices open to the underdeveloped countries. Professor Lewis seems to argue as though the industrial revolution in Western Europe and North America took place purely on the basis of balanced growth within a closed economy without any assistance from international trade; whereas the typical pattern of successful economic development seems to be characterized both by an expansion of agricultural output and by an expansion of exports. This seems to be true, not only for the pioneers of the industrial revolution but also for the followers, notably Japan and currently for Taiwan. Even if it is debatable whether or not one should regard foreign trade as 'the engine of growth', it would be difficult to ignore its humbler role as the 'handmaiden' of growth, serving as a check on the appropriateness of new industries by keeping domestic prices and costs in touch with external prices and costs.[1]

Turning now to the policy options open to the present-day underdeveloped countries, it is not clear why these countries should have to give up their 'trade option' in order to raise productivity in their domestic agriculture and domestic industry. In many cases it would seem quite feasible for them to raise domestic labour productivity by appropriate investment policies (or simply by reversing some of the discriminatory policies pursued against the agricultural sector) while maintaining a fairly liberal trade policy. The trade option and the domestic development

[1] I. B. Kravis, 'Trade as a Handmaiden of Growth: Similarities between the Nineteenth and Twentieth Centuries', *Economic Journal* lxvii (December 1970).

option would be mutually exclusive only when it is maintained that the latter requires to be pursued in a regime of autarky behind a wall of tariff and other trade restrictions, protecting both domestic industry and domestic agriculture. It is not clear how far Professor Lewis is prepared to move towards a policy of autarky in the pursuit of domestic balanced growth.

Finally we may touch briefly on Professor Lewis's ingenious argument that the underdeveloped countries would not be able to raise their per capita incomes merely by raising their productivity in the export sectors so long as wages in the export industries are tied to the low labour productivity in food production. This may be looked upon as a variant of the original 'Lewis model' in which the export sector instead of the domestic manufacturing sector is confronted with a horizontal labour supply curve from the agricultural sector. Professor Lewis now seems to be arguing that the upward turning-point in the labour supply curve will be perpetually pushed back by the high rate of population growth and that the only remedy is to shift the horizontal labour curve bodily upwards by raising domestic food productivity. This would raise the level of per capita income and the supply price of labour to the export sector; and, given conditions of constant costs, this would improve the factorial terms of trade of the country. As we have noted, successful economic development seems to be associated both with a rise in agricultural productivity and with an expansion of exports. It is clear that a rise in agricultural productivity has a vital part in economic development. But what is not clear is whether its function is to raise the wage level and improve the terms of trade (as Professor Lewis maintains) or to *prevent* wages from rising so as to sustain the country's competitive position in the export market. It may also be questioned whether a rise in agricultural productivity, while a necessary condition, is a sufficient condition for rapid economic growth, particularly for the majority of the underdeveloped countries whose domestic markets are small, and whether these countries would not need to rely on export expansion to overcome the narrowness of the home market. Given these considerations, it is not obvious why the underdeveloped countries should have to choose between the option for international trade and the option for domestic economic development instead of sensibly keeping both options open.

COMMENT

by Ian G. Stewart*

First and foremost let me express admiration for the grand, imaginative sweep of the paper, its comprehensive range, its penetrating analysis, its acute observation of historical events and economic contrasts. Surely Adam Smith would have approved so impressive and masterful an approach to the question why some nations have remained much less wealthy than others.

With the main conclusion and tenor of the paper I am very much in agreement—'the option to grow by example has always been more important than the option to grow by trade'. It would seem to agree with Harry Johnson's cogent dictum that 'fundamentally, the process of initiating self-sustaining economic growth is a process of effecting internal social and economic changes. The external trading environment may be influential in determining the relative difficulty of the process, but it is not crucial'.[1] Sir Arthur Lewis's reference to 'a failure of will' to 'reactionary landed aristocracies more interested in tribute than in growth' and the failure 'to evolve a modernizing élite, including both a professional and a managerial middle class, and also an industrial bourgeoisie' all accord with an orthodox, perhaps a conventional, mainstream of developmental wisdom. Especially vital, and I agree absolutely, is the requirement that 'ultimately the tropical world must complete its industrial revolution with a green revolution'—that agricultural productivity be raised somehow. The World Bank seems in recent years to have come more and more to this view, having previously regarded loans to agriculture as a financial abyss.

I confess that I am less than wholly convinced about the strand in the argument which deals with population growth, migratory movements of labour, and particularly the effects of frustrated immigration. Nineteenth-century, even twentieth-century data on population changes are often hard to come by or downright unreliable for many of the less developed areas, so that the influence of comparatively recent population changes tends to loom largest

---

* University of Edinburgh.
[1] Harry G. Johnson, *Economic Policies Towards Less Developed Countries* (Brookings Institute, 1967), chapter iii, 65.

in the neo-Malthusian calculation. But Western Europe's population experienced rapid growth in periods of the eighteenth and nineteenth century, with arguably more stimulus than hindrance to the emergence of new industrial and agrarian methods. We are led back to the failure of productivity, notably in agriculture, to keep pace with mounting populations in tropical countries. Moreover the demographic patterns to be found on the African continent differ markedly from the Indian and Chinese reservoirs of labour, yet Indian and Chinese real incomes can scarcely be any lower than those found, e.g. in Upper Volta or in Ethiopia.

I find more difficulty in following the argument (on pp. 142 and 143 of the paper) concerning 'the factoral terms of trade available to the tropics' taken in conjunction with the just price. To the extent that the barter, or commodity terms of trade offer more to the Nigerian peasant producer than the 750 lb. of grain per acre available at home, he can by free international trading escape from the trap of low food output, i.e. can consume at a higher level than his cousin growing food nearby. Opportunity cost valuations are nearly always under-estimations, either because factors are specific and earn rents or because there are 'vents for surpluses' through international or inter-regional exchanges in response to opportunity cost differences. The commodity terms of trade have not tended to put primary producers at a disadvantage, and there are reasons for adding that factoral terms of trade may diffuse productivity gain from the more technologically advanced countries to their (tropical) customers. It is a little difficult therefore to appreciate the 'fundamental sense in which the leaders of the less developed world denounce the current international economic order as unjust, namely that the factoral terms of trade are based on opportunity cost and not on the principle of equal pay for equal work'.

Sir Arthur invokes the medieval doctrine of the just price and by implication the just wage. I cannot resist quoting Gray's remark that 'here indeed is a very fine hare which, with no obvious asthmatic symptoms, is still gallantly breasting the uplands, pursued from afar by a great company of short-winded metaphysicians and economists'.[2] To rub the point home Gray goes on 'By the just wage was meant that rate of remuneration which was required to

[2] Sir Alexander Gray, *The Development of Economic Doctrines* (Longman Green, London, 1941), 51.

enable the worker to live decently in the station of life in which he was placed'!

This is picking on a point which is not central to Sir Arthur Lewis's argument, and I return in conclusion to full agreement with his view that agricultural progress is essential if tropical countries are to flourish, tempered by his observation that for some areas comparative cost advantage may lie with the production of consumer durables.

6

Mercantilism and Free Trade Today

BY J. MARCUS FLEMING*

INTRODUCTION

WHEN mercantilism is spoken of in a modern context it is commonly treated as embracing almost any departure from freedom of international trade. Piety, as well as prudence, suggests that I give the concept a somewhat narrower interpretation. The father of political economy, in whose honour we are met here, traced the various manifestations of mercantilist policy, which admittedly embraced most of the breaches of free trade practice of which he disapproved, to a single root in the fallacious ideas which the mercantilists entertained about money and the balance of payments. This is perhaps fortunate for me since the limitations of my own professional experience suggest that I should focus most of my remarks about modern mercantilism on those aspects of commercial policy most closely related to a balance of payments rationale.

Adam Smith treated mercantilism as a *system* of political economy.[1] Those who have researched in depth the economic policy prescriptions of merchants and others in the period of pre-industrial capitalism have naturally discerned a great many strands of thought, not all of which can be woven together into anything as unified as a system. To me, however, it appears that Smith isolated, quite successfully, the dominant feature of the ideology underlying the practices he wished to attack. For, of course, he was quite aware that mercantilist doctrine was a way of rationalizing, as being in the general interest, policies whose main

* Late Deputy Director of the Research Department of the International Monetary Fund. Mr. Fleming died on 3 February, 1976. His paper was read at the Conference by Mr. J. J. Polak, Economic Counsellor of the I.M.F.
[1] Book IV of the *Wealth of Nations*, in which mercantilism is discussed, is headed 'Of Systems of Political Economy'.

motivation lay in special interest, notably the desire of merchants and manufacturers to monopolize the home market. The core of the doctrine, as presented by Smith, was that a country could only enrich itself by acquiring the monetary metals, and that the way to acquire these—for a country without gold and silver reserves— was by measures of commercial policy, such as tariffs, export bounties, colonial preferences, and the like, designed to achieve a favourable balance of trade. Heckscher has tried to find an additional reason for the advocacy of a favourable balance of trade in what he calls the 'fear of goods', but where it is an exchange of goods and money that is in question it is not altogether easy to distinguish the desire to import fewer goods from a desire to import more money.[2] Perhaps the writers Heckscher had in mind thought of a favourable balance of trade as contributing to increased production, employment, and profits in the country without thinking of its influence being mediated through its effects on the money stock. If so, it prefigures a distinction which later became important in Keynesian theory between the direct influence of the foreign balance on the income flow and its indirect influence via the supply of liquidity.

Smith has been accused with some justice of exaggerating the extent to which the mercantilists identified money and wealth, though he is explicitly aware that they do not always do this, and mentions at least one other reason for which they recommend the accumulation of bullion, namely, to serve as a means of paying for foreign wars. Schumpeter[3] goes so far as to say that the mercantilists never equated money and wealth, but in the next breath he admits that they very often do imply that the export surplus or deficit is the only source of gain or loss for a nation, which comes to very much the same thing. However, it is probably true that Smith does not adequately explain the reasons why the acquisition of money or bullion appeared so desirable to mercantilists. Viner[4] gives a much fuller explanation, citing not only the role of bullion as a symbol of wealth, an emergency reserve, and a store of wealth, but also as a means to bringing about lower interest rates, more

[2] See E. Heckscher, *Mercantilism* (London, Allen and Unwin, 1935), Part IV, chapter 1.

[3] J. A. Schumpeter, *History of Economic Analysis* (London, Allen and Unwin, 1954), chapter 7, 361.

[4] J. Viner, *Studies in the Theory of International Trade* (New York, Harper, 1937).

active trade, greater output, and higher employment in a country. In what follows I shall lean a good deal on these particular elements in mercantilist thought.

To the practices of interventionism in commercial policy, practices which he treated under the rubric of the mercantile system, Adam Smith opposed his own philosophy of free trade. Several aspects of Smith's presentation of this doctrine are worth mentioning.

(1) Free trade is advocated in its unilateral form. Apart from consideration of defence it is assumed to serve the national interest as well as that of the international community.

(2) While Smith paid due regard to the virtues of free trade in bringing about the most advantageous distribution of labour and capital among alternative uses or employments, his special contribution was his emphasis on the role played by international trade in promoting a more intensive division of labour and a consequent rise in productivity through the opening up of new or wider markets.

(3) While very sensitive to the importance of giving employment, Smith regards the level of employment as determined by the supply and distribution of capital and is not responsive to mercantilist views as to the importance of monetary demand generated by a favourable balance of trade.

(4) Smith does not examine the question of freedom of capital movement, as distinct from freedom of trade. Had he done so he would doubtless have supported it from a cosmopolitan standpoint; but his own reasoning about the link between capital and employment would have made it difficult for him to support it in all circumstances from a national standpoint.

I do not propose to dwell on the triumph of free trade in Britain in the first half of the nineteenth century or what Viner called the intermission in the reign of mercantilism from 1846 to 1916.[5] Classical economics from David Hume onwards triumphed over the grosser fallacies of the mercantilists and revealed the attempt to accumulate money and treasure through a favourable balance of trade as a self-frustrating exercise, detracting from, rather than contributing to, the national wealth. Moreover, free trade chimed in with the interests of Britain as the pioneer industrial country,

[5] Op. cit., chapter 2, 118.

while the success of British industry conferred prestige abroad on the free trade ideas associated with that success.

When protectionism outside Britain revived in the form of higher tariffs later on in the nineteenth century, it was at least ostensibly on the basis of arguments that were far from absurd in the light of economic theory—industrial protectionism based on Friedrich List's elaboration of the infant-industry argument, and agrarian protectionism evoked by the rapid cheapening of ocean transport and justified on social or on military grounds that Adam Smith might not have rejected entirely out of hand.

Today, only a few disparate strands of the true mercantilist ideology survive. Gold still retains its role as a store of value for monetary authorities: less, however, as a war chest, or even as a means of securing essential supplies for a country in an emergency, than as a form of assets that is expected to rise in value in the long run relative to currencies. It remains to be seen whether its attractiveness will persist if its value is no longer steadied by the action of central banks but fluctuates according to demand and supply on the market.

A favourable balance of payments and a favourable balance of trade continue to be regarded as desirable, but this desire is no longer based on any confusion of money and wealth. It is, however, connected, if somewhat loosely, with one of the objectives entertained by some of the mercantilists, namely that of securing a sufficiently expansive development of money demand.

BALANCE OF PAYMENTS RESTRICTIONS

This brings me to the particular manifestation of modern economic policy that is most strongly reminiscent of mercantilist ideas and to which I shall largely confine my attention in this paper, namely, the use of restrictions on trade and payments for what are called balance of payments reasons. Such restrictions have usually taken a quantitative form—import licensing, quotas, exchange restrictions, tourist allowances, and the like—but sometimes also the form of advance import deposits, multiple exchange rates, or even of import duties. The essence of the balance of payments motivation for such measures is the desire to avoid running out of reserves, so as not to be placed before a choice of evils, the choice, namely, between curtailing demand, output, employment, and profits and allowing the exchange rate to depreciate. The first horn of this dilemma entered into the thinking of some of the true mercantilists, the second scarcely at all, since the option of depreciation was open to countries in the days of a metallic monetary system only through the cumbersome mechanism of a debasement of the coinage. Such debasements came to an end in England after the Tudor period. The option became much easier and more tempting after paper had replaced metal as a circulating medium and the monetary metals had been collected into central bank vaults.

It should be added that, though even in modern times the balance of payments justification has sometimes served as a screen for other motivations—protection of special interests, or social or developmental policies—this is much less true than during the mercantilist period proper. Special interests have found other rationalizations for the policies they advocate, and it is not so much from merchants and manufacturers as from politicians, bureaucrats, and occasionally economists that the pressure to apply such restrictions has come.

The inter-war period[6]

Balance of payments restrictions came to the fore during the inter-war period for two main reasons: highly disturbed conditions of international trade and capital movement, and the growth of rigidities in the internal cost structure impeding the correction of international disequilibria.

In the early 1920s, balances of payments in eastern, central, and part of western continental Europe were subjected to tremendous strains as a result of the carving up of new states out of old empires, the strongly resisted attempt to exact high reparations, and above all the development of hyper-inflation in many countries where public finances had broken down. For the most part,

---

[6] On balance of payments restrictions in the inter-war period, see various League of Nations publications, particularly *Report on Exchange Control* (1938); *Quantitative Trade Controls: Their Cause and Nature* (1943); *International Currency Experience* (1944). Also Margaret S. Gordon, *Barriers to World Trade* (New York, Macmillan, 1941), H. Ellis, *Exchange Control in Central Europe* (Cambridge, Mass., Harvard University Press, 1941), and J. Viner, *Trade Relations between Free-Market and Controlled Economies* (Geneva, League of Nations, 1943).

however, these strains were taken, not by trade and capital restrictions, but by exchange depreciations. The ex-enemy countries were limited in their freedom to raise tariffs and the techniques of exchange control had not then been perfected. Nevertheless, in Germany and other countries of central and eastern Europe, import restrictions set up during the First World War were retained in order to slow down the depreciation of currencies and thus to avoid the extra fillip to inflation and the deterioration in the terms of trade that were found to result from exchange depreciation.

Another factor making for balance of payments disequilibria during the 1920s was, of course, the determination of the United Kingdom and one or two other countries to restore their currencies to their pre-war parities with gold and the dollar. The difficulties resulting from the overvaluation of sterling were mitigated by the ability of the United Kingdom, as a reserve centre, to finance part of its deficits by accumulating reserve liabilities and by attracting private short-term funds from abroad through a tight interest rate policy. Nevertheless, the high resulting level of unemployment created a climate in which Britain's free trade tradition was bound to be undermined and protectionist sentiment was bound to grow. In the circumstances, it is a tribute to the strength of the tradition that the sentiment grew so slowly and manifested itself at first in such comparatively trivial forms as the McKenna duties, safeguarding duties, and the like.

A more general international factor tending to intensify payments difficulties in the 1920s was the scarcity of real reserves in the world. This was attributable in part to an increase in the demand for reserves, associated with enhanced instability in balances of payments, and in part to a decline in their rate of growth due to a rise in the prices of other goods and services relative to gold. The scarcity was lessened by the spread of the practice of holding reserves in the form of dollars and sterling, but this afforded only partial relief. Through the pervasive influence which it exercised in favour of monetary restraint, reserve stringency contributed to keeping unemployment relatively high and exercised a downward pressure on primary product prices even during the so-called boom of the late twenties. It is not surprising, therefore, that tariff protectionism, particularly in the agricultural sphere, should have tended to become more severe at this time.

It was in the 1930s, with the advent of the Great Depression, that balance of payments restrictions first appeared on a massive scale and in a variety of forms. With the collapse of primary product prices and the heavy unemployment that developed everywhere, countries become strongly desirous to have more favourable balances of payments on overall and especially on current account. Keynesian thinking reflected and encouraged a tendency to think of a favourable current account as a means to higher employment, and Keynes himself advocated revenue import duties prior to the devaluation of 1931.[7] Naturally enough, depression conditions also stimulated protectionism in the field both of industry and, particularly, agriculture.

As in the early 1920s, severe payments disequilibria developed, intensified by 'hot money' movements of funds out of countries where bank failures or currency devaluations were feared. The healthful flow of capital which had taken place from the United States to Europe in the later 1920s ceased and was reversed.

An interesting correlation—though not a perfect one—is observable between the extent to which countries subjected to balance of payments pressures resorted to restrictions and the nature of the currency experience they had gone through a decade before. By and large, countries like Germany which had had hyper-inflations were so impressed by the past association of exchange depreciation with inflation that they clung to an overvalued exchange rate despite the severity of their depression and had resort to the severest type of exchange restriction. France and other gold bloc countries, most of which had had milder inflations in the 1920s, adhered for a number of years to a fixed rate before they devalued; they mostly used import restrictions but not exchange controls.[8] And countries like Britain and the Scandinavians which, though they had experienced free floating and not experienced inflation, relied predominantly on exchange depreciation or devaluation, or pegging on a depreciated currency, together with the use of tariff measures, with but little in the way of quantitative restrictions. Cutting across this classification, however, many primary

[7] See the Report of the MacMillan Committee (Committee on Finance and Industry, Report, Addendum 1, 1931).

[8] Switzerland and the Netherlands were also members of this group, though they had no inflationary experience of their own. However, as close neighbours of countries that had suffered greatly from inflation they may have been particularly open to a 'demonstration effect'.

producing countries, in Latin America and elsewhere, were obliged by the collapse of their export prices to have resort both to exchange depreciation and exchange control.

The difference among countries in their attitudes towards exchange depreciation and the differences in the timing of their resort to it contributed greatly to the payments disequilibria which developed during the 1930s and particularly to the volume of disequilibrating hot money flows. The depreciation of one set of currencies made things more difficult for the countries left stranded with overvalued currencies. Nevertheless, the new-found flexibility of exchange rates probably helped to set the world as a whole on the path to recovery from the depression in two ways, first because the floaters and devaluers felt freer in adopting expansionary policies, and second because the rise in the currency and commodity value of gold helped to relieve the reserve stringency from which the world had been suffering.

As indicated, the spectrum of mercantilist devices more or less related to a balance of payments rationale was wide indeed. They ranged from general tariffs and Ottawa Agreements in Britain— belated manifestations of protectionism and economic imperialism for which the basic excuse of cost rigidity no longer existed after 1931—through import quotas in the gold bloc countries to exchange control in central Europe and Latin America.

Exchange control—the restriction of international payments, exchange transactions, and transfers of domestic balances among non-residents and the enforced surrender of exporters' earnings of foreign exchange—constituted the big contribution of the 1930s to the techniques of intervention. It had two special characteristics. It enabled governments to influence not merely trade flows but also, and indeed especially, capital flows. And it supplied a financial ambiance which provided an incentive for discrimination and for the balancing of international transactions on a bilateral basis. By this method residents could be prevented from exporting, foreigners from withdrawing, capital. Moreover, by applying to import payments restrictions more stringent than were applied to imports themselves, foreign suppliers might even be induced to provide financing. Sometimes, in order to obtain transfer of debt service, even countries like Britain that did not in general apply exchange controls applied them to exchange control countries like Germany. Clearing agreements sprang up among exchange control countries or between exchange control and non-exchange control countries in which currently accruing mutual claims were offset, though one side or the other would usually have to queue up to await payment.

As time passed, blocking of export proceeds and even queuing up of exporters for settlement tended to disappear and to be replaced by bilateral arrangements under which any balances accumulating in the hands of the bilateral surplus country were held by the monetary authorities of that country. Such an arrangement gave an incentive to each country, particularly the surplus country, to exempt the other from any import restrictions it might have. In this way countries with overvalued currencies could avoid some of the curtailment of trade that would otherwise have taken place, though on a distorted and discriminatory basis. True, both sides, particularly the surplus country, also had an incentive to restrict exports to the other if alternative hard currency markets were available, but the net effect was probably liberalizing. The protection against capital outflows by exchange control and the stimulus to exports afforded by bilateral balancing arrangements enabled some exchange control countries, such as Germany, to restore employment and output, despite extreme overvaluation, in a way that countries relying on trade controls were unable to do and to an extent that few of the flexible exchange rate countries could equal.

The practice of bilateral bargaining, facilitated by the existence of quantitative restrictions and exchange controls, gave to the larger countries such as Germany and Britain that directly or indirectly were able to exploit it, the advantages of discriminating monopsony. This bargaining power was used by both countries, mainly to improve the terms of trade, but in the German case also to achieve a shift in its markets and sources of supply to nearby countries. Britain had a particularly successful fling in the 1930s. Having large import surpluses with most of the exchange control countries, she was able to force them, through the threat of imposing clearing or import restrictions, to discriminate strongly in her favour in their own import policies. Moreover, she derived additional bargaining power from her transition from virtual free trade to tariff protection, and from the expansion of her currency area resulting from the desire of many countries to peg their currencies to a depreciated pound. One of the manifestations of this success was the intensification of imperial tariff preference which took place under the Ottawa Agreement.

The post-war period[9]

The lessons of the inter-war period regarding the appropriate role of balance of payments restrictions, as assessed by the best contemporary opinion, were reflected after the war in the Articles of Agreement of the Fund and the provisions of the G.A.T.T. Controls over capital movements, deemed indispensable for dealing with hot money flows, were regarded as legitimate, and indeed encouraged. Restrictions on current payments and trade were tolerated as temporary devices only, in the absence of adequate financing, pending corrective action through exchange rate adjustment or other means, and subject to the agreement of the Fund and the G.A.T.T. Exchange rate adjustment, though preferred to restriction, was itself subject to Fund consent in order to prevent the competitive exchange depreciation, inspired by mercantilist motives, that had marked the 1930s. This was the long-term regime envisaged at Bretton Woods, but it was recognized that the balance of payments situation as it existed at the end of the war would permit only a gradual dismantling of restrictions, and this was provided for in the transitional period arrangements.

The years immediately following the Second World War were marked by a severe balance of payments disequilibrium as between the United States and one or two other Western Hemisphere countries, on the one hand, and the other industrial countries, together with most less developed countries, on the other. The war and its aftermath led to a severe undervaluation of the dollar and a situation of more or less suppressed inflation in Europe and elsewhere. Suppressed inflation and the associated shortages for a time made exchange rate adjustment seem unlikely to be effective. Moreover, balance of payments assistance on an enormous scale from the United States, though not sufficient to eliminate the

[9] On balance of payments restrictions in the post-World War II period, see the Exchange Restrictions Reports of the International Monetary Fund, *The International Monetary Fund*, *1945–1965*, ed. J. K. Horsefield (I.M.F., Washington, 1969), chapters 6 and 10 by M. G. de Vries. Also J. H. C. de Looper, 'Current Usage of Payments Agreements and Trade Agreements' and 'Recent Latin American Experience with Bilateral Trade and Payments Agreements', both in I.M.F. *Staff Papers*, vol. iv, and M. G. de Vries, 'Multiple Exchange Rates: Expectations and Experiences', *Staff Papers*, vol. xii.

disequilibrium, provided in its way a further incentive to postpone adjustment.

In such a situation some restriction of imports and capital exports was inevitable for the great majority of countries. The appropriate financial framework for this was provided by a network of bilateral payments arrangements between countries and currency areas far more extensive than anything that had existed in the 1930s. Within this framework, trade was regulated by quantitative restrictions, undertakings to supply, state trading, etc. The bilateral payments arrangements, which usually provided for limited swing credits, provided a financial incentive for a mutual relaxation of restrictions. The degree of strict bilateral balancing involved in the system was tempered in the case of the United Kingdom by the practice of freely permitting transfers of sterling earnings between soft currency countries and the individual members of the sterling area and, after 1947, by the gradual extension of such transferability on a selective basis between soft currency holders outside the sterling area. The unfortunate attempt made by the United Kingdom in 1947, on the strength of a large loan, to restore the convertibility of sterling into dollars, thus exposing its exports to non-discriminatory treatment—and to do this without devaluation, without tying up the accumulated sterling balances, and without contracting the money supply—was one that was bound to fail, and Britain returned quickly to the bilateral fold. The events of 1947 do not, as Dr. Balogh has recently alleged, mark the early collapse of the Bretton Woods arrangements, but merely reflect a premature abandonment of the transitional period safeguards.

There is no doubt that the trade discrimination inherent in the system described had the advantage, at least in the short run, of enabling useful trade to flow that might otherwise have been suppressed. The objection to it was that it might blunt the incentive for the soft currency countries to take the necessary steps to achieve the sort of adjustment of their price levels and balance of payments that would enable them to get rid of restrictions altogether.

These fears were quite natural and logical, but they were not fulfilled. For this there were a number of reasons. In the first place, sterling was forced into devaluation in 1949, and with it went the other sterling area currencies and most of the European currencies also. An overvalued currency is always in a precarious position, no matter how strong a bastion of controls may be built around it. There is always a possibility that adverse developments in world markets and speculative capital outflows may bring it tumbling down. In this case, the U.S. business recession of 1948 was enough to do the trick. Many types of outflow from Britain could be prevented by capital controls and inconvertibility, but with a trade turnover as big as that of the sterling area a relatively slight shift in the timing of trade payments was enough to bring about the exhaustion of Britain's reserves.

These devaluations were very large. Indeed, from a longer-term point of view they were probably excessive. Once brought to the point of devaluation it seemed prudent to the authorities concerned to include a safety margin. This was an early example of how the system of adjustable par values, incorporated in the Bretton Woods Agreement of 1944, was likely to work, and how difficult it was to prevent competitive depreciation. However, a good foundation was laid for the correction of the dollar shortage and the elimination of restrictions and controls.

Other factors came in to reinforce the effect of the exchange rate adjustment. First came the rapid recovery of European productivity in the 1950s and 1960s from the low levels to which it had sunk in the immediate post-war period—a recovery that was given a powerful impetus by the capital investment made possible by Marshall Aid. And finally governments did gradually learn to control excess demand and give up the cheap money ideology that had prevailed in the Dalton era. In this way it became possible to prevent the gains of devaluation and productivity growth from being swallowed up by inflation. In this some countries, such as Germany and Belgium, which had had monetary reforms involving the radical curtailment of their money stocks, led the way, and Belgium, in particular, became a relatively hard currency member of the soft currency bloc—a fact which gave rise to some trade discrimination against it within the European area.

The semi-bilateralist phase in European recovery was followed by a phase of resolute liberalization and multilateralization on a regional basis. The improvement of the balance of payments position of the European countries, the continuance of Marshall Aid, and the paternal encouragement of the E.C.A. emboldened the members of O.E.E.C., in 1950, to take the leap of adopting multilateral settlement of their bilateral imbalances, leaving settlement to be made between regional surplus and regional deficit countries. This leap would have been impossible at the time without the setting up of the European Payments Union, which enabled these settlements to be made partly in credit (which pleased the deficit countries), partly in gold or dollars (which pleased the surplus countries). The multilateralization of settlements removed the incentive for discrimination in trade policy as among the members of the E.P.U. Non-discrimination, however, might conceivably have led to some restriction of trade among the softer currency countries. That this did not happen is due, first, to the buffer of E.P.U. credit and, second, to the organized effort to remove import restrictions within the O.E.E.C. which went by the name of the liberalization programme. This effort took the form, primarily, of removal of restrictions on prescribed percentages of imports, increasing through time, in different categories.[10] Individual O.E.E.C. countries increasingly extended O.E.E.C. liberalization also to specified soft currency countries outside the O.E.E.C. area. However, this liberalization was not at first extended in equal measures to imports from the dollar area, so that the result which the founding fathers of Bretton Woods had intended to achieve by the famous 'scarce currency clause' of the Articles of Agreement of the Fund was achieved in a very indirect way through the extension of liberalization within the non-dollar world. The result, which, of course, involved a discrimination against the United States, was carried out with the backing and approval of the U.S. authorities themselves—something that appears rather remarkable in these more contentious days.

Of course, there were some, including some within the Fund, who felt misgivings lest tolerance of discrimination against the United States might prove an obstacle to the balance of payments adjustment that would permit an all-round liberalization of quantitative restrictions. But the truth was that the actions necessary for this adjustment had already taken place, and in the course of the 1950s would work out their effects.

The 1950s witnessed the crumbling of inconvertibility in the world and the dwindling of restrictions in industrial countries on imports from the dollar area. Transferability of non-dollar currencies was not extended to the dollar area, nor were non-dollar

---

[10] There was also a liberalization programme for invisibles.

currencies generally made convertible, through exchange markets, into dollars, until 1958, but before that dollar settlements within the E.P.U. had been increasing in importance and a sort of indirect convertibility had sprung up through the transit trade and the London commodity markets. Moreover, from 1955 on, the Bank of England had been intervening in the market in support of transferable sterling. All this tended to erode the distinction between 'hard' and 'soft' currencies. At the same time, both in the O.E.E.C. and in the Fund, increasing pressure was brought to bear on countries to reduce differential restrictions on dollar imports. More importantly, the 'dollar shortage', the basic disequilibrium between the United States and other industrial countries, was disappearing—though some economists in Britain found that difficult to believe, possibly because the United Kingdom with its relatively low savings and productivity growth and its high employment objectives was having recurrent difficulties in balancing its own accounts with the rest of the world. Some remnants of balance of payments restrictions on dollar imports lingered on in Europe for a few years after the restoration of convertibility, but these had virtually disappeared by the end of the decade.

Restrictions in less developed countries

The removal or even reduction of balance of payments restrictions proved much more difficult in less developed than in industrial countries. Just after the war many of the former were in a strong balance of payments position because of the balances of foreign exchange which they had accumulated and been unable to spend during the war. However, they had also accumulated a backlog of import requirements, and within a few years most of them were getting very short of foreign exchange.

A number of factors combined to bring this about. In many cases, particularly in Latin America, governments pursued lax fiscal and monetary policies, partly because they were weak in the face of special interests and partly because of the urgency of expanding development expenditure. But while pursuing this inflationary course most of these countries were unwilling to maintain their competitiveness by an adequate depreciation of their currencies. Many of them had resort to multiple exchange rates. Others resorted to severe import restrictions which, in extreme cases, extended to the importation of materials and the throttling of the economy.

The reluctance to devalue sometimes reflected financial conservatism and a fear that depreciation would worsen the terms of trade and aggravate inflation, but it was also motivated by the desire to have a balance of payments excuse for policies that facilitated the raising of revenue, the protection of import-competing industry, the diversification of exports, or the cheapening of imports of capital goods and wage goods, and thus were deemed to promote economic development and social peace. In some countries, which developed an ideology of planning and interventionism as the royal road to development, quantitative import restriction was welcomed as a technique for controlling imports and the flow of materials and thus the direction of economic activity. In such cases we can say that rather than restrictions being the consequence of balance of payments difficulties, the payments difficulties were a means to the enjoyment of restrictions.

In E.C.L.A. in the 1950s and U.N.C.T.A.D. in the 1960s a rather sophisticated doctrine was developed according to which less developed countries were deemed to suffer from balance of payments difficulties of a structural sort that could not easily be relieved by devaluation.[11] This doctrine, not without foundation in fact, postulated that, owing to the relatively low income elasticity of demand for primary products as compared with manufactures and to the substitution of natural by synthetic products, there is a tendency for primary producers, particularly the less developed ones, to experience persistently deteriorating terms of trade and persistent balance of payments difficulties. Moreover, owing to price inelasticity in the demand for their products, primary producers as a group could not relieve these difficulties by devaluation or price adjustment without an unconscionable further deterioration in their terms of trade. Initially, the conclusion drawn from this argument, the validity of which has been a matter of some controversy, was that the developing primary producers should ration foreign exchange and encourage import-competing industries through suitably devised protective measures.

[11] See 'The Economic Development of Latin America and its Principal Problems', *Economic Commission for Latin America*, U.N. (1950); R. Prebisch, 'Towards a New Trade Policy for Development', U.N. (1964); M. J. Flanders, 'Prebisch on Protectionism: An Evaluation', *Economic Journal*, lxxiv (June 1964).

Later, in the 1960s, the conclusion was rather that the advanced industrial countries should relieve the balance of payments constraint of the less developed countries through the provision of aid and the preferential treatment of imports from the latter.

Whatever advantages currency overvaluation may have for the terms of trade of primary exporting countries taken collectively—and this is rather doubtful considering the supply conditions governing many primary products—there can be little doubt that it has proved an unfortunate policy for the countries adopting it, taken individually. Indeed, when it has resulted in multiple exchange rates and still more when it has resulted in quantitative import restriction it has distorted the economies and hampered the development of the countries concerned, discouraging the production of exports and of essential goods for the home market and encouraging the costly and inefficient production of less essential manufactures. There has indeed been, over the post-war period, a marked correlation among less developed countries in the rate of growth of per capita output and the degree of reliance on market mechanisms in preference to controls.

In the case of developing countries, a major role in the struggle against inflation, overvaluation, and balance of payments difficulties has been played by the International Monetary Fund, particularly in the 1950s and 1960s. Not only was the Fund itself in a position to offer relatively cheap financial assistance in the form of 3–5 year loans and stand-by credits as a bait to the adoption of appropriate adjustment policies, but commercial bank lenders, particularly in New York, fell into the habit of making their own financial assistance to these countries contingent on the obtaining of a stand-by credit from the Fund, which added considerably to the latter's 'clout'.

Policies insisted on by the Fund as a condition for stand-bys and drawings in the higher credit tranches have generally included the imposition of quantitative limitations on the expansion of central bank credit and particularly credit to the public sector; in addition, there have usually been conditions regarding the reduction or elimination of multiple exchange rates, and the devaluation or, frequently, the floating of exchange rates. In advocating these somewhat monetarist policies, the Fund generally found itself in alliance with the central banks and the finance ministries of the countries concerned, but not always with other parts of the government.

Progress in overcoming inflation and reducing payments restrictions in developing countries was slow at first but gained speed later. The second half of the 1950s and first half of the 1960s witnessed a widespread decline in the use of bilateralism and multiple exchange rates. Bilateralism, of course, lost much of its *raison d'être*, even for less developed countries, as the currencies of trading partners became convertible: however, it revived somewhat with the growth of trading connections with Communist countries. The less developed world found it harder to dispense with import restrictions: the quantitative kind were on the whole relaxed in the 1960s but were in part replaced by more refined techniques, such as import surcharges and import deposit requirements. In some important countries in Latin America, liberalization was fostered in the 1960s by the adoption of a system of sliding parities under which exchange rates were frequently adjusted to keep pace with relative inflation. On the other hand, the emergence, in Africa, of a large number of newly independent states was followed by the appearance of balance of payments difficulties and the adoption of restrictions in areas where trade had previously been relatively free.

Dollar deficit

While the 1950s witnessed the dwindling of the dollar shortage, the extrapolation of that movement into the 1960s, reinforced by the expansionism of the Kennedy and Johnson administrations, tended to increase the payments deficits of the United States to a point which gave rise to a certain mild anxiety in that country and evoked somewhat petulant reproaches about the exportation of inflation in one or two of the surplus European countries. That the anxiety felt in the United States was mild was due to the fact that, as the ultimate reserve centre, it could rely on financing a sizeable proportion of any deficits through the dollar accumulations of other countries, besides which it was still sitting on a sizeable fraction of the world's gold. This anxiety therefore did not find expression for a long time in any sort of commercial restriction. Indeed, in the Kennedy Round the United States took the lead in promoting a notable reduction of tariff barriers. The principal form in which it expressed itself was the imposition of restrictions on the outflow of capital through such measures as the Interest Equalisation Tax, the restrictions on direct investment financed from the United States, and the voluntary programme restricting the outflow of banking funds. These restrictions, though mercantilist on one interpretation, were entirely in accordance with the ideology of Bretton Woods, and since they exempted the developing countries and Canada from their scope were offensive to nobody except certain groups in the United States itself. An additional manifestation of balance of payments anxiety in the United States in the 1960s is found in the moral pressure exerted on official holders of dollars to refrain from converting them into gold, and in the decision in 1968 to terminate the gold pool and allow the value of gold in the private market to rise far above its official value. These developments had sinister implications for the future of the Bretton Woods arrangements.

To most countries outside the United States, the U.S. deficit in the 1960s provided a welcome, if somewhat inadequate, stimulus to world reserves of foreign exchange and contributed to the prolongation of the period of economic euphoria beginning in the 1950s. However, as I said, there were one or two countries, such as Switzerland and Germany, which felt, even in the early 1960s, that they were being subjected to inflationary pressures from an undue influx of reserves. These countries adopted various techniques to restrict the inflow of capital. Whether one regards this policy as anti-mercantilistic or mercantilistic depends on whether he regards the mercantilistic preoccupation with the balance of payments as relating to the overall balance or the current account balance. By preventing capital imports, these policies reduced the need for an exchange appreciation or rise in the price level which, had they occurred, would have entailed a deterioration in the balance of trade.

In the early 1970s the overvaluation of the U.S. dollar, masked in 1969 by inflows of funds of a cyclical character, became indisputable and apparently progressive to a point that alarmed the U.S. authorities, first because of its effect on the balance of trade and second because it threatened to overstrain the gentlemen's agreement of central banks not to convert their dollar accumulations and thus to exhaust U.S. gold reserves. This situation, it will be recalled, drove the United States into putting an end to convertibility in August 1971 and effectively devaluing in December 1971 and again in February 1973. It also led them to the imposition of a temporary import surcharge on balance of payments grounds in August 1971. The primary motive of all these actions was to improve the balance of payments of the United States either directly or by inducing other industrial countries to allow their dollar exchange rates to appreciate. The reluctance shown by some of these countries, particularly in 1971, to revalue their currencies, or allow them to appreciate, probably reflected, in part, a desire to avoid a deterioration in the current account balance at a time when business was not too brisk.

The period of rather widely generalized floating of exchange rates among industrial countries, which began in February 1973, is still very young and it is uncertain how long it will last. The primary producing countries generally continue to peg their currencies to one of the principal currencies or to a composite of currencies, but even for them exchange rate flexibility has greatly increased. In the 1930s resort to exchange depreciation by one group of countries had led to the imposition of restrictions of increasing severity on the part of other countries. The more generalized application of exchange flexibility in the 1970s, however, has had a very different effect, despite the fact that the system has been exposed to one of the biggest exogenous balance of payments shocks of all time in the form of the oil price increase in December 1973. It is true that, for non-oil-producing countries *as a group*, the so-called oil deficit on current account was matched by a corresponding surplus on capital account, as the O.P.E.C. countries invested their profits abroad or accumulated reserves in currency form. Nevertheless, there was plenty of scope for massive disequilibria within the group of non-oil countries themselves, and such did indeed tend to arise. The less developed countries, in particular, though initially protected from the impact of the oil price increases by high prices for their export products, suffered in 1975 a sharp deterioration in their terms of trade *vis-à-vis* industrial countries, and this coming on top of the oil price increase has put many of them into a very difficult position.

In spite of these disturbances there has thus far been remarkably little resort to restrictions by industrial or even by primary producing countries. This has been due to a combination of circumstances. Some of the credit must go to the much-abused Euro-currency market, together with the willingness of countries to borrow where necessary from the private market. Some of it must go to the system of managed exchange rate floating which, at some cost to exchange stability in the short term, has succeeded in containing disequilibrating capital flows, and has also permitted exchange rates to adjust in the longer run to differential rates of inflation. A good deal of credit also must go to international bodies, such as the I.M.F., the O.E.C.D., the G.A.T.T., and the E.E.C., which in their various ways have co-operated to resist a spread of restrictions. The Committee of Twenty of the I.M.F., in January 1974, called upon countries to refrain from responding to the oil deficit by escalating trade restrictions or by competitive depreciation,[12] and the O.E.C.D. ministers of the principal countries have, in two successive years, adopted a pledge to this effect.[13] Special facilities were set up, inside and outside the Fund, to help countries finance the payments deficits arising out of the oil price increases, and in the administration of its oil facility, both in 1974 and 1975, the Fund has been very firm in requiring borrowers to refrain from introducing import restrictions (quantitative or otherwise) or, where this seemed unavoidable, to apply them on a strictly temporary basis.

These influences have not been able entirely to prevent a recrudescence of restrictionism, but they have succeeded in keeping it within bounds. In general the new or intensified restrictions on imports have been selective rather than general in their application, and in only a few cases have they been used as a major instrument of adjustment. There has been a noticeable increase in the use of advance import deposit requirements, notably in the case of Italy; these are intended to affect domestic liquidity as well as the balance of payments. And many countries, notably the United Kingdom, have applied restrictions on imports competing with particular industries; these are in part protective in character. Only in a few cases have restrictions been used as a major instrument of balance of payments adjustment, and then their use has avowedly been temporary. Such restrictions, if of the quantitative type, can sometimes be justified as a means of avoiding the cost-inflationary effects of a too rapid exchange depreciation.

[12] See Communiqué of the January 1974 meeting of the Committee of Twenty in Rome.
[13] See Communiqués of O.E.C.D. ministerial meetings (O.E.C.D. Press Releases of 30 May 1974 and 29 May 1975).

CONCLUSION

Many of you will probably be thinking I have a tendency to look at the world through rose-coloured spectacles. Economists usually prefer the part of Cassandra to that of Pollyanna, but I appear to have reversed that preference. I have argued that the neo-mercantilism which arose in the inter-war period and culminated immediately after the Second World War, in the form of trade and payments restrictions undertaken on balance of payments grounds, has been whittled down in the course of time into a phenomenon of relatively minor and temporary importance. Let me summarize the main reasons for this. The spread of international organization and consultation has given increased leverage to the academic arguments against restriction by making it an issue of reciprocal rather than unilateral action. The fact that the largest payments deficits have fallen on countries in an exceptionally good position to finance them has made the avoidance of restrictions somewhat easier. But the principal factor has been the increasing flexibility of exchange rates, necessitated first by the existence of national price rigidities and secondly by the phenomenal increase in the international mobility of short-term capital which restrictions were clearly unable to control. Once floating rates had been adopted as the sovereign means of keeping over-all payments in balance, the retention of restrictions for the purpose of influencing the balance of current account payments as such became more difficult to justify.

Lest I be accused of exaggerating my thesis, I would say there has been a certain disassociation of mercantilist means or measures from mercantilist ends or motivations, though each taken by itself has, in some measure, continued to flourish. As we have seen, there have been times when countries have sought to improve the balance of payments in general, not by import restriction but by over-devaluation (or non-revaluation), or to improve the balance of trade in particular by restricting capital inflows and thus holding down the exchange rate. And, of course, there have been many cases in which trade restrictions have been applied with a protectionist rather than a balance of payments motivation.

Consciousness of my limitations has prevented me from extending my review over the field of commercial policy and protectionism in general. If I had done so I might have come to conclusions almost as optimistic on that subject. Progress towards trade liberalization in that broader area may owe rather more to deliberate international co-operative action and rather less to developments in the economic environment than in the narrower sphere of balance of payments restrictions. However that may be, I believe that it would be a mistake for economists today to direct too much of their attention to the question of freedom of international transactions as a means to economic welfare. The present-day world is full of evils and horrors, even in the purely economic sphere. But they lie in the areas of excessive population growth, persistent poverty in underdeveloped countries, and the conjunction of inflation and unemployment in countries in general rather than in that of impediments to international economic integration.

COMMENT
by Herbert Giersch*

1. Marcus Fleming has written an excellent survey of balance of payments oriented trade policies in the best British tradition. The sad fact that he is no longer with us adds to the reasons why I feel that it would be inappropriate for me to submit my comments in the form of criticizing specific points. Let me, instead, try to complement the paper and expand the subject a bit by looking at Mercantilism and Free Trade Today from a different angle.

2. In order to compensate for the absolute disadvantage of being one of the first speakers, if not the first, who does not live in the English-speaking world, I must exploit my comparative advantage, which arises from the fact that the country in which I reside happens to be the country about which I am least ignorant. That country solved its balance of payments problems a quarter of a century ago after it had received good economic advice from a two-man team which included the present Chancellor of the University of Glasgow. Since then West Germany has run a balance of payments surplus for most of the time. It was accumulating reserves, and until the dollar rate became flexible in 1971 the currency was clearly undervalued. Undervaluation of the currency with all its implications is perhaps exactly what mercantilist writers and

* University of Kiel.

merchants were aiming at, and what mercantilist politicians and statesmen believed to be the best strategy for economic growth. Let me, therefore, restate the subject of my comments by calling it 'Growth Policy and Free Trade Today'.

3. How closely this subject is related to Adam Smith's *Wealth of Nations* can be inferred from the following episode. When in 1971 the D-Mark was allowed to float upwards between May and December, the Institute for which I am responsible was made intellectually responsible for the Government's bold step. We received fairly unqualified criticism from export-oriented firms and their managers. The then President of the Federation of Industries at a press conference during the I.M.F. meeting in Washington went so far as to say that Professor Schiller by letting the dollar rate decline had damaged the West German economy more than Hitler had been able to do. In a mood of despair I re-read the *Wealth of Nations*, notably the chapters on Trade Restrictions in Book IV, and I found a number of sentences which gave me relief. Two of my collaborators inserted them as answers to questions they raised in a hypothetical interview with Adam Smith which was shortly afterwards published in the somewhat less renowned West German counterpart of Britain's *Economist*, the periodical *Wirtschaftswoche* (3. 12. 71).

Let me quote some of the sentences:

That foreign trade enriched the country, experience demonstrated . . . The merchants knew perfectly in what manner it enriched themselves . . . But to know in what manner it enriched the country, was no part of their business. (WN IV. i. 10.)

Comparing an undervaluation with export bounties, my collaborators could quote as an answer:

Bounties upon exportation are . . . frequently petitioned for . . . (WN IV. v. a. 1.) [But] whatever extension of the foreign market can be occasioned by the bounty, must, in every particular year, be altogether at the expence of the home market; as every bushel of corn which is exported by means of the bounty . . . would have remained in the home market to increase the consumption, and to lower the price of that commodity. (WN IV. v. a. 8.)

Instead of bushels of corn we were tempted to say beetles of VW.

Later it is stated that:

Consumption is the sole end and purpose of all production; and the interest of the producer ought to be attended to, only so far as it may be necessary for promoting that of the consumer . . . But in the mercantile system, the interest of the consumer is almost constantly sacrificed to that of the producer; and it seems to consider production and not consumption, as the ultimate end and object of all industry and commerce. (WN IV. viii. 49.)

With regard to the fear of unemployment Smith could be quoted as follows:

The undertaker of a great manufacture, who, by the home markets being suddenly laid open to the competition of foreigners, should be obliged to abandon his trade, would no doubt suffer very considerably . . . The equitable regard, therefore, to his interest requires that changes of this kind should never be introduced suddenly, but slowly, gradually, and after a very long warning. (WN IV. ii. 44.)

4. That seemed to us to imply that floating was better than abrupt parity changes of the Bretton Woods type, and we also felt it confirmed that proposals for a pre-announced crawl, which had been advanced since 1966 and which had been rejected out of hand by most responsible men, including central bank Governor Blessing, might have received at least the blessing of Adam Smith.

5. The implication of all this is that the Bretton Woods System with its delayed parity adjustments had permitted West Germany a quasi-mercantilistic policy of export-led growth which practically ended in 1971. The West German economic development from 1951 to 1971 would have ideally matched the objectives of mercantilist writers and practitioners. But, paradoxically, the mercantilist outcome was not due to any grand mercantilist design. On the contrary, the relatively fast development was accompanied by moves towards more *laissez-faire* in the fields of foreign trade, capital movements, and migration. Between 1951 and 1971 West Germany was able to make decisive steps towards free trade and factor mobility. The necessary or sufficient condition for this was the strength of the currency or, what amounts to the same thing, a trade union behaviour which allowed industry to become and remain highly competitive in foreign and domestic markets in spite of moves towards freer trade. This wage behaviour was rewarded with some time lag by a relatively fast increase in real wages, because it contributed to a high share of investment in GNP. It also induced an inflow of foreign capital and other factors complementary to domestic labour, such as technology from the United States and unskilled labour from southern Europe.

6. The example shows that an industrial growth policy need not be mercantilistic in the traditional sense. It need not introduce tariffs and import restrictions, to raise the marginal efficiency of investment in selective industries, if the supply of labour is sufficiently elastic and mobile, thanks to immigration or a more or less selective importation of guest workers. It does not require strong interference with relative prices and value productivities, if the political and legal system is sufficiently stable to limit the political risks of long-term industrial investments. It does not depend upon colonies, if there is a sufficiently free access to foreign raw material supplies and to export markets for manufactures. It does not need a large military (naval) base (or whatever the British Navigation Act was meant to protect) if the country has given up its military independence in favour of a more economical international security system. In fact, the destruction of the military system after the war increased the supply of entrepreneurs, after former officers had received a business training in appropriate institutions including the black market before the currency reform.

Any of the properties of old-fashioned mercantilism seems to have a good or better substitute in an open economy and an international framework that is conducive to both free trade and industrial growth. What has become more and more essential for growth is a domestic labour force which has properties complementary for mobile capital and which is prepared to allow the complementary factor to earn competitive rewards.

7. The process of industrial growth *cum* free trade, once it has started, is likely to be reinforcing for a number of reasons.

A country with a wage-determined competitiveness is an easy partner in negotiations for a common market, since it has little at stake in giving up its national sovereignty. A common market, on the other hand, is known to widen the scope for the division of labour and to increase potential competition.

In implementing a common market scheme, the country with an attractive wage policy can move ahead of others in abolishing restrictions on imports and capital flows. The additional doses of competition from abroad may contribute to keep industry sufficiently vigorous in spite of its possibly excessive competitiveness.

Moves towards more competition from abroad (either in the form of lowering import barriers or of revaluations) are an excellent substitute for price controls in conditions of high employment

(Haberler's incomes policy II). Together with the selective immigration of workers they help to improve the position of the Phillips curve.

If labour can be shown to gain in the medium run from wage restraint, it will be much more prepared to contribute to cost level stability, a factor which helps to keep the currency undervalued and thus to maintain a high marginal efficiency of investment in spite of capital inflows.

Once growth has accelerated, it helps to maintain a growth mentality in investment behaviour, in labour–management relations, and in the public at large. Tendencies towards a zero-sum mentality are kept in bounds.

8. Self-perpetuating industrial growth in one country or region may depend upon the existence of adverse conditions elsewhere. Once a country falls behind in the growth race, it finds it more and more difficult to remain sufficiently attractive to growth-minded factors of production, specifically to footloose (international) financial and human capital. The vicious circle may start from or may run through the following points:

(1) an overvaluation of the currency which depresses exports, industrial investment, productivity growth, and employment;

(2) excessive wage pressures which are bound to lead to unemployment;

(3) a resort to short-run remedies to unemployment which work via unanticipated inflation, but induce compensatory wage reactions after a time lag and, if often enough applied, tend to destroy money illusion and finally even exchange-rate illusion;

(4) the development of a mentality which considers growth too expensive relative to equality;

(5) excessive attempts at redistributing income through high marginal tax rates which depress the earning prospects for risk capital and for growth-minded entrepreneurs and which reduce the country's attractiveness to mobile resources;

(6) the control of capital exports which makes the country look like a capital trap, and the control of commodity imports which enables domestic producers to live the quiet life of a quasi-monopolist.

Apart from the control of capital exports, some of these features have become visible in the last couple of years in the West German economy.

9. Whether a country gains or falls back in the international growth race and whether it drifts toward the growth or the zero-sum mentality, depends also upon the average income elasticity of world demand for the products it offers. Dynamically, it is a problem of structural adjustment and the really essential part of the terms of trade issue. Let me state it this way: if a person, a farmer, an industrialist, or a statesman, complains about a persisting deterioration of his or his firm's or country's terms of trade, he makes—if he takes, as he should, the structure of demand as given—a statement about an inadequate structure of supply and, looking backward, a statement about a failure to meet an adjustment opportunity or requirement. When export prices fall relative to import prices, this can be due either to shifts in world demand or to strong competitors abroad who take advantage of a more appropriate factor endowment or a better technology. Individual firms can defend or improve their relative position by (1) process innovation, (2) product innovation, (3) changing the product mix, or (4) moving towards a better location. Countries and regions, which cannot move to a better location—almost by definition—must choose among the first three alternatives. If they fail to act, they will fall behind. Import barriers to protect structurally weak industries from foreign competition are most likely to slow down economic growth, at least in the longer run, but they are politically very popular, since pressures towards the protection of declining industries nowadays emanate from trade unions as well as from industrialists. Adam Smith would have made this point quite explicit, had he foreseen syndicalist developments in advanced countries. Growth policy is thus very often a politically unpopular long-run strategy for accepting the hardships of structural change.

10. There is little to be said against temporary protection as a means of granting adjustment time, apart perhaps from the objection that the need for adjustment comes unforeseen only in rare cases and that direct adjustment assistance for a definitely limited period might have lower social costs than import barriers.

To convey information about future needs for adjustment to decision makers in industry and the banking community requires structural projections, but this is a task which need not involve governments. It can be done much better by independent research institutes, preferably in competition. This is what we try to do at Kiel and elsewhere in the country. The 'invisible hand' to which Adam Smith referred does not function without costs; but if public funds were invested in gathering, synthesizing, and disseminating information about the imminent challenges from international markets, these costs could be considerably reduced. For an advanced country one can derive such information from international cross-section analyses which reveal where low-wage countries find their comparative advantage, or from a timely analysis of cases where producers from low wage countries have successfully invaded other advanced import markets. We need such international information systems to supplement and support the market mechanism for the benefit of the developing as well as the advanced countries. If there were more early retreats instead of defensive action by firms operating in sensitive fields in advanced countries, the developing countries would presumably feel much more encouraged to invest or to attract foreign investment for the purposes of increasing production and the supply to export markets. The firms starting an early retreat in advanced countries may be identical with those starting an investment and export offensive in developing countries. It would be interesting to know why this case of locational adjustment does not play a more important rôle and why it is not encouraged.

The answer may well be that politicians in the young nation states of the Third World consider—in agreement even with Adam Smith—that defence or independence is more important than opulence or economic development.

11. My last proposition refers to economic growth in the First and Third World taken as a whole.

If economic growth in the world economy is to be harmonious, with reasonable prospects for everybody to gain, it requires (1) outward-looking policies in the developing South, (2) forward-looking policies in the advanced North, and (3) a higher degree of capital mobility from North to South and a parallel transfer of adequate technologies.

Let me comment upon this proposition:

(a) The first part would be a forward-looking policy in the North (which includes North America, Scandinavia, and large parts of the European Community); it should be different from the policy of export-led growth, which West Germany pursued until 1971. On the contrary, it should be conceived to be complementary and thus conducive to a policy of export-led growth for countries that follow suit in economic development.

Maintenance assistance should be replaced by adjustment assistance to promote an advance retreat of resources from sensitive segments of the import market. This should, of course, be coupled with the abolition of protective devices (import barriers, conservating subsidies) that reduce the need for forward-looking adjustments.

The currency, instead of being undervalued, should be somewhat overvalued in relation to less developed countries. This second element is to invite strong competitive pressures from outside, and to give incentives to invest abroad rather than at home as far as traditional products and processes are concerned. It implies the earning, rather than the paying, of a seignorage gain in the international competition of currencies for use as a reserve medium.

The third element of a forward-looking policy would be institutional arrangements which are favourable to research, to product and process innovation, to risk taking, to the supply of risk capital, and to the formation of human capital in schools and enterprises. Here the trade-off between growth and equality may become relevant. As a pre-condition for rational policy decisions the electorate will have to be made aware that profits due to innovation (and speculation) are socially useful compensations for those who take the risk of capital losses and that their social function is to provoke explorations into the realm of new products and processes. The benefits will spread beyond the country; they include those external economies which arise from the fact that forward looking policies in the most advanced countries permit the others to follow suit on the path of export-led growth.

(b) The second part of the strategy consists in capital movements from high-wage to low-wage countries. They are to be a means of bringing the work to the workers and thus a counterforce to the migration from southern to northern Europe which was a characteristic of economic growth in the sixties and early seventies.[1]

---

[1] The argument that capitalist countries have an interest in liberalizing the international capital market rather than migration seems to be based on American rather than European experience.

Limits to migration from the South to the North of Europe emerge from the limits to industrial growth in the agglomeration areas of advanced countries, and from the costs of social integration on a continent that shows strong interest in preserving its cultural diversity and, therefore, a distinct resistance against the tendency of becoming an ethnic melting-pot. Under these conditions, factor movements to reduce productivity differentials between Europe and the Third World will have to take the form of capital movements rather than that of further migration of (guest) workers.

A possible objection to this is that a transfer of labour from a less developed to an advanced country is a transfer into an efficiency-oriented social atmosphere, which adds to productivity, whereas the transfer of capital in the reverse direction may entail a productivity loss, as long as the importing country or area lacks complementary factors, such as skilled workers, an adequate infrastructure, or an efficiency-oriented social climate.

The answer to this objection can only be a recommendation to make the necessary tests by freeing capital imports into less developed countries. If the latter do not attract enough capital, one surely will discover what complementary factors (that cannot be produced by spontaneous action) will have to be made available by governmental or inter-governmental intervention and co-operation.

Among the impediments to capital flows, I suspect, the fear of political change and the danger of expropriation without adequate compensation will be prominent. They might be limited by means of bilateral or multilateral treaties which provide insurance against such political risks. Any such arrangement—call it a Free Investment Area—should be a club open to all countries that are prepared to acept the rules of the game and to offer the necessary pledges. Openness in this sense (or a conditional M.F.N. clause) appears in given political circumstances to be the closest possible approximation to a world-wide system of capital mobility. A Free Investment Area is to be conceived as a system of horizontal (contractual) instead of vertical (hierarchical) relations, but it would in the end serve similar purposes as the Pax Britannica and the Pax Americana in the two previous centuries of capitalism. In the absence of such arrangements the less developed countries may grossly miss their goal of raising their share in world manufacturing from

7 per cent now to 25 per cent in the year 2000 and the advanced countries might in the longer run see themselves faced with an excess supply of capital which would force them to concentrate even more on labour-saving innovations and thus on a path of technological progress that would widen the gap between the technology of the North and what was needed in the South.

(c) The transfer of adequate technologies is perhaps the most difficult task, since experience so far seems to show that technology cannot be transferred except in the embodied form. New capital goods embody the relatively labour-saving technologies that match the factor endowment in advanced countries, and as far as second-hand equipment is concerned it appears to be capital-saving only if the complementary capital costs of stocking spare parts, and if maintenance and repair, which are rather skill-intensive, are left out of account. However, obsolescence in advanced countries, which is speeded up if product and process innovation accelerate, should be expected to widen the price differential between new and second-hand equipment and induce less developed countries to rely more on the technology embodied in the latter. It is surprising that multi-national corporations in their direct investment in less developed countries do not concentrate more on capital-saving, labour-using technologies. The reason can be either (1) that they are not maximizing their profits or (2) that they have to pay or to account for excessively high wages or (3) that capital and capital goods are too cheap for them in the less developed country because of an overvaluation of its currency (combined with relatively cheap import licences) or a subsidization of foreign investment (by the donor or recipient country) based on the sum invested rather than the number of jobs created. A failure to maximize profits may have several reasons. One of them is presumably the lack of openness of the economy which confers upon the investor, who has succeeded in jumping in, an unnecessarily high degree of monopoly and scope for waste; another is that target profits are deliberately reduced on political grounds and that this makes room for quite a number of non-economic considerations, including the preference of politicians and engineers for a technology that reflects the state of the art in advanced countries. Unless the market signals are set correctly (no overvaluation of the currency of the recipient country *vis-à-vis* the donor country; no wages above the equilibrium level and no subsidization of capital costs in recipient countries), there is little hope that any attempts at supplying adequate technologies, which could perhaps be induced, would be successful in finding an effective demand. In the transfer of technology as in other respects it seems that the world economy today is too much politicized— or mercantilistic—to let profit expectations develop among those who might be able to take care of what is most needed. In the absence of such profit expectations the task will fall upon governments and bureaucrats, which are probably not very efficient in this respect either.

My conclusion then is: There appears to be an alternative to the much discussed New International Economic Order, an alternative which is more in line with the thinking developed in the *Wealth of Nations*.

COMMENT

by W. M. Corden*

I should like to express deep regret that Marcus Fleming is no longer with us. He has made important contributions to trade theory and policy over a long period, and earlier to applied welfare economics. Remarkably, he produced this high-quality scholarly . work while working as an influential and busy national, and later international, civil servant. His ideas influenced James Meade in writing *Trade and Welfare*[1] and, through this, the methods of welfare analysis that he developed in an article published in 1951 have become widely used.

In this, his last paper, he has given us an admirable historical survey of trade restrictions, focusing on the balance of payments motivation for restrictions. I am sure that for many years it will be a valuable reference for students both of international economics and of economic history. Here I should like to develop and discuss two particular points raised in the paper. First, what are the *real* reasons, as distinct from rationalizations, for protectionism? And secondly, is it important that economists today direct their attention to the question of freedom of international transactions?

* Nuffield College, Oxford.
[1] J. E. Meade, *Trade and Welfare* (Oxford University Press, London, 1955).

Let me then begin with the first question. Marcus Fleming has written:

For, of course, he [Smith] was quite aware that mercantilist doctrine was a way of rationalizing, as being in the general interest, policies whose main motivation lay in special interest, notably in the desire of merchants and manufacturers to monopolize the home market.

There is a suggestion here that a distinction must be made between the *real* reasons for protection—which concern pressures from special interests—and the intellectual superstructure which then rationalizes these real reasons. Smith was concerned both with uncovering and exposing these real reasons and with demolishing the intellectual superstructure. Similarly, in Britain today—and in other countries—one can certainly distinguish the real reasons for protectionist pressures from the, often sophisticated, superstructure, the latter usually being the special concern of academics. But here I wish to concern myself with the *real* reasons.

The usual explanation runs in terms of the triumph of producer interests over consumer interests—the triumph of the small tightly organized group over the larger, more loose, group. I think this general approach originated with Smith. But there are two difficulties about this as an explanation.

(i) It is partial equilibrium. Protection benefits some producer interests but hurts others. Taking general equilibrium into account, export producers and *non*-protected import-competing industries are likely to lose from a tariff. Similarly, some consumers lose, but consumers of exportables may gain. Nevertheless, it can be argued that practical people think to an extent in partial equilibrium terms.

(ii) This approach does not explain why some producers get protection, and not others, and some benefit at particular times, and not at other times. Why does one pressure group succeed, and not another, and indeed why do some pressure groups not even try for protection?

So we need more exploration of this issue. Incidentally, I think Charles Kindleberger was one of the first to explore it with reference to the origins of European agricultural protectionism. I would like to try a hypothesis. I believe it explains a good deal of protectionism in the nineteenth and twentieth centuries.

The motive for protection is *conservative*—the preservation of sectional real incomes which would otherwise fall because of some shock. A war creates an infant industry, essentially accidentally. After the war, free trade would lead to destruction of the industry and hence severe falls in real incomes of the specific factors in the industry or factors intensive in that industry. There are many examples: the beginnings of American protectionism after the war of 1812, the Corn Laws after the Napoleonic Wars, Latin American and Australian protectionism after the First and Second World Wars. Similarly, depressions or recessions have this effect—as the recent recession has encouraged protection of the motor car industry in some countries, and as the agricultural depression of the 1870s encouraged agricultural protection in Europe.

Society accepts a 'conservative social welfare function'. I shall leave open the question as to whether this is a 'good' social welfare function. In practice its pursuit certainly leads to Pareto-inefficient policies. Furthermore, *trade* intervention, or even long-term subsidies, may not be cost-effective, given this social welfare function. Temporary and more direct measures, perhaps adjustment assistance, may be better. Smith did favour adjustment assistance. Of the historians I should like to ask whether any protectionism in the eighteenth century can be explained in these terms, and of the Smith scholars I should like to know whether Smith had thought along these lines of explanation.

I now turn to the second question. Is the issue of freedom of international transactions an issue of importance for economists today? Marcus Fleming has written—possibly his only really controversial statement in this paper:

I believe it would be a mistake for economists today to direct too much of their attention to the question of freedom for international transactions as a means to economic welfare.

The question then is whether we need today to fight a vigorous battle for Smithian ideas on the trade front. My answer has three parts to it.

Firstly, the present level of trade restrictions of the O.E.C.D. countries (with the exception of Australia and New Zealand, and perhaps the Common Agricultural Policy of the E.E.C.) is rather low. The welfare gains from removing them are not likely to be very great. The same applies to barriers to capital movements.

Of course there are particular cases, especially restrictions on clothing and textiles, and these damage the less developed countries.

The current Tokyo round of international trade negotiations (being conducted in Geneva) is not likely to yield great gains even if restrictions are reduced. Indeed, the process may even mobilize special interests, especially in the U.S., and make them excessively conscious of existing protective devices, as well as using up resources in lobbying, rent-seeking, and so on. To this extent I agree with Marcus Fleming.

Secondly, this is not true for many important less developed countries. I suspect that in a country such as India—indeed, notably in India—there may still be significant gains to be derived from reducing or removing completely existing restrictions—resource allocations gains, gains in fostering competition and so-called X-efficiency, and gains in reducing the costs of rent-seeking, of lobbying, and of a bureaucracy. The issues for less developed countries have been explored in the book by Little, Scitovsky, and Scott,[2] a book which has put the fundamental free trade theme, with lots of examples, and with vigour and confidence. One of my former Oxford students, a Marxian from Latin America, described it as a modern *Wealth of Nations*. And this makes the point that a modern *Wealth of Nations* would perhaps be more relevant— at least from the trade policy point of view—for less developed countries than for the developed countries.

Thirdly, and finally, to return to the O.E.C.D. countries, we may not need to fight a battle to reduce restrictions *further*, but the price of *keeping* the channels of trade and capital flows reasonably open is undoubtedly eternal vigilance—vigilance to prevent significant increases, for which the pressures are indeed eternal.

The greatest help to preventing increases in restrictions—as Marcus Fleming has written—is flexibility of exchange rates. This has saved the world from plunging massively into trade restrictions in 1974 and 1975. Nevertheless, the pressures are always there—especially when exchange rates get out of line, as the dollar–yen rate did in 1971, leading to protectionist pressure in the United States; or when there is a recession, as now.

I need hardly say that even in Britain the battle has apparently to be fought continuously, and can never be regarded as having

---

[2] I. M. D. Little, T. Scitovsky, and M. F. Scott, *Industry and Trade in Some Developing Countries* (Oxford University Press, London, 1970).

been won. Adam Smith would no doubt be glad to know that the general and prolonged application of import quotas is rather unlikely in Britain, having been explicitly rejected recently by the Government, and in any case being hardly compatible with membership of the E.E.C., as well as being highly likely to provoke retaliation from other countries—and of course the disapproval of the I.M.F. Possibly he would also be glad to know—in view of his strictures about the laziness of University Professors (though he referred to Oxford, not Cambridge)—that some academics in Britain have been exceedingly hard-working in building, refurbishing, or rediscovering the intellectual superstructure to justify protectionism.[3]

Let me conclude by repeating that, in my view, Marcus Fleming's last paper is outstanding as a historical survey that draws on the wealth of his experience, and applies his characteristically sound judgement. I feel sad that he is not here with us now.

[3] This refers to the advocacy of import quotas for Britain by the Cambridge Economic Policy Group, which has been given much prominence. See C.E.P.G. *Economic Policy Review* No. 1 (1975) and No. 2 (1976), Department of Applied Economics, Cambridge.

7

Competition: The Product Markets

BY P. SYLOS-LABINI*

IN this paper I will contrast Smith's view of the competitive process with modern developments and compare his expectations with what happened in the next two centuries. But, to do this, I must isolate the appropriate measure of value in which to make meaningful inter-temporal comparisons of prices and incomes. Therefore, the first part of the paper will be concerned with this fundamental problem, the solution of which is necessary to make an over-all appraisal of Smith's conception of competition and of economic growth. The main analytical lines for such an appraisal will be discussed in the second part of the paper.

I

1. Competition and monopoly

The distance between the static conception of competition, still prevailing in our time, and that of Smith is very large indeed: in the *Wealth of Nations* competition and economic growth are two aspects of one and the same process. More precisely, according to economists belonging to the marginalist tradition, the essential characteristic of competition is that the individual producer cannot modify the conditions of the market and, in particular, cannot modify the price. For Adam Smith, as well as for the other classical economists, competition is characterized by free entry; conversely, monopoly implies obstacles to entry. In the time of Smith, such obstacles were, first of all, of an institutional or legal type, such as 'the exclusive privileges of corporations, statutes of apprenticeship, and all those laws which restrain, in particular employments, the competition to a smaller number than might otherwise go

* Professor P. Sylos-Labini, University of Rome. The writer is grateful to W. A. Eltis, P. Garegnani, L. Meldolesi, and A. Roncaglia for their very helpful critical comments and suggestions; and to A. Skinner for help in improving his English style.

into them' (WN I. vii. 28), or the privileges granted to certain companies in the colonial trade (WN IV. viii. pt. III), or the high duties and prohibitions upon foreign manufactures (WN IV. iii. pt. II).[1] Such obstacles were to be attacked on the political and legislative plane. Smith, however, also considers other types of obstacle to entry: those determined by natural scarcities in agriculture and mining; those determined—temporarily—by secrets in manufactures; those—very important—determined by high costs of transport (see below, section II. 1). Still other obstacles to entry can be found in certain activities carried on in the towns, where, for technical reasons or for reasons of location, the number of manufacturers, workers, or tradesmen is small and cannot easily increase. In such a situation, the people concerned, just because they are very few, are likely to enter into a combination in order to raise the price of their products, or of their labour. Here again, however, the important element is not represented by the smallness of the number *per se*, but by the obstacles to entry, i.e. by the impossibility, or the great difficulty, for 'new rivals' to enter the market. The tendency to equality of wages and of profits in different employments (apart from the inequalities arising from the nature of the employments) presupposes free entry—or, as Smith sometimes says, with reference to both the product and labour markets, 'perfect liberty' (WN I. x. a. 1).

The obstacles to entry can keep the market price of particular commodities above the natural price and maintain not only profits but also wages above their natural rates for a long time.

When the quantity brought to market is just sufficient to supply the effectual demand and no more, the market price naturally comes to be either exactly, or as nearly as can be judged of, the same with the natural price . . . (WN I. vii. 11)

—where the effectual demand is the quantity demanded by all 'those who are willing to pay the natural price of the commodity, or the whole value of the rent, labour and profit' at their natural rates (WN I. vii. 8). The market price will rise above the natural price when the quantity of a given commodity which is brought to market falls short of the effectual demand, and fall below the natural price when the opposite is the case. Under competition, the market price can be higher than the natural price only for a limited period.

[1] References are to the Cannan edition (Methuen, 1930).

The concepts of natural prices and natural rates are inseparable from the concept of competition: in this respect, 'natural' and 'competitive' can well be considered as synonymous.

2. *The natural price and the natural rate of wages, profits, and rent*

To understand correctly Smith's conception of the natural price, it is necessary to realize that, unlike the point of view prevailing today among economists, Smith is considering not only the distinction between the short and long run, but also what we today would call—for different analytical purposes—'stages of development' which are indistinguishable from long historical periods. (When speaking of the short run, Smith says 'occasionally' or 'temporarily'; when referring to the long run, he uses either this expression or other equivalent ones, like 'considerable time'; when referring to the stages of development, Smith speaks of 'states', 'conditions', 'general circumstances of the society', or 'different periods of improvement'.)

According to Smith, the basic stages are three: progressive, stationary, and declining. (It should be clear that these three stages refer to a society which has already developed an exchange economy.) The progressive stage, on which Smith concentrates his attention, is often further divided. In brief, in discussing the behaviour of the natural and market price, Smith is using three, and not two, terms of reference: short run, long run, and stage of development. In the short run, the market price depends on supply ('quantity brought to the market') and demand. In the long run, under conditions of monopoly it depends on the same forces; under competition it tends to coincide with the natural price or, we may say, with the cost of production, with the proviso that, in a given historical period or sub-period, the natural price varies only if technology varies, whereas the natural rates of wages, profits, and rent are to be considered as constant. In passing from one stage of development to another, or from one sub-period to another, the natural price will vary as a result not only of technological changes, but also of variations in wages, profits, and rents:

The natural price itself varies with the natural rate of ... its component parts, of wages, profit, and rent; and in every society this rate varies according to their circumstances, according to their riches or poverty, to their advancing, stationary, or declining condition. (WN I. vii. 33.)

In Chapter vii of the first Book, Smith discusses systematically the behaviour of prices in the short and in the long run. In Chapters viii, ix, and x of the same Book, he discusses the behaviour of the 'natural rate' of wages, profits, and rent in the different periods and sub-periods of the 'progress of improvement'.

In analysing the variations of the natural rate of the 'three original sources of all revenue', Smith apparently uses the criterion of supply and demand; but it should be clear that his criterion has nothing to do with the one followed by the economists of the marginalist tradition, a criterion epitomized by two curves, one independent of the other. To clarify this point, let us consider very briefly some of the views set forth by Smith.

In the progressive stage of society, the demand for labour rises while 'the production of men' can only be increased under conditions of increasing cost, because each labourer has 'to bring up a greater number of children'. Therefore,

If [the] demand [for labour] is continuously increasing, the reward of labour must necessarily encourage in such a manner the marriage and multiplication of labourers, as may enable them to supply that continually increasing demand by a continually increasing population. (WN I. viii. 40.)

The demand for labour, according as it happens to be increasing, stationary, or declining, or to require an increasing, stationary, or declining population, determines the quantity of the necessaries and conveniences of life which must be given to the labourer; and the money price of labour is determined by what is requisite for purchasing this quantity. (WN I. viii. 52.)

The increase in the demand for labour can, for a time, raise wages to the level needed for a larger expansion of population; but, once this higher level is reached, it will remain there, even if demand continues to increase, so long as population and, therefore, the supply of labour increases at the same rate. However, when demand increases persistently faster than population, wages can continue to rise. One could say that the expansion of demand affects the cost of production of men; and it is this cost—the cost required by the general conditions of society—that regulates wages in a given stage of development. The increasing or declining state of the wealth of society also determines variations in profits, but in a direction often opposite to that of wages. As for rents, in the 'progress of improvement' they tend to increase, first, because the expansion of the demand for the produce of land comes up against the general scarcity of land itself (only in this broad sense Smith speaks of the rent of land as a monopoly price) and, second, because that expansion meets with particular scarcities (unimproved wilds to raise cattle, certain types of land fitted to some particular produce, mines). The said scarcities give rise to an increase in price and this makes it possible to increase production albeit at higher costs. However, when, given the stage of development, particular levels of rent for different types of land have stabilized, they become elements of costs (though in the course of historical time they are the result of increasing prices).

While wages, profits, and rent, then, are regulated by the variations of demand during the different stages of economic development, it seems that variations of this kind depend on the general conditions of society rather than on strictly economic forces. From this point of view, in each historical period, either the levels, or the rates of change, of wages, profits, and rent are given. In this sense, Marx is right in observing that those three elements 'determine autonomously'[2] the natural price, or, better, as Sraffa says, the natural price is arrived at by a process of *adding up* the wages, profits, and rent.[3] There is no doubt that, apart from a number of general remarks, Smith does not *analyse* the relations between wages, profits, and rent, and in particular we find in his work only hints as to the inverse relation between the wage rate and the rate of profit. Neither does he analyse the relations between these three elements and variations in the system of prices. Smith's theory of prices, however, would seem to be indeterminate rather than wrong. In any case, if we make use of Smith's analysis, we have to take into account his peculiar procedure (based on the tripartite division that I have mentioned, i.e. stage of development, long and short run); such a procedure, in Smith, seems to perform a role similar to that of the method of successive approximations adopted by later economists.

3. *The conditions of production and the measure of price changes*

The difference between the marginalist and the classical conception of competition is very large indeed, not only with regard

[2] Marx, *Theorien über den Mehrwert*, 2. Teil (Berlin, Dietz Verlag, 1959), X. B. 1.

[3] *The Works and Correspondence of David Ricardo*, edited by Piero Sraffa with the assistance of Maurice Dobb (Cambridge University Press, 1951), I. xxxv.

to the role assigned to free entry or to the obstacles to entry of actual or potential entrants ('new rivals')—a concept only recently rediscovered and put at the basis of the analysis of market forms— but also for deeper reasons.[4] Marginalist economists conceive the economic life as an 'arc', whereas classical economists view it as a 'circle' or as a 'spiral'. The former give to the psychological aspects of the behaviour of the consumers no less importance—in fact, even a greater importance—than to the conditions of production. The classical economists, on the contrary, consider the habits of the consumers as the result of the general conditions of society; besides, they do not conceive of consumption *in abstracto*; they distinguish between necessary and unnecessary—or between productive and unproductive—consumption, where the former, which is made possible by saving, is the consumption of 'productive labourers' and represents one set of the requirements for the repetition, or for the enlargement, of the social process of production. The other set of requirements is given by technology, which, by determining the quantity of productive labour to be employed, also helps to determine the amount of necessary consumption. The analysis of natural and market prices, then, should be conducted, not with reference to supply and demand as such, but with reference to the technological methods of production and to the conditions of necessary consumption.

We can here discuss particularly the changes in price that take place in the long run. In this context, effectual demand determines the amount to be produced: price is determined by the cost of production. If, in the course of time, effectual demand tends to increase (that is, if the extent of the market tends to expand) new and more efficient methods of production can be introduced, thanks to progress in the division of labour, and the 'natural price' thus decreases. But the effectual demand affects price only indirectly, that is, by determining changes in the methods of production. In Smith's words:

The increase of demand . . ., though in the beginning it may sometimes raise the price of goods, never fails to lower it in the long run.

---

[4] At present an increasing number of economists use the concept of entry in the analysis of market forms; but more than forty years ago Alberto Breglia was already making a systematic use of this concept ('Cenni di teoria della politica economica', *Giornale degli economisti* (February 1934)).

It encourages production, and thereby increases the competition of the producers, who, in order to undersell one another, have recourse to new divisions of labour and new improvements of art, which might never otherwise have been thought of.[5]

Cost and price reductions, then, are determined by an increase in the division of labour which is originated by a persistent expansion of the market. In other words, Smith's increasing returns are the result of irreversible changes, occurring in the course of time. This applies even to what we call today economies of scale: that is, to the advantages of an increasing division of labour and specialization of machines which are in turn made possible by the increasing size of individual firms (not necessarily of the individual plants)— provided we remember that these particular types of economies, which have become so important in the last hundred years or so, were of relatively little importance in Smith's time. Moreover, we should recall that viewed in a dynamic or more precisely in a historical perspective, such economies have a potentially destructive power with respect to competition (both in the classical and the marginalist sense), as Alfred Marshall and, after him, several other economists have correctly recognized.

Increasing returns, however, do not prevail everywhere; they prevail in manufactures and in certain agricultural productions, whereas in other types of production it is the tendency towards decreasing returns (a tendency also of a dynamic character) which prevails. The increase in production, which in this case takes place under conditions of increasing costs and price, is caused by the progressive expansion of demand. But, again, demand affects output directly and price only indirectly, by determining changes in the methods of production.

Since Smith intended to study the consequences of technological progress on relative prices, he needed a standard to be used in inter-temporal comparisons. Having discarded money as a proper unit, since the very conditions of production of the precious metals used as money undergo changes in the course of time, Smith adopts labour commanded, that is, he decides to take the wage rate of common labour as the unit. The idea, that the variations of this standard correspond to those expressed by labour embodied

---

[5] WN V. i. e. 26: 'Of the Public Works and Institutions which are necessary for facilitating particular Branches of Commerce'.

if the distributive shares are constant, is not new; but it is well to reflect on it.

Since for Smith, 'the whole price . . . resolves itself either immediately or ultimately into the . . . three parts of rent, labour and profit' (WN I. vi. 11), P, the price of a given commodity, can be seen as the sum of all revenues per unit of output.[6] If we call H the number of hours of labour directly or indirectly embodied in that commodity, W the wage rate per unit of time (per hour), and δ the ratio of total wages per unit of output and price, we have (measuring both P and W in terms of an abstract paper money or in terms of a given commodity):

$$WH = \delta P$$

If we compare the value of the commodity we are considering in two different periods, 1 and 2, and assume that owing to technical progress H_2 is smaller than H_1, then the ratio expressing labour embodied (H_1/H_2) is equal to the ratio representing labour commanded $\left(\dfrac{P_1}{W_1}\Big/\dfrac{P_2}{W_2}\right)$ if $\delta_1 = \delta_2$; i.e., if the share going to wages does not vary.

Ricardo and Marx maintain that Smith oscillates between the two standards (labour commanded and labour embodied) and that his theory of value is ambiguous or even inconsistent. In fact, on the one hand, Smith says that labour embodied regulates exchangeable values only 'in that early and rude state of society which precedes both the accumulation of stock and the appropriation of land' (WN I. vi. 1); on the other hand, Smith argues several times as if the two expressions were equivalent.

Now, there is no contradiction between the first point of view and the assumption that the two standards can be, and as a rule are, equivalent: the former implies $\delta = 1$ for all commodities; the latter implies a δ less than one and constant in the course of time for each commodity, but no longer equal for all the different commodities; the former refers to exchangeable value among

---

[6] This conception of Smith has been repeatedly criticized on the ground that 'a commodity residue' cannot be eliminated. This is true. But, as Sraffa has shown in his *Production of Commodities by means of Commodities* (Cambridge University Press, 1960), ch. vi, this 'commodity residue' can be made as small as we like by applying the method which he calls 'reduction to dated quantities of labour' which permits us to 'resolve' prices into wages and profits; for simplicity rents are neglected.

commodities, the latter refers to inter-temporal comparisons of the value of the same commodity. Although Smith does not explicitly make the assumption of a stable wage share, that assumption seems to be consistent with his views as to what happens in the 'progressive' state of a country's development. Indeed, given the reductions in labour inputs, that share can remain stable if the wage rate rises and if profits and rents vary in such a way as to keep constant the over-all non-labour share (if, for simplicity, we neglect rents, we might assume a constant share of profits even allowing for a fall in the rate of profit provided that, at the same time, we assume an appropriate increase of what today we call the capital–output ratio). After all, that assumption does not seem so far-fetched, if one thinks of the large literature intended to explain the relative stability of the wage share in modern times—say, in the hundred years preceding the Second World War.

Ricardo denies, at least as a rule, the equivalence between the two standards (labour commanded and labour embodied) mainly on the basis of the tendency towards decreasing returns from land, a tendency that Smith is far from considering universal in agriculture. In particular, Smith thinks that corn, in general, is produced under conditions of constant costs.

Let us consider Ricardo's argument. If the quantity of labour required to produce a given quantity of food and necessaries increases—says Ricardo—the money wage should increase in proportion to preserve the purchasing power of the labourer; but

food and necessaries in this case will have risen, if estimated by the *quantity* of labour necessary to their production, while they will scarcely have increased in value, if measured by the quantity of labour for which they will exchange. (*Works* I. i. 14.)

A numerical example may clarify the question. I refer to the conditions of production of corn in two situations and consider the consequences of both Ricardo's and Smith's assumptions. In both cases, wages increase; but in the case of Ricardo, such an increase is made necessary by the increasing costs of corn in terms of labour, whereas in the case of Smith, the increase of wages does not depend on this (the unit again is in terms of paper money or, if δ is taken as constant also in the case of the commodity used as money, in terms of a commodity produced with quantities of labour varying in inverse proportion to wages).

	RICARDO						SMITH				
H	W	HW	δ	$P = HW/\delta$	P/W	H	W	HW	δ	$P = HW/\delta$	P/W
1	5	5	0·25	20	4	1	5	5	0·25	20	4
2	10	20	0·50	40	4	1	10	10	0·25	40	4

Following Ricardo's assumptions of decreasing returns, constant purchasing power of wages in terms of corn (W/P), it is true, then, that the value of corn would rise if estimated by labour embodied (H) and it would not rise at all—according to his second assumption—if measured by labour commanded (P/W). (The rise of δ is the necessary consequence of the said two assumptions. For Ricardo, a rise of δ would imply a decline in the share accruing to profits.) But it is also true that, on the basis of Smith's assumptions, the two rules—labour embodied and labour commanded—are equivalent, even if the wage rate increases, provided δ remains constant.

The assumption that corn is produced at constant costs plays an important role in Smith's analysis in that it allows him to use the price of corn as a standard measure instead of the price of labour to make inter-temporal comparisons. Smith uses the former instead of the latter for practical reasons, because 'the price of labour can scarce ever be known with any degree of exactness', whereas the prices of corn 'are in general better known' (WN I. v. 22). Such a substitution is possible precisely because corn, which represents 'the principal part of the subsistence of the labourer', is produced at approximately constant costs.

This is the consequence of two contrasting forces: on the one hand, the real price of corn would tend to decrease owing to the increase of the productive powers of labour; on the other, the real price of corn would tend to increase because the real price of cattle, 'the principal instruments of agriculture', tends to increase. In early times cattle are almost free goods, because there are large areas of 'unimproved wilds'; later, the 'unimproved wilds' become insufficient and cattle have to be raised, to an increasing extent, by labour.[7] Moreover, the relatively high costs of transportation of corn—considerably higher than in the case of gold and silver—to some extent isolate the different nations;[8] a consideration which

[7] WN I. xi. e. 27: 'Digression concerning the Variations in the Value of Silver during the Course of the Four last Centuries'.

[8] See especially I. xi. c. 21 (Part II); I. xi. e. 38, IV. i. 12.

allows Smith to maintain that the forces affecting the cost of corn tend to compensate each other in every 'stage of development'. (Ricardo is very critical of Smith's corn standard; but nowhere does he discuss the arguments concerning the two contrasting forces or those concerning the comparative costs of transportation.)

Smith was aware that a precise balance between those two contrasting forces was out of the question; but he thought— correctly in my opinion—that silver, or gold, would have been a much worse standard when considering long historical periods, because in the course of time the value of these metals is bound to vary considerably owing to the discovery of new, abundant mines, or, on the contrary, to the gradual exhaustion of the existing mines (the volume of the traffic being supposed to be expanding). Silver, or gold, could be used only for relatively short periods; for long or very long periods, corn was to be preferred. To be sure, after the revolution in the means of transportation, which took place in the last quarter of the past century; after the gradual substitution of cattle as an instrument of agriculture by tractors and other machines, Smith's arguments no longer hold good. But, in Smith's time, these arguments were reasonable; moreover, he pushed his analysis back to the distant past.[9] This was not simply an instance of Adam Smith's method of putting all his arguments in an historical perspective; in my view, it was principally due to the fact that he was conscious of living in a period of great actual and potential economic and social change, so that long-run comparisons were important as a pre-condition for understanding the direction and the velocity of these changes. This appears clearly in chapter xi of Book I, where the corn standard is used to distinguish movements of prices due to the relative scarcity or abundance of silver from those determined by changes in the conditions of production. The point is that the 'progress of improvement' causes the 'real price' of certain commodities to rise and that of other commodities to fall (the 'real price' being the price in terms of labour or in

[9] In the long 'Digression concerning the Variations in the Value of Silver' included in chapter xi of the first Book, Smith considered the price of corn in the five centuries preceding his time and distinguished three periods, the second of which (1560–1640) is dominated by the so-called Price Revolution. On the basis of his assumptions, Smith attributed the variations in the price of corn mainly to variations in the value of silver, the former being the measure of the latter. Smith's interpretation, which has an important bearing on the study of price history, has never, so far as I know, been challenged by economic historians.

terms of corn); the behaviour of the real prices of the different
sorts of commodities can therefore be taken as an indication of the
stage of development reached by a country (as I said, for Smith the
theory of prices and the theory of economic growth intertwine).
More precisely, one of the main purposes of the long 'Digression'—where the corn standard is used precisely to isolate the
price changes due to the relative scarcity or abundance of silver—
was to eradicate the mercantilist opinion that the increase in the
quantity of gold and silver in Europe had in some way promoted
economic growth:

The increase of the quantity of gold and silver in Europe, and the
increase of its manufactures and agriculture, are two events which,
though they have happened nearly about the same time, yet have arisen
from very different causes, and have scarcely any natural connection
with one another. The one has arisen from a mere accident, in which
neither prudence nor policy either had or could have any share: The
other from the fall of the feudal system, and from the establishment of
a government which afforded to industry the only encouragement
which it requires, some tolerable security that it shall enjoy the fruits
of its own labour. Poland, where the feudal system still continues to
take place, is at this day as beggarly a country as it was before the
discovery of America ... Spain and Portugal, the countries which possess
the mines, are, after Poland, perhaps, the two most beggarly countries in
Europe ... Though the feudal system has been abolished in Spain and
Portugal, it has not been succeeded by a much better.[10]

In any case, it is clear that the corn standard works better than
the silver standard, considering the purposes Smith had in mind.
It is equally clear that the emphasis which Ricardo laid on decreasing returns from land is in some way connected with the conditions
of his times: the price of corn fluctuated on a very high level and,
presumably owing to the much higher costs and risks of transportation originated by the Napoleonic wars, the cultivation of
corn underwent, in England, a considerable expansion, with the
consequences envisaged by Ricardo.[11]

---

[10] WN I. xi. n. 1; 'Conclusion of the Digression'. (The above observations
imply a sharp criticism of the view, maintained by some economists and economic historians in our times, according to which the Price Revolution strongly
stimulated economic growth; see also below, section II. 1, on the relation
between profits and accumulation.)

[11] According to Smith, in the period 1700–1770, the average price of a quarter
of wheat fluctuated around the level of 40–50 shillings. From 1770 to 1790,
according to Tooke and Newmark, the average price did not vary very much;

All things considered, then, even if the corn standard lost much of its meaning after the transport revolution and the increased use of machinery in agriculture, it remains useful for the comparison of values 'at distant times and places' in the historical period studied by Smith and even until the middle of the past century. As a matter of fact, that standard is still used at present by economic historians, when they study the economy of relatively ancient periods. In any case, beginning with the second half of the past century, data concerning the price of labour were more complete and less unreliable than had been the case before and during Smith's time. And we should not forget that the corn standard was used by Smith only as a substitute for the labour standard.

4. *Different standards of value*

Smith was mainly interested in analysing the consequences of changes in technology on the value of different commodities in different times and places, whereas, as Sraffa has pointed out, 'the problem of value which interested Ricardo was how to find a measure of value which would be invariant to changes in the division of the product'.[12] In dealing with this problem, Ricardo started with labour embodied, but then modified his position by introducing, as a measure of value, an abstract money 'produced with such proportions of the two kinds of capital as approach nearest to the average quantity employed in the production of most commodities' (*Works* I. i. sec. VI. 3). The final step, along this route, has been Sraffa's standard commodity, which is, in fact, rigorously 'invariant to changes in the division of the product' in terms of its own means of production.

From the point of view of accumulation, the best standard is 'value', conceived as the property of a commodity to command labour: since the accumulation of capital consists, for Smith, in the progressive increase in the number of productive labourers,

that price jumped to much higher levels from 1790 to 1820, oscillating, first, around 60–70 shillings and, then, around 80–90 shillings per quarter, with peaks exceeding 100 shillings. In the following three or four decades the average price of wheat fell to its old level, oscillating around 55 shillings, without showing either a tendency to rise or to fall. T. Tooke and W. Newmark, *History of Prices* (6 vols., 1838–57) ed. by T. E. Gregory (London, P. S. King and Son, 1928).

[12] *Works* I. p. xlviii.

and since this increase (owing to progress in the division of labour) is necessarily accompanied by an increase in the efficiency of productive labourers, technical progress reduces the command of commodities over labour. It follows that the rate of increase in total output, or the 'annual produce', is higher, at least as a rule, than the rate of increase in the number of productive labourers (the possibility of making the assumption of an unchanged technology when total output increases is alien to Smith).

The distinction between 'labour commanded' and 'annual produce' corresponds to the distinction between 'value in exchange' and 'value in use', or else between 'value' and 'riches'.[13] In modern language: the best measure of 'value' is the wage deflator, whereas the best measure of 'riches' is the price deflator—both measures being necessarily approximate, but the former less than the latter. Smith started his great work with the consideration of 'riches', but then concentrated his analysis on 'values'; therefore, he was justified in using almost exclusively the wage deflator.[14]

In his Introduction and then in several points of his work, but always incidentally, Smith considered the behaviour of the 'annual produce' as such or in relation to the great body of consumers, i.e. to the whole population, or what we call today per capita income, the level of which depends, according to Smith, on the efficiency of the productive workers and on the proportion represented by such labourers of the total population. In modern language, if we call Y the 'annual produce' in money terms, P_y a price index, π_y over-all productivity, and E employment of productive workers directly employed in production, we have the following identity:

$$Y/P_y \equiv \pi_y E \qquad\qquad (a)$$

[13] The distinction between value and riches, which played an important role in classical economic theory, has become blurred in modern economic theory, which lays a much greater emphasis of utility (value in use), at the expense of the conditions of production, and of changes in these conditions in the course of time. J. B. Say can be rightly considered as the forerunner of such theoretical development; see Ricardo's forceful criticism of his views in *Works* I. xx. 14–16.

[14] If it is so, then Schumpeter's criticism of the concept of labour commanded is not well founded. Schumpeter thought that the choice made by Smith of this standard was due 'to his ignorance of the method of the index number, already invented in that time'. J. A. Schumpeter, *History of Economic Analysis* (Oxford University Press, 1954), ch. iii, section 4. (It is only true that the price deflator necessarily implies an index number, whereas this is not the case for the wage deflator if the wage rate of common labour is taken as the unit.)

Dividing both terms by total population, we have

$$Y_c \equiv \pi_y E_s$$

where Y_c is the real per capita income (real in the modern sense) and E_s the share of productive employment. By multiplying both terms of (a) by P_y/W_y we have

$$Y/W_y = \pi_y E P_y/W_y \qquad \text{(a')}$$

where W_y is wage per productive worker.

If we consider a price equation of the type

$$P = \alpha W_y/\pi_y \qquad \text{(a'')}$$

where $\alpha = 1+r$ (r being the rate of profit), we have, applying (a'') to the whole economy and substituting (a'') in (a),

$$Y/W_y = \alpha E \qquad \text{(b)}$$

This shows that variations of demand for productive labour—assuming as constant the distribution of income between profits and wages—correspond to the variations of the 'annual produce' measured in wage units.

If we take into account imported raw materials, the price equation becomes

$$P = \alpha(W_y/\pi + M), \qquad \text{(c)}$$

where M is the money value of raw materials per unit of output, and we have, with reference to the whole economy,

$$\frac{P_y}{W_y} = \frac{\alpha}{\pi_y} \cdot \frac{P_y}{P_y - \alpha M_y} \qquad \text{(d)}$$

Substituting (d) in (a') we have

$$\frac{Y}{W_y} = E\alpha \frac{1}{1 - \alpha M_y/P_y}. \qquad \text{(e)}$$

This shows that if we allow for imported raw materials, the conditions regulating the correspondence between the variations of demand for productive labour and those of the 'annual produce' measured in wage units are two: the stability of distributive shares, and that of the ratio between the prices of raw materials and those of finished products (assuming as constant the raw material input).

If we consider the amount of commodities commanded by labour, i.e. real wages (real in the modern sense), we have

$$W_y/P_y = \pi_y/\alpha \qquad (f)$$

or, if we use equation (c),

$$\frac{W_y}{P_y} = \pi_y\left(\frac{1}{\alpha} - \frac{M_y}{P_y}\right) \qquad (g)$$

This equation shows that, in an open economy, the variations of 'real wages' correspond to those of productivity, given α and given the ratio M_y/P_y (this ratio is relevant when considering the question of the terms of trade: see section II. 3); it also shows, given α and M_y/P_y, that the behaviour of P_y can coincide with that of W_y if productivity does not vary. In such a case, then, the variations of prices and those of wages go together and which deflator is used is a matter of indifference.

As is well known, Keynes prefers to use the wage unit rather than a price index on the ground that the 'general price level' is uncertain and 'undetermined' and 'more suitable in the field of historical and statistical description';[15] moreover, Keynes, like Smith, was interested in analysing the forces which regulate the volume of employment. Keynes, however, considers technology as given, so that, apart from its lesser uncertainty, the wage unit does not play, in his theory, the role it plays in Smith, for whom technological changes and the consequent increase in the 'productive powers' of labour were essential characteristics of modern economies. Besides, allowing for technological changes, the question arises of new goods which, especially in the long run, make any price deflator very ambiguous; in addition the appearance of new skills in the labour force gives rise to ambiguity, but this is much less serious. All things considered, then, the view that the wage unit in Keynes can be substituted by a price index is well founded, whereas it would not be so founded in the case of Smith. In any

[15] J. M. Keynes, *The General Theory of Employment, Interest and Money* (London, Macmillan, 1946), ch. iv. There are several points in common between Keynes and Smith. One is the wage unit; another is the very limited interest in the distribution of income and the great interest in the demand for labour; still another is the question of the relations between wages and prices. It must be said, however, that the similarities in the two theoretical constructions, though very interesting and to some extent significant, do not go very far. To mention only one important difference: Keynes, unlike Smith, was not interested in the economic consequences of technical progress.

case, though the wage unit is, in principle, a much better standard than the price deflator, it does not satisfy either that 'perfect precision—such as our causal analysis requires, whether or not our knowledge of the actual values of the relevant quantities is complete or exact' (Keynes, op. cit. 40). Such precision can, and must, be the prerogative of a standard to be used in measuring the changes in relative prices arising from changes in the distribution of income, given the technology.

In brief, we probably need three standards of value. We may use a price index as a deflator when we intend to consider the variations of the 'annual produce' or of 'riches'. We may use a wage unit (labour commanded) when we intend to consider the variations of the demand for labour or, more properly, the consequences of technological progress. (These two standards are necessarily approximate.) We must use a different, rigorous, standard when we intend to consider Ricardo's problem.

A final observation: 'Labour commanded', as a standard, is not only an analytical tool, the use of which is to be recommended in the theory of economic development, it also has certain practical uses. As a matter of fact, when we visit another country, we cannot rely on the exchange rate to compare the prices of goods in the country we live in and in the country that we are visiting: to make meaningful comparisons we are bound to use the rule of labour commanded, and we do use it, even if we are not fully aware of that fact. This becomes an even more stringent necessity if we visit a country in an entirely different stage of development or with radically different institutions.

II

1. *The competitive mechanism and the process of economic growth*

According to Smith, 'as art and industry advance', the prices of different commodities behave in different ways: certain commodities become dearer and dearer, whereas others tend to fall (when I say 'prices', I always mean 'real prices' or prices in terms of labour). Several sorts of rude produce belong to the first category: for example, 'cattle, poultry, game of all kinds, the useful fossils and minerals of the earth'. As a rule, vegetable food and manufactured products belong to the second category. The animal products grow dearer because, 'during a long period in the progress of improvement', the quantity of such commodities can increase only at increasing costs. (In this context, we are referring to stages of development and, therefore, we have to allow for both technological changes and for variations in the three component parts of the natural price.)

It is worth noticing that agricultural products are not concentrated in the 'increasing cost' category, but can be found in both categories—apart from corn, which is a special case. Thus, the effects of the division of labour, a process which works everywhere, tend to prevail in the case of most vegetable products, because the improvement in the methods of cultivation affects such commodities no less than corn and because they require less land (and, presumably, less use of cattle) than corn (WN I. xi. n, 'Conclution of the Digression'). 'As art and industry advance', therefore, the price of vegetable products would tend to fall less than the price of manufactures, since the scope for the division of labour in agriculture is naturally more restricted than in manufactures.[16]

The price of manufactures tends to fall, thanks to the increase in the 'productive powers' of labour, that is, to the decrease in the labour input, a decrease which, as a rule, is such as to more than compensate both the increase in the price of labour and the increase in the price of raw materials (WN I. viii. 56; I. xi. n. 12–13).

In the short run, it remains true that the market price of manufactures depends on supply, i.e. on the quantity brought to market, and demand. In the long run, the market price tends to coincide with the natural price which depends on costs, that is (referring to the price equation (c) of section I. 4), on the cost of labour (W_m/π_m) and on the cost of materials (M_m). (Since we are considering the manufacturing sector, here M_m is the money value of raw materials both imported and produced at home in other sectors.) If W_m increases but π_m rises more than in proportion, the cost of labour decreases and this decrease may be such as to more than compensate the increase (if any) in M_m.[17] The falling trend of prices of

---

[16] WN I. i. 4. Smith refers this observation to agriculture in general; I refer it to the fall in the real price of vegetable products compared to that of the price of manufactures, since it is quite clear that, in the case of animal products, the effects of the division of labour are more than counterbalanced by the adverse effects of natural scarcity and of increasing costs.

[17] Ricardo considers particularly this latter possibility; for the rest, he repeats almost literally Smith's concepts: 'The natural price of all commodities, excepting raw produce and labour, has a tendency to fall, in the progress of wealth and

manufactures, then, depends on the fall in the labour input, that is, on the rise in the 'productive powers' of labour, a rise which, in the opinion of Smith, was more rapid than that of the wage rate.

The wage rate in the short run depends on the demand for labour; it depends also on the price of provisions but, paradoxically, in the short run the wage rate and the price of provisions frequently vary in opposite directions.[18] In the long run, the level of wages depends on the 'trend' of the demand for labour and on the price of provisions; as a rule, the supply of labour will adapt itself to demand. In each stage of development, the purchasing power of wages in terms of provisions tends to be constant. The real price of labour tends to increase 'in the progressive state of the society', which implies an increasing accumulation of capital, that is, an increasing demand for productive labourers. In its turn, the accumulation of capital depends on profit, in the sense that profit is the pre-condition for accumulation. It is enough that profit be 'something more than what is sufficient to compensate the occasional losses to which every employment of stock is exposed': this is the lowest—the minimum acceptable or 'tolerable'—rate of profit (WN I. ix. 10, 18); for several reasons, too high a profit may represent a brake and not a stimulus to accumulation and the fall in the rate of profits, up to a point, can even speed up accumulation (see below). It is true that an 'extraordinary profit' may stimulate accumulation, but only if it is temporary; and it is temporary only if the entry is free and competition can work, though not immediately:

The establishment of any new manufacture, of any new branch of commerce, or of any new practice in agriculture, is always a speculation, from which the projector promises himself extraordinary profits. These profits sometimes are very great, and sometimes, more frequently,

population; for though, on the one hand, they are enhanced in real value, from the rise in the natural price of the raw materials of which they are made, this is more than counterbalanced by the improvements in machinery, by the better division and distribution of labour, and by the increasing skill, both in science and art, of the producers.' (*Works* I. v. 4.)

[18] The reason is that 'In years of plenty, servants frequently leave their masters, and trust their subsistence to what they can make by their own industry. But the same cheapness of provisions, by increasing the fund which is destined for the maintenance of servants, encourages masters, farmers especially, to employ a greater number.' The opposite is the case in years of scarcity. (WN I. viii. 45–6.)

perhaps, they are quite otherwise; but in general they bear no regular proportion to those of other old trades in the neighbourhood. If the project succeeds, they are commonly at first very high. When the trade or practice becomes thoroughly established and well known, the competition reduces them to the level of other trades. (WN i. x. pt. I, 43.)[19]

High *and* stable profits are always the consequence of monopoly, that is, of obstacles to entry; and monopoly—except in very special cases[20]—is damaging for economic growth, for several reasons, which often co-exist: (1) high price, (2) bad management, (3) extraordinary waste, and (4) reduction of revenue and, therefore, of savings.

(1) The monopolists, by keeping the market constantly under-stocked, by never fully supplying the effectual demand, sell their commodities much above the natural price, and raise their emoluments, whether they consist in wages or profit, greatly above their natural rate. (WN I. vii. 26.)

(2) Monopoly . . . is a great enemy to good management, which can never be universally established but in consequence of that free and universal competition which forces everybody to have recourse to it for the sake of self-defence. (WN I. xi. pt. I, 5.)

(3) Since the establishment of the English East India Company, for example, the other inhabitants of England, over and above being excluded from the trade, must have paid in the price of the East India goods which they have consumed, not only for all the extraordinary profits which the company may have made upon those goods in consequence of their monopoly, but for all the extraordinary waste which the fraud and abuse, inseparable from the management of the affairs of so great a company, must necessarily have occasioned. (WN IV. vii. pt. III, 91.)

(4) . . . as capital can be increased only by savings from revenue, the monopoly, by hindering it from affording so great a revenue as it would otherwise afford, necessarily hinders it from increasing so fast as it would otherwise increase, and, consequently from maintaining a

[19] This view—which was accepted in full first by Ricardo and then by Marx—anticipates quite clearly, though in a very embryonic way, the main thesis on innovations worked out by Joseph Schumpeter: Schumpeter's innovator is nothing else but Smith's projector. However, cf. WN II. iii. 26, II. iv. 15.
[20] As, for instance, in the case of a temporary monopoly, granted by law by means of a patent, of a new machine. (WN V. i. pt. III, art. I. 48.)

still greater quantity of productive labour, and affording a still greater revenue to the industrious of that country [the country that has established the monopoly of the colonial trade]. (Ibid., § 57.)

In Smith's conception, then, the fall in the rate of profit was a positive phenomenon *if* it was a reflection of the gradual elimination of monopolistic barriers of various kinds, especially those determined by laws and by institutions; that is, a positive phenomenon provided that it was a reflection of increasing competition and provided that it did not fall to the minimum acceptable level. When the rate of profit is approaching this level, however, stagnation is not the necessary outcome: with very low profits, capital would go in the direction of foreign trade or would 'disgorge itself' into the carrying trade, both at home and abroad (WN I. ix. 9–10; II. v. 35). The tendency of profits to fall, then, has, in Smith, not only a different cause but also a different effect than in Ricardo, for whom, in the long run, the fall in the rate of profit would simply bring accumulation to a halt (*Works* I. vi. 28). There are, however, two more possibilities indicated by Smith: one is given by 'the acquisition of new territory, or of new branches of trade', which may check and, for a time, even reverse the tendency of profits to fall; the other is given by the export of capital (WN I. ix. 12 and 10), which (we can infer) would increase the revenue of the investors or of the lenders, but it would certainly not contribute to the accumulation of capital in the home market. In any case, if it is true that very low profits are a consequence of the great prosperity of a country, it is also true that very low profits discourage further accumulation.[21] The rate of profit, then, would approach the minimum level and accumulation would tend to stagnate 'in a country which had acquired its full complement of riches' which 'is consistent with the nature of its laws and institutions' (WN I. ix. 15): a peculiar type of stationary state that in modern language would be described as one of economic maturity.

Competition, then, is seen by Smith as a process, at the end of which there is a kind of stationary state, but in the course of which there is an almost uninterrupted process of economic growth.

All events—spontaneous and political—that reduce monopolistic

---

[21] Compare this interpretation with that proposed by G. S. L. Tucker in his book *Progress and Profits in British Economic Thought, 1650–1850* (Cambridge University Press, 1960), ch. 4.

barriers of one kind or another and thus increase competition, contribute to sustain economic growth. Thus, the restoration of free importation, by gradually reducing import duties, the abolition of the exclusive privileges of the great companies in the colonial trade, and the repeal of the statute of apprenticeship— that is, the elimination of what are 'real encroachments upon natural liberty'—are all measures (extremely difficult to introduce) of a kind which will promote economic growth. On a different ground,

Good roads, canals, and navigable rivers, by diminishing the expence of carriage, put the remote parts of the country more nearly upon a level with those in the neighbourhood of the town. They are upon that account the greatest of all improvements. They encourage the cultivation of the remote, which must always be the most extensive circle of the country. They are advantageous to the town, by breaking down the monopoly of the country in its neighbourhood. They are advantageous even to that part of the country. Though they introduce some rival commodities into the old market, they open many new markets to its produce. (WN I. xi. pt. I, 5.)

Falling prices of those productions where the effects of the division of labour can prevail over the effects of natural scarcity, rising wages, and falling profits (with the qualifications above mentioned): these, for Smith, are the main aspects of a process of growth, which is characterized by the competitive mechanism.

The statistical picture of the past century seems to bear out Smith's expectations: during two periods (1800–1815 and 1850–1870) prices tended to rise, as a consequence of external events, like the Napoleonic Wars and the American Civil War, and also, probably, of fluctuations in the rate of increase of the monetary stock. But the fundamental trend of most prices was downward. To make appropriate comments, it is advisable to exclude the first two decades, which were strongly influenced by the Napoleonic Wars, and to distinguish the following eighty years into two sub-periods, from 1820 to 1870 and from 1870 to 1900, or, more precisely, 1897, when the long-term fall of prices came to an end. The reason for this subdivision is that in the seventies the transport revolution (railways and steamships) asserted itself in the most advanced countries of the world, with consequences which were particularly marked in the agricultural markets.

The following are the main trends in the two sub-periods:[22]

	1820–1870	*1870–1897*
1. Agricultural prices		
1a—vegetable products	declining	declining
1b—wheat	stationary	declining
1c—animal products	first stationary, then slowly rising	declining
2. Prices of exports (mostly manufactured products) (A)	falling	falling
3. Prices of imports (mostly primary products) (B)	first slowly falling, then stationary	falling
4. Terms of trade (A/B)	falling	stationary
5. Wages in manufacturing	first stationary, then slowly rising	rising

The behaviour of prices and wages during the first sub-period corresponds almost exactly to Smith's expectations; even the expectation of a fall in the price of vegetable products which was slower than the fall in the prices of manufactures seems to be borne out by the facts. In the second period, there are certain exceptions: the prices of wheat and of animal products are falling. In Smith's conception, such behaviour would only be possible assuming a rapidly developing relative scarcity of the metal used as money—gold in that period. If, as I think, this can be accepted, at most, as a subsidiary hypothesis, the main explanation is the rapid fall in costs due to the transport revolution, which opened world markets both to the vegetable products of North America and to the animal products of South America. A third exception, perhaps, is given by the behaviour of the terms of trade: since most of the exports of the United Kingdom were—and still are—manufactures and most of the imports were—and still are—primary products, the terms of trade should have been falling, as has happened in the first sub-period; instead, they were stationary. Such behaviour can be explained by the transport revolution only in part, and I will reconsider this question later on.

[22] Sources: B. R. Mitchell (with the collaboration of P. Deane), *Abstract of British Historical Statistics* (Cambridge University Press, 1962); A. Imlah, 'The Terms of Trade of the United Kingdom 1793–1913', *Journal of Economic History* (1950), n. 2; K. Martin and F. G. Thackeray, 'The Terms of Trade in Selected Countries, 1870–1938', *Bulletin of the Oxford Institute of Statistics* (November 1948).

Apart from these three exceptions, the behaviour of other prices and of wages corresponds to Smith's expectations also in the second sub-period. In this sub-period, even the rate of interest seems to behave in the way that Smith would have expected in a mature economy. Another indication of such Smithian maturity was the notable increase of investment abroad.

On the whole, in the past century, the competitive mechanism seems to prevail. The structure within which such a mechanism works is characterized by relatively small firms and easy entry, by the absence, or irrelevance, of trade unions, by the relatively modest size of State revenue and expenditure, and, of course, by extremely limited State intervention in the economy.

2. *A comparison between the past and the present century*

The modern picture has radically changed: small firms can be found, in great numbers, in agriculture and in the retail trade; but agriculture, in countries like the United Kingdom, today represents a tiny fraction, both of total income and of total employment; and the retail trade (apart from great imperfections in this area; imperfections not absent in the time of Smith and not ignored by him) is not, and has never been, a leading sector in economic growth. Not only banking and insurance, but also several branches of industry are dominated by large firms that, as a rule, are organized in the form of joint stock companies, though their legal framework is different from the one existing in Smith's time.[23] Trade unions, which were prohibited in those times,[24] have

---

[23] It is well known that Smith was very critical of joint stock companies, as he knew them. It is perhaps less known that Smith was in favour of joint stock companies in the case of four activities, the operations of which were 'capable of being reduced to what is called routine', that is, banking, insurance, canal and aqueduct construction and management. Apart from these activities, Smith was utterly sceptical as to the capacity of joint stock companies to prosper or even to survive for long, at least in foreign trade, without exclusive privileges granted by law: 'Without a monopoly, however, a joint stock company, it would appear from experience, cannot long carry on any branch of foreign trade. To buy in one market, in order to sell with profit, in another, when there are many competitors in both; to watch over, not only the occasional variations in the demand, but the much greater and more frequent variations in the competition, or in the supply which that demand is likely to get from other people, and to suit with dexterity and judgement both the quantity and quality of each assortment of goods to all these circumstances, is a species of warfare of which the operations are continually changing, and which can scarce ever be conducted successfully, without such an unremitting exertion of vigilance and attention, as cannot long be expected from the directors of a joint stock company' (WN

[*See overleaf for note 23 cont. and note 24*]

been organized and are today very powerful. In several branches of industry production has been carried out by a decreasing number of firms of an increasing size, that is, a process of concentration has taken place. Certain companies which had acquired, for technical reasons, one sort or another of monopolistic power, have been nationalized; several prices are administered by public bodies, especially in the field of public utilities. More generally the intervention of the State has acquired a very large and continuously growing importance. Large corporations, powerful trade unions, and growing State intervention are all phenomena variously linked together and, fundamentally, are all the result of the same objective process, that is, of the process of concentration.

At the origin of this process, we do not find changes in 'utility' or in the tastes of the consumers; we find changes in the conditions of production, i.e. technological progress, which has influenced the whole of economic life, including—directly or indirectly— changes in the habits of consumers. In the final analysis, at the root of the process of concentration we find a particular kind of division of labour: an increasing specialization of operations co-ordinated within organizational units of increasing size. This kind of division of labour has given rise to various types of 'economies of scale'; not only economies of scale in the strictly technological and organizational form, but also what we may call commercial, financial, and even 'scientific' economies of scale (since only very

V. i. e. 30, 'Of the Public Works and Institutions which are necessary for facilitating particular Branches of Commerce'). This passage shows very well that Smith's conception of competition is neither idyllic nor aseptic, like the conception of most contemporary economists—with the exception of Schumpeter, Rothschild, and a few others. Not even the division of labour, so much praised for its positive effects on economic growth, is seen by Smith as an idyllic process. (WN V. i. pt. III, art. II. 50.)

[24] 'The masters, being fewer in number, can combine much more easily; and the law, besides, authorises, or at least does not prohibit their combinations, while it prohibits those of the workmen.' The combinations of the masters, however, 'are frequently resisted by a contrary defensive combination of the workmen; who sometimes too, without any provocation of this kind, combine of their own accord to raise the price of their labour. Their usual pretences are, sometimes the high price of provisions; sometimes the great profit which their master makes by their work. But whether their combinations be offensive or defensive . . . They are desperate, and act with the folly and extravagance of desperate men, who must either starve, or frighten their masters into an immediate compliance with their demands . . . those tumultuous combinations . . . generally end in nothing, but the punishment or ruin of the ringleaders.' (WN I. viii. 12, 13.) The labour market: *quantum hodie mutatus ab illo*!

*l*arge companies can afford to organize costly laboratories for applied scientific research). The process of concentration has given rise, first, to large joint stock companies, then also to cartels and —mainly through mergers—to trusts and conglomerates. The process of concentration, in certain activities, has surpassed national boundaries and acquired world dimensions, giving rise to multinational corporations and accelerating the rate of change in the structure of world trade and of the international division of labour.[25]

In such a situation, the market form prevailing in industry— and, particularly, in manufacturing industry—is certainly no more Smith's competition, though it would be misleading to say that it is similar in character to Smith's monopoly. In a great number of activities, particularly in industry, which is the most dynamic sector of the economy, a novel market form has emerged, oligopoly, that partakes of some of the characteristics of monopoly and of some of those of competition, as several contemporary economists have pointed out. We find oligopoly not only in highly concentrated industries producing homogeneous commodities, but also in industries producing highly differentiated commodities.

In the industrial markets where oligopoly prevails, entry is not free: the main obstacle to entry is given by the size of output to produce or to sell economically—a size large in relation to the extent of the market. (In differentiated industries, costly and risky advertising campaigns need, first, to be launched and then to be repeated in order to break into the market; therefore, large sales are necessary to recoup these costs, which represent a variety of overhead costs.)

If the main obstacle to entry is given by the size of the output the individual firm must produce in relation to the extent of the

[25] The multinational corporations operating in 'new manufactures' and in 'old established manufactures' base their dominating position mainly on one kind or another of economies of scale, which are the outcome of a long process of division of labour. A third category of multinational corporations operating in agriculture and mining in certain underdeveloped countries base their dominating position upon concessions backed by political power, for the exploitation of natural resources; such corporations enjoy advantages very similar to those 'exclusive privileges' granted to the joint stock companies operating in the colonial trade in the time of Adam Smith. On the other hand, certain multinational corporations operating in manufactures enter into dealings with governments either to sell a part of their products to them or to influence their behaviour; it seems that in such dealings 'fraud and abuse' are the rule.

market, then that obstacle shifts, so to speak, if the market expands. In the said conditions, we cannot assume, not even as the result of a long-run tendency, a unique level of cost of production for all the firms; we have to allow for different cost levels in different firms. The larger the size of output, the lower the cost; but, given the extension of the market, the larger the size, the more difficult is the entry of a new firm. On these contradictory elements the industry finds a sort of dynamic equilibrium, that is, a situation acceptable to all firms. Such a situation changes either because the market expands, or because costs vary, or both (the market expansion necessarily implies cost changes, whereas the opposite is not true). In any case, costs represent the logical basis of two concepts —the entry-preventing price and the elimination price—which are essential to analyse both price determination and price variations.

In competition, the expansion of production can take place *either* because demand expands—an expansion which in the course of time promotes cost and price reductions—*or* because costs are reduced and these reductions, which generate an 'extraordinary profit', attract competition and promote an expansion of production. In both cases, the result is a greater production and a lower price. Owing to the obstacles to entry in oligopoly, the first route to growth—demand—becomes more and more important relative to the second one. And demand can increase not only 'naturally' (as a consequence of an expansion originating in private firms or in foreign demand) but also 'artificially' (e.g. public expenditure and public orders to firms). The cost reductions are transformed into price reductions only when they depend on innovations accessible to all firms or when they depend on the reductions in the prices of the means of production, especially labour and raw materials. As for the cost of labour, it falls when money wages increase less than productivity—or, as Smith puts it, when the reduction in the quantity of labour more than compensates the increase in wages. But this behaviour, which Smith considered to be the rule in a rapidly expanding economy, is today less and less frequent, owing to the great power which has been acquired by the unions.

In oligopoly, as well as in competition, prices depend on costs; but, unlike competition, prices depend on costs not only in the long run but also in the short run. The difference is very important indeed, because it is this dependence that largely explains why technological progress does not give rise any more to a downward trend of prices, at least in industry. As a matter of fact, the prices of raw materials being constant, technical progress reduces costs only if wages do not rise or if, as Smith assumes, wages rise less than in proportion to the reduction of labour input. The Smithian case still occurs today, but more and more seldom; as a rule, owing to the market power of the trade unions, the cost of labour either remains constant or increases, and consequently prices or, more precisely, wholesale prices, either remain constant or, much more often, increase. Retail prices increase even when wholesale prices remain constant, because wages increase at similar rates all over the economy, but the efficiency of labour in retail trade increases less than the general average; moreover, services increase in proportion to wages. Today as in the past, the Smithian ratio P/W tends to decrease, as a consequence of technical progress; not only wages, however, but also prices tend to rise (the former more than the latter). In modern conditions inflation is a tendency arising from the very structure of the product markets, as well as of the labour market.

In the new conditions, demand—in the sense of market size—has not only a strategic role in economic growth; it has an essential role also in short-run changes of income and employment. The fact is that in competition, when demand falls, price falls, since firms cannot do anything to prevent that fall. In oligopoly, firms, and particularly the leading firms, which control sizeable shares of the market and must be concerned with the behaviour of total demand, can avoid a price fall by reducing their output; they can also avoid a price rise when demand increases. As a matter of fact, the leading firms normally command a certain amount of unused capacity to face seasonal fluctuations and the long-run increase in demand, if such an increase is expected; the unused capacity can also serve as a deterrent against potential entrants. Therefore, an increase of demand normally determines an increase of output and not of prices; if prices increase this occurs because costs increase.

The outcome of all this is that, under contemporary conditions, a considerable price fall can take place only during a severe slump in output and employment, whereas in the past century a price fall was a normal occurrence and only exceptionally accompanied by an interruption of the process of economic growth. Money wages, which, in the past century, were fluctuating with the business cycle, although on a rising trend, have in our century shown an increasing downward rigidity. After the Second World War, absolute decreases are practically absent in all advanced countries; what is left to be explained is the change in the rate of increase.

Technological progress and product differentiation, then, have progressively increased the obstacles to entry in a growing number of markets; and, though such a trend has been to some extent counterbalanced by decreasing transport costs, all things considered, the market power of many firms has increased. This, however, has only in certain periods and in certain countries given rise to a general increase in profit margins, since the market power of the unions has increased not less and, especially after the Second World War, even more than the market power of the firms. The consequence has been an increase not only of the wage rate but also in the share of wages in the national income and, correspondingly, a reduction in the profit share, at least in the industrial sectors of several countries. In any case, the market power of the unions depends on that of the firms.

Since the market power of the modern oligopolistic firms is not, as a rule, the result of legal or institutional obstacles to entry, but of obstacles determined by the very process of economic growth, it cannot be progressively reduced in the way Smith suggested for the monopolies of his own times. Yet, that power is often enhanced by laws and agreements of various kinds, which can be attacked on the legal and political plane. Besides, the reduction of protectionist barriers between country and country—a typically Smithian prescription—can, to some extent, reduce that power. On the whole, however, the structure of contemporary advanced economies, characterized by giant corporations, powerful trade unions, a large State apparatus, poses problems of economic policy completely different from those envisaged by Adam Smith. In truth, we can learn not so much from his prescriptions, as from the nature of his approach, which is at once theoretical and historical and points to the necessity of studying economies in their over-all movements.

3. *The terms of trade and underdeveloped countries*

I have already noted that, whereas during the first sixty or seventy years of the last century the terms of trade of the United

Kingdom had a tendency to fall (that is, they moved 'against' British exports, mostly manufactured goods, and in favour of imports, mostly primary goods), in the last thirty years of the century the terms of trade remained about stationary. I also noted that the falling trend corresponded to Smith's expectations, whereas the stationary trend does not, because, according to him, the rate of increase in the 'productive powers' of labour is higher in the case of manufactures than in the cases of agricultural and mineral products; that is, in the latter case, the increase in productivity is unable to compensate, or more than compensate, the effects of natural scarcity.

In this century, it appears that the terms of trade of those industrialized countries that import most of the raw materials they use have until very recently remained stationary or, more probably, have risen, that is, they have moved in favour of manufacturers and against primary products.

As is well known, the question of the terms of trade is a very controversial one, especially if we consider, on one side, the industrialized countries and, on the other, the countries which base their economy on the production and export of a limited number of primary commodities. Here it is enough to observe that if it is true that the rate of increase in productivity has been higher in industrialized than in underdeveloped countries, then stationary terms of trade will increase the gap between the two categories of country; it is an indication that the fruits of technological progress have been largely 'captured' by labourers and other income earners of industrialized countries. (The different behaviour of productivity depends not only or not so much on the nature of agriculture or on grounds of natural scarcity, as on the much slower technological progress of the poorer countries.)

All in all, the present-day relations between advanced countries and underdeveloped countries resemble those between 'towns corporate' and the country as described by Smith:

The government of towns corporate was altogether in the hands of traders and artificers; and it was the manifest interest of every particular class of them, to prevent the market from being overstocked, as they commonly express it, with their own particular species of industry; which is in reality to keep it always understocked. Each class was eager to establish regulations proper for this purpose, and provided it was allowed to do so, was willing to consent that every other class

should do the same. In consequence of such regulations, indeed, each
class was obliged to buy the goods they had occasion for from every
other within the town, somewhat dearer than they otherwise might
have done. But in recompence, they were enabled to sell their own just
as much dearer; so that so far it was as broad as long, as they say;
and in the dealings of the different classes within the town with one
another, none of them were losers by these regulations. But in their
dealings with the country, they were all great gainers; and in these
latter dealings consists the whole trade which supports and enriches
every town. (WN I. x. pt. II, 18.)

Certainly, the direction of the trend in the terms of trade is not,
in itself, a decisive factor for the development of underdeveloped
countries; Kindleberger's 'capacity to transform', i.e., the capacity of an economy to adapt itself and to exploit the changing
conditions of the internal and international markets, is even
more important. It is also true, however, that an adverse or even a
stationary trend in the terms of trade is an additional brake on the
development of underdeveloped countries. Moreover, their high
and relatively rigid specialization is itself a consequence of the
domination of certain advanced countries, so that the behaviour
of the terms of trade *and* the rigidity of the specialization are to
be analysed together.

It seems that in recent years the movements of the terms of
trade have often been against the advanced countries and in
favour of underdeveloped countries; the most striking change of
this kind has been that of the price of oil. Owing to the greater
political strength of the underdeveloped countries on the world
plane, a political strength that has been enhanced by the rivalry
among the great powers; owing also to certain natural scarcities
which are beginning to appear, in spite of technological progress
in agriculture, in mining, and in the invention of substitutes; and
further to the instability of the 'dollar standard' and the consequent higher 'propensity to speculate' in raw materials—considering all these forces and changes, it is possible that the terms
of trade between manufactures and primary products will tend to
move more and more often in favour of the latter products. Such
a tendency, if it asserted itself, would create new economic hardships for the advanced countries.[26] But it is to be feared that

[26] It is worth reflecting on the equation (g) mentioned in section I. 4, concerning real wages (real in the modern sense): if we consider M_y as the price of

any process through which countries which are at present underdeveloped will move towards equality with respect to the now
advanced countries will be long, difficult, and painful for all.
And since most of the underdeveloped countries in ancient or in
recent times were colonies, it is well to enlarge the scope of our
thoughts and reflect on the following important observations of
Adam Smith:

The discovery of America, and that of a passage to the East Indies
by the Cape of Good Hope, are the two greatest and most important
events recorded in the history of mankind. Their consequences have
already been very great; but, in the short period of between two and
three centuries which has elapsed since these discoveries were made,
it is impossible that the whole extent of their consequences can have
been seen. What benefits, or what misfortunes to mankind may hereafter
result from those great events, no human wisdom can foresee. By uniting, in some measure, the most distant parts of the world, by enabling
them to relieve one another's wants, to increase one another's enjoy-
ments, and to encourage one another's industry, their general tendency
would seem to be beneficial. To the natives, however, both of the East
and West Indies, all the commercial benefits which can have resulted
from those events have been sunk and lost in the dreadful misfortunes
which they have occasioned. These misfortunes, however, seem to have
arisen rather from accident than from any thing in the nature of those
events themselves. At the particular time when these discoveries were
made, the superiority of force happened to be so great on the side of the
Europeans, that they were enabled to commit with impunity every
sort of injustice in those remote countries. Hereafter, perhaps, the
natives of those countries may grow stronger, or those of Europe
may grow weaker, and the inhabitants of all the different quarters of
the world may arrive at that equality of courage and force which, by
inspiring mutual fear, can alone overawe the injustice of independent
nations into some sort of respect for the rights of one another. But
nothing seems more likely to establish this equality of force than that
mutual communication of knowledge and of all sorts of improvements
which an extensive commerce from all countries to all countries
naturally, or rather necessarily, carries along with it. (WN IV. vii. pt.
III, 80.)

Smith's conception of social life, I have already noted, is by no
means idyllic and contrasts quite decidedly with the conventional

imported raw materials and P_y as the price of finished products, it appears that
an increase in the ratio M_y/P_y brings about—*ceteris paribus*—a diminution either
of real wages or of the rate of profit.

optimism that would prevail later on; yet his conclusions, as well as his recommendations, are never pessimistic. In this particular but extremely important case, we can accept Smith's conclusion provided we recognize that, under modern conditions, 'an extensive commerce' as such is not enough to promote equality, even if we take into account all the qualifications accompanying that conclusion. Smith himself, in another respect, points out that that 'liberty and independency' which was arrived at by the inhabitants of the towns 'much earlier than the occupiers of land in the country', was the pre-requisite of the rise and progress of the towns in Europe, after the fall of the Roman Empire (WN III. iii. 3). After the end of the Second World War, several colonies or quasi-colonies have, in fact, acquired some sort of 'liberty and independency'. But this is only a pre-requisite of a process of development that under modern conditions will necessarily be very different from all the processes analysed in the *Wealth of Nations*. Even the processes of development which are taking place in our time in advanced countries are very different from those studied by Smith. All this, however, does not mean that to-day the *Wealth of Nations* can interest only historians of economic thought or students of economic history. Because, to try to understand the societies in which we live, we have to try to understand, on the theoretical plane, the logic of their movements in long or very long periods. And, in this direction, the approach developed by Adam Smith in his great work can still give us invaluable help today.

COMMENT

by C. K. Rowley*

By a perpetual monopoly, all the other subjects of the state are taxed very absurdly in two different ways; first, by the high price of goods, which, in the case of a free trade, they could buy much cheaper; and secondly, by their total exclusion from a branch of business, which it might be both convenient and profitable for many of them to carry on. It is for the most worthless of all purposes too that they are taxed in

* University of Newcastle-upon-Tyne.

this manner. It is merely to enable the company to support the negligence, profusion, and malversation of their own servants, whose disorderly conduct seldom allows the dividend of the company to exceed the ordinary rate of profit in trades which are altogether free, and very frequently makes it fall even a good deal short of that rate. (WN V. i. e. 30, *Of the Public Works . . . necessary for facilitating particular Branches of Commerce.*)

This quotation perhaps better than any other captures Smith's attitude towards competition and monopoly in the product market and presages all recent discussion on management discretion, X-inefficiency, and satisficing behaviour in the presence of substantial market power. It denies the theoretical relevance of all attempts to determine monopoly power by reference to the rate of profit—a lesson alas! which has been ignored by succeeding generations of economists. It emphasizes—as Sylos-Labini has correctly stated—the reliance placed by Smith upon free entry as the basis of competition and of obstacles to entry as the *sine qua non* of monopoly. It is the failure to appreciate the essential dynamics of the Smithian competitive process which is the central weakness both of the more elegant neoclassical approach and of Lange–Lerner socialism. Arguably, this lack of appreciation is a key determinant in the present economic decline of the United Kingdom as economists vie with each other in devising yet more sophisticated instruments of government intervention not as a buttress to competition but in a futile and damaging quest for the marginal conditions that constitute their sacrament. It is indeed ironic that the bicentenary of Adam Smith is celebrated in this country by an industrial policy that in every significant respect is an insult to the *Wealth of Nations*. But, as Smith himself has wryly commented: 'There is a great deal of ruin in a Nation' (Letter 221, addressed to Sir John Sinclair, dated 14 October, 1782). Against this background, let me comment upon certain aspects of Sylos-Labini's paper.

1. *Competition and monopoly*

It is important to stress, perhaps to a greater degree than does Sylos-Labini, that Smith viewed the principal impediments to competition as emanating from government itself, most especially in the form of exclusive privileges granted to corporations and of high duties and prohibitions placed upon foreign manufacturers.

It is also important to note that Smith was far more aware than have been many of his successors of the close interaction between economics and politics and of the disproportionate political influence of well-organized pressure groups:

> It cannot be very difficult to determine who have been the contrivers of this whole mercantile system; not the consumers, we may believe, whose interest has been entirely neglected—but the producers, whose interest has been so carefully attended to; and among this latter class our merchants and manufacturers have been by far the principal architects. (WN IV. viii. 54.)

Recognition of this interface between the protected minorities and the political process is important for an understanding of the conspiracy between the bureaucrats and the unionized labour interests which so imperils both our economic performance and our civil liberties at the present time. Those private-sector industrialists who have glimpsed the nature of this nexus are now actively engaged in obtaining bureaucratic status for their own enterprises, if not by outright nationalization then by encouraging the Government to take on a financial interest via the National Enterprise Board. In consequence, antitrust policy is a terminal case in the present United Kingdom context.

2. *The natural price and the natural rate of wages, profits, and rent*

Sylos-Labini offers an important insight into Smith's view of the market mechanism in stressing the very flexible time-dimensions within which the latter analysed the behaviour of supply and demand. It is a weakness as well as a strength of neoclassical economics that the time-dimensions are so tightly defined and that, for the most part, the less precise 'stages of development' phase is either ignored or paid a footnote attention. Indeed, when analysing such issues as long-run marginal cost pricing for public enterprise, the neoclassical strait-jacket gives rise to ludicrous implications, as economists such as Turvey and Littlechild now recognize. Smith was much too well-informed ever to fall into such a formalist trap.

Sylos-Labini exaggerates the difference between Smith and the neoclassicals on the issue of the criterion of supply and demand. Neoclassical economists readily accept the existence of a positively sloped supply curve of labour with respect to the real wage and, in the long run, accept that this implies an appropriate theory of population. Interdependence between the supply curve and the demand curve is not at all alien to neoclassical economics, as Sylos-Labini appears to suggest. Nor, especially recently, has neoclassical economics restricted itself exclusively to the analysis of 'strictly economic forces' as any issue of *The Journal of Political Economy* will bear witness, though it has not sold itself out to Marxist dialectics despite the pressure applied from Cambridge, England. The essential message from Smith—to the effect that prices will tend towards the level dictated by the efficient cost of production in the absence of monopoly restrictions—is quite consistent with the neoclassical predictions. It is tragic that this important insight is not at all reflected in British market policies at the present time.

3. *The extent of the market and technological changes*

As Sylos-Labini correctly points out, increasing returns, viewed by Smith as prevailing in manufactures and in certain agricultural productions, did not constitute a threat to competition since they were negligible at that time, even by reference to eighteenth-century markets. Indeed, Smith's increasing returns were more the fruit of technical progress than of the extended division of labour and, as such, not necessarily related to the scale of production in the sense of neoclassical economics. Certainly, those like Kaldor, who rely upon increasing returns to destroy the logic of neoclassical economics, will find precious little in the *Wealth of Nations* to support their propositions. Once again, much confusion has arisen in the attempt to compress Smithian dynamics into a rigid framework of comparative static analysis.

4. *The competitive mechanism and the process of economic growth*

Smith had a clear view of the relationship between competition and economic growth and—as Sylos-Labini demonstrates—his central predictions are not falsified by reference to nineteenth-century experience. Whether the relationship would stand up to twentieth-century scrutiny, given the systematic corrosion of the competitive mechanism and its replacement by bureaucratic socialism is a moot point, and one deserving of further scrutiny.

Without denying Sylos-Labini his interpretation that profits high *and* stable are always the consequence of monopoly I would emphasize that Smith was in no way committed to the notion that profits low *and* stable are indicative of competition. As my introductory quotation indicates, Smith was fully apprised of the possibility that potential profit might be subverted by the factors of production or squandered in sloth in monopolistic markets.

5. *A comparison between the past century and our century*

Sylos-Labini's interpretation of market changes since the *Wealth of Nations* was written has a distinctly Galbraithian flavour, with large multi-national multi-product oligopolies consolidating their market shares via mergers, manipulating their markets and protecting themselves from new entry via advertising, with prices largely unresponsive to changes in demand, even in the short run, and with such competition as remains relying upon over-all market expansion for its delicate and transitory life. I do not entirely share his viewpoint, nor do I accept, as he appears to do, the inevitability of the Galbraithian nightmare. It is true that merger-sponsored concentration has been extensive in Britain since 1945. But recent evidence suggests that scale economies in production do not justify current levels of concentration. For example, George and Ward clearly indicate that for 41 industries the leading U.K. firms on average are 2·2 times as large as their West German counterparts—and they are hardly more competitive! The recent merger boom is closely associated with bureaucratic socialism in Britain and concentration could be substantially reduced by anti-trust policy with consequential improvements in efficiency in production in many manufacturing industries if the public was alert to its true predicament. There are encouraging signs that the shrine of scale economies no longer is sacrosanct in view of the depressing recent experience of our largest enterprises.

Nor do I accept Sylos-Labini's assertion that prices are entirely cost-determined in oligopolistic markets. As Stigler and Kendall have shown, effective prices are much more flexible through the cycle than list price movements would suggest. The widening of the British market with entry into the European Economic Community should encourage additional price flexibility even in markets which formerly were well protected.

In conclusion, I suggest that Adam Smith would be appalled by present British industrial policy were he to revisit us for the bicentenary. But he would reject out of hand the inevitability of bureaucratic socialism that is so depressing a feature of Sylos-Labini's paper. Competitive capitalism has taken a beating in post-war Britain, and indeed now it is in a far from healthy condition. But bureaucratic socialism has not provided the voters with their much-coveted economic growth. There is a ground-swell of opinion deeply concerned at the erosion of natural liberty in this country and sceptical of the economic case for bureaucratic socialism. I retain a Smithian optimism that the people will recognize before it is too late the coincidence of government expansion and economic decline, and that bureaucratic socialism will be reined in and then cut back in the twin names of liberty and economic efficiency.

COMMENT

by A. Nove*

Before turning to Professor Sylos-Labini's interesting and thought-provoking paper, I would like to make a few remarks concerning the impact of Adam Smith in Russia. His influence, exercised through two Russian students who attended his courses in Glasgow, is the subject of a paper by Dr. A. H. Brown in a symposium linked with the present occasion.[1] By the beginning of the nineteenth century Smith's work was the talk of society. In Pushkin's *Eugene Onegin*, the hero, a man-about-town, is shown to be well acquainted with it, as the following quotation amply demonstrates. I quote the first few lines in Russian to show that it is poetry in the original. The rhymed English version is my own, with apologies to any literary purists (from stanza 7).

> Braníl Goméra, Feokríta,
> Zató chitál Adáma Smíta
> I byl glubókii ekonóm.
> Tó yest' umél sudít o tom
> Kak gosudárstvo bogatéyet
> I chem zhivyót, i pochemú
> Ne núzhno zólota yemú
> Kogdá 'prostói prodúkt' iméyet . . .

* University of Glasgow.
[1] 'Adam Smith's First Russian Followers', *Essays on Adam Smith*.

Theocritus and Homer bored him
But Adam Smith he read right through.
In economics he was learnéd
He knew how wealth of nations grew,
What they produce, and why they need
Just 'simple products' and not gold.
Advice his father failed to heed;
The family estates were sold.

Pushkin was not only Russia's most famous poet but a widely educated man. He had been taught about Adam Smith at the *lycée* at Tsarskoye Selo. A textbook he used, on public finance, written by N. Turgenev (not to be confused with the novelist Ivan Turgenev), contains the following passage:

Those who study political economy, called Smithian or critical, learn to believe only in research and reason and simple common sense, in all that is natural and not artificial. They would see that welfare is based on freedom, and that evil comes when busybodies try to think and act for others and impose petty tutelage. Those seeking the causes and nature of the wealth of nations are presented with the vast experience of times past.[2]

This is typical of the impact of Smith on the Russian liberal-minded gentry of the period. One more quotation may be proper, possibly the first instance of economics being regarded as a dismal science. It comes from the anonymous memoirs of a fellow-student of Pushkin's at the *lycée* of Tsarskoye Selo:

In 1818 political economy and severity of deportment were in fashion. We considered it improper to dance . . ., and had no time for the ladies. But everything soon changed; the French quadrille replaced Adam Smith. (Brodsky, ibid., 65.)

Now on to Sylos-Labini's valuable paper and to some thoughts to which it gave rise.

Firstly, I began to speculate on the odd fate of the word 'competition'. As he points out 'the difference between the marginalist and the classical conception of competition is very wide indeed'. It seems to me that the marginalists, or more precisely the general equilibrium theorists, have so defined perfect competition as to eliminate the very possibility of competition. For Adam Smith

[2] N. Brodsky: *Pushkin's novel Eugenii Onegin, a Commentary* (Moscow, 1957), 64.

and his successors it was a process of struggle. Producers devise methods 'in order to undersell one another'. To use Sylos-Labini's words, 'Smith's conception of competition is neither idyllic nor aseptic'. People are hurt, new firms try to elbow their way in. Bankruptcies occur. There has to be some spare or under-used capacity, for, if there is not, how can anyone compete, in the sense of trying to grab a larger share of the market, an activity which firms under competitive conditions are prone to in real life? The textbook's perfect competition is neither perfect nor competition. It is a logical construct with certain useful mathematical properties. Its other uses seem to me to be small, its capacity to divert our students from real issues considerable. It does seem to me to be a misuse of language to have the words 'imperfect competition' describe even the most competitive sectors of our economy. In real life almost every competitor is trying to persuade his potential customers that his goods are better, his after-sales service more reliable, than those of his rivals. Yet to some purists even a peasant crying out that his melons are superior to those of other peasants is 'differentiating the product' and is well on his way to becoming an oligopolist. Such a definition has confused our analyses of real oligopoly, where competition is indeed substantially restricted.

Of course it is true, as Sylos-Labini points out, that in most sectors of manufacturing industry what we have is 'no more Adam Smith's competition'; genuine oligopoly is very common. The degree of power over output, prices, and the market, varies widely in the real world. A total monopoly is about as unreal as perfect competition. But the *degree* of monopoly power can certainly have effects. I recall a sad remark made to me a few years ago by a Czech economist: 'Why is a capitalist monopoly so much more efficient than a socialist monopoly?' His answer to his own question was: 'Because there is nothing so monopolist as a socialist monopoly'. Adam Smith was quite right to stress the vital importance of freedom of entry into the industry. In the West, hard though it is in some sectors of industry for a newcomer to establish himself, at least it is legal for him to try, and the policies of the established oligopolists with regard to prices, the volume of output, and technical progress are affected by the need to discourage the would-be entrant from entering. The Soviet-type industrial ministry or manager is surrounded by a kind of impenetrable tariff wall. The customers are attached to their suppliers by the planning agencies and cannot go elsewhere. No autonomous unit can decide to enter the industry. Under sellers' market conditions the producer has the whip hand, the customer (be he another factory or an ordinary citizen) becomes often reduced to the position of a suppliant. Under these conditions monopolistic distortions flourish, unless combated by administrative measures, which are hard to define or enforce.

In analysing modern Western economies, and in comparing their operations with those in Communist countries, it is surely both useful and important to be conscious of the extent of real or potential competition or monopoly, both of the power of the monopolist and of his possibility for using it. Nor should one over-look, as some textbook-reared students (and even some of their teachers) are apt to do, the dimensions of quality, reliability, punctuality, and service. These things may be automatically attended to under competition because of the consequences of loss of goodwill, but goodwill has no commercial meaning if it can neither be lost nor transferred, if the customer cannot go else-where. If it is more convenient for the producer for razor-blades to be rather blunt, there will be no 'commercial' reasons for them to be sharp, without competition, or an imposed standard of sharpness, unless there is a sense of duty (a sentiment which plays no part in modern economic analysis).

One point did worry me a little, especially because of the stress on production. I do not know whether this is a query which should be addressed to Adam Smith or to Sylos-Labini, and it is this. After citing Adam Smith to the effect that 'the demand for labour determines what are the necessaries and conveniences of life which must be given to the labourer', one seeks in vain the link between this and the *production* of the necessaries and conveniences of life. Sylos-Labini himself states that 'wages, profits, and rent depend on the general conditions of society rather than strictly economic forces', and quotes Marx approvingly in this connection. But what of the level of output? The real price of labour, we are told, tends to increase 'in the progressive state of society', and also that this implies the increasing *accumulation of capital*, which *depends on profit*. How is such a dynamic model consistent with a fall in the profit rate, which is presented as the natural consequence of higher incomes of the labourers? Why is it assumed that the necessary increase in output will be forthcoming, as if this is an automatic response to demand? Surely, the wage rate does *not* just depend on 'demand for labour and the price of provisions': it depends decisively also on the production of goods and services?

All this has its contemporary aspect. I have seen sophisticated mathematical models in which real wages and output are independent variables. We have all heard trade union militants blithely ignoring the connection between real wages and productivity, while exaggerating the possibilities of income redistribution. I have also seen (Western) analyses of the Soviet economy in which an enhanced rate of increase in consumption is made dependent upon a decline in the level of investment, with not a word about how one achieves a large increase in the output of consumers' goods and services without additional investment (the point, of course, is what one invests in).

Sylos-Labini makes very interesting use of the *Wealth of Nations* in his discussion of the terms of trade of underdeveloped countries. However, at least for this reader of his paper, there seem to be several different aspects of the problem perhaps insufficiently distinguished. One, strongly backed by a quotation from Adam Smith, relates to the dimension of national power and to colonial status. In this model terms of trade are altered by armed might, as when a conqueror puts his foot on the scales. A second and quite different point relates, in Sylos-Labini's words, to 'the capture of the fruits of technological progress by labourers and other income earners of industrialized countries'. For this to take place Adam Smith's 'superiority of force' is not required. What seems to be implied is that successfully pressed claims for higher wages by workers in industrialized countries force up costs and prices. This was a point made by the neo-Marxist economist, Emmanuel, in his book on unequal exchange. It was made in another way by Sir Arthur Lewis at this conference. In *this* model the power element refers more to the power of trade unions inside industrialized countries, and of course the resultant inequalities require barriers to migration to maintain them. Thirdly, there are the quite different questions such as the over-production of cocoa, the development of synthetics, and other factors which affect the demand for, and price of, certain commodities, and therefore the terms of trade of the developing world. Finally, there is productivity: output per head. It seems to me important to distinguish these strands in the argument.

But I have no intention at all of ending on a critical or carping note. This was a most useful presentation. Sylos-Labini's own work is that of an economist who is very much and very usefully of this world, and we should thank him for coming to this conference and showing us the modernity and relevance of Adam Smith.

8

The Labour Market

E. H. Phelps Brown[*]

WHEN Adam Smith entered on his study of mankind in the business of daily life, there was a method he took for granted. The very title of his work reminds us of it: not 'Principles of Political Economy' but 'The Wealth of Nations'. He thought and wrote with 'different ages and nations'[1] in his mind's eye. Avid of information, observant, retentive, and reflective, whether in the voyaging of his mind in the long years of his classical studies, or in his bodily travels through countries of his own day, he was a natural user of the comparative method.

We in our turn can use his work to apply that method: we can ask how the economies he knew compare with those of today, and how his understanding compares with our own of the enduring problems of society.

One of those problems that particularly concerns the labour market is social inequality. In an economy like ours in which seven-eighths of the national income consists of earnings, and incomes policy has raised insistently the question of how much each should get relative to others, social inequality presents itself prominently as inequality of pay. But under this there still lies the formerly more prominent question of why the national product comes to be divided as it is between pay, profits, and rent. These are the two questions we shall take up here. Smith recorded his observations about both of them. We can look at them through his eyes, so as to be able to compare the economies of his time

---

[*] Sir Henry Phelps Brown, Professor Emeritus, London School of Economics, London. The author is indebted to Laurence Hunter and Andrew Skinner for valuable comments which have enabled him to correct and improve his text at a number of points.

[1] WN I, Introduction & Plan of Work, 3 § 8. Page references to the WN are to E. Cannan's edition in 2 vols. (Methuen, University Paperbacks, 1961). The page numbers are those of vol. i, except such as are prefixed with ii.

with those of today, and his views of their workings with our own. In doing this we shall be looking first at the labour market, and then at the economic and social structure in which that market operates.

I

Why do different occupations command different rates of pay? Why, as the phrase goes, do dons earn more than dustmen? Adam Smith's first answer was that the pay of each occupation is fixed and from time to time changed by the interplay of supply and demand. Any restriction of supply keeps the pay up. 'Had the Universities of Oxford and Cambridge been able to maintain themselves in the exclusive privilege of graduating all the doctors who could practise in England', Smith wrote to Dr. Cullen,[2] 'the price of feeling the pulse might by this time have risen from two and three guineas, the price which it is now happily arrived at, to double or treble that sum.' Similarly with the 'statutes of apprenticeship and other corporation laws . . . which, when a manufacture is in prosperity, enable the workman to raise his wages a good deal above their natural rate' (WN 70; I. vii. 31)— this natural rate being the one that would prevail under free competition (WN 70; I. vii. 27). With curates and dons it was the other way about: these occupations were flooded with men educated on charitable foundations. Curates had to have a 'long, tedious and expensive education', but because so many got it free, the church was 'crowded with such people who, in order to get employment, are willing to accept of a much smaller recompence than what such an education would otherwise have entitled them to',[3] and curates earned no more than journeyman masons or shoemakers. As for the dons:

the time and study, the genius, knowledge, and application requisite to qualify an eminent teacher of the sciences, are at least equal to what is necessary for the greatest practitioners in law and physic. But the usual reward of the eminent teacher bears no proportion to that of the lawyer and physician; because the trade of the one is crowded with indigent people who have been brought up to it at the public expense; whereas those of the other two are encumbered with very few who have not been educated at their own. (WN 148; I. x. c. 38.)

[2] J. Rae, *Life of Adam Smith* (London, Macmillan, 1895), 278. Letter 143, dated 20 September 1774.

[3] WN 145; I. x. c. 34 ('Inequalities occasioned by the Policy of Europe').

These were some of the numerous ways Smith noted in which 'the policy of Europe' disturbed the differences of pay that would otherwise prevail in a competitive market where the movement of labour into any occupation was neither subsidized nor obstructed. But there still would be differences of pay in such a market, for entrants would take account not only of the money offered by each occupation, but also of its 'particular nature', and according as that nature was attractive or repellent they would present themselves in greater or less number, and so receive less or more pay.[4] The judge accepts the honour in which he is held in lieu of part of the salary otherwise due in money (WN 119; I. x. b. 24: ii. 240; V. i. b. 19); but the butcher must earn more than other tradesmen, because his is 'a brutal and odious business' (I. x. b. 2). Reckonings of this kind, in which individuals take combined account of the pay and the nature of each occupation, lead to the adjustment of differences of pay in the market, through the mobility of labour—the mobility of entrants and, in the longer but not the shorter run, the mobility of those already occupied. If one occupation offers more than others, taking pay and amenities or deterrents together, then labour will move into it in greater numbers, and bring the pay there down, while the consequently reduced supply raises it elsewhere. The upshot is that the net advantages offered by all occupations tend to equality, and the differences in pay are only such as will offset differences in the non-pecuniary rewards that occupations offer, and in the difficulty of qualifying for and following them.

But this conclusion was never stated by Smith in so many words. That was not his way. He was recording tendencies he saw at work in the world around him, but they would have led to the conclusion we have drawn here only if they operated without obstruction and if there were no conflicting forces; and he observed plenty of these.

Among the obstructions, besides those artificially erected by 'the policy of Europe', are some inherent in human nature. 'Man is of all sorts of luggage the most difficult to be transported': hence great differences in what was paid for the same work in different places, with 'the common price of labour' in London three times

---

[4] WN I. x. b, 'Inequalities arising from the Nature of the Employments themselves'. See also Albert Rees, 'Compensating Wage Differentials' in *Essays on Adam Smith*.

what it was in the Highlands (WN 84; I. viii. 31-4). Once people had taken up an occupation, moreover, they were not disposed to leave it in a hurry, or found it hard to do so: if the demand for an occupation dropped and the pay fell below the level needed to attract entrants, some of those who were 'bred to the business in the time of its prosperity' would hang on even for the rest of their lives (WN 70; I. vii. 31). Because of this immobility of labour, at least in the short run, the ups and downs of demand brought sharp movements in pay: a public mourning, for example, would raise the wages of tailors and lower those of the workers in coloured silks and cloths (WN 67; I. vii. 19).

Movements of that sharp kind are only prominent instances of the movability of rates of pay that Smith generally presupposed when he envisaged the working out of natural rates in a competitive market; but he also noticed the rigidity of custom. 'In many places the money price of labour remains uniformly the same sometimes for half a century together' (WN 83; I. viii. 30). He was largely right, at least for a sheltered and traditional industry like building: in the Thames valley the predominant wage of the building craftsman remained the same for 120 years, from 1412 to 1532; and in Smith's own century it had remained the same for 20 years, from 1710 to 1730, and again for 37 years, from 1736 to 1773.[5] Perhaps too we are not just reading a feature of our own times back into the past, if we see an implicit reference to the rigidity of custom in Smith's observation that the rise and fall of the general level of real wages leaves differentials unchanged (WN 160; I. x. c. 63).

We said that in Smith's account of how differences of pay came about, the tendency to equalize net advantages not only comes up against such obstructions as we have just noticed, but also has to bear the impact of other forces. One of these is bargaining power. This was not exerted through collective bargaining, for though both masters and men had a propensity to combine, the men's combinations were ineffective because they could not hold out nearly so long as the masters. 'In the long run the workman may be as necessary to his master as his master is to him; but the necessity is not so immediate' (WN 75; I. viii. 12). To force the issue speedily, therefore, the men would resort to outcry and tumult, which only brought the law down on them: the end would be only 'the punishment or ruin of the ringleaders' (WN 76; I. viii. 13). The masters, then, themselves 'always and everywhere in a sort of tacit, but constant and uniform, combination, not to raise the wages of labour above their actual rate' (WN 75; I. viii. 13: I. x. c. 61), could have it their own way: sometimes they even entered into combinations to lower wages, and sometimes the men yielded without resistance. How was it, then, we may ask, that as Smith observed elsewhere (not altogether in agreement with what he had had to say about customary rates), 'Since the time of Henry VIII . . . the wages of labour have been continually increasing'? (WN 100; I. ix. 6.) The answer was that in times of expansion, when the funds destined for the maintenance of labour were overflowing, the masters abandoned their combinations and competed for scarce labour by bidding up the rate (WN 77; I. viii. 17). But in more balanced times the pay that any one workman could get would depend on the bargain that he could make singlehanded with a master, and here the form of bargaining power came in that depended on each party's judgement of how much the other needed him, and on the intensity of each man's determination. Thus in a year of bad harvest, although the cost of living was up, the workman would be willing to take less, and the master would find him 'more humble and dependent' (WN 93; I. viii. 48)—because there was unemployment in the air. Something at all times depended on 'the easiness or hardness' of particular masters, and this was one reason for men being paid at different rates for doing the same work in the same place (WN 87; I. viii. 34).

There were other forces whose impact Smith noticed. Indeed he needed to invoke them if his account of pay was to cover the range of occupations, high paid as well as low. His observations as we have followed them so far were mostly applicable to manual workers, the 'workmen' of whom he invariably speaks in the contexts we have quoted. But two other forces that he invokes at particular points go to account for the higher earned incomes. One of these is the cost of education and training; the other is status.

For a manual trade, Smith said, however skilled, 'long apprenticeships are altogether unnecessary. The arts, which are much superior to common trades, such as those of making clocks and watches, contain no such mystery as to require a long course of instruction.' (WN 137; I. x. c. 16.) A few weeks' instruction, perhaps even a few days' would be enough, even though it would take longer to acquire the needed dexterity of hand. (One thinks of the composing rooms of *Izvestia* and *Pravda* today, largely staffed, we are told, by women with six months' training.)[6] But however unnecessary the full rigour of apprenticeship, it does impose a cost, and the craftsmen's differential over the labourer is no more than what is sufficient to compensate the superior expense of their education. But 'education in the ingenious arts and in the liberal professions, is still more tedious and expensive. The pecuniary recompense, therefore, of painters and sculptors, of lawyers and physicians, ought to be much more liberal: and it is so accordingly.' (WN 115; I. x. b. 9.) 'Ought to be': why? One possible reason—but it is a matter of fact, not of propriety—is that the high cost of education greatly reduced the supply of labour to those occupations; and certainly Smith had stressed this effect of apprenticeship. But here, I think, it is propriety that he has in mind: education has given the labour in question a high quality, and it is only right and proper that high quality should command a high price. This is indeed how most people, if not most economists, think today: highly trained and skilled labour is seen as valuable inherently, deserving of high reward just because it is highly trained and skilled, not paid highly as a fact of the market because people are prepared to pay a good price for its handiwork. If 'one species of labour requires an uncommon degree of dexterity and ingenuity, the esteem which men have for such talents, will naturally give a value to their produce, superior to what would be due to the time employed about it.' (WN 53; I. vi. 3.) In the Soviet-type economies today the basic principle of pay, the Marxian rule under socialism, is that pay should be proportioned to the quantity and *quality* of labour; to which is now added its complexity. In Western countries job evaluation is increasingly used, at all occupational levels, to rank jobs and order their pay according to their requirements of training, experience, responsibility, and the like, that is, according to the quality of the labour they call for. The economist would say that this is a short cut: supply and demand in the market having set prevailing rates

[6] G. Polanyi and J. B. Wood, *How Much Inequality?* (Institute of Economic Affairs, 1974), 74.

upon the various components of personal productivity, a reckoning of the package of components called for by a particular job will give a fair indication of what relative pay the market will generally set on it. But to most laymen it appears as it did to Smith that there is a direct and equitable link between the quality of the work and the pay: it is only right and proper that the more highly trained should be more highly paid, not because their work is more productive, but because it is more estimable.

This brings us near the other force that goes to explain the higher earned incomes, namely the esteem that men have for status, and their sense that to each occupation there corresponds a certain station in life which the pay of the occupation should enable those who follow it to maintain. Smith invoked this principle incidentally when he discussed the size of the standing army that a country can keep up.

As the soldiers are maintained altogether by the labour of those who are not soldiers, the number of the former can never exceed what the latter can maintain, over and above maintaining, in a manner suitable to their respective stations, both themselves and the other officers of government and law . . .[7]

It is this principle again that really underlies his argument that we must pay highly those whom we must be able to trust unreservedly.

We trust our health to the physician; our fortune and sometimes our life and reputation to the lawyer and attorney. Such confidence could not safely be reposed in people of a very mean or low condition. Their reward must be such, therefore, as may give them that rank in the society which so important a trust requires. (WN 118; I. x. b. 19.)

It cannot be meant that we take care to pay our lawyers high enough fees to enable them to maintain a superior station in life. The active principle must be, that we see high fees as the right and proper payment for their high qualifications; and the judgement that persons of such qualifications should be entitled to maintain a superior station in life only runs parallel to that. In another passage Smith himself was clear that it was not high status that attracts high pay, but high pay that helps confer high status. If lawyers and doctors, he said, were subsidized as heavily as

[7] WN ii. 218; V. i. a. 11 ('Of the Expence of Defence').

ordinands are in their education, their swollen numbers 'would oblige them in general to content themselves with a very miserable recompense, to the entire degradation of the now respectable professions of law and physic' (WN 147; I. x. c. 36). In the *Theory of Moral Sentiments* he had been emphatic that what drives us on to get rich is the prospect of status that being rich will bring— 'To be observed, to be attended to, to be taken notice of with sympathy, complacency, and approbation, are all the advantages which we can propose to derive from it'.[8] But Smith also saw pay and status as rising and falling together as effects of a common cause: when teachers of the sciences became more plentiful in the age or two after Aristotle, he said, the competition between them 'probably somewhat reduced both the price of their labour and the admiration for their persons' (WN 149; I. x. c. 39). But whichever way we may take the causality to run through the link between pay and status, or if we think the two go together because both depend on scarcity, the fact that they do go together has been commonly taken to show that they do so as of right. Opinion today is probably changing, but Smith drew attention to a principle of propriety that at least until a recent date has been widely accepted, and can hardly have failed to affect the fixing of pay.

We have here an instance of the variety of Smith's perceptions.[9] A little way back we saw him arguing that the high honour accorded to certain occupations made men willing to follow them for less pay; now he notes that high honour and high pay go together. The two observations are not inconsistent, but he made the first as an economist following the interplay of supply and demand, the second as a sociologist entering into the normative judgements of man in society.

This ambidexterity is typical of Smith's handling of the pay structure. His account relies in part on the interaction between the supply of and demand for each kind of labour. But, he says, these market forces may be blocked by the rigidity of custom or overridden by bargaining power. That those people, however, whose occupations stand high in the social scale are also highly paid owes less in his view to market forces than to widely held beliefs about what it is only right and proper to accord to persons of

[8] TMS I. iii. 2. 1 ('Of the origin of Ambition, and of the Distinction of Ranks').
[9] I owe this point to Andrew Skinner.

eminent accomplishment and high social standing. At a time when the course of economic events has made us increasingly aware of the limitations of abstract and mechanistic theory, Smith's gift of empathy, his power of entering imaginatively into the workings of human nature, make him an instructive guide to our own world of labour.

Yet there are one or two points of fact and analysis in which the economist of today must state a difference from him.

The outstanding difference of fact lies in the contrast between the weakness of the trade union in Smith's day and its power in ours. We have seen how he regarded combinations of workmen as impotent. In recent years Great Britain, like Jugoslavia, has been an economy in which the organized employees of most grades have in practice enjoyed a substantial measure of autonomy in the pushing up of their pay. Why this change? One reason is that the power of the strike has grown, through the increase in the resources available to maintain the striker and his family, and through the extension of the coverage of stoppages, both directly and through the increased integration of industry, so that one group of strikers can dislocate so much of the economy that the damage they inflict vastly exceeds the cost of meeting their claim. Instead of Smith's masters, the employers are now mostly themselves employees; their approach has been administrative rather than acquisitive, and they have been operating in a world in which the commitment of governments to full employment has until quite recently provided an assurance, borne out by experience, that a rise in labour costs that has to be covered by higher prices will do their business less harm than the stoppage they will suffer if they stand out against it. Nor in any case have they combined to make a stand: what Smith reported about the strength of combination among masters and workmen has been inverted. Full employment, again, has brought a change of outlook, a nerve, a readiness to wield powers of disruption which were often actually present in earlier days, but resort to which was inhibited then by the anxiety diffused by unemployment. The law, too, which in Smith's day was effective—savagely so—in putting down combinations, is unable to apply criminal sanctions against strikers even in their hundreds, still less to impose a settlement by making strikers in their hundreds of thousands go back to work. Public opinion nowadays is often with the strikers, because so many of the public are trade unionists themselves. The conception of the role of the trade union formed when hungry men were struggling against stern masters has persisted, and the halo of the Tolpuddle Martyrs rests on the brows of airline pilots. Moreover we are all trade unionists today: our standard of living in a time of ever rising prices depends for most of us on our own next claim, and we see other claimants not as competitive with us, as they really are, but as comrades in arms. The great majority of the electorate are trade unionists, and no politicians of any party in their election manifesto care to promise that if returned they will see to it that forthcoming claims are settled for as little as possible. Of all these changes since Smith's day, in the standard of living and support, in industrial structure, the law, and attitudes throughout society, it is probably the change in attitudes that counts for most. Could he come back he would be impressed powerfully by the loss of that spirit of subordination to whose origins he devoted some pages of his account 'Of the Expence of Justice'.[10] We have yet to learn how to manage the business of the economy without it.

Besides this difference in the working of the labour market, we can notice two ways in which our understanding of that working differs from Smith's. One is that we miss in him any appreciation of how the supplies of young people to different occupations depend on the social class of their parents. He showed how, as between certain occupations, the one that is more disagreeable or despised must pay more, by way of compensation. But, as John Stuart Mill said, in the 3rd edition of his *Principles*:[11]

It is altogether a false view of the state of facts, to present this as the relation which generally exists between agreeable and disagreeable employments. The really exhausting and the really repulsive labours, instead of being better paid than others, are almost invariably paid the worst of all, because performed by those who have no choice.

Smith had not remarked that the tendency to equalize net advantages holds only for occupations between which entrants do have a choice. True, in his Glasgow Lectures he had noticed that the more arduous occupations were often paid less, not more.

The opulence of the merchant is greater than that of all his clerks,

---

[10] WN ii. 232–36; V. i. b. 3–12 ('Of the Expence of Justice').
[11] (1852) II. xiv. i.

though he works less; and they again have six times more than an equal number of artisans, who are more employed. The artisan who works at his ease within doors has far more than the poor labourer who trudges up and down without intermission. (LJ(B) 213; Cannan 162–3.)

But Smith did not repeat this observation in the *Wealth of Nations*. He did notice how easy it was for 'people of some rank and fortune' to acquire accomplishments, and how hard for 'the common people',[12] but he did not draw out the implication that the range of occupations accessible to most entrants is limited by their social brackground. Cairnes[13] thought that this limitation divided entrants into 'non-competing groups'. Probably there has always been some overlap between groups, and children are by no means all tied down to, or privileged to retain, the occupational level of their parents: the western economies show a great deal of intergenerational mobility, upwards and downwards. But taking occupational levels as they are commonly ordered by pay and status, we find that intergenerational mobility is still greatest between adjacent levels. Evidence has accumulated to suggest that this is so because the genetic endowment of children, the development of their potential by the style of their upbringing in the home, the schooling they get and their capacity to profit by it, the expectations with which they enter into employment, all these vary systematically with the occupational level of their parents. It did not seem so to Smith, at least until the child was six or eight years old. When the future philosopher and common street porter first 'came into the world', he said (WN 19–20; I. ii. 4), 'and for the first six or eight years of their existence they were perhaps very much alike, and neither their parents nor playfellows could perceive any remarkable difference'. But from that age onwards different kinds of education and then of employment did make a difference; and it was these, and not heredity and home, that were responsible for 'the very different genius which appears to distinguish men of different professions'. Smith did indeed recommend the extension of elementary education at, in part, the public expense. But we have come to see that the possibilities of reducing the inequality of pay by providing greater

[12] WN ii. 304–05; V. i. f. 52 ('Of the Expence of the Institutions for the Education of Youth').

[13] J. E. Cairnes, *Some Leading Principles of Political Economy Newly Expounded* (London, Macmillan & Co., 1874), I. iii. 5.

equality of educational opportunity are limited: a child's ability to avail himself of that opportunity depends so much on his geno-type and his early upbringing in the home.

The other consideration that the economist of today misses in Smith's explanation of the working of the labour market is the link between pay and productivity. He did notice that link in one direction, when he remarked that the 'liberal reward of labour . . . increases the industry of the common people' (WN 91; I. viii. 44): men work better when they are well paid and in good health and spirits. But he did not follow the link in the other direction, the one taken by more recent economic analysis when it finds that the pay of any kind of labour tends to equality with its marginal value product. There is a passage, it is true, in which he contends that the countryman is so evidently 'superior' to the townsman—we might take that to mean 'more productive'—that only 'cor-poration laws and the corporation spirit' could account for the country labourer's wages being lower than the townsman's here, instead of higher as they were in China and India (WN 142; I. x. c. 24). But usually, as we have seen, Smith held that pay depends on the nature of the employment, and the value of the product follows from the pay rather than the pay being derived from the value of the product. He took productivity only in the sense of physical causality, so that labour as the active factor was responsible for the whole product. The other factors, land and capital, were able to exact a share of this, but what they got did not depend, any more than what the labourer retained, on a separable and attributable contribution to value added. But this brings us to his view of the distribution of the national product between pay, profits, and rent—the second of the two main ques-tions that we set out to look at through his eyes.

II

What is most remarkable in Smith's account of the share of labour in the product is the way he loaded Marx's gun for him.

To begin with, he saw the product as being at all times wholly that of the labourer, but only in the 'original state of things' was the labourer generally able to enjoy it. In an advanced society, in which land was appropriated and most employment depended upon advances from a master's stock, only the self-employed, the 'single independent workman', 'enjoys the whole produce of his own labour, or the whole value which it adds to the materials on which it is bestowed' (WN 74; I. viii. 9). It would follow that rent and profits are exactions, tolls levied by robber barons whose strongholds command the road that most workmen, being property-less, are obliged to take. Smith did in some places take very much this view; but being aware as always of the many-sided nature of things, he also allowed that both land and capital may contribute to production.

Of rent he said bluntly at first that it is extorted. 'As soon as the land of any country has all become private property, the land-lords like all other men, love to reap where they never sowed, and demand a rent even for its natural produce.' (WN 56; I. vi. 8: I. viii. 6.) But later he said too that 'in agriculture . . . nature labours along with man; and though her labour costs no expense, its produce has its value, as well as that of the most expensive workman': so 'rent may be considered as the contribution of those powers of nature, the use of which the landlord lends to the farmer' (WN 384; II. v. 12). But when he is dealing with wages, Smith treats rent as a deduction from the produce which, if there were no landlords, would rightfully accrue to the worker.

Similarly with profits. There are passages in which Smith allowed by implication that capital contributed to the produce. In the paragraph which is a sacred text for the human capital theorists of today, and in which he compared the education and training of a man with the building of a machine, he clearly thought that productive capacity was being built into both, and he wrote as if the machine itself would produce the profit on the capital sunk in it:

when an expensive machine is erected, the extraordinary work to be performed by it before it is worn out, it must be expected, will replace the capital laid out upon it, with at least the ordinary profits. (WN 113; I. x. b. 6.)

Again, at the outset of Book II on stock (WN II, Introduction), he held that as stock accumulates 'the same quantity of industry produces a much greater quantity of work'—whether it is through the productivity of the machines through which capital is applied or the concern of the capitalist to apply it efficiently. Yet when he wrote of the productivity of land, he contrasted agriculture with manufactures—'in them nature does nothing; man does all' (WN

385; II. v. 12). And when profits first appear, it is as the 'second deduction from the produce of the labour': the master shares in the product of the workmen because 'they stand in need' of him 'to advance them the materials of their work, and their wages and maintenance till it be completed' (WN 74; I. viii. 7, 8).

Qualifications or inconsistencies apart, this is a picture of exploitation. There is one passage in which Smith said as much outright. In new colonies, he said, the plenitude of land makes all the difference.

> In other countries, rent and profit eat up wages ... But in new colonies, the interest of the two superior orders obliges them to treat the inferior one with more generosity and humanity; at least where that inferior one is not in a state of slavery.[14]

The theory of the division of society into a property-owning class and a property-less proletariat, and of the exploitation of the one by the other, was here to be had for the taking.

Smith also provided ready for use the materials of the theory of surplus value. There were three essentials. One was the reduction of different kinds and qualities of labour to different quantities of a common stuff—Marx's 'homogeneous, socially necessary labour time'. Smith held that this was done near enough in practice by 'the higgling and bargaining of the market' (WN 35–6; I. v. 4), so that if the craftsman was paid half as much again as the labourer, we could take it that there was half as much again of the common stuff of labour in an hour of the craftsman's work. He could support this with the view he also held, that any man who works for an hour, whether he is skilled or unskilled, 'must always lay down the same portion of his ease, his liberty, and his happiness' (WN 37; I. v. 7). This subjective uniformity of the hour of labour enabled him to use labour as the unit in which to measure all values. This was the second essential. Marx's systematizing mind applied it to the value of labour itself. A man's pay was as valuable as the goods and services he bought with it, and their value was measured by the amount of labour embodied in them. But here comes in the third essential: Smith's finding that the real wages of common labour fluctuated about the subsistence level and could never remain above it for long indicated that the value of the labourer's work was less than the value of his produce. Thus

---

[14] WN ii. 76–77; IV. vii. b. 3 ('Causes of the Prosperity of new Colonies').

Smith's labour theory of value was used to show that the exploitation of man by man under capitalism did not arise from any human malignity or conspiracy, but was inherent in the very nature of employment.

Not that Marx omitted to impute malignity, or at least the determination of the exploiters to order the affairs of society so as to uphold their power to exploit; and here again he could draw on Smith. Almost in so many words, Smith stated the Marxian view of the superstructure of government as erected upon the infrastructure of the relations of production, when he contended that it was the coming of inequality of fortunes that made civil government necessary and provided it with its essential function, the protection of property.

It is only under the shelter of the civil magistrate that the owner of . . . valuable property . . . can sleep a single night in security. He is at all times surrounded by unknown enemies, whom, though he never provoked, he can never appease and from whose injustice he can be protected only by the powerful arm of the civil magistrate continually held up to chastise it. (WN ii. 232; V. i. b. 2.)

The rich . . . are necessarily interested to support that order of things, which can alone secure them in the possession of their own advantages . . . Civil government, so far as it is instituted for the security of property, is in reality instituted for the defence of the rich against the poor, or of those who have some property against those who have none at all. (WN ii. 236; V. i. b. 12.)

We might add, for good measure, that Smith's distinction between productive and unproductive labour (WN 351; II. iii. 1) was also taken over by Marx. It has been said to have been a factor in raising the pay of the skilled manual worker in the Soviet-type economies to a higher level than in the west relatively to the pay of the white-collared; though others will see in this also the need under the Leninist strategy to maintain a broad basis of support for the party among the manual workers. Perhaps too it marks the freedom of the Soviet planners to adjust differentials to the relative supplies of different kinds of labour in an educated community—an adjustment that has been put off in the west by the uninterrupted sway of customary differentials and the ability of free trade unions to defend them.

Surveying all these facets of Smith's thought that were taken over by Marx, we may wonder how it came about that the writings of so respectable a member of society should have lent themselves to the purposes of a revolutionary.

It may have been that with part of his mind at least Smith accepted Mandeville's contention that what seemed the gross inequities of society really worked out to the common good: so that he was free to characterize them unsparingly without implying that they should be swept away. At least there was a remarkable argument in his *Theory of Moral Sentiments*, to the effect that the rich

consume little more than the poor, and in spite of their natural selfishness and rapacity, though they mean only their own conveniency, though the sole end which they propose from the labour of all the thousands whom they employ, be the gratification of their own vain and insatiable desires, they divide with the poor the produce of all their improvements. They are led by an invisible hand to make nearly the same distribution of the necessaries of life, which would have been made, had the earth been divided into equal portions among all its inhabitants ... When Providence divided the earth among a few lordly masters, it neither forgot nor abandoned those who seemed to have been left out in the partition. (TMS IV. i. 1. 10.)

But in his *Lectures* Smith had prefaced his account of the division of labour by remarking how very unequally it allocated its burdens and its fruits: '. . . there is no equal division, for there are a good many who work none at all. The division of opulence is not according to the work . . .' (LJ(B), 213; ed. Cannan 163.) In fact, throughout the scale, the more laborious the task, the lower the income. In the *Wealth of Nations*, again, he allowed that many who 'do not labour at all . . . consume the produce of ten times, frequently of a hundred times more labour than the greater part of those who work' (WN, Introduction & Plan of Work, 2; § 4).

Probably we need look for no consistency here. Smith's mind dwelt apart: its speculations were unconstrained by the proprieties of his daily life; the freedom with which he laid about landlords in his rhetoric did not disturb his natural respect for the house of Buccleugh. It may be, too, that those subversive thoughts of his about labour, pay, and profits that Marx was to take up are thoughts that to this day arise in the minds of us all when we first consider these things, especially if we are not men of property ourselves. Much of Marx's authority lies in his having presented views whose *naïveté* gives them wide appeal, through an awe-inspiring medium of theoretical obfuscation.

Here we must leave labour and the labour market; yet it is hard to leave the company of Adam Smith. In studying what he had to say we have heard his voice, and been drawn towards his endearing habit of thought and speech. It is the habit of a clubbable man, imaginative and conversible, one with whom a question or an observation would start a train of thought that he delighted to follow where it led, and to express with an expansive and persuasive vigour. He is said to have been slow of speech at his first entry on a topic, and then as he warmed to it to have become magisterial, even lengthy. On both counts perhaps he would hardly be welcome today on the panel of a Brains Trust or Any Questions; yet, but for that, how well suited to such discussions his mind would be, with its breadth of observation and its keen insights. Those insights, it is true, were not systematized. In our present study we have seen how often what he says as he expounds one thesis hardly agrees with what he says by the way on the same subject as he enlarges on another theme. He was exposed to the danger that besets all of us who like to express our thinking forcibly, that the expression will run away with the thought. Nor was he by nature a logician, stating premisses in terms rigorously defined, and building on them a coherent and consistent structure of abstractions. Since his day economists have become increasingly practised in doing that. Their constructions provide an important means of checking error in our thinking: but on the positive side they have proved sterile, of little application, even misleading in their application, to the real world, not least the world of labour. 'Undoubtedly we are inclined', Georgescu-Roegen has said, 'to attribute to reality a far greater degree of orderliness than the facts justify.'[15] Adam Smith did not make that mistake. He saw the many-sidedness of truth, the iridescence that baffles our endeavours to see things in primary colours, the turbulent confluence of many currents of causality in the stream of time and history. That is why his work lives on.

[15] Nicholas Georgescu-Roegen, *Analytical Economics: Issues and Problems* (Harvard, Harvard University Press, 1966), 123.

COMMENT

by L. C. Hunter*

Professor Phelps Brown has chosen to focus on two aspects of Adam Smith's view of the labour market which well typify Smith's contribution to economics as a whole. The economist in Smith was able to identify certain long-run forces operating on the determination of the wage level and the factoral distribution of income, and he was able to codify these in such a way as to provide a framework within which others who followed him could elucidate and develop our understanding. Thus Smith observed the long-run influence on wage levels deriving from the growth of income and capital (demand) and from population growth (supply). But he was able also to draw the important theoretical distinction between the wage rate as a generalized aggregate and the wage structure, and it is in this latter area particularly that he displays what Professor Phelps Brown has referred to as his sociological insight, his interest in the concrete phenomena of practical life. In an extensive qualification of the role of market forces, Smith drew attention to the importance of custom and status, the influence of education and training, and even in a limited way the relevance of bargaining power. Indeed, in this area of investigation he effectively laid out a skeleton map of the subject which still stands today, altered inevitably in detail and illustrations, but quite adequate as a guide to any introductory course in labour economics.

This is worth a little further discussion. Central to Smith's whole approach to wage differentials is the concept that we now know as the equalization of net advantages. Thus he argued that occupations carrying high status or social esteem would tend to attract a reduced monetary compensation, and vice versa. Jobs which required a long and expensive education or training would carry a higher rate of payment in compensation for the outlay of time or money: but note that a distinction was carefully drawn between occupations like law and medicine where that cost was privately borne (and thereby commanded a high [private] rate of return),[1] and other occupations (teachers and the clergy)

---

* University of Glasgow.

[1] Smith also observed, however, that 'honour makes a great part of the

where the expense was more typically borne publicly, to be reflected in a much lower rate of payment.[2] Two other equalizing
factors were observed by Smith: first, the effects of income
security which helped to explain differences in *rates* of pay between
those holding jobs in steady trades and those working in irregular
employments; and second, the influence of risk, as reflected in
the varying probabilities of success offered by different employments and the trade-off between a high chance of modest income
and a small chance of very large rewards.[3]

Finally, Smith drew attention to the need for certain occupations
embodying a large amount of trust or public responsibility to confer a high income. Here, perhaps, one finds Smith's observations
less relevant to the present scene, for as Professor Phelps Brown
rightly observes opinion (on the positive association between pay
and status) is probably changing. More generally, one may be a
little critical of Smith's conception of the role played by social
esteem in fixing pay relativities. For he tends to assume that tastes
(which affect the appraisal of net advantages, for example) are
formed in a uniform mould, so that butchers, hangmen, and
theatrical performers were all equally regarded as occupations
carrying social disapproval or distaste. We would now recognize
more variety in individual values and tastes, and in consequence
of that a modification of the view that such occupations need
extraordinary financial compensation: if there are people with
tastes different from the social norm, sufficient to meet the demand
for particular services, the need for a differential disappears.[4]

So far we have dealt only with occupational differentials which
arise in conditions of 'perfect freedom'. (Smith actually went
further and required three additional conditions: (i) that the employments should be long established and well known; (ii) that
there should be no boom or slump; (iii) that the occupations
concerned should be the main employments—'moonlighting'

---

reward of all honourable professions'. WN (ed. Cannan 1930), i. 102; I. x.
b. 2 ('Inequalities arising from the Nature of the Employments themselves').

  [2] In this, of course, we have an obvious parallel with modern human capital
analysis of returns to investment in education.

  [3] For an up-to-date treatment of these very points, see Milton Friedman,
Price Theory: A Provisional Text (Frank Cass & Co. Ltd., London, 1962),
Chapter 11.

  [4] For a more extended treatment of this, see Albert Rees, 'Compensating
Wage Differentials' in *Essays on Adam Smith*, 339–40.

was apparently a phenomenon even at that time. In short, Smith was concerned with the analysis of long-run equilibrium under freely competitive conditions.)[5] We would now classify these differentials as 'equalizing'; that is, as differences in pay which were compensation for different characteristics of the occupations.

Going on from this, however, Smith also noticed other sources of pay differences which were not equalizing, but which came about from restrictions on competition, and were treated under the heading 'policy of Europe'. This category of non-equalizing differences we would also recognize today, and in many respects the same sorts of consideration apply. For Smith, there were three important factors here: restrictions on competition by the control of entry to trades through apprenticeship (which he regarded even then as quite unnecessary); artificial augmentation of supply through subsidies to education costs; and obstructions to occupational and geographical mobility.[6] The effects of these interferences with free market processes were inevitably to create wage differences which persisted because the normal equilibrating forces of mobility could not take effect, and as a result shortage and surplus of labour could exist virtually alongside one another, and adjustments to increases or decreases in employment opportunity were impeded.

If we add to this Smith's appreciation of the importance of custom,[7] the influence of bargaining (albeit at that time primarily between master and workman rather than on the collective basis we are so familiar with today), and his explicit recognition of the analogies between investment in physical and human capital, we have a very satisfactory guide to the territory of labour economics at the present day. We might also note that Smith, like Marshall over a century later, sought to identify the distinctive characteristics of the employment of labour and capital, and although Marshall made a more successful and succinct appraisal, Smith was undoubtedly aware of the main distinctive features.

The durability of Smith's observation is all the more remarkable because of the changes that have taken place in the economic system at large, and the labour market in particular. It is worth

[5] WN i. 116–18; I. x. b. 41–47.

[6] WN i. 120–21; these problems are considered at length in I. x. c ('Inequalities occasioned by the Policy of Europe').

[7] Cf. Phelps Brown, p. 246.

reflecting on the fact that whereas we now take for granted the existence of a well organized and institutionalized labour market, the concept of a developed market mechanism must have been unknown in Smith's time. He himself gives us no account of what we would regard as an institutionalized labour market (apart from the controls on mobility already discussed). While Smith was obviously keenly aware of the variation in wage rates among occupations and between different parts of the country, it would be unwise to assume that this sort of detailed information was characteristic of the average worker. The constraints on access to what we would regard as a basic education were severe, and thereby interfered with free occupational choice. Apart from the artificial restraints on geographical movement, and Smith's observations on the apparently inherent immobility of labour, there was the added fact of the difficulties and expense of travel.

Perhaps above all, the factory system was still embryonic and small-scale, with the main onset of mechanization and large-scale enterprise still to come. As this type of industrial organization has grown up, it has of course brought a whole new set of considerations into the reckoning. For a start, it must surely have played a role in facilitating trade union organization and so, as the legal framework began to accommodate it, made possible the development of collective bargaining. The grouping of large numbers of workpeople together under a single employer also created a problem of wage differentials *within* the organization, and from that has emerged our understanding of the internal labour market and its various processes, a central feature of our contemporary study of the labour market and industrial relations.

It is this vastly more sophisticated labour market organization, growing up to meet the needs of a changed industrial system, which has led us to take up for closer examination the role of information in the labour market, the process of job search by workers and employee search by employers. The development has also, of course, brought its problems. With increased division of labour, the bargaining power even of small groups is enhanced, and the importance of pay comparisons—so critical in our present-day wage system—is heightened. The possibilities of trade union organization have corrected the imbalance in bargaining power between master and worker, but in so doing they have increased the scope for conflict and raised expectations of success through industrial action.[8] Thus although we are still uncertain about the extent of the differential wage achieved by unionization, we are in little doubt about the general direction of the effect. In our present situation, the rightness of the new balance we have reached is still in doubt, and as Professor Phelps Brown so justly remarks, we have yet to learn how to manage the business of the economy as it is currently organized in the absence of the 'spirit of subordination' which was one of the stabilizing influences remarked upon by Smith.

The other complementary change which would perhaps be most striking to Adam Smith if he were to return today is the large and increasing involvement of government in the labour market. While the strength of this varies from country to country, we cannot fail to recognize the growth of active government intervention in labour market processes. It is true, even in Britain, that until the early 1960s government intervention was largely passive and Smith might well have approved of most of what was then being done to try to create an improved mechanism for clearing the market. The last fifteen years or so have seen a marked change in Britain and most of the European countries, with government's activities going far beyond the creation of background conditions which would allow more efficient deployment and redeployment of labour resources. Thus we have a plethora of bodies concerned with employment services, training, health and safety, industrial relations, and pay levels and structures, to say nothing of the extended role of government as an employer in its own right. In short, we have increasingly come to *expect* governments to have explicit policies for employment, for the establishment of a framework for wage bargaining (if not actual regulation of wage levels and relativities themselves), and for the direction of change of the industrial relations system. It is extremely doubtful if Smith would have found it easy to accept this sort of development.

Having emphasized in these last paragraphs the difference between the labour market conditions of his day and our own, we must admit that it is quite remarkable that so much of Smith's labour market analysis has preserved its relevance today. We must, of course, beware of overdrawing his contribution. Perhaps

[8] This, of course, would have implications for Smith's theory of distribution since it means that the wage-fund is negotiable.

the greatest deficiency was in his treatment of labour demand, where his value theory, based essentially on cost of production, caused him to turn away from the productivity line of analysis and perhaps delayed the development of the marginal productivity proposition which incidentally helped to neutralize the Marxian critique of distribution under capitalism; and as Professor Phelps Brown has expressed it (254), Adam Smith clearly helped to load Marx's gun, through his own distribution theory. Nor should we overrate (as is sometimes done) his 'fatherhood' of such modern developments as human capital theory which, after all, took nearly another two hundred years before they began to emerge in a fruitful form. But equally, we cannot underplay the importance of his contribution in setting out the essential topography of labour economics as we know it today, despite the primitive level of labour market organization with which he was familiar. Were Smith to have done no more, he would surely have deserved a place of honour in the history of our subject.

COMMENT

by D. I. MacKay*

It is impossible in a brief comment to do justice to the paper by Phelps Brown who has shown, like Smith himself, an ability to inform theoretical speculation with acute observation of the complex reality which is the labour market. For the most part, I find little to disagree with in what Phelps Brown has to say. Yet, to retain some of your interest, I have to differentiate my product. This, as is so often the case in academic debate, may tend to emphasize the point of departure rather than the wide area of agreement. If so, I apologize, but the initiated will recognize both the wide area of agreement and also the importance of the point of departure.

In the first part of his paper Phelps Brown suggests that Smith's concept of net advantages, and the light that this throws on wage differentials, has to be amended in the light of the substantial institutional changes which have occurred in the labour market. We all know the passage which summarizes the concept and which

* Heriot-Watt University, Edinburgh.

is still the accepted starting-point for the discussion of occupational differentials:

The whole of the advantages and disadvantages of the different employments of labour . . . must, in the same neighbourhood, be either perfectly equal or continually tending to equality. If in the same neighbourhood, there was any employment evidently either more or less advantageous than the rest, so many people would crowd into it in the one case, and so many would desert it in the other, that its advantages would soon return to the level of the other employments. (WN I. x. a. 1.)

We are also familiar with Smith's analysis of the causes of occupational wage differentials—social esteem, the cost of training, income security, and risk—all of which figure prominently in contemporary analysis. The richness of insight and detail in Smith's analysis has been ably demonstrated by Professor Phelps Brown and by Professor Hunter and requires no further elaboration here. Of greater interest is the qualification which Smith immediately attaches to his original statement of the concept of net advantages. Having expressed a general tendency towards equalization of net advantages, he immediately qualifies the statement in the next sentence as follows:

This at least would be the case in a society where things were left to follow the natural course, where there was perfect liberty, and where every man was perfectly free both to chuse what occupation he thought proper, and to change it as often as he thought proper. (WN I. x. a. 1.)

Mobility, as Hicks has observed, is the guarantor of the interrelation between wage rates, and restrictions on such mobility will cause non-compensating wage differentials to emerge and persist.[1] Such restrictions are numerous and they were numerous, too, in Smith's day—regulation of the supply of labour to an occupation, custom and tradition, the social costs which inhibit the movement of human 'luggage' (WN I. viii. 31), are all explicitly recognized by Smith.

These factors remain important today. There are many studies which testify to the regulations which restrict the supply of labour into apprenticeships, the legal profession, or a host of other occupations. Inter-generational mobility, as the work of Kelsall

[1] J. R. Hicks, *The Theory of Wages* (Macmillan, 1932), 79.

and Glass and many others have shown, remains strongly influenced by social class and background.[2] The persistence of
substantial regional differentials in income and employment
opportunities, in the U.K. and in many other industrialized
countries, reflects the psychological costs which inhibit mobility.
Much remains the same, but Phelps Brown suggests there is one
crucial difference above all others—the emergence of strong,
well-organized unions negotiating for wage increases and highly
centralized bargaining procedures. As he puts it:

> The outstanding difference of fact lies in the contrast between the
> weakness of the trade union in Smith's day and its power in ours (251).

Let it be clear that this *is* a major difference. There has been some
change in the balance of power between the employer and the
employee. Our understanding of the workings of the labour market
would be seriously incomplete if we neglected the existence and
exercise of union 'bargaining power'. Academic research provides
plenty of examples of the impact of such power. The existence of
a substantial union/non-union wage differential in the United
States has been well documented by the work of Lewis, Rees, and
others. I am glad to report on a novel study, shortly to emerge from
Smith's own *alma mater*, which provides empirical evidence of the
existence of a union/non-union differential in Britain.[3] Industrial
relations literature abounds with references to coercive comparisons, fair relativities, and the like, concepts which are often given
driving force by union organization. Again, unions regulate the
supply of labour to many occupations, help to structure the working of the internal labour market, impose restrictions on the
mobility of labour, and negotiate national bargains which restrict
the freedom of the individual employer and employee.

Most of this is well documented and few labour economists
would dispute that unions exercise a significant influence in these
fields. Yet there is one point on which I would differ with Phelps
Brown. The examples of union power referred to, reflect the view
that unions can and do influence the mobility of labour and its
utilization. Unions do influence *relative* prices. This impinges on
the efficiency of the economy and is therefore important. It is

[2] R. K. Kelsall (ed.), *Graduates: The Sociology of an Elite* (London, Methuen,
1972), and D. V. Glass (ed.), *Social Mobility in Britain* (1954).
[3] Charles Mulvey, 'Collective Agreements and Relative Earnings in U.K.
Manufacturing in 1973' (forthcoming).

here, in resource allocation and utilization, that the main effects of the exercise of the monopoly power are felt. However, the impact on relative prices is a 'once-for-all' effect, which cannot lead to continuing inflation. I do not share the view, which seems to be supported by the argument advanced by Phelps Brown, that unions are the major cause of the inflationary pressure evident in so many economies in the post-war period. Nor, indeed, do I share the view that they are, in the United Kingdom, the major source of resource misallocation.

The so-called 'modern Keynesian position' is that unions can use their monopoly power not only to prevent a reduction in money wages, but also to exert upward pressure on wage levels, even in the face of adverse labour market conditions. It has long been accepted that money wages are sticky downwards. I think it was Phelps Brown himself who once put it that the trade unions were more effective as the 'anvil' than as the 'hammer'. Nowadays, it is common to accept that they can also apply the hammer! Of course, wage rises without any change in monetary and fiscal policy will cause unemployment. However, it is argued, even appreciable rises in unemployment will have little effect in moderating inflation. Inflation can only be curtailed by unemployment levels which are socially and politically unacceptable. This new view of political economy is, then, that inflation is institutionally determined in the factor markets and then passed on to product markets. As inflation has an institutional cause, an institutional remedy is required. This remedy is an incomes policy, backed by legal restrictions.

I suspect that Phelps Brown would accept the major propositions in this argument and hence the remedy proposed. Certainly many labour economists would accept the propositions advanced. I do not. It seems to me more than unlikely that unions can be properly regarded as the chief cause of a rate of inflation as high as that experienced in recent years. The origin of inflation has been an incipient tendency for governments of both parties to increase public expenditure at a rate faster than the real growth of national income. Increased expenditure has been financed in two ways. First, by the printing press, which is inflationary in the classic sense. Second, by a refusal to adjust tax thresholds in the light of rising prices. In the last decade, real disposable income has risen very slowly and has even fallen appreciably for a significant number of groups. Increased money supply and increased pressure in the labour market, by groups attempting to maintain or increase real disposable income, give us an inflation which is neither purely demand, nor purely cost induced. The principal architect of the inflation is the central government, a proposition which, I feel, Adam Smith himself would endorse. After all, as he put it:

Great nations are never impoverished by private, though they sometimes are by public prodigality and misconduct. (WN II. iii. 30.)

It is the highest impertinence and presumption, therefore, in kings and ministers, to pretend to watch over the œconomy of private people.

For kings and ministers

are themselves always, and without any exception, the greatest spendthrifts in the society. Let them look well after their own expence, and they may safely trust private people with theirs. (WN II. iii. 36.)

Few monetarists would disagree with this sentiment!

One consequence of this behaviour has been a very rapid rate of inflation. To boot, inflation, unindexed taxes, and egalitarian incomes policies have together brought about a massive redistribution of post-tax income, far greater than anything ever achieved by union action alone, and a compression of differentials which will discourage risk taking and investment in human capital. Increased public expenditure has resulted in a much expanded public sector in which the growth of employment and incomes has outstripped the rewards available in the risk-taking sector of the economy. The burden has to be borne by a contracting market sector with contracting profit margins due to the imposition of rigorous price controls. The massive maldistribution of resources which will result owes little to the unions.

To escape from our present difficulties, a short-run incomes policy may be a necessary evil, and I would certainly argue that it is. However, a long-run incomes policy will result in a further misallocation of resources. The central authority is not competent, and never will be competent in our type of society, to administer a long-run policy. Moreover, to concentrate on an incomes policy as such, mistakes the real cause of our present difficulties. Finally, and most telling of all, repeated experience in this and other western economies clearly indicates that a long-run policy simply will not work.

As with most economists, I will not hesitate to invoke the great and the good on my side. More seriously, it is at least arguable that if Adam Smith was alive today he would be much more concerned with the extension and the exercise of the monopoly powers of the central government, rather than with the exercise of the monopoly power of the unions. It is the misuse of the powers of central government and the pursuit of short-run palliatives rather than long-run remedies, which has brought us to our present situation. No doubt the unions have contributed their piece, but theirs is the supporting rather than the starring role.

This is not to say that Smith would take the same view of government intervention as was appropriate in the late eighteenth century. Much has changed and Smith, like all great economists, was able to adapt his theories and policy prescriptions to the world as it is. In some matters he would have changed his opinion. For example, as Sir Eric Roll has observed, he would be unlikely still to hold the view that the Post Office 'is, perhaps, the only mercantile project which has been successfully managed by, I believe, every sort of government'.[4] He would not, I think, have changed his general position, but I wonder where he would now find an exception to prove his general rule!

[4] Sir Eric Roll, 'The *Wealth of Nations* 1776–1976', *Lloyds Bank Review* (January, 1976).

9

Public Goods and Natural Liberty

BY JAMES M. BUCHANAN*

According to the system of natural liberty, the sovereign has only three duties to attend to; three duties of great importance, indeed, but plain and intelligible to common understandings: first, the duty of protecting the society from the violence and invasion of other independent societies; secondly, the duty of protecting, as far as possible, every member of the society from the injustice or oppression of every other member of it, or the duty of establishing an exact administration of justice; and, thirdly, the duty of erecting and maintaining certain public works and certain public institutions, which it can never be for the interest of any individual, or small number of individuals, to erect and maintain; because the profit could never repay the expence to any individual or small number of individuals, though it may frequently do much more than repay it to a great society. (WN IV. ix. 51.)

METHODOLOGICAL DISTANCE

ADAM SMITH was an applied welfare economist. He carried with him a conceptual model for the idealized working of the economy, which, although flawed in some of its particulars, can still teach much to modern students. Smith did not, however, seek to accomplish his didactic purpose by elaborating his theoretical model. Instead he applied the analysis variously, sometimes repetitively, but always with great skill to the actual economy in which he lived. The starting-point remained always the institutions that he observed, the effects of which were to be explained, along with the effects that might be forthcoming under alternative arrangements.

Modern economic theorists proceed quite differently. They

* Virginia Polytechnic Institute and State University. The writer is indebted to his colleagues Victor Goldberg, Gordon Tullock, Richard Wagner, and E. G. West, and to Warren Samuels of Michigan State University, for helpful comments on an earlier version of this paper.

analyse abstract and formal models which may bear little or no relationship to the institutions that may exist. (Indeed it is this disparity between the conceptual models and reality that often makes the attempted derivation and testing of empirically refutable hypotheses seem bizarre.) In their elaboration of the formal structures, modern economic theorists have been able to develop precise logical taxonomies that have helped to clear away mental cobwebs. Rigour abounds, even if sometimes in proofs that seem deep in the pure mathematics of conceptual systems.

It is helpful to lay out this methodological distance between Adam Smith and modern economists before getting at the subject matter posed for me in this paper, namely, Smith's conception of public goods and externalities. Given his way of proceeding, we should not expect to find in the *Wealth of Nations* precise definitions of these now-important concepts in theoretical welfare economics.[1] To see whether or not Smith had such concepts embedded in his analytical structure at all, we must approach his work indirectly. We must first ask: what would Smith's major work look like if he possessed no concept of public goods, no idea of external effects? And how would the work that was informed by the equivalent of these modern concepts be different from that which was not so informed?

LIBERTARIAN ANARCHISM

We begin to get an answer to the first of these questions by looking at the analysis of modern economists who explicitly deny the potential relevance of external effects, who see no conceivable agenda for state or collective action emerging from public characteristics of any activities, who reject all attempts to derive an 'economic theory of government', an 'economic logic of collective action'. Modern libertarian anarchists, sometimes called property-rights anarchists, approximate to this description, and they are perhaps best exemplified by Murray Rothbard. His book, *For a New*

---

[1] The distinction between Smith's approach and that of modern economists is stressed by A. Macfie in his comparison of what he calls the Scottish method with the scientific or analytical method. As Macfie suggests, Smith was not 'consciously concerned with building a logical model'. Instead he was 'curious about people, about men at work, about comparative institutions . . .' Cf. A. L. Macfie, *The Individual in Society: Papers on Adam Smith* (London: Allen and Unwin, 1967), 29.

Liberty,[2] offers an opportunity for comparison and contrast with the *Wealth of Nations*. Is Rothbard the modern analogue to Adam Smith? Little or no exegesis is required to answer such a question emphatically in the negative. Adam Smith was far too realistic to argue that markets would emerge and would function effectively in the absence of a legal framework.[3] One of the most important lessons of the 1776 masterpiece is the linkage between the *general* security of property (including the enforceability of contracts) and the functioning of markets, a security that could only be provided by the vigilant protection of the sovereign.[4] Smith was a sufficiently good historian and also sufficiently close to the insecurity of the pre-Enlightenment era to avoid the mistake of assuming that property rights and contracts are secure in nature and that they could be preserved through the emergence of voluntary association.

'LAWS AND INSTITUTIONS' AS PUBLIC GOODS

We need, therefore, to go no further than Smith's repeated insistence on security to prove that some concept of externality and/or publicness must have been embodied in the analysis.[5] The following passage makes clear that the 'laws and institutions' of a

[2] Murray Rothbard, *For a New Liberty* (New York: Macmillan, 1973). David Friedman also belongs in this libertarian-anarchist camp, although his analysis is somewhat less extreme than that of Rothbard. See David Friedman, *The Machinery of Freedom* (New York: Harper and Row, 1973).

[3] This statement requires no qualification for the WN. In his TMS, Smith may be interpreted as suggesting that something akin to the idealized libertarian anarchy *could* emerge, if only *all* men would adopt the behavioural norms laid down. However, Smith does not suggest that all men will, in fact, act in this way. And, indeed, he specifically states that government is required because they will not do so. 'What institution of government could tend so much to promote the happiness of mankind as the general prevalence of wisdom and virtue? All government is but an imperfect remedy for the deficiency of these.' Adam Smith, *The Theory of Moral Sentiments*, with an Introduction by E. G. West (New Rochelle: Arlington House, 1969), 269; IV. i. 2. 1.

[4] 'It is only under the shelter of the civil magistrate that the owner of that valuable property, which is acquired by the labour of many years, or perhaps of many successive generations, can sleep a single night in security. He is at all times surrounded by unknown enemies, whom, though he never provoked, he can never appease, and from whose injustice he can be protected only by the powerful arm of the civil magistrate continually held up to chastise it.' WN (Modern Library Edition), 670; V. i. b. 2.

[5] When we force Smith's treatment into these modern terminological categories, the advantages of clarity must be offset against the necessary losses in generality.

society are directly responsible for the economic well-being of its members.

China seems to have been long stationary, and had probably long ago acquired that full complement of riches which is consistent with the nature of *its law and institutions*. But this complement may be much inferior to what, with *other laws and institutions*, the nature of its soil, climate, and situation might admit of. A country which neglects or despises foreign commerce, . . . cannot transact the same quantity of business which it might do with different laws and institutions. In a country too, where, though the rich or the owners of large capitals enjoy a good deal of security, the poor or the owners of small capitals enjoy scarce any, but are liable, under the pretense of justice, to be pillaged and plundered at any time by the inferior mandarines, the quantity of stock employed in all the different branches of business transacted within it, can never be equal to what the nature and extent of that business might admit. . . .

A defect in the law may sometimes raise the rate of interest considerably above what the condition of the country, as to wealth or poverty, would require. *When the law does not enforce the performance of contracts*, it puts all borrowers nearly upon the same footing with bankrupts or people of doubtful credit in better regulated countries. . . . Among the barbarous nations who over-ran the Roman empire, the performance of contracts was left for many ages to the faith of the contracting parties.[6]

In this passage, Smith makes several points, directly or indirectly, that are worth noting. The well-being of a society is a function of its basic laws and institutions; these are variable and subject to explicit modification; there is nothing sacrosanct about those laws and institutions that emerge in what may be called the natural process of social evolution;[7] and, finally, the basic laws and institutions must be (or should be) equally available to all persons and groups within a society. These characteristics can be applied

[6] WN 95; I. ix. 15, 16. Italics supplied.

[7] In this interpretation, Smith differs from the position that seems to be taken by F. A. Hayek, who holds Smith up as one of the discoverers of the notion that efficient results need not be willed or planned. This is indeed one of Smith's basic insights into the functioning of a market economy. But, in my view, Hayek extends this notion too far when he applies it to the emergence of law itself. See F. A. Hayek, *Law, Legislation, and Liberty*, vol. I, *Rules and Order* (Chicago: University of Chicago Press, 1973). My interpretation of Smith's position is supported by E. G. West in his 'Introduction' to the Arlington House edition of TMS, cf. p. xii.

with relatively little change to 'public goods' in their modern formulation. Such goods (1) enter the utility functions of individuals, (2) can be varied in quantity by the decision-makers for the collectivity, (3) may be provided inefficiently or not at all in the absence of collective action, and (4) must be (or should be) made generally available to all members of the community.

Somewhat surprisingly perhaps, early applications of the modern theory of public goods did not include explicit reference to the legal structure, to the basic 'laws and institutions' organized for the protection and enforcement of individual rights and contracts. In one sense, the protection of property is a private good, largely if not exclusively beneficial to the individual whose rights are secured. 'Publicness' emerges, however, when protection enforcement takes the form of 'law', generally available to all persons, which delineates a structure of reciprocal rights, and which allows the capture of the major scale advantages of joint action.[8] The neglect of this seemingly important aspect of public goods theory is explained, in part, by the same reasons that explain the failure of modern economists to examine legal structures generally. They have implicitly assumed that a well-ordered and functioning 'protective State' of a particular sort exists, within which voluntary market arrangements emerge and generate allocative and distributive results. This has allowed attention to be concentrated on the possible 'failures' of such arrangements. It is from this 'market failure' emphasis of post-Pigovian welfare economics that the modern theory of public or collective-consumption goods emerged, notably in Samuelson's seminal paper in 1954.[9] Early applications and examples were, therefore, designed to demonstrate efficiency limitations of voluntarily-organized markets, even when trading arrangements are ideally protected in a well-functioning legal order. Many of the alleged 'failures' of markets stem, however, from the inefficient assignment of property rights and not from some inherent characteristic of the activities in question. David Hume's meadow drainage (a famous 'publicness' or 'commonality' example which was certainly known to Adam Smith) does not take place because the meadow is held in common. There is no necessary 'publicness' quality of swamplands. A reassignment of property rights to bring

[8] This is recognized by Smith. Cf. TMS 501; VII. iv. 35.
[9] Paul A. Samuelson, 'The Pure Theory of Public Expenditure', *Review of Economics and Statistics*, xxxvi (Nov. 1954), 387–9.

the interrelated land parcels under single ownership could, in fact, ensure that voluntary action would accomplish efficient results. In modern public goods theory, attention has been placed on the costs of exclusion, along with the advantages of joint consumption. The explicit provision of external defence and internal protection are now commonly cited as examples of genuinely public goods, a classification that would have been accepted directly by Smith, who listed these two specific activities as the first and second duties of the sovereign.[10]

Smith's work was fully informed with an understanding of the concept that we now call 'publicness'. There is, none the less, an important difference between the essentially negative emphasis of modern economists on particular instances of market failure, even in a legal order, and Smith's positive emphasis on the 'laws and institutions' required to make markets work. Smith comes closer than many moderns to the recognition that general law, itself, represents the best example of 'publicness'.[11] The commonality or non-excludability features of law, of the whole legal framework, emerge directly from the very definition itself—rules and regulations that are generally applicable to all persons and groups in the community. Law may arise from custom, from conventional modes of behaviour that have become established by usage, but, as noted above, Adam Smith clearly allowed for the possibility of conscious modification and change. Again, almost by definition, law cannot be changed by voluntary action on the part of one or a few persons. In this sense, law embodies polar or extreme publicness. A person who voluntarily adopts a rule that restricts his own behaviour secures zero benefits while possibly conferring pure external economies on others in the community. In a formal way, therefore, we might say that 'markets fail' in generating the 'public good' that law represents, with law here conceived in its widest meaning as the whole set of legal institutions. To Smith, however, this would have seemed a bizarre way of

---

[10] See WN 653, 669; V. i. a. 1, V. i. b. 1.

[11] This treatment of 'law as a public good' has only been recently developed. See, in particular, William Riker, 'Public Safety as a Public Good', in *Is Law Dead?*, edited by E. V. Rostow (New York: Simon and Schuster, 1971), 379–85; Thomas R. Ireland, 'Public Order as a Public Good', typescript (Chicago: Loyola University, 1968). My own book, *The Limits of Liberty* (Chicago: University of Chicago Press, 1975), develops the 'publicness' of law as one of its main themes.

putting a simple point. Without law, markets will not even come into existence, at least in any meaningfully efficient sense. Law is antecedent to market co-ordination, to the economic activity of agents, to the working of Adam Smith's invisible hand.

For those 'laws and institutions' which render private holdings secure against both external and internal aggression and invasion, which enforce the performance of contracts, and which facilitate trade, Smith's treatment is wholly consistent with modern public goods analysis. As we move beyond these limits, however, the difference in emphasis mentioned above becomes relevant. Smith's observations led him to recognize the prospect that particular laws, particular rules, applicable to the whole society, might be 'public bads' rather than 'public goods'. His primary attention was turned toward securing a relaxation or removal of the restrictions on the free flow of commerce, on the abolition of the constraints on 'natural liberty'.[12] By contrast, economists in the early post-Pigovian tradition tended to neglect the 'public bads' which political interferences in markets can generate. Only with the relatively recent advent and spread of the theory of public choice, the extension of economic analysis to political choice, has this element of applied welfare economics returned to the corpus of scientific discussion in economics.[13]

AGENDA FOR POLICY

A comparison between Adam Smith's agenda for economic policy and that of the early post-Pigovian public goods or externality theorist warrants our attention. As we know, Smith's ubiquitous argument called for the dismantling of state interferences with the

[12] Smith's position is not wholly consistent with the modern strand of discussion and analysis, which has been called 'property-rights economics'. In some of the representative works in the latter tradition, 'efficient' institutional forms, including the structure of property rights, are somehow predicted to emerge, independently of explicit or conscious collective action. This is related to the Hayek position noted above.

[13] I shall not discuss public choice analysis and applications further in this paper. This subdiscipline emerged in the years following World War II, and notably in the United States. In some respects, it is constructed on the failures, analytical and practical, of theoretical welfare economics. It matches its own theory of 'government failure' against the traditional welfare economist's theory of 'market failure'. Public choice theory has gained adherents due to the post-Arrow collapse of 'social welfare function' constructions, and due perhaps more importantly to the demonstrable failures of political correctives to market forces.

working of markets. The post-Pigovian, uninfluenced by latter-day public choice analytics, offered arguments, at least by implication, for an extension of state action, for corrections for market failures. To an extent, the real world setting of 1776 dictated Smith's policy agenda, and any plausible ordering of priorities should have called for a reduction in the scope and range of ill-conceived and often unworkable mercantilist controls.[14] Had Adam Smith lived in a relatively pure *laissez-faire* age, where a minimally protective state confined itself largely to the enforcement of property rights and contracts, it is not difficult for us to imagine him constructing a catalogue of market abuses or failures and calling directly for corrective action. Smith was not a doctrinaire libertarian, and he would have supported legislation for anti-monopoly action, for the definition of the monetary unit, for the regulation of banking, for public utility operation and/or regulation, for minimal public education, for standardized weights and measures, for grade labelling, for limited building codes, possibly for publicly supplied information and support for the arts.

The other side of the comparison is the more puzzling. In the late twentieth century, we do not live in anything that remotely resembles a *laissez-faire* world. We live instead in a veritable maze of governmental rules and regulations, which begin to approach even if they do not yet exceed those present in the world of Adam Smith. The intellectual question lies in the general failure of modern-day welfare economists to address more explicitly the 'public bads' which political interferences with trade represent. Why have so many modern economists continued to call for an extension in the range of political controls when their demonstrable inefficacies are self-evident? What has gone wrong with their agenda for economic policy? Why have so many of them remained relatively silent about minimum wage restrictions, legally-protected strike threat systems, rent controls, income policies, price ceilings on crude oil and natural gas, agricultural price supports, publicly subsidized idleness, cartelized transportation networks, restricted licensing for trades and professions, bureaucratic dicta-

---

[14] Cf. Jacob Viner, 'Adam Smith and Laissez Faire', in *The Long View and the Short* (Glencoe, Illinois: Free Press, 1958), 232. The reading of Viner's essay, initially published in 1928 in celebration of the 150th anniversary, has the effect of shortening intellectual history on the one hand while dramatically pointing up the changes that have taken place in policy history over the half-century.

tion of product quality, product safety, product innovation, hiring practices, educational organization, and countless other restrictions on 'natural liberty'?[15]

An Adam Smith returned after two centuries in 1976, viewing the world as now, and applying his allegedly primitive conceptions of economic order, would surely duplicate his policy priorities of 1776. The *Revised Wealth of Nations* that he might write would probably pay scant if any attention to market failures. It would, instead, contain much criticism of the ineffectiveness of existing and proposed political-governmental nostrums. In careful discussion of example after example, in repetitive application of the elementary verities, such a returned Adam Smith would lay bare the genuine social costs of the interferences with natural liberty. What a challenge this notion of a returned Adam Smith presents! Where is the young economist willing to devote the decade to the task?

NATURAL LIBERTY AS A PUBLIC GOOD

The restrictions on 'natural liberty' surely constitute 'public bads', from which it follows that their removal would be equivalent to the production of 'public goods'. And surely these 'public goods' would increase the utility of persons in the community more than the sometimes piddling adjustments that are suggested for correcting minor market distortions. Smith would quickly discern that, now as then, markets 'fail' largely because they are not allowed to work because of overt political-governmental restrictions. It follows from this that the first steps toward making markets work more efficiently involve removing the restrictions. But are we not forcing the argument somewhat to place Smith's discussion in a public goods context here? Once we accept, with Adam Smith, the publicness attributes of any law, the general applicability to all members and groups in the community, it is relatively straightforward to

[15] A cynical response would be to suggest that many modern economists do not, in fact, fully understand the principle of market co-ordination, and, because of this, have no intellectual faith in the 'natural economic order'. Macfie suggests that the shift in emphasis here can be traced back to the Benthamites. See A. L. Macfie, op. cit. 157. To state the same point somewhat more charitably, some part of economists' acquiescence can be explained by their implicit, if erroneous, assumption that the restrictions serve as correctives to what they conceive to be relative disparities in the economic power of participants in an unconstrained market order.

translate almost all of his discussion into the terminology of public goods analytics. No person or small group can, independently and voluntarily, modify an existing legal rule, but such action can be taken by the collectivity, acting on behalf of all persons.

We may ask why economists have not discussed governmental restrictions on markets in a public-goods framework. Why have we introduced the lighthouse, as our classic public goods example, while continuing to discuss the restrictive licensing of taxicabs in orthodox efficiency analysis? In the classroom textbook model, without explicit collective action, no lighthouse will be constructed.[16] But without explicit collective action, an existing restrictive licensing scheme will remain in being. The 'public good' that its removal represents will not be produced, making the example analogous in this respect to the lighthouse case.

It will be useful to develop this public goods interpretation of governmental interference with markets in more detail. In so doing, we may be able to identify a source of the economist's frustration with political process. Why does building a lighthouse seem so different, at first glance, from the removal of the licensing of taxicabs? The dilemma of the fishermen seems to be more general; no single person finds himself willing to build the lighthouse, even though, if constructed, *all* fishermen might benefit. Clearly, this is not the case with the removal of taxicab licensing. While this step would surely improve over-all efficiency in the economy, only *some* members of the community will secure benefits; *some* members will clearly be harmed. But the lighthouse example can readily be rigged to make it fully analogous even here. Those fishermen who know precisely where the shoals are, or who might have technically advanced sounding devices, presumably benefit from the absence of the lighthouse, and these persons would possibly be harmed by the production of the public good, which, in itself, would benefit other fishermen, and, in the net, would increase the efficiency of the economy. Public goods analysis can allow for negative evaluations on the part of some of those who must, by definition, share in the quantities that are ultimately provided. In the public goods framework of analysis, however, the

---

[16] For a discussion of the economic history of lighthouses and the history of lighthouses in economics, which raises questions about the appropriateness of this stock example in public goods theory, see R. H. Coase, 'The Lighthouse in Economics', *Journal of Law and Economics*, xvii (October 1974), 357–76.

presence of negative evaluations on the change that is under consideration implies, at least indirectly, that compensations should be made, as necessary, to secure general agreement. This implication becomes explicit in the Wicksell–Lindahl variant of public goods analysis. By contrast, if the removal of restrictive devices, say a tariff, is discussed in the orthodox manner, the modern economist elevates his efficiency norm into a position of overriding significance, and tends to recommend repeal without mention of potential compensations. It is small wonder that his proposals tend to fare badly in the arena of practical politics. George Stigler has suggested that, in these respects, Adam Smith was little different from those who have followed him.[17] In Stigler's interpretation, Smith did not present either a positive or a normative theory of public choice, or governmental-political process. This interpretation of Smith has been challenged by E. G. West, who explains Smith's lack of attention to the more direct 'politics of policy' by demonstrating his emphasis on constitutional structure, on the basic laws and institutions within which policy measures are taken.[18] West's interpretation is fully consistent with the broadened conception of 'public good' attributed to Smith here.

USURY LAWS AND MARKET RATES OF INTEREST

To this point, I have suggested that Adam Smith's applied welfare economics was informed by an understanding of the concepts of public goods and externalities and that, although the order of policy priorities differed, his agenda for policy action was not dramatically divergent from that of modern economists. But it would indeed be surprising if the two-century gap, during which intellectual paradigms have shifted and economic science has

---

[17] Stigler argues that Smith did not fully develop a self-interest theory of the emergence and maintenance of governmental restrictions on markets. Cf. George Stigler, 'Smith's Travels on the Ship of State', *History of Political Economy*, iii (Autumn 1971), 265–77; *Essays*, chapter xii.

[18] E. G. West, 'Adam Smith's Economics of Politics', *History of Political Economy* (forthcoming). Even at the most direct level, however, there is at least one case in which Smith seems to have been fully aware of the necessity to satisfy the self-interests of affected parties. See Smith's interesting letter to Dundas concerning free trade for Ireland, in which the possibilities of compensation to vested interests are indirectly raised. The letter is cited in full in John Rae, *Life of Adam Smith* (1895; New York: Augustus M. Kelley, 1965), 353–5. Letter 201, dated 1 November 1779.

developed, produced no specific conflicts in the treatment of particular issues. We can find one such conflict in Smith's treatment of interest. As we might expect, he was highly critical of legal prohibitions on the payment of interest. But, surprisingly, Smith was unwilling to allow interest rates to find their market equilibrium levels. In the markets for money, Smith lost his pervasive faith in 'natural liberty'.

His argument warrants serious consideration, especially since it can be translated into something akin to a modern externality analysis. Smith seemed to lend support to legal ceilings of money rates of interest, provided that these rates were set 'somewhat above the lowest market price' (WN 339; II. iv. 14), but not greatly above it. He suggested that rate ceilings below the lowest market price would have the same inhibiting effects on trade as outright prohibitions of interest payments. But why did he support legal ceilings at all, even if fixed just above the lowest market rates? He did so because, if rates were allowed to go higher than this

the greater part of the money . . . would be lent to prodigals and projectors, who alone would be willing to give this high interest. Sober people, who will give for the use of money no more than a part of what they are likely to make by the use of it, would not venture into the competition. A great part of the capital of the country would thus be kept out of the hands which were most likely to make a profitable and advantageous use of it, and thrown into those which were most likely to waste and destroy it. (WN 339–40; II. iv. 15.)

If we translate this into modern jargon, Smith is saying that loans made for productive investment generate external economies because of the effects on capital formation and on economic growth. By contrast, loans made for strictly consumption purposes exert no such spillover benefits. As the citation indicates, Smith predicted that the high-risk *consumption*-loan demanders would be effectively rationed out of money markets. Implicitly, he assumed that high-risk investment loans were not important, an assumption that would surely be questioned in an age of rapid technological change. Even under his assumptions, however, in this instance, Smith may have revealed less sophistication about the pressures of market forces than usual. But, apart from the particulars of his proposal, the basic issue is worth discussion. Does investment generate external economies? Smith was, of course, writing decades before the advent of marginal productivity analysis, before the 'wheel of exchange' in an economy was closed by the addition of factor pricing to product pricing. In a fully competitive world, owners of factors receive marginal productivities, including the owner of investment capital. In this pure model, there are spill-over benefits from investment activity but these are not Pareto-relevant.[19] In the world that exists, or could exist, however, the rate of investment, and capital formation, that will emerge from private decisions depends on the institutions within which such decisions are made. And whereas there may be no Pareto-relevant external economy exerted by private decisions made at the margins of adjustment within a given institutional setting, the inframarginal changes in behaviour that might be produced by modifying the institutions themselves may well qualify under the Pareto-relevancy criterion. In the impure world where lives are finite, however, where bequests emerge even from rational life-cycle plans, and perhaps more importantly, where collectivities claim increasing shares in incomes generated, the inframarginal external economies from investment and capital formation must be acknowledged. These seem likely to become increasingly relevant for policy in a world now widely characterized as threatened by capital 'short-age'. Few modern economists would follow Smith in seeking to correct for these by the imposition of legal ceilings on interest rates, but the widespread introduction of subsidies to investment reflects the basic thrust of his argument.

PRODUCTIVE AND UNPRODUCTIVE LABOUR

Smith's somewhat confusing and often-criticized distinction between productive and unproductive labour can be interpreted in a manner similar to that applied to his defence of legal ceilings on interest rates. Productive labour is that which is applied to the replacement, or accumulation, of capital or stock, which includes the replacement of, or additions to, inventories of finished con-sumables. Although he did not specifically discuss it, we may presume that Smith would have also added the labour that goes into the production of human capital here. Unproductive labour is that which produces utility that vanishes upon the instant of its

[19] For a discussion of the distinction between Pareto-relevant and Pareto-irrelevant externalities, see J. M. Buchanan and W. C. Stubblebine, 'Exter-nality', *Economica*, xxix (November 1962), 371–84.

production, where the acts of production and consumption are simultaneous. The externality applies to the act of employing labour. The person who employs labour productively confers external benefits on others in society; the person who hires the menial servant does not. Hence, 'every prodigal appears to be a public enemy, and every frugal man a public benefactor.' (WN 324; II. iii. 25.)

Adam Smith did not, however, use the external economy of investment as a basis for collective interference with the natural liberty of individual choice, as he did in the case of the interest rate. For strictly private decisions, Smith expressed his willingness to allow persons to choose freely, presumably on the grounds that, on balance, the observed rate of capital accumulation was sufficiently high as to warrant a policy stance of inaction.[20] The context of his discussion leaves little doubt, however, but that in some set of circumstances different from that which characterized the Scotland and England of the eighteenth century, he might well have suggested either the subsidization of saving-investment or the penalization of consumption spending. Although he did not expressly examine the bases for taxation in his separate treatment of taxes, we may conclude from Smith's general argument that he would have looked with favour on proposals to levy general taxes on expenditures or consumption rather than on incomes.

Specific policy implications did emerge, however, from the alleged external economies involved in capital accumulation, even if these did not take the form of interferences with private decisions to save and to spend. These implications stem directly from Smith's admirable propensity to establish his policy priorities in the order of their observed importance, a propensity already noted. The concentration of outlay on unproductive labour was observed to lie in the public or governmental rather than in the private sector of the economy.

---

[20] It might also be possible to interpret Smith's aversion to abnormally high rates of profit in an externality setting, where, once again, he derived no inferences for policy interferences with natural liberty. While recognizing the allocative function of above-normal profits, Smith emphasized that very high profits tended to generate prodigality in behaviour, to 'destroy parsimony'. Although he does not apply an externality framework, Rosenberg stresses this aspect of Smith's discussion. See Nathan Rosenberg, 'Some Institutional Aspects of the *Wealth of Nations*', *Journal of Political Economy*, lxviii (December 1960), 557–70; especially 558.

Great nations are never impoverished by private, though they some-times are by public prodigality and misconduct. The whole, or almost the whole public revenue, is in most countries employed in maintaining unproductive hands. Such are the people who compose a numerous and splendid court, a great ecclesiastical establishment, great fleets and armies, who in time of peace produce nothing, and in time of war acquire nothing that can compensate the expence of maintaining them, even while the war lasts. Such people, as they produce nothing, are all maintained by the produce of other men's labour. When multiplied, therefore, to an unnecessary number, they may in a particular year consume so great a share of this produce, as not to leave a sufficiency for maintaining the productive labourers, who should reproduce it next year. The next year's produce, therefore, will be less than that of the foregoing, and if the same disorder should continue, that of the third year will be less than the second. Those unproductive hands, who should be maintained by a part only of the spare revenue of the people, may consume so great a share of their whole revenue, and there-fore oblige so great a number to encroach upon their capitals, upon the funds destined for the maintenance of productive labour, that all the frugality and good conduct of individuals may not be able to compen-sate the waste and degradation of produce occasioned by this violent and forced encroachment. (WN 325 f; II. iii. 30.)

The proclivities of those 'who pretend to watch over the economy', who 'are themselves always, and without exception, the greatest spendthrifts in the society' impose external costs on all remaining members. Smith strongly infers that check-reins must be placed on those extensions of the public sector beyond those limits which ensure that individuals' 'uninterrupted effort to better their own condition' is 'protected by law and allowed by liberty to exert itself in the manner that is most advantageous' (WN 329; II. iii. 36).

Modern economists may be justifiably critical of Adam Smith's apparent over-emphasis on the prodigality of government. He seemed to overlook the potential productivity of specific collective outlays, although elsewhere in his treatise he clearly allowed for public investment in what we now call 'social overhead capital'. He recognized the advantages of capital investment in roads, bridges, canals, and other similar projects. His concentrated references here to government profligacy apply to defence out-lay, to the maintenance of the bureaucracy, and to the public provision of transfers.

In this age of massive bureaucracy, accompanied by apparently exploding rates of increases in government spending, it seems highly doubtful that a returned Adam Smith would greatly change his policy priorities, even upon a sophisticated understanding of modern public goods and externality analysis. Reluctantly, perhaps begrudgingly, he might acknowledge that the modern technology of war makes the maintenance of a large defence establishment essential. But can we really doubt but that his major animus would be directed toward the bloated budgets which seem to have got beyond the control of the bumbling politicians of our time? The modern economist may reject Smith's central notion that capital accumulation in a setting of natural liberty protected by law provides the key to economic development, or even that such development is, in itself, a desirable objective. What the modern economist cannot do, at least consistently, is to propose further interferences with natural liberty for the avowed purpose of stimulating capital investment while at the same time continuing to ignore the stifling effects of public sector expansion. As Gordon Tullock has remarked, government should take its foot off the brake before it hits the accelerator. Adam Smith would surely have agreed.

COMMENT

by E. J. Mishan*

According to Professor Buchanan's speculations, if Adam Smith were alive today 'his major animus would be directed toward the bloated budgets which seem to have got beyond the control of the bumbling politicians of our time'. Indeed, Buchanan continues, 'the modern economist cannot, at least consistently, . . . propose further interferences with natural liberty for the avowed purpose of stimulating capital investment while at the same time continuing to ignore the stifling effects of public sector expansion'.

As an aspirant to the status of 'modern economist' I shall, of course, take care to avoid the charge of inconsistency, although as it happens, I find myself in agreement with the priority he would give to natural liberty today. Indeed, my comments on his stimu-

* London School of Economics.

lating essay tend toward another crucial question: whether the modern economist can consistently support both continued economic growth and a system of natural liberty. As is expected of me, I shall eventually express doubts about the possibility. But I will take a little time working myself into the mood, initially by addressing myself to some questions raised by Buchanan's discussion of public goods.

I

Although a person of Buchanan's eminence in political economy is obviously conscious of the distinctions to be made in talking of public goods, they need to be more clearly etched for my purpose than for his. Let us then draw distinctions between the broad notion of a public good, a public sector good, and the economist's more exclusive definition of a public good which, following my practice, we shall henceforth refer to as a *collective* good.

An economist's definition of a collective good has to be functional with regard to allocative considerations. Although controversy of a minor order surrounds the definition, we can make do with that which perceives the collective good as a service the cost of which cannot be allocated among the beneficiaries on any economic principle—at least in the absence of congestion costs, or other spillovers, that may be generated in its consumption, the marginal increase of which can then be attributed to the additional person. Formally, the collective good can be treated as an external economy with the understanding that whereas the latter is perceived to arise as an incidental side effect from economic activity, the collective good proper is purposely designed as economic activity.

In general, collective goods can be a part of the public sector of the economy or else a part of the private sector, and within the private sector they can either be handled by the market or be politically assigned. The larger the costs of building in 'excludability'—which costs vary with technical progress—the more likely is the collective good to appear in the public sector of the economy; though, of course, it could conceivably be politically assigned or 'farmed out' to a private organization. It is also true that private goods can be produced either in the private or the public sector of the economy. As a result of public sentiment about what is 'right and proper' many services that would be defined as private goods—those generated by public utilities, by hospitals and health centres, by educational institutions—are today to be found in the public sector of the modern economy.

Finally, there is the broad idea of a public good as a social desideratum. Such attributes as high employment, stability, peace, cohesion, and liberty can be regarded as socially desirable. Setting aside possible conflicts in the endeavour simultaneously to pursue all these aims, the economist continues to believe that he can make useful contributions to some of them, for instance, high employment and stability and, perhaps less directly, to such objectives as domestic peace and liberty.

At a time when the British government's share of net national expenditure is about 60 per cent, and the American government's share is approaching 50 per cent, the dangers and disadvantages eloquently argued by many liberal economists today, in particular by Hayek, Friedman, Brittan, and by Buchanan himself, are becoming all too evident. This is the theme to which I shall address myself, though I shall make a short detour first in order to gather some useful material.

II

Although, interpreted narrowly as the uniqueness of the (partial) optimal position irrespective of the distribution of property rights, the so-called Coase Theorem is far from novel,[1] his leisurely discussion in his 1960 paper on the alternative ways of dealing with spillovers, and the influence of law on the outcomes, marks the beginning of a more systematic consideration of all those incidental costs, briefly referred to as *transactions costs*—an umbrella term covering such diverse but related expenditures as bargaining costs, the costs of setting up and maintaining market institutions, costs of protecting property, costs of policing, costs of calculating and collecting taxes, costs of monitoring and regulating, etc.[2] Such costs do not lend themselves to elegant formalization, but in any serious discussion of the large issues of allocation, equity, and freedom, they cannot be too heavily emphasized. It is one of the great

[1] To the best of my memory, this theorem was common knowledge in the London-Oxford-Cambridge graduate seminar, 1947–8 which included then, as students, Baumol, Graaf, Hahn, Turvey, and myself.

[2] Ronald Coase, 'The Problem of Social Cost', *Journal of Law and Economics* (October, 1960).

achievements of Chicago's *Journal of Law and Economics* to have brought such crucial matters to the fore in the continuing debate on private enterprise and the role of the state.

A pragmatic approach might seem to suggest that, in so far as resource allocation is concerned at least, we should promote economic arrangements carrying the smallest transaction costs. For some instances, however, it is altogether conceivable that such costs are so high that they will swamp the otherwise net gains in any movement to optimum. In that case it is clearly more economic to 'stay put' and bear with the lesser evil—the misallocation, say, arising from adverse spillovers. But just where one 'stays put' depends upon the existing law. Spillover-permissive laws entail costs of enforcement as also would spillover-repressive laws. And to move away from the polar solutions implied by each—unchecked market output in the former case, zero output in the latter —requires transaction costs which, as stated, may be economically unwarranted. Some ideal investigation would reveal to us which sort of law on balance was superior on allocative grounds.

There are problems enough here without as yet taking account of the intangible costs of government bureaucracies with which the economists mentioned earlier are rightly concerned. What I am suggesting here is that some of these intangible costs can be traced to the post-war growth of external diseconomies or 'collective bads' in modern societies. And I am suggesting further, first, that these 'collective bads' are likely to grow in urgency and, secondly, that some economists, particularly those of the Chicago School, have an ideological block against proper assessment of the implications. In consequence, they continue to be somewhat intemperate in their attack on 'environmentalists' for invoking more government intervention when, as they believe, the market itself would be able to cope with the situation.

However, much of the economic literature on the subject is not very pertinent to developments, concerned as it is with A's actions on B, and perhaps also with B's on A, when A and B are two persons or two firms or two industries. In such instances, bargaining is not impractical, and the question of equity is often uncertain. But in modern affluent-effluent societies, the issues that arouse environmentalists are related to the growing range of disamenities and hazards that afflict large populations in consequence of expanding industry and technology. Whether, in these emerging conditions, markets, even competitive markets, tend to optimal solutions—whether, indeed, there is, on balance, a social gain—is, in my opinion, doubtful, and, at best, controversial. Moreover, since the impact on the welfare of millions of people is substantial, the question of equity cannot continue to be brushed aside. And what is most important of all, and what is just beginning to be realized, any form of solution to these kinds of developments that spring from man's increasing scale of intervention in the biosphere, and often take the form of overt conflicts of interest, necessarily entails government intervention. As economist Ronald Ridker wrote in 1972 in the introduction to a recent Report commissioned by the U.S. Congress:

Conservation of our water resources, preservation of wilderness areas, protection of animal life threatened by man, restrictions on pollutant emissions, and the limitations on fertilizer and pesticide-use, all require public regulation. Rules must be set and enforced, complaints heard and adjudicated. True enough, the more we can find means of relying on the price system, the easier will be the bureaucratic task. But even if effluent charges and user fees become universal, they would have to be set administratively, emissions and use metered, and fees collected. It appears inevitable that a larger proportion of our lives will be devoted to filling in forms, arguing with the computer or its representative, appealing decisions, waiting for our case to be handled, finding ways to evade or move ahead in the queue . . .

III

Since technology was a much more primitive affair in his day, Adam Smith was reasonably conversant with its progress—which cannot be said of economists, possibly not even of scientists, today. But since we are playing the game of speculating what Smith would think and say were he alive today, largely by reference to the text of the *Wealth of Nations*, let us assume that his interest in modern technology would have continued undeterred by the proliferation of new journals and new specialisms. If so, Smith would not only be looking with incredulity at the range of annoyances that people today are empowered by technology to inflict on one another, despite increasing government regulation. He would also be looking at advances in the computer industry, in supersonic air travel, in fast breeder reactors, in new weapons, and at the research being done in microbiology, in the laboratory production of hybrid genes, and at the extensive marketing of new drugs and food additives, and of chemical fertilizers and pesticides. He would, I presume, be impressed by an increasing spectrum of hazards of varying imminence and severity, many of them likely to invoke, indeed to warrant, government intervention. For if history has shown anything, it has shown that ordinary people rank security higher than freedom.

The tree of science has produced many fruits, but today it also casts a lengthening shadow on the human prospect. In the increasingly close-knit and dangerous world we are rapidly developing, the public will, I believe, continue to demand increased government surveillance, monitoring, regulation, control, and protection.

It is an ironic commentary on man's vision that the erosion of liberty we discern as we approach the close of the second millennium A.D. can be traced directly to the process of continued economic growth, that process on which, since the Enlightenment of the eighteenth century in which Adam Smith lived, men of goodwill founded their hopes for a brighter future.

COMMENT

by *Alan Williams**

$$1776 + 13 = \dots?$$

I have interpreted the change in the title of Jim Buchanan's paper from that originally advertised ('Public Goods and Externalities') as an invitation to stress the political philosophical aspects of Smith's views on the role of the state (pardon me, 'sovereign') rather than the consequential mechanics of his embryonic welfare economics. I hope that my co-discussant, Ed Mishan, will pursue the complementary course of concentrating on the more direct challenges to modern welfare economics that Jim Buchanan has tossed into our laps, though I will come back to these at a general level at the end of my comments.

Peacock and Rowley recently warned that:

it is an illusion to infer that Paretian welfare judgements lead to non-authoritarian solutions in matters of economic policy simply because

* University of York.

they are derived from individual preferences. Nor should it be inferred, as too often is the case, that those who deviate from consensus economics on matters of this kind necessarily are to be classified as intellectual fools or authoritarian knaves.[1]

Despite the 'necessarily' in the last sentence, if anyone is to fit that description, however, it is likely to be me, since I do have a strong paternalistic streak and easily get confused by philosophical discourse, and I would therefore plead to have that taken into account as an extenuating circumstance if you cannot stomach what follows.

Devils are notoriously good at citing scripture, so let me join the assembled throng and present the two passages from the *Wealth of Nations* that will serve as the text for my little homily. The first is from Book IV, Chapter ix and immediately precedes the passage that Buchanan cites at the head of his paper:

All systems either of preference or of restraint, therefore, being thus completely taken away, the obvious and simple system of natural liberty establishes itself of its own accord. Every man, as long as he does not violate the laws of justice, is left perfectly free to pursue his own interest his own way . . . (WN IV. ix. 51.)

If we delve further into what Adam Smith means by 'justice' in this context (as next expanded in Book V, Chapter i, Part II) it will be seen to have the hallmark of his times:

Men who have no property can injure one another only in their persons or reputations . . . Envy, malice, or resentment, are the only passions which can prompt one man to injure another in his person or reputation. But the greater part of men are not very frequently under the influence of those passions . . . But avarice and ambition in the rich, in the poor the hatred of labour and the love of present ease and enjoyment, are the passions which prompt to invade property, passions much more steady in their operation, and much more universal in their influence. Wherever there is great property, there is great inequality . . . and the affluence of the few supposes the indigence of the many. The affluence of the rich excites the indignation of the poor, who are often both driven by want, and prompted by envy, to invade his possessions. It is only under the shelter of the civil magistrate that the owner of that valuable property, which is acquired by the labour of many years, or perhaps of many successive generations, can sleep a single night in security. He is at all times surrounded by unknown enemies,

[1] *Welfare Economics: A Liberal Restatement* (Martin Robertson, 1975), 1–2.

whom, though he never provoked, he can never appease, and from whose injustice he can be protected only by the powerful arm of the civil magistrate . . . (WN V. i. b. 2.)

I will attempt to focus the discussion by a piece of breath-taking abstraction which may well serve merely to underline Buchanan's observations about the 'methodological distance' between the splendour of 1776-style political economy and the parsimony of 1976-style welfare economics.

Let us suppose that we all believe that it is a 'good thing' if the opportunity set ('scope for self-fulfilment') of individuals in a society is maximized. Let us further suppose, for the purposes of this discussion, that there are only four relevant realms within which such opportunities exist, the economic, the political, the social, and the legal. Within each realm each individual faces constraints on his freedom of action. Not all of them need be binding. For instance, a very poor man may find that only the economic constraints effectively influence him, for he has not the means to engage in actions which might be precluded by other constraints. Conversely, a rich and socially influential man may find the legal restraints upon his freedom of action the most irksome. Thus for a person's *effective* freedom to be maximized we need to discover which constraints impair his self-fulfilment most, and ask ourselves what, if anything, we should or could do about them.

One of the side-conditions which we might, as a society, *choose* to bear in mind in deciding whether we *should* loosen any of these constraints might be an egalitarian notion that we would try to ensure that the scope for self-fulfilment in each realm was much the same for everybody and, Pareto notwithstanding, would not improve matters for one person unless we could do so for all. Yet another consideration which we would *have* to bear in mind in deciding what we *could* do is that the 'production possibility frontier' between the various realms of 'freedom' will limit what is feasible for the society (e.g. enforcement of strict equality before the law may be very costly, i.e. reduce individuals' economic freedom, and may indeed be impossible if great inequality persists in the other three realms).

Returning now to Adam Smith, his position could be crudely epitomized as mainly concerned with the maximization of freedom in the legal realm, subject to a strong egalitarian side-condition in that realm. He believed that this would in itself maximize freedom in the economic realm, but was not concerned with inequalities in that realm, except to the extent that they might threaten the power of the legal authority. Inequality in the political and social realms he accepted as part of the natural order. (See the section of Part II of Chapter i of Book V (WN V. i. b. 3) describing 'the principal causes which naturally introduce subordination', viz. superiority of personal qualifications, of age, of fortune, and of birth.) Hence 'justice' was essentially a matter of equality before the law, with the content of law to be as unrestrictive as possible with respect to 'natural liberty'.

Buchanan seems to be of much the same mind, except that I suspect he would go a step further and say that whether or not legal freedoms (equally distributed) enlarge economic freedom, we should still pursue them. Indeed, we should do so even at considerable cost in the economic realm, because freedom from legal restraint is a good in itself, and equality in the legal realm is our main protection against a maldistribution or misuse of political power. Economic and social inequality is thus seen as obnoxious only when it threatens to undo the legal order by leading a sufficiently numerous group of citizens to believe that 'a detour into anarchy and out again into a new constitutional contract'[2] will probably leave them better off.

But now let us suppose that we are considering a community in which the primary good is to maximize economic and social freedoms, subject to a side-condition about equality in each of those two realms, and that the other two realms (the legal and political) are seen as instrumental to that purpose. Our perspective is now very different, and consequently so might be our policy priorities. For instance, we might feel it necessary to offer discriminatory legal protection to women, or Negroes, or Jews, or the disabled, or the poor, or the ignorant, to offset social and economic discrimination. We might also be prepared to sacrifice some of our less valuable legal freedoms (e.g. the right to a trial by jury for parking offences) in exchange for better health services, and risk having this caricatured as selling our birthright for a mess of pottage. This, it seems to me, is the general thrust of modern welfare economics, with its deeply ingrained utilitarian streak, as

[2] James M. Buchanan, *The Limits of Liberty* (University of Chicago Press, 1975), 85.

embodied in its practical manifestation, the use of cost–benefit analysis for public policy evaluation.

Although from this different perspective I can share many of Jim Buchanan's (and Adam Smith's) views about desirable social reforms, I am also able to see some problems to which their perspective seems to blind them. In particular, it does not generate confidence in the applicability of the eighteenth century's perspectives to the twentieth century's problems when acknowledged social responsibilities such as the alleviation of the adverse consequences of unemployment and redundancy are still to be dismissed pejoratively as 'publicly subsidized idleness' as if all fault lay with the individual victim. Nor am I impressed when a reincarnated Adam Smith is exhorted to spend his time laying bare 'the genuine social costs of the interference with natural liberty' rather than the more challenging task of seeking methods of manipulating the economic system so as to enhance social cohesion and fellow feeling.

I recognize that the price of freedom is eternal vigilance, and I am glad that we have indefatigable vigilantes like Jim Buchanan whose activities enable me to be a 'free rider'! But there are other freedoms to worry about besides the one that is the focus of his attention and, nostalgic Bicentennials apart, the parallels between 1776 and 1976 should perhaps not concentrate too exclusively upon 'Liberty', but, anticipating 1789 (and 1989), pay equal attention to 'Equality' and 'Fraternity'!

10

Adam Smith on Public Finance and Distribution

BY R. A. MUSGRAVE*

ADAM SMITH, in the *Wealth of Nations*, paints a sweeping panorama of economic activity, public as well as private. While focus is on the private sector and markets are guided by the invisible hand, Smith was no economic anarchist. Governmental activity forms an inherent part of his system of natural liberty. As laid out in the introduction to Book V, the sovereign must provide for a system of laws which assures the sanctity of property and sets the rules by which exchange and the division of labour can flourish. Moreover, provision must be made for defence, public works have to be undertaken, and public education must be provided for the common people. Were I to report on how Smith viewed the provision of public services, the conduct of my 'allocation branch' of the budget, I might have viewed Chapter i of Book V as a fore-runner to the modern theory of social goods. Even though his view of the matter was not as incisive as that of Hume, externalities might well be built into the Smithian system, setting a limit to what the invisible hand can handle.[1] But my assignment is to deal with the distribution and not the public service function of the fiscal system and on this aspect very little is to be found in the *Wealth of Nations*. My task, therefore, differs from that of my colleagues in this symposium. Whereas they may claim that Adam Smith anticipated all that was to come, my first task must be to inquire why the distribution issue was so largely

---

* H. H. Burbank Professor of Political Economy, Harvard University.

[1] Hume offered an uncannily modern conception of the social goods problem including the absence of preference revelation and the free rider issue. See David Hume, *Treatise on Human Nature* (1740) III. ii. 7, as quoted in Alan Peacock, 'The Treatment of the Principles of Public Finance in the *Wealth of Nations*', in *Essays on Adam Smith*.

omitted from Book V. Thereafter, I will sketch how, Adam Smith notwithstanding, this issue became a major concern of fiscal theory, how distribution-oriented policies came to assume strategic, if not dominant, importance, and how our past master might have felt about these developments.

I

DISTRIBUTION IN SMITH'S FISCAL SYSTEM

Before examining Smith's view of the fiscal system, it is well to take a look at the fiscal environment in which he worked. A sketch thereof is given in Table 1. At the beginning of the decade in which the *Wealth of Nations* appeared, the British national income was approximately £130 million.[2] With public expenditures of £12 million, the expenditure to national income ratio stood somewhat below 10 per cent, a ratio not very different from that prevailing up to the World War I years. Of the expenditure total of £12 million, 40 per cent went for debt service and 33 per cent for military purposes (1770). Of the remaining 27 per cent, £1·3 million went for poor relief, leaving £1·9 million for other purposes, half of which was accounted for by the civil list. Poverty-related programs were thus a major expenditure item, accounting for nearly half of what is left after deducting the 'uncontrollable' outlays of interest and defence. Yet there is no consideration of the finance of poor relief in Book V, and Smith's earlier critique of the settlement laws is directed against the resulting immobility of labour without consideration of the adequacy of support levels.[3] With poor relief provided in kind, transfer payments as a category do not appear in Smith's fiscal system. Only in his treatment of education does he consider public responsibilities toward the poor.

[2] We use 1770 (rather than 1776) as our reference point so as to view the fiscal structure as it was prior to the subsequent expansion in defence outlays. The British National Income for 1801 was estimated at £232 million. See B. R. Mitchell, *Abstract of British Historical Statistics* (Cambridge University Press, 1962), 366. With prices about doubling between 1770 and 1800 (ibid., 468) this was equivalent to about £160 million in terms of 1770 prices. Allowing for the growth in real income from 1770 to 1800, this seems in line with Hollander's 1770 estimate of £127 million. See S. Hollander, *The Economics of Adam Smith* (University of Toronto Press, 1973), 127.

[3] See Adam Smith, *The Wealth of Nations*, E. Cannan, ed. (Methuen, London, 1904), i. 137–142; I. x. c. 45–59 ('Inequalities Occasioned by the Policy of Europe'). All references to Adam Smith are to this edition.

TABLE I

The Structure of Public Finances in 1770 (in £000 sterling)

A. *Expenses*

Net Expenditures, United Kingdom (1770)

1	Debt Charges	4,836	
2	Defence	3,863	
3	Civil List	898	
4	Other Civil Government	927	
5	Total		10,524
6	Expenditures on Poor Relief (1776)	1,531	
7	assumed for 1770		1,300
	County Expenditures (1792)		
8	Jails; vagrants, constables	113	
9	Bridges	33	
10	Other	77	
11	Total	223	
12	assumed for 1770		150
13	Estimated total, 1770		11,974

B. *Receipts*

Receipts, United Kingdom (1770)

14	Customs	2,841	
15	Excises	5,139	
16	Stamps	336	
17	Post Office	162	
18	Land and Assessed Taxes	1,796	
19	Total		10,274
20	Poor Rates Receipts (1776)	1,720	
21	assumed for 1770		1,500
22	County and Police Rates (1792)	218	
23	assumed for 1770		150
24	Estimated total, 1770		11,924

[Source:

Lines 1–5: See B. R. Mitchell, *Abstract of British Historical Statistics*, 390.

Line 6: ibid. 410.

Line 7: Assumed on basis of same source.

Lines 8–11: ibid. 411.

Line 12: Assumed on basis of same source.

Lines 14–18: ibid. 388.

Line 20: ibid. 410.

Line 21: Assumed on basis of same source.

Line 22: ibid. 411.

Line 23: Assumed on basis of same source.]

He notes the need for public education as a means of relieving the condition of the common people, suffering from the dulling effects of industrial labour, and argues in favour of extending the Scottish system of publicly supported parish schools to England (WN ii. 270; V. i. f. 55). However, this goes to prove the exception rather than the rule, there being little or no concern with distributive expenditure policy in the rest of Smith's fiscal system. Nor did he view taxation as a redistributive device, since tax equity, as we shall note presently, was interpreted in benefit rather than ability terms.

How can this omission be explained, given the image of Adam Smith as so worldly-wise and generous a thinker? The answer may be found in the twofold constraint imposed by (i) the system of moral sentiments in which Smith and his time viewed the conduct of society, and (ii) the system of economic relationships by which he held the state of distribution to be determined. Neither was amenable to the inclusion of distribution issues in the system of public finances and both must contribute to explain their omission.

Distribution in the Theory of Moral Sentiments

Adam Smith's view of what today would be called distributive justice cannot be garnered from the *Wealth of Nations*, or certainly not from this source alone. Though this work is rightly considered his supreme achievement, he was also the author of a *Theory of Moral Sentiments*. While the *Theory* was published 17 years earlier, it would be a mistake to consider it a youthful aberration, lest the more hard-headed author of the *Wealth of Nations* be embarrassed thereby. Certainly, Smith himself did not take this view, since the *Theory* underwent six revisions, the last being published in 1790, the year of his death. In order to understand what is not said in the *Wealth of Nations*, I must begin, therefore, by considering what was said in the *Theory of Moral Sentiments*, inviting, as it were, the older brother to the birthday party.[4]

---

[4] Indeed, an analysis of his view of public finances and certainly of his view of the role of the state should allow for the *Theory of Moral Sentiments* as well as for the *Wealth of Nations*. The otherwise fine contributions by Alan Peacock (op. cit.) and George Stigler, 'Smith's Travels on the Ship of State', in *Essays on Adam Smith*, Part I, suffer from drawing on the latter work only. For a

Adam Smith, the moral philosopher, weaves in this work an intricate web of motivations, values, and rules of conduct. While man is more concerned with his own happiness than that of others, his tendency to selfish action is constrained by his desire for approbation by the 'impartial spectator'.[5] Reflecting the opinion of others and 'his representative, the man within the breast', the spectator will monitor one's conduct and induce one to respect certain virtues including those of justice, prudence, and beneficence.

Justice, in Adam Smith, is seen in commutative rather than distributive terms. It is a 'negative virtue', which consists of the duty not to injure someone else (TMS 117; II. ii. 1. 9). Offence against justice is resented by the observer and calls for punishment. The claim to justice can be enforced by the injured party. *Prudence*, 'the capacity to take care of oneself' is not 'one either of the most endearing or of the most ennobling of the virtues', yet it is considered respectable and approved by the observer (TMS 316; VI. i. 14). Indeed, 'the sober and deliberate action which it demands, the willingness of that prudent man to sacrifice present satisfaction in expectation of the future', is the fuel which drives economic progress and which generates the wealth of nations. Prudence, as socialized self-interest, has a strategic place in the natural order of things and as such differs from mere selfishness. *Beneficence*, finally, is the highest of all virtues.[6] The extension of generosity, affection, and kindness is a voluntary act which, as distinct from justice, cannot be enforced. Given freely, it secures the applause of the impartial spectator. But man is capable of limited beneficence only. It is extended most readily to family and friends, followed by neighbours and perhaps the nation, but hardly to humanity at large. Love of humanity, though the greatest of virtues, is hardly in man's grasp. Perfection is not within reach, and prudence distrusts 'the man of system' who pursues utopian goals and cannot suffer deviation from his 'ideal plan'. He is more likely to create disorder than to do good (TMS 342; VI. ii. 2. 17).

fuller interpretation of Smith, drawing on both works, see 'Adam Smith Heute und Morgen', Horst Claus Recktenwald, *Kyklos*, xxviii (1975), 5–22.

[5] See Adam Smith, *The Theory of Moral Sentiments*, with an introduction by E. G. West (Arlington House, New Rochelle, New York, 1969), 119; II. ii. 2. 1.

[6] Ibid. 117; II. ii. 1. 9. In Smith's system, it is the virtue of beneficence, rather than that of justice, which bears close relationship to distributive justice.

Smith's structure of moral sentiments, like that of his friend Burke, thus rests on a conservative position. But though man is entitled, by the Lockean system of natural liberty, to the fruits of his labour, beneficence retains a major role.[7] While expressed mainly in terms of friendship, sympathy, and esteem, there is no suggestion that beneficence might not also take the form of material support. Why, then, does not this expression of virtue find a place in Smith's view of the fiscal system? Its absence is explained by the voluntary nature of beneficence, a virtue which will be rewarded with sympathy but cannot be enforced. Transfers to the less fortunate, though laudable in Smith's moral system, must be of the voluntary or Pareto-optimal type, calling for implementation by charity rather than by a mandatory process of budgetary redistribution.[8] People may choose to share their riches with their neighbours, but they cannot demand that others do so. The virtue of giving is with the giver and the view of equality as a social good is disallowed. The voluntary exercise of beneficence in turn is limited by human frailty, so that the scope of charity is restricted.

The pressure on beneficence is relieved, however, by two further considerations. One is psychological in nature, and holds that the state of distribution has little to do with the level of welfare because little is gained from the consumption of luxuries. The other derives from the economic order which leaves only a limited degree of freedom in affecting the state of distribution. On both counts, the significance of distributive concern (*qua* economic beneficence) is thus reduced.

Distribution and Welfare

Consider first the unimportance of excessive possessions. The individual's unceasing desire for wealth, so Smith tells us, is based on a deception. The landlord who surveys the riches of his

[7] In LJB 149 ff., ed. Cannan, 106 ff., Smith sets forth various ways of acquiring property, viewing entitlement to the fruits of one's labour in a Lockean spirit. However, Smith the practical man is impatient with the abstract construct which derives natural law from the condition which prevails 'in the state of nature—as there is no such state existing', LJB 3; ed. Cannan, 2. See also the *Wealth of Nations*, i. 123; I. x. c. 12 and ii. 43; IV. v. b. 43.

[8] This aspect of inter-individual utility inter-dependence has received intensive consideration in recent years. See H. H. Hochman and J. D. Rogers, 'Pareto Optimal Redistribution', *American Economic Review* (September, 1969).

fields and in imagination himself consumes the whole harvest, does not realize that the 'capacity of his stomach bears no proportion to the immensity of his desires, and will receive no more than that of the meanest peasant' (TMS 264; IV. i. 1. 10). In later terms, the marginal utility of income is taken to fall to zero after a certain minimum level is reached. Smith thus rejected the view of his friend Hume, who recognized that the gains to the poor, from redistributing a given total income, would exceed the losses of the rich.[9] What then is the motivation behind industry and the striving for wealth? 'Do they imagine', so Smith asks, 'that their stomach is better or their sleep sounder, in a palace than in a cottage?' 'The contrary', so he answers, 'has so often been observed, and indeed, is so very obvious . . . that there is nobody ignorant of it' (TMS 70; I. iii. 2. 1). The true motivation, rather, is provided by the desire to win the admiration and notice of others. Only kings are fit for happiness or tragedy; the poor man is ashamed of his lot and goes unnoticed. This Veblenesque drive explains why men undergo the toil and anxiety which they must suffer to improve their lot, and in the process, give up 'all that ease, all that careless security, which they otherwise could enjoy' (TMS 72; I. iii. 2. 1). But the deception thus worked by human avarice has its positive function: it lends stability to the social structure and provides the driving force 'which rouses and keeps in continual motion the industry of mankind' (TMS 263; IV. i. 1. 10). The gain, it appears, is not in wealth itself but in the dynamic process of enhancing it. In short, inequality serves an important function and happily does so at little opportunity cost.

The Economic Laws of Distribution

I now turn to the second constraint on distribution policy, which is posed by the functioning of the economic system. Here we have two models to deal with, one dominant in the *Theory of Moral Sentiments* and the other in the *Wealth of Nations*. Both shade into each other, but there are important differences as well.

1. Beginning with the *Theory of Moral Sentiments*, Smith's view is that by the nature of things, a more or less egalitarian end result ensues, no matter how unequal may be the start. Viewing equity in terms of consumption rather than income, he argues that

[9] See David Hume, *Essays and Treatises on Several Subjects* (London, 1752), ii. 229.

the rich can consume but little more than the poor. The rest of the riches they must distribute among those who provide

the different baubles and trinkets which are employed in the economy of greatness; all of whom thus derive from his luxury and caprice the share of the necessities of life which they would in vain have expected from his humanity or his justice. The soil maintains at all times nearly that number of inhabitants which it is capable of maintaining. The rich . . . consume little more than the poor . . . Though they mean only their own conveniency . . . They are led by an invisible hand to make nearly the same distribution of the necessaries of life which would have been made had the earth been divided into equal portions among all its inhabitants; and thus, without intending it . . . advance the interest of the society, and afford means to the multiplication of the species. When providence divided the earth among a few lordly masters, it neither forgot nor abandoned those who seemed to have been left out in the partition . . . In ease of body and peace of mind all the different ranks of life are nearly upon a level, and the beggar, who suns himself by the side of the highway, possesses that security which kings are fighting for.[10]

The economic reasoning of this remarkable passage lends itself to various interpretations. The argument is not simply that because the rich can consume only little, little is taken away from the poor. (One wonders, in this context, how large a share of national output went, at Smith's time, into the consumption of baubles and trinkets?) It is held also that population size will adjust itself to what the land can produce so that improved means of production, in the long run, will not raise wage rates but merely expand population. This is the Malthusian-like mechanism, which in amended form reappears in the *Wealth of Nations*. Moreover, it is *because* the rich pay for the production of baubles and trinkets that the poor can earn the necessities of life. Presumably, they could not do so (or population would have to be smaller) without there being a demand for luxuries by the rich. But why could not the resources used to produce trinkets be used to produce amenities for the poor? Is it that the trinkets (or the emulation called forth by their possession) are needed as a reward for entrepreneurial industry, or is there a pre-Keynesian hint of potential

[10] *The Theory of Moral Sentiments*, 264–5; IV. i. 1. 10. The 'all is for the best' flavour of this passage foreshadows Mrs. Alexander's 19th-century hymn, 'All things bright and beautiful, all creatures great and small, all things wise and wonderful, the Lord God made them all. The rich man in his castle, the poor man at his gate, God made them, high or lowly, and ordered their estate.'

under-consumption, due to incapacity of the poor to generate sufficient demand? Here, as in other passages, there are many facets to Smith's reasoning and it is not easy to disentangle them.

Viewed as an expression of moral sentiments, one wonders whether the quoted passage would have satisfied the impartial observer. He might well have viewed it as an apologetic for not confronting the issue of distributive justice more squarely; or he might have taken it to reflect Smith's Calvinist dislike of trinkets, leading him severely to underestimate the elasticity of demand for opulence, not unlike in this respect to the low esteem in which a more recent colleague holds the modern pleasures of affluence. However this may be, it is significant to note that Smith did not rest the case simply by reference to the natural law of entitlement and just acquisition. Rather, the invisible hand is invoked—this being one of the two instances where, to my knowledge, he does so—to show that inequality is, after all, less unequal and avoidable than it seems to be.[11]

2. Turning to the richer and more complex analysis of the *Wealth of Nations*, we now find the issue of distribution viewed as a theory of factor shares, rather than one of inter-individual assignment. As such it is an integral part of the theory of value, with product and factor prices linked in a general equilibrium system. At the same time, factor shares in the late eighteenth century reflected economic classes, more nearly so than they do today, so that the economic theory of factor pricing also doubled as a social theory of distribution among economic groups.

Moreover, the theory of factor shares is now seen in a dynamic setting. In the long run, population size, via changes in the rate of infant mortality (WN i. 81; I. viii. 39–40), still responds to any deviation of actual from subsistence wage, until the latter is restored. But two further considerations apply, both of which are favourable to labour: (i) while the capital stock increases, the demand for labour rises and with the resulting increase in labour supply lagging behind, wage rates are temporarily increased. It is not the level of the capital stock that matters, so Smith argues in his chapter on wages, but its rate of increase (WN i. 71; I. viii. 22). (ii) In the process, there may result an upward shift in what is considered an acceptable subsistence. This will retard population

---

[11] The other occurs in the discussion of product markets (*Wealth of Nations*, i. 421; IV. ii. 9).

increase and permit the new equilibrium to be reached at a higher wage rate.

In combination, these two provisos may be read as compatible with a marginal productivity theory of wage determination, but taken separately they differ in their implication. Whereas the gains under (i) are contingent on continued growth, those from (ii) would remain even if expansion ceases. However this may be, Smith points with satisfaction to the fact that British wages have risen well above the subsistence level (WN i. 75–7; I. viii. 28–32) and that increased productivity has permitted the frugal peasant to live as well as an African king (WN i. 14; I. i. 11). The poor, as well as the rich, stand to gain from economic expansion, although it is not evident how the share of the poor will fare in the process.

We are left with two models of distribution theory which yield rather different results. In the *Theory*, the poor remain poor but distribution does not matter greatly because excess consumption is useless. In the *Wealth* they can gain from economic development and such gain is applauded. This makes it somewhat difficult to identify the 'true Mr. Smith', but both versions are similar in that neither leaves much scope for adjusting the state of inter-individual distribution.

Smith's Welfare Function

Before proceeding to the application of this analysis to tax policy, let me speculate briefly on how Smith would have written an individual's utility function and how he would have approached the design of a social welfare function.

A person's happiness, so Smith might have argued, would be a function of (i) the necessities of life which he consumes, including some conveniences and superfluities which are enjoyed by even 'the meanest labourer' (TMS 70; I. iii. 2. 1). To this would be added (ii) the satisfaction gained from the exercise of beneficence, as well as (iii) that derived from the envy of others for one's riches, offset more or less by the additional toil and burdens assumed in securing it. Finally, there might be a term reflecting (iv) the pride or satisfaction derived from being a part of the harmonious order which the system of natural liberty provides.

Asked further to write the social welfare function reflective of his natural order, Smith, after protesting so unproductive an activity, might well have adopted the utilitarian pattern of assigning a weight of 1 to each individual, and he might not have objected to comparing levels of utility or happiness. But he would have found no occasion to assign differing social weights to successive units of income since he thought such differentials to be spurious. The marginal utility of income schedule as we have seen drops to zero after a certain level of income is reached.

Turning to the social welfare function, would welfare be viewed in terms of average or total welfare? Smith does not offer an explicit discussion of the 'utilitarian' formula of maximum happiness for the largest number (the *Wealth of Nations* somewhat preceded Bentham's formulation) but he did call his major work the *Wealth of Nations* and not the *Wealth of Man*. Moreover, the economic process of accumulation (more about which later) is said to 'serve the interest of Society, and afford the means to the multiplication of the species' (TMS 265; IV. i. 1. 10). But even if population growth were added as a term to the social welfare function, Smith's linkage between welfare and distributional change would operate via its effects on accumulation and population size, rather than via the effects of redistribution among a given population. Yet, it is precisely the latter that is the essence of the modern distribution problem.

Implications for Tax Policy

How, then, does his theory of factor pricing and income shares relate to the role of tax policy, and especially its bearing on the state of distribution? The first of his four maxims of taxation (equality, certainty, convenience of payment, and economy in collection) demands that the tax system be equitable, but equity is defined as distributional neutrality:

> The subjects of every State ought to contribute toward the support of the government, as nearly as possible, in proportion to their respective abilities, that is in proportion to the revenue which they respectively enjoy under the protection of the State. The expense of government to the individuals of a great nation, is like the expense of management to the joint tenants of a great estate, who are all obliged to contribute in proportion to their respective interests in the estate. (WN ii. 310; V. ii. b. 3.)

This passage may be read as either an ability-to-pay or a benefit based view of tax equity. The 'that is' clause nicely begs the issue since if ability-to-pay depends on income, and income is earned under the protection of the State, the two versions may be said to yield the same result. But other passages suggest that he ranked the benefit principle in the primary role. Moreover, Smith calls for a distribution of the tax burden in *proportion* to income, with a slight nod in the direction of progression (ii. 327; V. ii. e. 7). Finally, we note that equity is seen in terms of income (i.e. 'revenue from *all* sources'), rather than in terms of consumption. Indeed, consumption taxes are criticized because 'they do not always fall equally or proportionably upon the revenue of every individual' (WN ii. 378; V. ii. k. 58). Contrary to his view of utility *qua* consumption in the *Theory*, Smith now sides with the Haig–Simons rather than the Fisher–Kaldor school of tax-base theorists.

Given the premise of proportional rates, Smith would have no need to call for a global-type income tax. A schedular-type tax, with wages excluded but all other schedules subject to the same rate, would do. He did not, however, support an income tax as he opposed the taxation of profit income, and his anti-income-tax position lent authority to the case against Pitt's income tax of 1799.[12] This followed from his notions of tax incidence as based on his theory of factor shares. A tax on wages, so he argues, would be 'absurd and destructive' because it would either come to be absorbed by the landlord in reduced rent as in the case of agricultural labour or by the consumer as in the case of industrial labour (WN ii. 349; V. ii. 2). With wages at the subsistence level, a decline in the net wage below this level calls forth a decrease in labour supply, with the gross wage rising until the net wage is returned to the old level. As a result, the return to other factors is reduced and this being the case, they might as well be taxed in the first place.[13] The underlying assumption is that the wage rate cannot fall below subsistence, even though this may be at a customary rather than a minimum level. Evidently, the acceptable minimum can rise in the process of development, but thereafter

[12] See William Kennedy, *English Taxation, 1640–1799* (London, Bell and Sons, 1913), 149.

[13] More specifically, Smith argues that it is better to tax these other sources because the maintenance of net wages at subsistence will call for a percentage increase in the wage rate which exceeds the rate of tax. While the latter point is correct, it hardly justifies the conclusion that *therefore* it is better to use other taxes in the first place.

cannot be depressed. However this may be, the population response is still the key factor in the argument.

The rent of land, on the other hand, is a fit object of taxation.
The land tax ranks high, as 'it does not appear likely to occasion
any other inconvenience to the landlord, except always the considerable one of being obliged to pay the tax' (WN ii. 318; V. ii.
c. 19). Essentially the same holds for taxes upon the produce of
land which finally are also paid by the landlord. Taxes on the rent
of houses are divided between the ground and building rent component of the base. The tax on ground rent is borne by the owner
of the land, but the tax on building rent causes capital to move to
other uses, with the burden passing to the landlord and the consumer of housing. In all, taxes on house rent are good taxes even
though they may bear more than proportionally upon the rich.

Taxes upon profits, finally, are of questionable merit. That part
of profits which is needed to pay interest is in the nature of a rent
income, so that the tax thereon cannot be passed on. The tax is
economically feasible but its administration would call for an
intolerable inquisition. The remaining part of profits 'in most
cases . . . is no more than a very moderate compensation' and is
needed to reward the employer for his risk and efforts (WN ii.
331; V. ii. f. 2). Such taxation would interfere with the reward for
prudence and retard economic growth. Profits, therefore, are not
a proper subject of taxation.

Turning to taxes on consumable commodities, a distinction is
drawn between taxes on luxuries and taxes on necessaries, defined
to include 'not only those things which nature, but those things
which the established rules of decency have rendered necessary to
the lowest rank of people' (WN ii. 355; V. ii. k. 3). Taxes on
necessaries operate in the same manner as a direct tax upon the
wages of labour and are self-defeating. 'The middling and superior
ranks of people, if they understood their own interest, ought
always to oppose all taxes upon the necessaries of life, as well as all
direct taxes upon the wages of labour' (WN ii. 357; V. ii. k. 9).
They themselves must pay such taxes. Taxes upon salt, leather,
soap, and candles are rejected accordingly. Taxes upon luxuries,
however, are paid by the consumer. Though not paid in proportion to all revenue received, they permit the individual flexibility
in his tax payments. They are 'perhaps, as agreeable to the three
first . . . maxims . . . as any other' (WN ii. 379–80; V. ii. k. 60),

and though they offend the fourth, this is unavoidable and must be taken into the bargain.

This summary, to be sure, does not pretend to offer a full evaluation of Smith's incidence analysis. While the chapters on incidence reflect inconsistencies inherent in various parts of Smith's distribution theory, they are nevertheless impressive in their heroic endeavour to view the problem of incidence (as the Physiocrats had done) in general equilibrium terms. A splendid but defective model of factor pricing, to paraphrase Schumpeter in his 'Review of the Troops', produced positive if mistaken answers to incidence theory.[14] For our purposes the upshot of the matter is that there are only two viable tax bases, i.e. rent and luxury consumption.

The burden of approved taxes thus seems to fall on the progressive side of Smith's proportionality rule. Landlords with the highest income are hit from both the income sources and the spending uses side. Profit recipients, the next highest group, pay on the spending side only but are taxed relatively heavily on luxury consumption. The common people in turn pay no tax, except through their limited consumption of amenities. With incidence thus determined by the nature of economic forces, the first maxim has only limited application. Taxes, it would seem, have to be placed where the economy can absorb them.

But theorizing aside, what was the actual tax structure which existed in Smith's time? One-third of revenue (see Table 1) was derived from taxes falling on the rent of land and housing, while the other two-thirds came from customs duties and excises. With levies on malt, beer, and sugar the main revenue producers, the tax structure relied to a significant degree on items below the luxury level.[15] However, Smith thought of these as amenities rather than necessities, with taxes thereon borne by the consumer. While the impact of the tax structure in its reliance on customs duties and excises was not as equitable as he might have liked it to be, he thought it preferable to the continental system. Moreover, in matters of applied tax policy Smith was rather pragmatic.

[14] Joseph Schumpeter, when evaluating the Ricardian model, noted that 'it is an excellent theory that can never be refuted and lacks nothing but sense'. See 'The Review of the Troops', *Quarterly Journal of Economics* (May 1951), 161.

[15] See Stephen Dowell, *History of Taxation and Taxes in England* (Reprints of Economic Classics, Kelley, New York, 1965), iii. 207.

After the good taxes have been fully utilized, so he tells us, the less desirable ones must be resorted to.[16]

While Smith does not discuss expenditure incidence, his logic would have led to similar conclusions on the expenditure side. Leaving aside the difficult question of how to allocate the benefits from defence and debt service, remaining outlays, as noted before, were in substantial part directed at the very poor (workhouses), with the remainder going largely to the very rich (civil list). But in the context of his economic system, Smith would have been led to conclude that poor relief in the end could not raise the standard of living of the poor but merely siphon income from the landlords and sustain a larger population. In short, there was little economic scope for the exercise of beneficence through the budget, even if redistribution through the mandatory use of taxation had been defensible. Moreover, by retarding the rate of growth, the lot of the poor might well have been worsened.

II. THE POST-SMITH RECORD

Having sketched the role of redistribution in Smith's view of the public sector, I can find little which anticipates subsequent developments, be it at the level of fiscal theory or of practice. The mechanism of population response, so central to his incidence theory, ceased to function or became reversed, and consumer stomachs learned to expand in line with the vast increase in *per capita* income that occurred in the Western world. While the relationship between the size of the pie and its slicing remained an acute issue, the range of distributional policy options proved much greater than the Smithian view had suggested. Along with this development, the strictures of natural law, which would guarantee innate property rights in differential ability and inherited wealth, gave way to a more flexible view of what the optimal state of distribution should be. All this combined with the rise of popular democracy, a shifting balance of political power, and rising fiscal centralization to render distributional concerns of growing importance to fiscal policy.

[16] See the *Wealth of Nations*, ii. 390; V. ii. k. 80. Given this premiss Smith (contrary to Stigler's stricture, op. cit.) did allow for revenue adequacy as part of his system of tax maxims.

The Distribution Issue in Fiscal Theory

Just as the theory of social goods is an extension of the benefit view of tax equity, so is the theory of fiscal redistribution an extension of the ability-to-pay doctrine. Though the benefit theory need not be incompatible with progressive taxation, the rising case for progressive taxation, as a measure of redistribution, belonged to the ability-to-pay tradition. While earlier writers had interpreted ability-to-pay to call for regressive, proportional, or progressive taxation,[17] a more systematic interpretation of the doctrine began only with John Stuart Mill. Construing taxation according to ability-to-pay as taxation which imposes equal sacrifice, Mill called for equal proportional sacrifice, mistakenly thinking that this would also result in least total sacrifice.[18] Matters were straightened out by Edgeworth, who distinguished between equal absolute, equal proportional, and equal marginal sacrifice, and who noted the equivalence of the latter as an equity rule with least total sacrifice, thus coinciding with the criterion of fiscal efficiency.[19] These concepts were developed further by Pigou who thought equal absolute sacrifice the proper equity rule.[20] However, there was no simple and obvious relationship between the various equity rules and the case for progressive taxation. Assuming comparable and equal marginal utility of income schedules, equal marginal sacrifice would call for maximum progression (levelling incomes down from the top until the necessary revenue is reached) provided only that marginal utility falls as income rises. Equal absolute sacrifice in turn would call for progressive, proportional, or regressive rates depending on whether the elasticity of the schedule exceeds, equals, or falls short of unity. Equal proportional sacrifice, finally, poses a more complex case so that no simple relationship follows. But though it seems reasonable to assume that marginal income utility declines, there is no intuition regarding the rate of decline, thus leaving the issue of progressivity

---

[17] For a survey of this literature see Edwin R. A. Seligman, *Progressive Taxation in Theory and Practice.* (*American Economic Association*, June 1894.)

[18] See John Stuart Mill, *Principles of Political Economy*, ed. W. J. Ashley (Longmans, Green, and Company Ltd., London, 1921), 804.

[19] See F. Y. Edgeworth, *Papers Relating to Political Economy* (MacMillan and Co., London, 1929), ii. 100.

[20] See A. C. Pigou, *A Study in Public Finance* (3rd ed., MacMillan, London, 1951).

(and with it appropriate changes in the distribution of income) an open question.

This theory of tax equity thus leads to a wholly inconclusive position. Beyond this, it came to be attacked on more basic grounds. The *old* welfare economics, of which ability-to-pay theory was an inherent part, came to be rejected in its entirety because the very premiss of interpersonal utility comparison came to be considered non-operational and meaningless (a critique by which I was never wholly persuaded). The *new* welfare economics proposed to deal with problems of welfare in terms of efficiency only, while shunning issues of distribution. Distribution, to post-Robbins economic theory, became a non-issue. Society would benefit if A gains without a loss to B, and this was about all that could be said. A social welfare function was designed which would record a gain in welfare as a move to the efficiency frontier, thus separating welfare economics as an efficiency issue from any justice content.

But economics as a social science cannot entirely detach itself from major social problems. It is not surprising, therefore, that economists are now in the process of replacing the new with a still *newer* welfare economics. A social welfare function is postulated which (i) values the utility derived by various individuals of equal income equally and (ii) assigns social weights to the marginal utility of income, letting these weights decline as income rises. Consequently, the crude measurements of inequality by such devices as the Gini coefficient may be supplemented by a more meaningful measure which reflects the social gain that can be obtained from equalization.[21]

In the newer welfare economics, the framework of the old sacrifice theory is essentially re-established, with the difference (perhaps more formal than real but satisfying the scientific conscience of the profession) that it avoids the hurdle of interpersonal comparison and empirical determination of income utility functions. The new approach, however, makes some important additions. Discussion of the fiscal distribution issue is no longer restricted to the allocation of tax burdens, with revenue limited to the size of the public service budget, but is seen in more general terms. The target becomes optimal income distribution, the design of an optimal tax-transfer system, not merely the optimal

---

[21] See A. B. Atkinson, 'On the Measurement of Inequality', *Journal of Economic Theory*, ii (1970), 244–63.

collection of a fixed amount of revenue. Moreover, the new analysis systematically allows for the efficiency costs of redistribution, those responses which Pigou had referred to as announcement effects and which linger in the shadows of Smith's fourth maxim. Concurrent with this development in economic analysis, philosophers have re-examined the distributional implications of the contractarian tradition and have focused on a maximin rule of distribution.[22]

Given this framework and based on certain assumptions, devotees of the newer welfare economics have been busy computing what would constitute an optimal state of distribution and the required scope of redistribution.[23] These results have given a more concrete flavour to the debate, but they depend on the nature of the underlying assumptions, mainly (i) the shape of the social welfare function by which outcomes are evaluated, (ii) the distribution of earnings capacity, the results of which are to be adjusted, and (iii) the shape of a uniform utility function, maximization of which determines the individual's response (in choosing between goods and leisure) to tax and transfer policies. Finally, (iv) a linear tax function is assumed. The results suggest that the optimal degree of redistribution even under the extreme Rawlsian criterion of maximin (where a zero value is assigned to gains obtained by anyone but the lowest on the scale) is less than might have been expected, but these results depend on the underlying assumptions. In particular, I remain uneasy about the arbitrariness which is introduced in choosing a particular (Cobb–Douglas or constant elasticity) utility function, in assuming it to be uniformly applicable to all individuals, and in operating with a linear tax schedule only. I appreciate that these assumptions are needed to formulate a workable model and I admire the mathematical ingenuity which went into this construction, but I remain as yet hesitant to draw policy conclusions. Nevertheless major progress is being made, and one wonders how Adam Smith would have viewed it. Two responses may be ventured.

First of all, Smith would have held that the utility function by

[22] See J. R. Rawls, *A Theory of Justice* (Harvard University Press, Cambridge, Mass., 1971; Oxford University Press, 1972).

[23] See the contributions by A. B. Atkinson and E. Sheshinski, in *Economic Justice*, E. S. Phelps, ed. (Penguin, 1973). Also see R. Cooter and E. Helpman, 'Optimal Income Taxation for Transfer Payments', *Quarterly Journal of Economics* (November 1974).

which short-run labour supply is determined permits a goods–leisure trade-off only above subsistence, and that the long-run schedule must allow for population response. Second, Smith would have felt very uneasy about the simplified leisure–goods trade-off on which the current models are based. He would surely have argued that the response will differ between various types of labour and that effects upon the dynamic role of entrepreneurship and capital accumulation must be distinguished from effects on the supply of common labour. Finally, and most important, he would have rejected the very notion of an optimal distribution of income which is to be attained by a process of non-voluntary redistribution. For him the state of distribution, as noted before, was set by the system of natural liberty (property rights in the fruits of one's ability and industry) and the objective forces of the economic system (factor pricing and population response), an order which was to be amended only by voluntary redistribution based on the virtue of beneficence, but not by budgetary meddling. Given redistribution of that type, efficiency costs do not arise, so that the problem of dead weight loss would be limited to the response to taxes imposed to finance public services. For such finance, the benefit principle would apply, with a compromise to be reached between equity and the other three maxims. The newer welfare economists would be applauded in implementing the fourth maxim, but this would only be part of the story.

The Distribution Issue in Fiscal Practice

If Adam Smith would have been displeased with the introduction of mandatory redistribution schemes into fiscal theory he would have been dismayed by the revolutionary changes in fiscal practice which occurred over recent decades. These developments are shown in Tables 2a and 2b using the U.S. and U.K. as illustrations, with more or less similar pictures to be found in other Western countries. We note that budget patterns changed relatively little over the century and a half following the *Wealth of Nations*. The share of the public sector in GNP was not much higher in the 1920s than at the time of Adam Smith, but drastic changes began in the 1930s and gained pace in the post-war years. The construction of the modern welfare state, heralded in the mid-1940s by Beveridge's *Full Employment in a Free Society*, placed social service expenditures in the centre of budgetary policy. What had seemed hardly worth mentioning in the *Wealth of Nations* became the core of the fiscal issue. The public sector share (see Tables 2a and 2b) rose from below 15 per cent of GNP in the mid-twenties to a 1974 level of 33 per cent for the U.S. and

TABLE 2a

Rise of Social Expenditures: (a) United Kingdom

	1770	*1890*	*1910*	*1938*	*1955*	*1974*
As percentage of G.N.P.						
Public Expenditures, total[a]	12	9	13	30	37	44
Total, excl. Defence and Interest	3	5	8	17	23	35
Social Services	1	2	4	11	16	25
Transfers	n.a.	1	1	7	7	15
Purchases[b]	n.a.	8	12	23	30	25
As percentage of Public Expenditures						
Social Insurance and Assistance	n.a.	n.a.	n.a.	17	16	21
Education	n.a.	n.a.	n.a.	9	11	13
Other Social Services[c]	n.a.	n.a.	n.a.	11	16	23
Total, Social Services	13	22	31	37	43	55
Transfers	n.a.	7	13	21	26	35
Purchases	n.a.	93	87	79	74	57
As percentage of Public Expenditures, excl. Defence and Interest						
Social Insurance and Assistance	n.a.	n.a.	n.a.	30	26	27
Education	n.a.	n.a.	n.a.	15	17	17
Other Social Services	n.a.	n.a.	n.a.	20	27	30
Total, Social Services	43	40	50	65	70	74
Transfers	n.a.	13	21	37	42	44

[*Source*: For 1775 see Table 1. For 1890–1955 see Alan T. Peacock and Jack Wiseman, *Growth of Public Expenditures in the United Kingdom* (Princeton University Press, 1961), 83, 86, 92. For 1974 see C.S.O., 1975 *National Income Bluebook*, Table 52. A G.N.P. base at market price of £82,000 million is used. Using a market price base of £70,000 million, the over-all expenditure ratio is 40%.

[a] Excludes (1) lending and borrowing, and (2) public corporations which, in a more detailed analysis, should be partly included.

[b] Includes interest on public debt.

[c] Includes outlays on health, housing, and food subsidies.]

44 per cent for the U.K. The share of the social expenditure items in total public expenditures rose from around 30 per cent to 50 per cent or more, with a substantially higher ratio if defence and interest are excluded from the base. Indeed, this increase in social service expenditures accounted for the entire gain in the rising ratio of public expenditures to GNP which has occurred (especially in the U.S.) over the last two decades. To be sure, a substantial part of the growth has been in transfers, so that the real share of government in GNP has not expanded accordingly. But this is only a natural by-product of the rising importance of

distributional considerations, and does not detract from their increasing weight in budget patterns.

TABLE 2b

Rise of Social Expenditures: (b) United States

	1902	1927	1940	1950	1960	1973
As percentage of G.N.P.						
Public Expenditures, total	7	10	18	23	27	32
Public Expenditures, excl. Defence and Interest	5	8	14	13	15	23
Social Services	2	3	5	6	9	15
Transfers	n.a.	n.a.	3	5	15	10
Purchases[a]	n.a.	n.a.	15	18	22	22
As percentage of Public Expenditures						
Social Insurance, Assistance, and other	7	7	14	10	18	30
Education	18	22	16	15	14	18
Total, Social Services	25	29	30	25	32	48
Transfers	n.a.	n.a.	15	25	19	30
Purchases[b]	n.a.	n.a.	85	75	81	70
As percentage of Public Expenditures, excl. Defence and Interest						
Social Insurance, Assistance, and other	10	19	18	18	33	39
Education	25	17	21	27	25	23
Total, Social Services	35	36	39	45	58	62

[*Source*: See R. A. Musgrave and P. B. Musgrave, *Public Finance in Theory and Practice* (McGraw-Hill, New York, 1976), 2nd ed., 137.

[a] Interest is included in purchases.

[b] The over-all expenditure ratio for 1974 is 33 per cent, and the ratio excluding defence and interest is 24 per cent. 1973 rather than 1974 figures are used because the necessary breakdown for the latter is as yet unavailable.]

A similar, though less pronounced development has occurred on the tax side of the budget picture, where the rise of the direct tax share in total tax revenue signalled increased reliance on progressive taxation. Using again the U.S. and U.K. as points of reference, this development is shown in Table 3. In the U.K. the income tax share rose from 36% in 1913 to over 40% in later years, an increase which occurred at the cost of the share contributed by local rates. In the U.S. the income tax share rose from 11% at the beginning of the century to 30% in 1927 and 50% today. The sharp increase which occurred during World War II was largely at the cost of the property tax share, reinforced by a decline in the contribution of indirect taxes. These developments, combined with the increasingly progressive rate structure of the income tax, suggest a widening departure from Adam Smith's rule of pro-portionate taxation, at least on the surface. However, in recent years there has developed a significant counter-tendency, i.e. the rising importance of the payroll tax, especially in the revenue structure of the United States.

TABLE 3

Composition of Tax Structure

(All Levels of Government)

	United Kingdom[a]			United States[b]			
	13/14	*38/39*	*74/75*	*02*	*27*	*50*	*74*
Direct	36%	42%	43%	11%	31%	53%	49%
Indirect	31	28	29	37	18	24	17
Local Rates	33	17	10	52	49	13	12
Pay Roll	—	12	18	—	2	10	22
Total	100	100	100	100	100	100	100

[*Source:*
[a] See A. R. Prest, *Public Finance in Theory and Practice* (5th ed.), 168, 199 and for 1974, *C.S.O. Annual Abstract* (1975), Tables 330 and 331.
[b] See R. A. Musgrave and P. B. Musgrave, *Public Finance in Theory and Practice*, 2nd ed., 208, and U.S. Department of Commerce, *Survey of Current Business* (July 1975).]

In order to measure the over-all distributive effects of taxation, a comparison must be drawn between the pre- and post-tax distributions of income; or, preferably, the existing post-tax distribution may be compared with that under a proportional tax structure. This is a speculative undertaking involving theoretical judgement regarding incidence, supported in part by only limited empirical evidence. In some instances, especially with regard to the corporation and property taxes, there remains substantial room for controversy, and long-run results may differ from those applicable to the short run. Nevertheless, the typical conclusion is that the tax structure as a whole (and Adam Smith would have been pleased with this) tends to be proportional over the larger part of the income range. Such is the case for estimates based on British,[24] U.S.,[25] and Swedish[26] data. The British estimates, which

---

[24] See Central Statistical Office, *Economic Record* (December 1974). Also see J. S. Nicholson, 'The Distribution and Redistribution of Income in the

[*See overleaf for note 24 cont. and notes 25, 26*]

exclude corporation tax and allocate rates in line with rental expenditures, show some degree of progression for household incomes up to £800 (1973 levels) but become more or less proportional above this level. The U.S. data, which include all taxes and are available for a variety of incidence assumptions, follow a more or less similar pattern. Progression depends in particular upon the treatment of the corporation and the property taxes, but remains modest even if the most favourable assumptions for progressive results are made. Given a more or less proportional effective rate curve, it is not surprising that the Gini coefficient applicable to post-tax income is but slightly more equal than that applicable to pre-tax income.

Turning to the expenditure side of fiscal redistribution, the rise of transfer payments and of social services has made for an increasingly redistributive pattern. Estimates for a variety of countries, including U.K., U.S., and Sweden, show the benefit to income ratio to decline sharply as income rises. While a host of new difficulties arise in an attempt to allocate expenditure benefits, it is evident that they cannot be neglected. Indeed, the major redistributive effects of budget policy operate via the expenditure side. Expenditure equity, it appears, is more important than the traditional focus on tax equity.

But it is not enough to consider the tax and expenditure sides in isolation. To obtain the net result, both sides must be combined. Relating the net of benefit and taxes to earnings (before tax and transfers), 1973 data for the U.K. show a net benefit rate falling from 700% at the lower end of the scale to zero at an income level of about £1,200 and a rising net burden rate thereafter, reaching 26% above a £3,750 level. U.S. estimates for 1968 present a similar pattern with the break-even point at around $8,000, approximately the mid-point in the family earnings scale. Throughout, the post-budget distribution of income (earnings plus expenditure benefits minus taxes) is more equal than the distribution

United Kingdom' in *Poverty, Inequality and Class Structure*, D. Wedderburn, ed. (Cambridge University Press, 1974).

[25] See J. A. Pechman and B. Okner, 'Who Bears the Tax Burden?', *Brookings Institute* (Washington, D.C., 1974); and R. A. Musgrave, Karl E. Case, and Herman Leonard, 'The Division of Fiscal Burden and Benefits', *Public Finance Quarterly* (July 1974).

[26] See P. Franzen, K. Lövgren, and I. Rosenberg, 'Distribution Effects of Taxes and Public Expenditures in Sweden', *The Swedish Journal of Economics*, 77 (1975), No. 1.

of earnings only (excluding benefits and before deducting taxes), and throughout the net gain in equality is substantially larger than if the comparison is limited to taxation effects only.

Nevertheless, the over-all impact as measured by the change in Gini coefficient is still modest. This had led observers to note that the redistributive process involves a great deal of churning with a relatively small net effect. This, however, overlooks the fact that the resulting increase in the percentage of income received by, say, the lowest decile or quartile in the income scale is very substantial. As weighted by a social welfare function, the resulting degree of equalization thus proves much larger than suggested by the resulting unweighted change in Gini coefficient.

Smith might have been pleased with this result, finding support of the poor closer to his virtue of beneficence than a more broadly based egalitarian goal. But, in line with the winds of current thought, he would have stressed the linkage between distribution policy and accumulation, arguing that all factors stand to gain from more rapid growth, which growth may well be retarded by redistribution. Even so, he would have to revise his view of the mechanism by which the distribution issue is related to growth, as well as his set of moral sentiments by which the case for reduced inequality can be argued or rejected. The wealth of nations, as Smith well knew, is not independent of its distribution; but the same wealth, in the last resort, belongs to the individuals that comprise the nation and thus cannot be assessed without assignment among them.

COMMENT

by A. R. Prest*

Professor Musgrave's paper is an elegant synthesis of what the great man actually said, whether in 1759 or in 1776, about the normative and positive aspects of distribution and what he might have said of modern theoretical and empirical developments in this area if he were alive today. I propose to say something under each of these headings.

Under the first, Professor Musgrave gives the impression, inten-

* London School of Economics.

tionally or unintentionally, that Adam Smith's views on this subject do not add up to a great deal. Thus the search for a normative theory of distribution amid the concepts of justice and beneficence in the *Theory of Moral Sentiments* is found not to be a very profitable one; it is stated (304) that Smith had nothing to say on the distribution of income by size as distinct from that by factor shares; and the well-known fence-sitting act in respect of ability-to-pay versus benefits-received principles is reviewed at some length (307).

I am very much aware that beauty is in the eye of the beholder when it comes to textual exegesis, especially with a work which has acquired a semi-biblical reputation over the last 200 years. Nevertheless, I think that Professor Musgrave is a shade unfair on Adam Smith in that rather more is said on these topics than would appear from his account. This comes out clearly enough if one looks more closely at Chapter i of Book V of the *Wealth of Nations*, which Professor Musgrave puts on one side as relating to social goods provision (296). In fact there are passages there which show the keenest of eyes for distributional matters. Thus we are told:

> For one very rich man there must be at least five hundred poor, and the affluence of the few supposes the indigence of the many. The affluence of the rich excites the indignation of the poor, who are often both driven by want, and prompted by envy, to invade his possessions.[1]

One in five hundred. Given that exactly 0·2 per cent of income recipients had a pre-tax income in excess of £12,000 per annum in the U.K. in 1972/73,[2] this seems a reasonably pertinent comment. And the latter part of the passage fits in perfectly with the so-called philosophy underlying the so-called social contract in the Britain of today, the grounds for campaigning for a wealth tax and so on.

In the same chapter we are given an extremely good account of the factors making for class distinctions. Would anyone today want to add much to the four which are enumerated—differential ability, age, fortune, and birth?

It also seems to me that Adam Smith goes rather further than

---

[1] WN ii. 199 of the Everyman edition (J. M. Dent & Sons, London, 1910); V. i. b. 2 ('Of the Expence of Justice').

[2] Of 28·4 million tax units, 56,000 were above the £12,000 mark. *National Income and Expenditure*, 1964–74 (Central Statistical Office, H.M.S.O., London, 1975), Table 28.

Professor Musgrave allows in endorsing the ability-to-pay principle of taxation. Thus in WN V. ii we have the following well-known and often-quoted passage:

A tax upon house rents, therefore, would in general fall heaviest upon the rich; and in this sort of inequality there would not, perhaps, be anything very unreasonable. It is not very unreasonable that the rich should contribute to the public expense, not only in proportion to their revenue, but something more than in that proportion.[3]

Or in discussing taxes on carriages and turnpike tolls we have the following passage in Chapter 1 of Book V:

Whatever exigency of the state therefore this tax might be intended to supply, that exigency would be chiefly supplied at the expense of the poor, not of the rich; at the expense of those who are least able to supply it, not of those who are most able.[4]

Or, looking at another chapter, we have a clear glimpse of the principle of international equity when discussing the responsibilities of other countries towards the public debt incurred by Great Britain (V. iii. 88). With respect to the U.K. income tax it is probably a fair guess that he would not have liked the idea of returning an income total to the authorities. But neither did his contemporaries—so much so that Pitt's global return had to be abandoned in favour of the schedular system in Addington's version of the tax in 1803.

Of course, this is all a matter of interpretation and of emphasis. Perhaps the difference between Professor Musgrave and myself is that he is inclined to characterize a glass which contains half the quantity of liquid which it might hold as half-empty; I should say it was half-full.

On the second topic, what the great man might have said, there is scope for enormous fun or enormous inconclusiveness depending on the way one chooses to play the game. But given Smith's own description of the *Wealth of Nations* as 'a speculative work', (V. iii. 68) there is some justification for playing the game.

I should like to start here with something which Professor Musgrave omits—the changes in the factor distribution of income in modern times. Adam Smith, with his emphasis on the undesirability of taxing profits, would have been concerned with, and

[3] WN ii. 324; V. ii. e. 6 ('Taxes upon the Rent of Houses').
[4] WN ii. 216; V. i. d. 13 (Article I).

indeed alarmed at, the way profits have fallen sharply as a proportion of factor rewards in recent years in the U.K.[5] One can hardly think that he would have regarded this as the passport to rapid growth of the economy. On the other hand, he would not, one suspects, have been surprised to find that the distribution of earnings from employment shows a remarkable constancy over the years, with the ratio of, for instance, the lowest decile to median income being more or less unchanged in the U.K. from 1886 to 1974.[6]

Turning to some of the changes which are mentioned by Professor Musgrave, it seems reasonable to think that Smith would have viewed the latter-day growth of public expenditures with more than a little concern—and especially if he was confronted not just with the 1974 figures for the U.K. as given in Table 2a but also with those for 1975.[7] However, he might not have been entirely surprised at the long-run tendencies shown in the table; after all, we are told in Book V, Chapter 1 that

> The first duty of the sovereign, therefore, that of defending the society from the violence and injustice of other independent societies, grows gradually more and more expensive as the society advances in civilisation.[8]

Perhaps the relative price effect should be renamed the Adam Smith effect!

What his views *would* have been on the estimates of the redistributive effects of government revenues and expenditures, it

[5] A convenient summary covering the period 1950–72 is given in G. J. Burgess and A. J. Webb, 'The Profits of British Industry', *Lloyds Bank Review* (April 1974). For later figures see *The Budget 1976* (Confederation of British Industry, London, 1976). It is, incidentally, by no means clear that the statement by Professor Musgrave about the correspondence between factor shares and social classes in the eighteenth century can be fully justified. There were still a lot of peasant farmers, and the enclosure movement was by no means complete at the time Adam Smith was writing. See above, 304.

[6] Royal Commission on Distribution of Income and Wealth, *Report* No. 1, Cmnd. 6171 (July 1975), 57.

[7] Public expenditure (from Table 57 of the 1975 *Blue Book*, but excluding loan transactions) was 54 per cent of factor cost G.N.P. in 1974 (or 49 per cent if public corporations are omitted as in Table 52), the preliminary figure for 1975 being 56 1 in the former case. It would be better to take percentages of G.N.P. at market prices (the result being a reduction of the 1974 49 per cent figure to 45 per cent) but this would then necessitate adjustments to the historical data to ensure comparability.

[8] WN ii. 197; V. i. a. 42 ('Of the Expence of Defence').

is impossible to say. What one can say is what they should have been. I have argued for many years[9] that these calculations, especially when they purport to cover the revenue and expenditure sides jointly, are of exceedingly little value or meaning. I am pleased to report progress, even if rather slow progress, in gaining adherents to this view. Thus Professor Shoup argued that

The effect of an entire public finance system on the distribution of disposable income and wealth cannot be known; the question itself is meaningless.[10]

And the first report of the Royal Commission on Income and Wealth stated, after describing the standard assumptions on which taxes are allocated to different income groups:

While we believe that these assumptions might be acceptable in respect of estimates of the incidence of marginal changes in taxation, they are unlikely to hold in respect of the total effect of direct and indirect taxation. (Op. cit. 65.)

Some valiant work has also been done recently by Mr. M. S. Levitt of the U.K. Treasury and O.E.C.D. in pointing to the neglect of the effects of indirect taxes on the real value or purchasing power of saving and the importance of this omission for the usual calculations about the progressiveness of such taxes.[11] Perhaps some day one will be able to welcome Professor Musgrave to the club of the unbelievers; he is after all the originator of the modern theory of incidence and, most especially, the principle that the concept is indivisible, there being no sense in trying to separate the impact effects of taxes on the distribution of income from their long-run effects.[12]

[9] See e.g. 'Statistical Calculations of Tax Incidence', *Economica* (August 1955), and 'The Budget and Interpersonal Distribution,' *Public Finance*, Parts I and II (1968).

[10] *Public Finance* (Aldine, Chicago, 1969), 577.

[11] M. S. Levitt, 'The Redistribution of Income: A Comment', *Royal Economic Society* (1974 Conference Proceedings, forthcoming).

[12] Cf. *Theory of Public Finance* (McGraw-Hill, New York, 1959), 228.

COMMENT
by A. B. Atkinson*

Adam Smith's most celebrated contribution to public finance is undoubtedly his four maxims for taxation, which still appear in many modern textbooks on the subject.[1] That his formulation of the objectives of government policy should have attracted so much attention would, one feels, have come as a surprise if he had been here today. Smith himself made no great claims for them, describing them simply as having 'evident justice and utility' (WN ii. 312; V. ii. b. 7)[2] and noting that they had been followed by all nations. As Hicks later put it, the canons of taxation 'have had a fame which perhaps they hardly deserved, since they appear to have been mainly a reflection of contemporary opinion'.[3] Or, to quote Kennedy:[4]

It has sometimes been supposed that the publication of the *Wealth of Nations* brought to the world a new revelation of the principles of taxation, and that it immediately affected the policy of the Chancellors of the Exchequer. But this is a serious misconception. [What Smith did was to give] a wider intellectual sanction to a set of opinions already very influential.

The four canons of taxation are, therefore, probably better viewed as systematization of prevailing opinion; none the less, it is still most interesting to ask, as Professor Musgrave has done, how Smith's views relate to modern treatments of the role of taxation. How far do the considerations which were paramount in the late eighteenth century remain of importance today, and are there aspects which have tended to be overlooked in the modern literature? Such questions are particularly relevant in view of the fact

* University of Essex.

[1] A sample of widely used texts showed that the maxims are discussed in U. K. Hicks, *Public Finance* (3rd edition, Cambridge University Press, 1968); R. A. Musgrave, *The Theory of Public Finance* (McGraw-Hill, New York, 1959); A. R. Prest, *Public Finance* (5th edition, Weidenfeld and Nicholson, London, 1975); and C. S. Shoup, *Public Finance* (Weidenfeld and Nicholson, London, 1969).
[2] All page references, unless otherwise indicated, are to the *Wealth of Nations*, ed. Cannan (Methuen, London, 1904).
[3] Op. cit. 117–18.
[4] W. Kennedy, *English Taxation 1640–1799* (F. Cass, London, 1913), 141.

that many current theoretical contributions, particularly with regard to optimal taxation, draw inspiration from welfare economics in general rather than from the public finance tradition.

1. *Fiscal Theory*

The recent developments have typically seen the design of tax structure in terms of the goals of equity and efficiency, objectives which may in broad terms be taken as corresponding to Smith's Maxims I and IV. The former, or the notion that citizens contribute in relation to 'abilities' or 'revenue', is derived from a very different view of distributive justice from that which finds expression in most modern treatments. This aspect has been discussed most interestingly in the paper, and I do not wish to pursue it further, except to note that although the maxim as stated calls for proportionate taxation, there is, as the author notes, a later suggestion that 'it is not very unreasonable that the rich should contribute to the public expense, not only in proportion to their revenue, but something more than in that proportion' (V. iii. e. 6). In this context it should be remembered that Pitt's income tax of 1799 was progressive in the sense of being limited to upper incomes and that this feature did not attract widespread criticism.[5]

The efficiency aspect—Maxim IV—is much closer in spirit to the modern notion, and the wording indeed corresponds closely to the concept of excess burden:

> Every tax ought to be so contrived as both to take out and to keep out of the pockets of the people as little as possible, over and above what it brings into the public treasury. (WN 311; V. ii. b. 6.)

It is the trade-off between such a minimization of burden and its equitable distribution (Maxim I) which has received most attention in recent optimal tax theory. As Musgrave comments, the results obtained depend sensitively on the way in which the problem is formulated—on the extent of differences in pre-tax incomes, on the response of individuals to taxation, on the redistributive values of the government, on the amount of revenue to be raised, and on the range of taxes at the government's disposal.

---

[5] Cf. Kennedy: '*distributively* the Income Tax was an expression and not a contravention of the typically eighteenth century view of the equitable distribution of taxation.' (Op. cit. 171.) The endorsement of progression in the sense of increasing *marginal* rates of tax was, of course, quite a different matter.

At the present time, it would therefore be hard to draw up anything corresponding to Adam Smith's prescriptions. Nevertheless, the recent theoretical literature does offer some insights. To take just one example, the analysis of optimum income taxation by Mirrlees[6] has brought out that high *marginal* rates of tax at the top of the income scale are not necessarily implied by a redistributive tax policy. From the point of view of equity, it is *average* tax rates that are relevant, and marginal rates are relevant only in so far as they affect the average rate higher up the scale. This is illustrated by one of Mirrlees's examples (Case 5) where the marginal tax rate falls from 35–40 per cent to 20 per cent; and the schedule is close to proportional at a rate of 20 per cent over the range of the top 1–10 per cent. These results depend crucially on Mirrlees's particular assumptions (for example, those concerning labour supply) and for this reason need to be treated with considerable caution.[7] It is none the less interesting in the present context that the maximization of a utilitarian social welfare function in a simple model of labour/leisure choice, assumptions which as Musgrave notes would not have been liked by Smith, can lead to a tax schedule not too dissimilar in shape (although at a different level) from Pitt's income tax at the upper end. What is, of course, different is that the Mirrlees optimum tax would have a substantial negative tax payment to the bottom quartile.

In concentrating on the efficiency/equity trade-off, the optimal taxation literature has tended to ignore certain important considerations, and Smith's further Maxims II and III draw attention to aspects which should receive more prominence. The first of these—that 'the tax which each individual is bound to pay, ought to be certain, and not arbitrary'—has many obvious applications. One less obvious one is to the payment of social security benefits, where it can be argued that the uncertainty surrounding eligibility is one reason for the ineffectiveness of means-tested benefits, such as Family Income Supplement, in reaching all those entitled. Maxim III—that 'every tax ought to be levied at the time, or in the manner, in which it is most likely to be convenient for the contributor to pay it'—is particularly relevant when considering

---

[6] J. A. Mirrlees, 'An Exploration in the Theory of Optimum Taxation', *Review of Economic Studies* (1971).

[7] See N. H. Stern, 'On the Specification of Models of Optimum Income Taxation', *Journal of Public Economics* (1976).

intertemporal aspects. Too often it is assumed that there is a perfect capital market and hence that the timing of a given present value of payments or receipts is a matter of indifference to the taxpayer.

2. *Fiscal Practice*

Professor Musgrave feels that Smith 'would have been dismayed by the revolutionary changes in practice which occurred over the recent decades'. On the tax side, these are seen to be largely the rise in direct taxation and 'the increasingly progressive rate structure of the income tax'. Now, as Professor Musgrave himself has shown so clearly elsewhere, this latter aspect depends on what one means by progression:[8]

> While most people feel that income-tax progression increased, the concept of 'increased' or 'decreased' progression is ambiguous . . . Statements about changes in the pattern of progression are useful only if accompanied by a definition of the particular measures used.

If, for example, one defines progression in terms of marginal rates of tax, then there can be little disagreement that these have increased markedly over, say, the past 50 years. But, as noted earlier, the redistributive impact of taxation depends not so much on marginal rates as on average rates, and the latter seem the proper basis for the definition of progression. Here again, as Musgrave and Thin show, there are a variety of possibilities; however, it is possible to narrow the field if we are willing to assume that the government's concern is with the Lorenz curve of disposable income.[9] It then follows that the degree of progression is neutral with respect to equal proportionate changes in disposable income.[10]

If we apply this to the income tax rates over the past five decades, we can measure how revolutionary have in fact been the changes in fiscal practice. To this end, the table below shows income tax (and surtax) as a percentage of pre-tax income at

[8] R. A. Musgrave and T. Thin, 'Income Tax Progression 1929–1948', *Journal of Political Economy* (1948).

[9] This means in effect that the government's concern with dispersion is independent of average incomes. This assumption is clearly open to question. See, for example, S. Ch. Kolm, 'Unequal Inequalities', *Journal of Economic Theory* (1976).

[10] See Jakobbson, 'On the Measurement of the Degree of Progression', *Journal of Public Economics* (1976).

different relative earnings levels, where overall disposable incomes have been adjusted for the change in the total tax burden, by setting the tax on average earnings at the level prevailing in 1974–75. In other words, it compares the tax schedule in 1974–75 with that in earlier decades on the assumption that the latter would have been increased in a Lorenz-neutral fashion (i.e. by a proportionate reduction in all disposable incomes). From this it appears that there has been a shift towards the higher income groups, taking the period as a whole. However, there has not been the inexorable trend away from proportionate taxation which Professor Musgrave suggests has taken place.

Adjusted Tax as % of Income at Different Levels
(Normalized so that tax on average earnings = 1974–75 level)

	¾ Average Earnings	Average Earnings	Twice Average Earnings	Four Times Average Earnings
1925–26	22	22	23	26
1938–39	22	22	24	31
1951–52	18	22	33	40
1961–62	18	22	30	34
1971–72	18	22	27	32
1974–75	18	22	27	38

[*Note*: tax liability for a married couple with all income earned by husband, no adjustment for relief and allowances other than the earned income relief.]

As we have seen, it is debatable whether Smith really favoured proportionality; but even if he did, there have been decades when the tax structure appears to have been moving his way.

The calculations above take no account of the possible shifting of taxation. As Professor Musgrave notes, there have been a number of studies in this country of the overall incidence of taxation by Nicholson and others, and he himself pioneered such work in the United States. Given the historical perspective of his essay, it is a little surprising that he does not refer to the estimates by Samuel over 50 years ago.[11] These show, for example, that in 1913–14 taxes represented a higher percentage of income for a family (with 3 children) with earnings of £100 a year than for

---

[11] Lord Samuel, 'The Taxation of the Various Classes of the People', *Journal of the Royal Statistical Society* (1919).

a family with £1,000 a year. The comment made by the Minority Report of the Colwyn Committee that the figures 'show very little progression' sounds familiar today.[12]

These estimates are, as Professor Musgrave points out, 'a speculative undertaking involving theoretical judgement regarding incidence'. It is probably in this respect that Smith would have been most dismayed. His own treatment of taxation policy is founded firmly on a general equilibrium view of the economy, and shifting is in the forefront of the analysis. Whatever the deficiencies of his theory, he would—one feels—have been disappointed to learn that the incidence of major taxes is still a matter for controversy.

Smith's treatment of incidence should indeed be regarded as his main contribution to the analysis of taxation. With the theoretical vision embodied in the *Wealth of Nations*, he was able to clarify fiscal questions of the day, and to provide contemporary views on taxation with a rationale hitherto lacking. At the same time, it would be fair to say that these questions were not his main concern. Constable, another of this year's bicentenarians, was once rebuked by a patron for not giving his house sufficient prominence in the painting he had commissioned. Constable replied that 'it was a picture of a summer morning, including a house'. Of the *Wealth of Nations*, it may perhaps be said that it was 'an economic treatise, including taxation'.

[12] Colwyn Committee on National Debt and Taxation, *Report*, Cmnd. 2800 (H.M.S.O., 1927).

Public Policy and Monetary Expenditure

BY R. C. O. MATTHEWS*

OTHER speakers at this conference have discussed the great themes treated by Adam Smith. They have considered how far his ideas have been justified by later thinking and later events. My assignment is a different one. I have to discuss a great theme rather little treated by Smith. A major question, therefore, must be how far his neglect of it has proved justified.

The notion of total monetary expenditure—effective demand—is, naturally, absent from Smith. He did, however, have quite a lot to say about money and banking. I propose, therefore, to divide my remarks into two parts, speaking first about money and banking, and secondly in more general terms about aggregate demand.

First, then, about money and banking.

At the Grand Dinner held on 31 May 1876 by the London Political Economy Club in honour of the 100th Anniversary of the publication the *Wealth of Nations*, the prevailing view among the speakers was that little more remained to be done in economics. One exception was noted by the Chairman, Mr. Gladstone. 'It appears at least to me', he said, speaking with unusual diffidence, 'that perhaps the question of the currency is one in which we are still, I think, in a backward condition.'[1] Twenty years ago, when Keynesian orthodoxy prevailed with little challenge, it might have seemed unlikely that the same thought would be expressed on the 200th anniversary. Now, however, we are again conscious of acute disagreements.

I shall refer later to some of the more radical of these disagree-

---

* Master of Clare College, Cambridge.

[1] Political Economy Club, *Revised Report of the Proceedings at the Dinner of 31st May, 1876* (London, 1876), 46.

ments. Yet in spite of them many of the disagreements of which we are conscious on the strictly monetary side pertain more to the choice of theoretical framework than to actual conclusions, whether on the positive or the normative side.

Let me recite some basic points of agreement. It is believed by most economists that monetary factors are not major determinants of the long-run rate of growth of real income. It is agreed that monetary factors have often played a major role in business cycles and that misjudged monetary policy can cause or aggravate cyclical instability. On the normative side, it is not disputed that the control of the money supply is a public responsibility.

A major disagreement on the positive side has been the extent to which increases in the money supply have been responsible for the upward trend in prices in the post-war period, and in particular for its acceleration since the late 1960s. Even on this the disagreement is not as radical as it once appeared. On the one hand, the monetarists—or at least their leader—no longer hold that post-war increases in the money supply were brought about by purely technical and easily avoidable errors in monetary management; they recognize that increases in the money supply reflected more deep-seated pressures on government from the public. On the other hand, anti-monetarists do not dispute that if governments had somehow been able to withstand those pressures, the price rise would probably have been halted, though possibly at a high real cost.

On the normative side, too, the differences in practice are less radical than might be supposed. A seemingly major disagreement is whether the control of the money supply should be discretionary or whether the Government's role should be neutral. But given the scale of the Government's own borrowing and lending operations, neutrality is hard to define, let alone practise. So purely mechanical guidelines are not usable, and the exercise of some sort of discretion can scarcely be avoided.

I should like to ask three questions suggested by a comparison of our present-day consensus on monetary matters and the position adopted by Smith. These questions are:

1. Why is the control of the money supply held to be a public responsibility?
2. Is the long-run rate of growth unaffected by monetary forces and monetary policies?

3. What are the consequences of short-run increases in the rate of growth of the money supply?

The answer to the first question, why control of the money supply is a public responsibility, is uncontroversial, but it prepares the way for consideration of the other two.

There is a paradox in present-day controversies that often passes unobserved, at least in popular writings. Those who argue most strenuously against restriction of commercial freedom of action in other sectors are the ones most insistent on the need for tight control of the money supply, that is, tight control over a particular class of private sector commercial activities, namely those involving the issue of debts acceptable in the settlement of transactions. Indeed in popular discussions 'monetarism' is often identified with avoidance of public intervention in the working of markets. Of course this is a vulgar identification—those doctrines are not inherently connected. However, the same people do tend to hold them.

Smith, who also recommended some control over banking, was well aware of the conflict. Speaking of his proposed prohibition of the issue of small notes, he said:

> To restrain private people, it may be said, from receiving in payment the promissory notes of a banker, for any sum whether great or small, when they themselves are willing to receive them; or, to restrain a banker from issuing such notes, when all his neighbours are willing to accept of them, is a manifest violation of that natural liberty which it is the proper business of law, not to infringe, but to support. Such regulations may, no doubt, be considered as in some respect a violation of natural liberty.

His reply amounted to saying that in this case, as in some others, a divergence does exist between private and social net product:

> Those exertions of the natural liberty of a few individuals, which might endanger the security of the whole society, are, and ought to be, restrained by the laws of all governments; of the most free, as well as of the most despotical. The obligation of building party walls, in order to prevent the communication of fire, is a violation of natural liberty, exactly of the same kind with the regulations of the banking trade which are here proposed. (WN II. ii. 94.)

This is rather general. It does not say exactly why the money supply is held to require public control, i.e. where the divergence between private and social interest arises. The following answer is not in Smith's idiom, but I imagine he might have accepted the substance of it.

A Walrasian general equilibrium system describes the forces determining relative prices, and hence, under a commodity money system, absolute prices also. However, commodity money is inherently inefficient. There will therefore be a tendency for competition to cause it to be replaced as a medium of exchange by bank money, i.e. debts of financial intermediaries. In the absence of any central control, the natural result would be a pure credit economy. In such an economy, the issue of any one bank's debts would be limited by competition, and each bank would need to hold some reserves. But this would not impose a limit on the total amount of bank debt, because these reserves could perfectly well consist of claims on other banks. In such a system competition causes financial intermediation to be thoroughly efficient in all respects except one: the absolute level of prices is indeterminate.[2] The consequent uncertainty affecting inter-temporal transactions is a source of inefficiency that is not self-correcting. Hence the need to regulate the supply of money as a means of anchoring the general price level. Smith's formula for regulation was to ensure that commodity money did remain the chief medium of exchange, by prohibiting the issue of small notes. The modern formula is to control bank activity by requiring banks to keep reserves in a form and of an amount that commercial prudence alone would not necessarily dictate.

In either case, the free working of competition in financial markets is being interfered with. The question then arises whether this interference obstructs—whether it has obstructed—the growth in the wealth of nations, in one or other of the many ways that Smith and present-day advocates of the free market have delighted to point out in relation to other forms of government interference. This brings us to our second question: is the rate of long-run economic growth indeed independent of monetary forces, including Government action in the monetary sphere, as is commonly believed?

We have perhaps got a rather one-sided view of this as a result of placing too much emphasis on money as a quantity, as

[2] J. G. Gurley and E. S. Shaw, *Money in a Theory of Finance* (Washington D.C., Brookings, 1960), 253–6.

contrasted with banking as an activity. Smith avoided such mis-placed emphasis. His treatment of banking is in quite other terms from his treatment of the silver question: he did not try to subsume them both under the heading of the money supply. In the main-stream of modern economics, possible damage to growth from monetary malfunctions has usually been seen as likely to arise either from excessive overall demand and hence inflation and ill-effects arising therefrom, or else (as in Keynes) from unemploy-ment, brought about by too tight a control over the money supply in face of downward inflexibility of wages. The unemployment in the latter case comes about, according to the theory, because a shortage of real balances causes there to be a high marginal convenience yield on money, and this in turn discourages invest-ment by establishing a high standard to which the marginal efficiency of investment must conform. The long-run growth rate may or may not be reduced in the latter case, but anyway there is a loss of output.

Of course, inflation and unemployment are great issues, and in the second part of my paper I shall have something to say about their relation to growth. But they are not the only relevant issues. The asset holder's margin between money and other assets is not the only margin at which adjustments may take place. To take one instance. In Smith's day the chronic shortage of coin (due chiefly to an inappropriate price ratio between gold, silver, and copper) caused much time to be spent 'riding round the country in search of money to pay wages'[3]—the eighteenth-century equivalent of the excessively numerous trips between savings banks and deposit banks at one time held by Friedman to be the chief consequence of a non-optimum money supply.[4]

This was a static non-optimality. Potentially more important for economic growth in Smith's day was the discouragement afforded by shortage of coin to any activities that involved payment of wages on a large scale. This was a discouragement to the develop-ment of manufacturing and the division of labour. It was miti-gated by the activities of issuers of tokens, bankers, counterfeiters, and other suppliers of near-money. It was this substitute supply

[3] T. S. Ashton, *An Economic History of England: the 18th Century* (London, Methuen, 1955), 173.

[4] M. Friedman, 'The Optimum Quantity of Money' in *The Optimum Quan-tity of Money and other Essays* (London: Macmillan 1969), 1–50.

that Smith had in mind in his primarily anti-mercantilist but at the same time by implication decidedly anti-monetarist observation 'the attention of government never was so unnecessarily employed, as when directed to watch over the preservation or increase of the quantity of money in any country'. I call this anti-monetarist because of course such substitute activities tend to frustrate the central purpose of controlling the money supply, as well as alleviating harmful by-products of the control.

Shortage of circulating medium is not the only possible harmful by-product. Forces affecting the total liabilities of banks affect also their assets. This was a point prominent in the Report of the Radcliffe Committee, who saw the banks as being in some respects more sharply demarcated from other financial institutions on the asset side than on the liability side. In so far as other financial intermediaries are not perfect substitutes for banks in their lending, forces affecting the rate of growth of bank deposits will affect the activities that are financed by borrowing from banks.

These are potential inefficiencies in financial markets. If we regard banking merely as one service industry among many, they may seem a second-order type of consideration. In terms of real inputs employed, banking is not such a very large industry, and it is on the face of it not so terribly important if its productivity is 10 per cent or even 50 per cent below what it could be. However, because of the role of banks, as intermediaries, in the allocation of investible resources, the effects of inefficiencies are capable of being more pervasive than the effects of inefficiencies in other sectors. Suppose for example that innovation is among the activities financed by bank loans. Then restrictions on banks will restrict innovation and economic growth. It is easy to describe phases of economic history when bank finance did play an innovatory role. Schumpeter indeed held that this was true by definition. In his model innovation is due to New Men, who by virtue of their newness cannot use self-finance. Money and banking therefore play an important part in the Schumpeterian system.[5]

Schumpeter's was a schematic picture, and on his own reckoning did not necessarily survive the institutionalization of innovation. The important point, however, is that financial intermediation, of which banking is a major part, is not a mechanical activity. Its efficiency can be greater or less and subject to more or less

[5] J. A. Schumpeter, *Business Cycles* (New York, McGraw-Hill, 1939), 109-23.

innovation and improvement over time. The effects may be large. For example the development of bill finance, organized largely through banks, has often been held to have made a major contribution to the growth of trade in the first quarter of the nineteenth century. *Per contra*, the failure of investment banking to develop in Britain later in the century has often been blamed for industrial retardation.

In answer to my second question, then, I conclude that we may have been too ready to agree that what are called monetary forces are neutral in their effects on long-run economic growth. The banking and financial institutions most favourable to growth will change over time; they cannot be confidently foreseen, and may be difficult to identify even after the event. As a matter of policy, we cannot be sure that the attempt to anchor the price level by monetary policy, i.e. government intervention in the finance market, is necessarily less prone to create distortions than attempts to achieve the same result by government intervention in other markets, e.g. the labour market. *A priori* logic does not speak in a clear voice on that issue. The answer depends on the empirical characteristics of different markets, and the conclusion is not necessarily the same in all times and places.

I come now to my third question, what are the consequences in the short run of increases in the money supply. What I want to discuss is one particular aspect of that question that was prominent in the *Wealth of Nations* but is much less talked of today.

A central feature in Smith's treatment—for example in his account of the history of the Ayr Bank—is the notion of 'over-trading' (WN II. ii. 57). This concept keeps recurring in discussions of eighteenth- and nineteenth-century booms and crises, and to some extent lived on into the twentieth century. Smith's definition was in terms that do not now stand examination, describing a maximum permissible gearing ratio. In this particular case it is more helpful to try to identify what was in the back of his mind, and in those of others who followed him, than to scrutinize his formal definition.

Over-trading is not a perfectly clear concept. There are several elements that are conceptually distinct, albeit associated in practice: excessive gearing (typically based on short-term borrowing); over-estimate of future returns; and speculation, i.e. dependence on the expectation of rising prices. In descriptions of actual events the concept was defined in the light of hindsight and provided much occasion for moralizing. The damage, in the form of losses to shareholders and creditors as well as to promoters, was attributable partly to their own folly and stupidity but also partly due to the over-expansion of credit.

'Over-trading' carries suggestions of overdoing things, in rather the way that 'over-heating' does in present-day discussions. It is important to appreciate, however, that the meaning of the two concepts is quite different. There is no suggestion in Smith that the troubles caused by the Ayr Bank had anything to do with running into a full employment bottleneck. The ill-effects of sudden increases in the money supply were seen by him, and by many later commentators, as lying in the quality of the business they financed, rather than in general over-inflation of demand.

Was this simply a mistake? Was it confusing a minor symptom for the basic cause? Certainly there was an element of straightforward logical error, expressed in the 'real bills' doctrine that credit could never be over-expanded provided that it was limited to financing commercially sound activity. On the other hand the notion can be related to what seems to me one of the most valuable of Friedman's contributions, namely his analysis of the path by which increases in the money supply enter the system.[6]

It enters in the first instance through particular channels, the banks, or in the old days the market for bills of exchange. It is only gradually that it is diffused more evenly throughout the economy. Hence the effects in the first instance are disproportionately concentrated on types of assets or activities that are customarily financed through those channels. There is limited scope for increasing the supply of these assets or the number of these activities. Businesses do not usually have on the shelf unlimited numbers of well-considered projects of a kind suitable for bank finance, waiting to be carried out as soon as banks release the funds. In the short run, the marginal efficiency of investment is likely to show quite sharply diminishing returns, even if there are no particular bottlenecks in the labour market. So if the amounts of extra finance are large, they will go either into bidding up the prices of existing assets (shares or commodities or real estate) or else into low-priority investment projects. Hence the way is

[6] M. Friedman, 'Money and Business Cycles' in *The Optimum Quantity of Money and Other Essays*, 189–236.

prepared for the familiar drama of price rise, speculation, and collapse. The property boom and secondary bank crisis of the 1970s show that this drama has not ceased to be enacted in our own times. Full employment is not a necessary condition for this kind of speculation boom to develop. Indeed manufactures and services, where the effects of full employment are most likely to impinge, are never likely to be the chief subjects of speculation.

In determining whether this kind of speculative boom happens, much depends on the speed with which the increase in the quantity of money takes place. If the wave of new liquidity is strong and sudden, its chief effect may be its impact on what stands in its immediate path, that is to say there may be over-trading in Smith's sense. If it is milder but longer-sustained, the more important consequence may be the rise in the overall water level. That is to say general excess demand. In either case the effect is likely to be different from an increase in demand arising from a non-monetary source, such as an increase in exports or in the marginal efficiency of investment.

The danger of banks financing 'over-trading' is the counterpart of the need for them to finance innovation. It may be difficult to ensure that there is bank finance for the Schumpeterian New Man without opening the door to the Smithian Chimerical Projector; indeed they may be one and the same person—innovators often bankrupt themselves. I suspect the dilemma may have been particularly acute in eighteenth-century Scotland. The lending policies of banks, as described by Smith, were so cautious, that innovators may well have found difficulty in getting loans, except at times when the whole system was saturated with liquidity.

In answering, then, the question about the consequences of short-run increases in the money supply, the main point I want to make is the same one as that I made earlier about the long-run effects of monetary forces: namely, that regard has to be had to qualitative as well as quantitative aspects. Despite all the vast institutional changes since Smith's day, it is still true that the way the banking system develops and is controlled both in the short run and in the long run affects the direction of expenditure as well as its total amount. The effects may be good or bad. Of course it was a mistake when Banking School theorists held that it was only the direction of expenditure that could be affected by banking institutions and policy. But it is also a mistake to regard misdirection of expenditure as a mere manifestation of excessive aggregate expenditure.

I now come to the second part of what I have to say. In talking about monetary forces, I have, perhaps, cheated, by emphasizing their relationship to matters other than aggregate expenditure, and so bringing the discussion more into line with the *Wealth of Nations* but further from my assigned topic. I now turn to consideration of aggregate expenditure as such and its relation to the wealth of nations, particularly in relation to the under-utilization of resources.

Adam Smith did not believe that market forces ensured full employment. But his explanation of unemployment lay in a wages-fund, capital-shortage type of theory rather than in terms of effective demand. Why he should have devoted little attention to effective demand can easily be understood when it is recollected how that concept—or its equivalent—first became current.

This was in connection with business cycles. In 1776 the business cycle had not yet become established as a regular phenomenon, or at least had certainly not yet been diagnosed as such. In the course of the next hundred years, however, it became apparent that what had first been seen as spasmodic and occasional crises were incidents in a more regular and continuous alternation of periods of good trade and dull trade. It was seen, too, that they gave rise to industrial unemployment quite different in nature from the chronic rural under-employment of the Speenhamland counties or the chronic urban under-employment of Dickens's London. The question therefore arose about the reasons for this phenomenon and its long-run significance. Let me trace, in the most summary way, and from a chiefly British standpoint, how thought and events evolved thereafter. I concentrate on the questions of the influence of effective demand on the *level* of income, through the degree of utilization of resources, on the one hand, and its influence on economic *growth* on the other.

The consensus among economists up till 1914 was that the significance of cycles was second-order, though not negligible. They would have conceded that these fluctuations did cause hardship to labour in certain industries and also that occasional exceptionally severe recessions, like those of 1842 or 1886, could push up to a significant degree the average level of unemployment over an entire cycle. Fluctuations in effective demand were not seen as affecting to an important extent the rate of growth of real national income or as bringing about *chronic* under-utilization of resources. Most nineteenth-century economists would probably have been quite sympathetic to the notion that the level of unemployment fluctuates around a 'natural' level.

Of course, not everyone saw cycles in this light. On the one hand Marx saw them as the successive steps towards the final crisis of capitalism; on the other hand, Schumpeter (whose formative years date him as a pre-1914 economist) saw them as the steps on the ladder of capitalist economic development. But most economists saw cycles as just fluctuations around a path that was otherwise determined. Even when the problem of chronic unemployment became prominent in the early twentieth century, the Webbs and Beveridge, for example, saw it as essentially a fault of industrial organization. In sub-titling his 1909 book *Unemployment: A Problem of Industry*, Beveridge was taking a stand against those who thought it was a problem of the individual unemployed man; there was no suggestion that it was a problem of aggregate demand.

In the inter-war period, the discussion took a new turn. In the 1930 edition of his book Beveridge described the change in the phenomenon to be explained in Britain:

Up to the war [World War I] labour supply and labour demand run in a well-established relation. The former grows steadily; the latter on the whole as fast, but unsteadily . . . They are like two bicyclists, one proceeding straight and soberly along one side of a narrow road, one proceeding less soberly in a series of wobbles, but never falling off the road altogether and always coming back from the ditch side to rejoin his companion . . . In 1921 the lines of labour supply and labour demand begin again in a different relation. Only in one year out of the nine since then does labour demand use above 90 per cent. The drunken bicyclist may not wobble so much as he did, but has taken to riding permanently in the ditch.[7]

Concern with this problem of chronic unemployment led to Keynesian theory and the doctrine that the average level of utilization of resources might be *persistently* too low, on account of demand deficiency, and the associated doctrine that this could be

---

[7] W. H. Beveridge, *Unemployment: A Problem of Industry 1909 and 1930* (London, Longmans, 1930), 347–8.

cured by government policy.[8] I suppose that in the heyday of Keynesian economics, it would have been held that demand management would have been capable of correcting nineteenth-century business cycles, as well as correcting the chronic demand deficiency of the inter-war period; but most Keynesian economists probably thought that business cycles in the old days hadn't been too bad anyway, and this intellectually interesting question has not been much discussed.

Under-utilization of resources was the great preoccupation of the inter-war period. The theory of growth was rather lost sight of. So there was not much explicit discussion of whether aggregate demand affected the long-run growth of income as well as its level. In so far as the link between growth and demand was discussed, it related more to the opposite direction of causation, namely the possibility that the depression of demand might be due to exhaustion of the underlying growth potential, as analysed in the stagnation thesis.

The consensus in the 1950s and early 1960s reflected the predominantly good economic experience of that time. The average level of resource utilisation had been high. There might be debate on how much this was *directly* due to government regulation of aggregate demand, and it might be held that government was actually responsible for the persisting cycles. But there was not much doubt in most people's minds that regulation of demand could prevent the recurrence of serious under-utilization if it threatened. Less clear was the prevailing doctrine about the relation between demand and growth. The historically high growth rates achieved in most countries were, I suppose, thought by many economists to have something to do with high demand pressure, and of course some blamed the comparatively poor British growth performance on the stop-go cycle. However, there did not exist any consensus on this aspect, nor any well-articulated theory.

Finally, in the last ten years, the success of the monetarist counter-revolution has brought about an astonishing change. In

---

[8] As Professor Wilson has recently reminded us, the claims made for policy were modest. The more ambitious notions of the role of fiscal policy really came from *How to Pay for the War* and from the actual experience of World War II rather than from Keynes's pre-war writings. T. Wilson, 'The Natural Rate of Unemployment,' *Scottish Journal of Political Economy*, (Feb. 1976), 99–107.

this country, at least, the fight is still being fought, and the Keynesian citadel has not yet fallen; the course of the battle, moreover, is confused by some skirmishes, *within* the citadel, between those who interpret Keynesian economics in an equilibrium sense or in a disequilibrium one; and it is further confused by the activities on the flank of a separate group of insurgents who bear the Cambridge flag but whose allegiance between the main parties of attackers and defenders sometimes seems in doubt. The doctrines of the counter-revolutionaries are close to those of the nineteenth century and in some ways to the 'Treasury view' of the 1930s. Doctrines have been revived that undergraduate students in the 1950s, reading the controversies of the 1930s, used to marvel that any sane man could have held: that increasing government expenditure does not reduce unemployment in a depression and may very well increase it; that a major part of unemployment is due to the personal characteristics of the unemployed; and so on. The central doctrines, as they relate to real income, are familiar. The long-run rate of growth of real income is determined on the supply side. The cause of chronic under-utilization of resources, if its occurs, is a too high real supply price of labour, not, as supposed by Keynesians, a too high supply price of new capital (interest rate). Cycles are mainly due to mistakes of the central bank. Presumably it would be conceded that *some* tendency to fluctuation may arise from other causes. There is some unclearness on this point in the doctrine; in particular British monetarists (who unlike Friedman have not shown much interest in history) have not made clear whether they think nineteenth-century British business cycles were due to avoidable monetary mismanagement or whether they were due to other causes but were not bad enough to worry about *except* when magnified by monetary mismanagement.

So in the hundred years since Mr. Gladstone spoke at that dinner, the trend of thought has been round in almost a complete circle, with a few excursions thrown in as well. In reviewing these trends, it is difficult to avoid the impression that changes in received doctrine owed more to changes in the practical problem of the day—unemployment in the 1930s, inflation today—than they did to improvements in logical reasoning or in empirical analysis. Significant influence must also be accorded to two individuals, Keynes and Friedman, whose genius, like that of Smith, lay as much in their powers of persuasion as in their intellectual originality. In these controversies, the empirical evidence has seldom seemed to all parties unequivocal; and on the *a priori* side, if out-and-out monetarism rests on some pretty special and dubious assumptions, the same is true of orthodox textbook Keynesianism. It is perhaps because changes in thought have owed much to fashion and to changes in current problems, rather than to the orderly and rigorous march of economic science, that they have not carried universal conviction: the triumph of the Keynesian revolution left Robertson sulking and unconvinced, and if the Chicagoan counter-revolution turns out to carry the day there will still be plenty of sulking and unconvinced Keynesians.

The situation is an unsatisfactory one. The following are perhaps the two extreme positions regarding the influence of aggregate demand and public policy on the degree of utilization of resources and on growth. The limitations of our scientific knowledge are shown by the fact that both positions are reasonably tenable, as are others that lie somewhere between them.

1. Neither the growth rate nor the average degree of utilization of resources is affected by aggregate demand. The only important *real* manifestation of the effects of variations in aggregate demand is the business cycle. Attempts to remedy that by conscious regulation of demand will only make matters worse. Not merely is this true now—it was always true. The inter-war unemployment in the U.K. was due largely, if not wholly, to excessively high real wages. It would not have been reduced by public spending.

2. The other extreme position is a minority view and it has not been so elaborately formulated. There are elements of it in the writings of Lord Kaldor, who, paradoxically, has traced them back, through Allyn Young, to Smith—paradoxically, because the idea is on the face of it close to mercantilism. Not merely does effective demand influence the long-run rate of growth; it is its sole determinant. If demand grows (or at least if demand for the right things grows, permitting an extension of the market and a more refined division of labour), output will grow: otherwise not. Technical progress, capital accumulation, and changes in the labour force do not as such necessarily have any effect on the growth rate actually achieved. In the absence of growth in demand, exogenous supply side changes will lead in the short run merely to changes in the degree of utilization, and in the

longer run will lead to their own reversal. Hence well-judged manipulation by government of demand and its direction is crucial not only to the degree of utilization of resources but also to growth.

In the extreme form I have stated doctrine 2 is perhaps scarcely tenable. But consider one aspect of it, that relating to the labour force. Is it really so clear that exogenous changes in the rate of growth of the labour force have any effect on the rate of growth of GNP (let alone GNP per head)? Are we really convinced that if demographic forces had made for rather faster population growth in Britain in the last hundred years, it would have made much difference to the rate of growth of GNP? Would it have made any difference at all? There are various hypotheses about the ways in which an extra supply of labour *may* generate extra demand for itself; but at the *a priori* level, they do not sound overwhelmingly convincing, especially in the absence of any government full employment policy. Empirically we do in the long run find *some* signs of relationship between population growth and growth of GNP; but the correlation is chiefly due to those countries and periods, like the United States in the nineteenth century, of which it can plausibly be held that the high population growth was the result of high growth of demand rather than the other way round.[9]

I do not myself take this sceptical view about the effects of labour force growth on growth of GNP, but I think a case can be made for it. The way would then be open for an interpretation of growth that would chiefly emphasize capital accumulation, *à la* Smith; but alternatively the way would also be open to an interpretation of growth that would allow demand to share pride of place with technical progress, taking technical progress in the broadest sense, corresponding to Smith's 'improvements', and making due allowance for the need for an institutional and legal framework congenial to improvements.

I asked at the beginning whether Smith's comparative neglect of aggregate demand had proved justified.

The first aspect of the question concerns the *level* of income, as affected by unemployment and by distortions due to inflation, the second aspect concerns the *growth* of income. It was reasonable for *Smith* to neglect the first aspect, because in his day it had not yet manifested itself as a major problem. Subsequent events have

[9] See data in S. Kuznets, *Modern Economic Growth* (New Haven, Yale University Press, 1966), 64–5.

shown that it is a more important problem than he could have foreseen. At various times there have been doubts whether unemployment and inflation really *are* all that important, and whether they are not in fact very subordinate to growth, which in turn is mainly independent of them. This thought is present in Marshall, and was prominent in the 1960s. It is easily shown that a few per cent of lost output caused by unemployment is compensated by a very small number of years growth. I suggest that this is too narrow a view of the aims of economic activity. Unemployment, perhaps even more than inflation, has capricious distributional effects, and so can create relative deprivation that is not offset by growth. Moreover (to borrow again the jargon of our sister science) unemployment interferes with role-fulfilment. So simply maximizing the discounted sum of output is not an adequate criterion. The level of aggregate demand is on any reckoning a public policy issue, if only because wrong policies can cause or aggravate cycles. What the public policy should be, and what trade-off if any exists between high employment and price stability, is, of course, another matter.

On the second aspect, growth: Smith's implicit answer is that aggregate demand is not an important determinant. I have expressed some doubts about this, first in talking about the links between innovation and the expansion of bank credit, secondly in more general terms in asking whether supply side forces can be relied on to translate themselves into reality. Despite these doubts, my guess is that Smith was more right than wrong on this aspect. But the issue is far from proven.

COMMENT

by R. A. Gordon*

In view of the time limitation imposed on discussants, I can hardly do justice to the interesting paper that Robin Matthews has just presented. I can only pick out a few points for brief comment. I shall follow the author in considering, first, the role of money in the dynamics of economic activity and, second, the

* University of California.

broader topic of how and to what extent changes in aggregate demand influence economic instability and growth.

First, as to the effect of monetary influences on the rate of economic growth. I thoroughly agree with Matthews when he speaks of 'Too much emphasis on money as a quantity, as contrasted with banking as an activity . . .', at least so far as concerns the effect of financial influences on the rate and pattern of economic growth. Indeed there is a reciprocal relation here that perhaps Matthews does not sufficiently emphasize. Not only does the changing environment of financial institutions affect the volume and composition of real investment, but the reverse is also true. I might cite as one example the recent study by Davis and North of the ways in which felt needs generated by investment opportunities in the United States in the nineteenth century led to various financial innovations.[1] Incidentally, Adam Smith was not unaware of the possibility of increasing the level of real output through financial innovations; witness his discussion of the effect of substituting bank notes for gold and silver in Book II, Chapter ii. Moreover, given the city in which we are meeting, I cannot refrain from quoting the following few words from the same chapter of the *Wealth of Nations*. 'I have heard it asserted,' writes Smith, 'that the trade of the city of Glasgow, doubled in about fifteen years after the first erection of the banks there' (WN II. ii. 41).

I shall pass fairly quickly over Matthews's discussion of the short-run effects of increases in the money supply, a treatment which begins with Smith's discussion of 'over-trading'. I must confess that I find little new in this discussion, which leads to a conclusion that I think we should all immediately accept; namely, that the short-run effects of monetary expansion depend on the pattern and quality of credit expansion as well as on its total amount.

Let me turn now to the second half of Matthews's paper, which is concerned, in effect, with the evolution of macroeconomics since the *Wealth of Nations*. With apologies to the author, I feel obliged to begin by offering a mild objection to what seems to me to be an overly narrow focus in this part of his paper. It is true that we are gathered here at a great British (and Scottish) university to

[1] L. E. Davis and D. C. North, *Institutional Change and American Economic Growth* (London, 1971).

celebrate the two hundredth anniversary of the book that made Britain the centre of economic thought in the Western World for more than a century and a half. None the less, I think that Matthews concentrates a bit too much on merely British experience in illustrating his arguments. And in considering the eventual re-cognition of the role of aggregate demand in the generation of economic instability and growth, one should not ignore, as he does, the contribution of Swedish economists, from Wicksell on. And, of course, there are others in other countries who might also be mentioned.

This concentration on British experience leads the author to say that 'Under-utilization of resources was the great preoccupation of the inter-war period.' This may have been true of Britain, but it was certainly not true of the United States until after 1929. And even in the United Kingdom, there was until 1931 a tragic pre-occupation with restoring and maintaining the pre-war parity of the pound. I might add also that while it is true that growth theory was largely ignored before World War II, Harrod's initial pre-sentation of his multiplier–accelerator growth model was made in 1939, although it did not attract wide attention until the publica-tion of his L.S.E. lectures shortly after the end of the war.

In this connection, I am surprised that Matthews has nothing to say about the proliferation of growth models after the war. In particular, the Solow–Swan neoclassical growth model, which substituted a conventional production function for the artificial simplicity of the accelerator in the Harrod–Domar model, involved the study of the interaction of aggregate demand and aggregate supply in a useful way.

I should like to mention also two other important post-war developments in the empirical study of growth. One, based largely on work at the National Bureau of Economic Research, involved the attempt to measure the relative contributions of capital and labour to the growth of total output in the United States and the discovery of the mystifyingly large 'residual' that could not be explained by the increase in the supply of inputs. The other was Edward Denison's work which, in effect, sought to explain this residual. His first volume sought to do this just for the United States, but in *Why Growth Rates Differ*, he made a comparative study of the sources of post-war growth in most of the major industrial countries. I must add, however, that these studies are concerned primarily with the determinants of aggregate supply, whereas Matthews's concern, so far as growth is concerned, is with the role of aggregate demand.

In his concluding paragraphs, Matthews summarizes what he considers to be two extreme positions with respect to the influence of aggregate demand and public policy on resource utilization and growth. At the one extreme, aggregate demand does not matter; at the other, only aggregate demand matters. To me, both extreme positions seem hardly worth discussing. We live today, as our ancestors did in Adam Smith's time, in a dynamic interdependent world in which aggregate demand and aggregate supply, as well as the demand and supply for particular goods and services, interact in complex and continually changing ways that reflect the changing institutional environment.

Let me end by adding that I wish our author had not neglected the inflation problem as much as he has. In a paper entitled 'Public Policy and Monetary Expenditure', comments on the role of aggregate demand—and also aggregate supply—in determining the rate of inflation would be as appropriate as concern with growth and cycles.

COMMENT

by R. S. Sayers

I read Professor Matthews's paper with great admiration; this for a variety of reasons, not the least being that though one might have expected the final paper in this celebratory Conference to sum up the fruitfulness of Smith's work in this area, Matthews has instead chosen to emphasize the importance of unanswered questions.

As economists, economic historians, and political economists— and all these are under the great umbrella of Adam Smith—we have found an amazing range of interest in the *Wealth of Nations*. I myself read it just fifty years ago; I read it again last autumn and I have of course learned yet more of it by listening to the papers here in these few days. Looking back to my own reading, though I learned something of eighteenth-century England, and more of eighteenth-century France (practically nothing of eighteenth-century Scotland), I had originally let myself be fascinated by the operation of the Invisible Hand, but came at last to extreme discomfort at the gaps in the argument.

Simplifying almost (I hope not quite) to the point of caricature: the most damaging gaps arise from insufficiency of exploration (*not* omission) of the time factor in the economic processes and neglect of the instability of expectations. Decisions on production involve commitment—largely irretrievable—of real resources for varying lengths of time, some of them very long. Expectations can be extremely jumpy: their time-focus can shorten and lengthen in ways that bear no relation to the periods of commitment of real resources. The result is that instead of an Invisible Hand steadily leading from the pursuit of self-interest to the attainment of the public interest, we are at the mercy of a shaky, fidgety hand groping its way through the mists of time.

Smith would assuredly have become aware of this if he had contemplated the phenomenon of the trade cycle. Not that we can accuse him of failing in this: for, though one can find cyclical elements in earlier fluctuations, it has been rightly remarked that the trade cycle came into our history only after 1776. If Smith had seen all this, his passages on money would have been more interesting, just as contemplation of a century of trade cycles inspired the outburst of monetary theory—and of a simplistic monetarism—to which I was exposed in my undergraduate years. As it was, Smith's monetary passages are unsatisfying. He perceived that unregulated pursuit of private interest would lead to unhealthy growth of banking and credit, and he glimpsed the instability of this credit. For remedy he hankered after commodity money; he does not seem to have appreciated that, as the monetary quality is created—imposed—by the public itself, the irrepressible ingenuity of self-interest would always create a superstructure of credit with instability enough to make any control—whether of quantity or quality—extremely difficult, as well as confusing its objectives.

In the second of Smith's two centuries this relative weakness of monetary methods of control has become of graver moment largely because successful growth in the wealth of nations has carried with it a shift in political power which has magnified the pressures with which any monetary—or for that matter, fiscal—policy has to cope. Incidentally, I find myself a little impatient with the argument whether the damaging pressure originates in the magnification of public expenditure or in the use of trade union power, for I believe that both these are manifestations of one and the same deeper shift of objectives and balance of power in our society.

The comparative weakness of monetary instruments of control is important also because economic fluctuations involve heavy unemployment, and this is not just a waste of resources but is in itself a source of human misery which is the antithesis of the wealth of nations, a misery that cannot be compensated in any measurable way by a subsequent gain in economic growth. Further, the weakness of monetary control is important because fluctuations have a bearing on growth. The relationship between economic fluctuations and growth is exceedingly complicated. There are many cross-currents in the argument: I remember, for instance, Dennis Robertson arguing that we have to have unsustainable booms because without them we should never get the really big capital constructions on which growth partly depends.

I have started many hares: you are all rareing to get home, and anyway I am quite out of breath. I have said enough to show you that I abundantly share Robin Matthews's discontents, and I can perhaps best sum up by reverting once more to my undergraduate days. In the late 1920s Keynes, who was then getting interested in the Cambridge activities of Isaac Newton, was talking to us in his Monday evening club about undue reliance on Marshall, on whose *Principles of Economics* we were being very strictly brought up. Keynes remarked that Cambridge mathematics had suffered for 200 years from the shadow of Isaac Newton, and he begged us to beware of letting Cambridge economics suffer similarly from the shadow of Marshall. (No-one foresaw that the greater danger might be the shadow of a taller man than Marshall.) We, this weekend, have been looking at Adam Smith through 200 years. It has not all been shadow, but let us be careful! Perhaps we should, after the great benefits the University of Glasgow has enabled us to draw from this weekend, turn with new zest to the questions that will remain unanswered when we have all read the Glasgow Edition of the *Wealth of Nations*.

Index of Authors

Addington, H., 37, 321
Alverez, A., 41n
Anderson, James, 38
Aristotle, 250
Arkwright, Richard, 2, 5n, 13, 25, 31–2
Arrow, K., 95 and n
Ashley, W. J., 311n
Ashton, T. S., 2 and n, 10, 334n
Atkinson, A. B., 312n, 313n
Auckland, Lord (W. Eden), 31, 37

Backman, J., 29n
Bacon, Lord, 28, 29
Bagehot, W., 49n, 51 and n, 53, 55 and n, 61 and n
Bailey, Samuel, 46
Balassa, 155
Balogh, T., 174
Barbour, Violet, 21n
Baring, 47
Barkai, H., 64 and n
Baumol, W. J., 67 and n, 288n
Belshaw, H., 150 and n
Bentham, J., 60 and n
Bentley, Thomas, 7, 8, 13, 15 and n, 19, 20n, 21n, 22n
Beveridge, W. H., 314, 340 and n
Black, J., 5
Black, R. D. C., 52n, 63, 66, 67, 70, 71–2
Blaug, Mark, 1n, 33 and n, 65 and n
Blessing, Governor, 187
Bohm-Bawerk, 65
Bonar, J., 37n, 56n
Boserup, E., 147n
Boswell, James, 7, 36
Boufflers, Comtesse de, 36
Boulding, K. E., 63n
Boulton, Matthew, 5 and n, 7, 8, 19, 20 and n, 25, 30
Bowden, W., 29n
Bowley, M., 46 and n, 62n
Brady, A., 47n
Braun, R., 24 and n, 25n
Bray, Charles, 23
Brems, H., 64n

Brendt, R. B., 74n
Breglia, A., 205n
Brittan, S., 93n, 288
Brodsky, N., 238n
Brown, A. H., 237
Brown, L., 47n
Buccleugh, Duke of, 4n
Buchanan, James M., 88n, 283n, 286, 287, 288, 291, 292, 293–95
Burgess, G. J., 322n
Burke, Edmund, 8, 36, 37, 63, 69, 301

Cairncross, A., 105n
Cairnes, J. E., 51 and n, 60 and n, 253 and n
Campbell, R. H., 38n
Campbell, T. D., 74n
Cannan, E., 4n, 6, 35n, 56n, 57–59, 67 and n, 71, 243, 253, 258, 261n, 297n, 301n, 324n
Cantillon, R., 38
Carl, 7, 18
Carpenter, K., 1n
Carus-Wilson, E. M., 21n
Case, K. E., 318n
Chalmers, G., 38
Child, J., 38
Clark, J. M., 56n
Coase, Ronald, 1n, 280n, 288n
Coats, A. W., 52n, 107n
Cobden, 127
Cochrane, Andrew, 2, 36
Colbert, Abbé de, 37
Cole, W. A., 2
Constable, 329
Cooter, R., 313n
Cordasio, F., 38n
Cromer, Lord, 145
Cort, H., 17
Cullen, Dr. William, 244

D'Alembert, 36
Dalton, H., 56n
Darby, Abraham, 5 and n, 17
Dardel, P., 16n
Davenant, C., 38
Davis, L. E., 346n

List of Guests Attending

Professor K. J. W. Alexander
Sir Douglas Allen
Professor G. C. Allen
Professor A. B. Atkinson
Mr. F. J. Atkinson
Professor A. D. Bain
Professor A. Bajt
Mr. W. R. Ballantyne
Professor R. H. Barback
Mr. R. H. Barclay
Professor H. Barkai
Professor and Mrs. P. Barucci
Miss M. Berg
Professor R. D. C. Black
Dr. J. O. Blair-Cunynghame
Professor C. Blake
Professor and Mrs. M. Blaug
Professor A. I. Bloomfield
Professor and Mrs. J. A. Bottomley
Professor M. Bowley
Dr. L. Boyle
Professor The Lord Briggs
Mr. S. Brittan
Professor W. R. Brock
Professor C. V. Brown
Professor E. Brunner
Professor J. C. Bryce
Professor J. M. Buchanan
The Rt. Hon. A. Buchanan-Smith
Sir Alexander Cairncross
Ms. F. Cairncross
Professor G. C. Cameron
Professor R. H. Campbell
Professor T. D. Campbell
Mr. N. Carmichael
Professor W. W. Chambers
Professor P. Chamley
Professor S. G. Checkland
Mr. W. Clark
Mr. E. J. Cleary
Professor A. W. Coats
Professor W. M. Corden
Mr. J. K. Cordy
Professor B. A. Corry
Mr. A. Y. W. Cowie
Mr. M. F. Dealtry

Mr. J. Deykin
Mr. C. Diaz-Alejandro
Mr. L. Dicks-Mireaux
Mr. J. H. Dollan
Professor R. S. Downie
Professor P. J. Drake
Mr. W. A. Eltis
Professor Dr. G. Fabiunke
Mr. D. E. Fair
Sir Robert Fairbairn
Professor G. R. Fisher
Professor L. Fishman
Mr. J. S. Flemming
Professor D. Flint
The Rt. Hon. Gerald Fowler
The Rev. Allan D. Galloway
Professor M. Gaskin
Mr. J. M. A. Gee
Professor Dr. H. Giersch
Sir Andrew Gilchrist
Professor A. Gill
Mr. F. Gillanders
Mr. G. Glass
Professor C. D. Goodwin
Professor R. A. Gordon
Professor W. M. Gordon
Professor J. C. Gunn
Sir Douglas Haddow
Professor W. Hagenbuch
Lady Hall
Professor C. D. B. Harbury
Professor P. E. Hart
Dr. R. M. Hartwell
Professor F. A. von Hayek
Dr. K. H. Hennings
Professor R. J. Hirst
Mr. P. A. Hoare
Professor S. Hollander
The Rt. Hon. Sir Geoffrey Howe
Professor and Mrs. W. S. Howell
Professor L. C. Hunter
Dr. R. T. Hutcheson
Mr. C. Johnson
Professor J. Johnston
Professor T. L. Johnston
Professor H. W. de Jong

The Rt. Hon. Sir Keith Joseph
Professor The Lord Kaldor
Professor N. Kawashima
Mr. J. B. Kay
Dr. J. R. Kellet
Professor C. M. Kennedy
Mr. P. Kilborn
Professor C. P. Kindleberger
Sir Arthur W. Knight
Dr. C. J. Larner
Mr. F. Layfield
Professor Sir A. and Lady Lewis
Professor H. F. Lydall
Professor A. I. MacBean
Mr. J. McCargow
Mr. M. C. MacLennan
Dr. R. G. L. McCrone
Bailie McCulloch
Sir Donald MacDougall
Sir Frank McFadzean
Miss P. M. McGill
Mr. L. McGrandle
Professor D. I. MacKay
The Rev. Johnston R. McKay
Professor W. J. M. Mackenzie
Mr. M. B. McLachlan
Mr. A. R. Macmillan
Mr. H. McRae
Professor F. Machlup
Dr. A. Maddison
Dr. D. Martin
Professor F. Martin
Professor S. Matsukawa
Professor R. C. O. Matthews
Professor and Mrs. J. E. Meade
Professor R. L. Meek
Professor G. M. Meier
Professor Dr. H. Meissner
Mr. A. M. L. Mill
Professor J. Bennett Miller
Professor R. Millward
Mr. J. Milne
Professor H. Mizuta
Mr. A. Moncrieff
Professor R. A. Musgrave
Professor H. L. Myint
Professor S. D. Nisbet
Dr. A. R. Nobay
Sir Fraser Noble
Professor A. Nove
Professor D. P. O'Brien
Professor M. Olson
Professor H. M. A. Ontiri

Dr. S. C. Orr
Professor J. R. Parkinson
Professor G. B. Parry
Professor A. T. Peacock
Mr. A. F. Peters
Professor G. H. Peters
Sir Henry and Lady Phelps Brown
Dr. M. Pickford
Mr. J. J. Polak
Professor A. M. Potter
Professor A. R. Prest
Professor R. A. Rankin
Professor D. D. Raphael
Professor H. C. Recktenwald
Mr. A. B. Richards
Professor F. W. Rimmer
Mr. C. J. Risk
Professor The Lord Robbins
Professor Sir Austin Robinson
Professor P. Robson
Sir Eric Roll
Professor R. Rose
Professor N. Rosenberg
Professor I. Ross
The Rt. Hon. William Ross
Professor D. C. Rowan
Mr. A. M. Russell
Professor T. M. Rybczynski
Professor C. T. Sandford
Mr. J. R. Sargent
Professor R. S. Sayers
Professor and Mrs. P. Schwartz
Professor Dr. and Mrs. R. Schwertfeger
Professor D. Simpson
Professor R. Sinz
Dr. L. Sirc
Mr. A. S. Skinner
Mr. A. Slaven
Professor P. G. Stein
Professor D. Stevens
Professor I. G. Stewart
Professor G. Stigler
Mr. G. Suzuki
Dr. P. Swinbank
Professor P. Sylos-Labini
Professor P. Thal
Mr. M. D. Thornton
Mr. and Mrs. M. Tivegna
Professor W. B. Todd
Mr. P. F. della Torre
Dr. R. C. Tress
Mr. S. Tsuru

Professor The Lord Vaizey
Miss V. van Valkenhoef
Sir Douglas Wass
Professor E. G. West
Mr. W. P. D. Wightman
Professor A. Williams
Sir Charles Wilson
Professor J. S. G. Wilson

Professor T. Wilson
Professor D. M. Winch
Mr. J. R. Winton
Professor J. Wiseman
Professor J. N. Wolfe
Mr. G. D. N. Worswick
Dr. M. Zinkin